PAPAL BANKING IN RENAISSANCE ROME

This book is dedicated to my mother
in memory of her enthusiasm for
all things

Papal Banking in Renaissance Rome

Benvenuto Olivieri and Paul III, 1534–1549

FRANCESCO GUIDI BRUSCOLI

ASHGATE

Published by
Ashgate Publishing Limited
Gower House
Croft Road
Aldershot
Hampshire GU11 3HR
England

Ashgate Publishing Company
Suite 420
101 Cherry Street
Burlington, VT 05401-4405
USA

Ashgate website: http://www.ashgate.com

British Library Cataloguing in Publication Data
Guidi Bruscoli, Francesco
Papal banking in Renaissance Rome:Benvenuto Olivieri and Paul III, 1534–1549.
– (Studies in banking and financial history)
1. Olivieri, Benvenuto, 1496–1549 2. Banks and banking – Italy – Rome – History – 16th century 3. Bankers – Italy – Rome – Biography 4. Bankers – Italy – Florence – Biography 5. Taxation, Papal – History – 16th century 6. Papacy – History – 1447–1565 7. Papal States – History – 1417–1605
I. Title
332.1'0945632'09031

Library of Congress Cataloging-in-Publication Data
Guidi Bruscoli, Francesco.
[Benvenuto Olivieri. English]
Papal banking in renaissance Rome: Benvenuto Olivieri and Paul III, 1534–1549 / Francesco Guidi Bruscoli. p. cm. – (Studies in banking and financial history)
Translation of: Benvenuto Olivieri: i mercatores fiorentini e la Camera Apostolica nella Roma di Paolo III Farnese, 1534–1549.
Includes bibliographical references and index.SSCD STAFF: After verifying and end-stage processing, send to SSCD office for DTOC shelf
Based on the author's thesis (doctoral) – Università degli studi di Bari, 1998.
1. Olivieri, Benvenuto, 1496–1549. 2. Finance, Public – Italy – Papal States – History – 16th century. 3. Finance – Italy – Papal States – History – 16th century. 4. Catholic Church. Camera Apostolica. I. Title.

HJ1188.P3613G84 2007
332.10945'609031–dc22

2006032400

ISBN 978-0-7546-0732-8

Printed and bound in Great Britain by MPG Books Ltd, Bodmin, Cornwall.

Contents

List of Tables

Preface

The publication of this book would not have been possible without the generous contribution of the *European Association for Banking History e.V. (EABH)*, which in June 1999 awarded me the Young Scholar Prize for PhD theses in the subject of economic and banking history. The thesis (*Un banchiere fiorentino a Roma durante il pontificato di Paolo III (1534-49): Benvenuto Olivieri*) was written for a *Dottorato di Ricerca – X ciclo* in Economic History organized by the University of Bari between 1995 and 1998. I am therefore grateful to the commission and its president Antonio Di Vittorio, who followed my research for those three years. In particular, I am grateful to Marco Spallanzani, who was my tutor for the thesis and has since been following all my work closely.

The text was modified, updated, and then published in Italian: *Benvenuto Olivieri, i* mercatores *fiorentini e la Camera apostolica nella Roma di Paolo III Farnese (1534-1549)* (Florence: Olschki, 2000). Soon after, the process of revision and translation began, but unfortunately this required far longer than initially planned. I thank the Fondazione Carlo Marchi, sponsor of the Italian edition, which has kindly approved the publication of the book also in English.

In the meantime, I expanded on certain topics and wrote a series of articles. In 2001, when I found new sources concerning the cloth trade between Germany and Italy, I revised and added to an article that had previously appeared in German, and published 'Drappi di seta e tele di lino tra Firenze e Norimberga nella prima metà del Cinquecento', *Archivio Storico Italiano*, CLIX (2001): 359-394. Two years later I published an essay on the financing of the 'national' church of San Giovanni dei Fiorentini over the period extending from the first projects to the final steps in the 1730s ('*Se questi pagassino sarebbe già principio* … Il difficile finanziamento della chiesa di S. Giovanni dei Fiorentini in Roma', in A.M. Falchero-A. Giuntini-G. Nigro-L. Segreto (eds), *La storia e l'economia. Miscellanea di studi in onore di Giorgio Mori* [2 vols, Varese: Lativa, 2003], I, pp. 355-369), which has then been considerably enriched and then published in *Quellen und Forschungen aus den italienischen Archiven und Bibliotheken,* 86 (2006): 294-320 ('S. Giovanni dei Fiorentini a Roma. Due secoli di finanziamenti tra pontefici e granduchi, prelati e *mercatanti*'). More recently, following a conference held at Avignon in 2004, the proceedings of which are still in press, I wrote an article on the connections between merchant-bankers and the Apostolic Chamber in the sixteenth century that presents tables showing the many tax-collecting farms (*appalti*) and the *mercatores* involved during the pontificate of Paul III. The information is taken both from Florentine and Roman documents and from published materials ('Mercanti-banchieri e appalti pontifici nel Cinquecento', in A. Jamme-O. Poncet (eds), *Offices, écrit et papauté (XIIIe-XVIIe siècle)* [Rome: Ecole Française de Rome], forthcoming).

This book is a translation of the Italian version with a few modifications, in particular some cuts in *A Note on Moneys* and in Chapter 2, part 4, new bibliographical references in the footnotes and the elimination of the longest quotes from primary sources, substituted by English syntheses. As far as archival documents are concerned, the only additions were a *Libro del Provveditore* in the collection of the Archivio di San Giovanni dei Fiorentini of Rome, and a few volumes of *Notarile Antecosimiano*, held by the Archivio di Stato of Florence, which led to some modifications of Chapter 2, section 2, concerning the Olivieri family's activity in Nuremberg. However, the text has remained largely unchanged, inasmuch as the latest publications on the subject have not modified the main arguments and conclusions presented by my research. The bibliography at the end of the volume includes only the studies actually cited in the text. I have omitted, among others, an interesting festschrift in honour of Ciro Manca, which came out in the same year as *Benvenuto Olivieri* (D. Strangio (ed.), *Studi in onore di Ciro Manca* [Padua: Cedam, 2000]): particularly relevant for this subject are the essays by F. Colzi, R. De Rita, L. Palermo, F. Piola Caselli and D. Strangio.

Deserving of special mention is a volume on Bindo Altoviti (A. Chong-D. Pegazzano-D. Zikos (eds), *Raphael, Cellini & A Renaissance Banker. The Patronage of Bindo Altoviti* [Boston: Isabella Stewart Gardner Museum, 2003]), a banker who had previously received surprisingly little scholarly attention. He, along with Filippo Strozzi, was one of the two main Florentine merchant-bankers in Rome in the first half of the sixteenth century; Benvenuto Olivieri worked with both at different stages of his career. This much-needed publication (in two languages, English and Italian) analyses many aspects of Altoviti's life and activity as well as his well-known patronage. Especially relevant for this study, however, is the essay by M.M. Bullard ('Bindo Altoviti, Renaissance Banker and Papal Financier', pp. 21-57).

The translation of this book at times was made particularly challenging as a result of cultural, historical and economic differences unique to this period; sometimes exact translations do not exist, therefore I have elected to leave these terms in the original Italian. Among the colleagues who gave me useful guidance, I would like to thank here in particular Jim Bolton and Richard Goldthwaite.

The translation is by Nicola Hargreaves.

F.G.B.
Florence (Italy), Spring 2007

List of Abbreviations

AASGF	Archivio dell'Arciconfraternita di S. Giovanni dei Fiorentini of Rome
ASF	Archivio di Stato of Florence
ASR	Archivio di Stato of Rome
ASV	Archivio Segreto of the Vatican
ASVR	Archivio Storico del Vicariato of Rome
BAV	Biblioteca Apostolica of the Vatican
BNCF	Biblioteca Nazionale Centrale of Florence

A Note on Moneys

In the 1530s and 1540s, two gold coins were mainly used in the Papal State: the *scudo d'oro in oro* and the *gold cameral ducat*. While the fineness of the latter reached 1,000/1,000 (=24 carats), that of the *scudo d'oro in oro* was 916.7 (=22 carats); this, added to the slightly different weight of the two coins, implies that the ducat was worth somewhat more than the *scudo*.[1]

Both the *gold cameral ducat* and the *scudo d'oro* were issued with the value of 10 *giuli*, a silver coin that had been the fulcrum of the monetary reform carried out by Julius II in 1504. In the course of time the intrinsic characteristics of the *giulio* were modified more than once and the modification almost always consisted in a devaluation. Consequently, the value of the gold coin with respect to that of silver also changed, on the one hand because of the fluctuation in value between the two metals, and on the other because of the progressive devaluation of the *giulio*. Despite the fact that the gold coin was in circulation, the accounts were kept in an 'ideal' coin of the unchanging value of 10 *giuli*. With these fluctuating values in mind, the bankers opened an account called 'Premiums on coins and gold' ('*Aggi d'ori e di monete*'), in which they recorded the difference between the *scudo d'oro* and its value in terms of silver coin (the '*scudo di moneta*'), listing on the *Dare* side fluctuations in favour of the company and on the *Avere* side any losses that could be attributed to the exchange rate.

---

1 For further details see: J. Delumeau, *Vie économique et sociale de Rome dans la seconde moitié du XVIe siècle* (2 vols, Paris, 1957-59), II, pp. 655-676, based on the rare volume by G. Garampi, *Saggi di osservazione sul valore delle antiche monete pontificie* (Rome, 1776); E. Martinori, *La moneta. Vocabolario generale* (Rome, 1914, reprinted Rome, 1977), esp. pp. 128, 134-135, 183-184, 458, 462-465; F. Muntoni, *Le monete dei papi e degli Stati pontifici* (4 vols, Rome, 1972-73), I, pp. iv-vii; E. Stumpo, *Il capitale finanziario a Roma fra Cinque e Seicento. Contributo alla storia della fiscalità pontificia in età moderna (1570-1660)* (Milan, 1985), pp. 23-42.

Introduction

This book examines the professional life of Benvenuto Olivieri, a Florentine merchant-banker who lived in Rome in the second quarter of the sixteenth century. By that time very close relations had been established between the Apostolic Chamber, which managed the papal finances, and the *mercatores romanam curiam sequentes*, or, in other words, as the name suggests, those merchant-bankers whose business activities were dedicated almost entirely to serving the papal finances. These relations had developed gradually over time, to be definitively consolidated in the decades following the end of the Great Schism.

Naturally, the important role played by the merchant-banking companies in the area of papal finances has not been ignored in the literature dealing with this epoch. Of the various volumes published, two well-known, albeit not very recent, books can be singled out as being of particular relevance as they both discuss in some detail the papacy's need of and reliance on the merchant-bankers in the fourteenth and fifteenth centuries. The first was written by Yves Renouard at the beginning of the 1940s and the second by Jean Favier in the mid-1960s.[1] Also worth mentioning are several somewhat more recent articles that analyse various aspects of the relations in the fifteenth century between the Roman curia and private merchant-banking companies, above all Florentine: those that provide a general overview include various papers by Michele Cassandro, Luciano Palermo and Arnold Esch.[2] Again referring to the fifteenth century, some excellent work has also been done on the

1 Y. Renouard, *Les relations des Papes d'Avignon et des compagnies commerciales et bancaires de 1316 à 1378* (Paris, 1941); J. Favier, *Les finances pontificales à l'époque du grand Schisme d'Occident, 1378-1409* (Paris, 1966). More recently, also: F. Piola Caselli, 'L'espansione delle fonti finanziarie della Chiesa nel XIV secolo', *Archivio della Società Romana di Storia Patria*, CX (1987): 63-97.

2 See in particular: M. Cassandro, 'I banchieri pontifici nel XV secolo', in S. Gensini (ed.), *Roma capitale (1447-1527)*, Atti del IV Convegno di studio del Centro studi sulla civiltà del tardo Medioevo, San Miniato (Pisa) 27-31 October 1992 (Pisa, 1994), pp. 207-234; L. Palermo, 'Banchi privati e finanze pubbliche nella Roma del primo Rinascimento', in *Banchi pubblici, banchi privati e monti di pietà nell'Europa preindustriale. Amministrazione, tecniche operative e ruoli economici*, Atti del Convegno, Genoa 1-6 October 1990 (2 vols, Genoa, 1991), I, pp. 435-459; A. Esch, 'Bankiers der Kirche im grossen Scisma', *Quellen und Forschungen aus italienischen Archiven und Bibiliotheken*, 46 (1966): 277-397; Id., 'Die Kirchenstaatsfinanz und das Bruttoprodukt der grossen Handelsunternehmen (14.-15. Jh.)', in A. Guarducci (ed.), *Prodotto lordo e finanza pubblica (secc. XIII-XVIII)*, Atti della 'Ottava settimana di studi', Prato 3-9 May 1976 (Florence, 1988), pp. 487-506; Id., 'Florentiner in Rom um 1400. Namensverzeichnis der ersten Quattrocento-generation', *Quellen und Forschungen aus italienischen Archiven und Bibliotheken*, 52 (1972): 476-525. In the bibliography are also included several studies of merchants in Rome during the Renaissaince by Ait, Esch and Palermo, as well as works by F. Arcelli: 'La costituzione della compagnia di Antonio della Casa e Jacopo di Michele di Corso Donati presso la corte pontificia (1438-1440)', *Studi*

Medici bank; worth mentioning in particular is Melissa Bullard's research, and the volume by Raymond De Roover, which contains a rich, well-documented section on the Roman branch of the Medici bank and on its relations with the Papacy.[3]

These works on the relationship between the Papacy and bankers in the fifteenth century are essential background to the present volume, which instead concentrates on the first half of the sixteenth century. This was a key period because, as we shall see, it was during this time that the Apostolic Chamber relied on private bankers' money at levels which had not been experimented with before. This in turn led to the necessity of finding increasing sources of income, both to support the growing financial needs, and to repay the *mercatores* who were making loans in order to cover them. It is not a mere chance, therefore, that exactly in this time many important posts (depositary, treasurers, custom officers, etc.) fell into the hands of private merchant-bankers, who therefore became increasingly influential in determining the papal fiscal policy; an additional way to raise money was created through the institution of public debt, which would then 'explode' after the second half of the century.

However, with regard to the Cinquecento, while a number of historians have written specifically on Florentine bankers in Rome, virtually none makes more than a passing mention of the relations between the bankers and papal finance. The only happy exceptions are perhaps Melissa Bullard's works on Filippo Strozzi and Bindo Altoviti. In her book on Strozzi, Bullard, using both private and Chamber sources, examines the life and the political relations of this important historical figure, and in so doing furnishes some interesting information about the papal contracts of this period, in which Strozzi, under the patronage of Pope Clement VII, was heavily involved.[4] Bullard's recent essay on Bindo Altoviti fills a gap, as previously the only work dedicated to the great banker was the book by Coriolano Belloni, which is very short, out-of-date and provides only very marginal information about the history of the bank.[5] Pierre Hurtubise's research into the Salviati family, even though it concentrates on the socio-political rather than financial-economic aspects,

---

Romani, 45 (1997): 5-26; and *Il banchiere del Papa: Antonio della Casa mercante e banchiere a Roma, 1438-1440* (Soveria Mannelli, 2001).

3 M.M. Bullard, *Fortuna della banca medicea a Roma nel tardo Quattrocento*, in S. Gensini (ed.), *Roma capitale (1447-1527)*, pp. 235-251; by the same author see also Chapter 7 (*Financing the pope's debt*) of the volume *Lorenzo il Magnifico. Image and anxiety, politics and finance* (Florence, 1994), pp. 189-214. R. De Roover, *The Rise and Decline of the Medici Bank (1397-1494)* (New York, 1966), esp. pp. 194-224.

4 M.M. Bullard, *Filippo Strozzi and the Medici: Favor and Finance in Sixteenth-century Florence and Rome* (Cambridge, 1980).

5 M.M. Bullard, 'Bindo Altoviti, Renaissance Banker and Papal Financier', in A. Chong-D. Pegazzano-D. Zikos (eds), *Raphael, Cellini & A Renaissance Banker. The Patronage of Bindo Altoviti* (Boston, 2003), pp. 21-57. The volume contains other essays on the life and patronage of Altoviti, in particular two essays by D. Pegazzano: 'Il Gran Bindo Huomo Raro et Singhulare: The Life of Bindo Altoviti' (pp. 3-19) and 'A Banker as Patron' (pp. 59-91). C. Belloni, *Un banchiere del Rinascimento, Bindo Altoviti* (Rome, 1935). Bindo Altoviti is also mentioned by A. Stella, under 'Altoviti Bindo', in the *Dizionario Biografico degli Italiani*, (Rome, 1960), II, pp. 574-575 (his son is also included in this volume: 'Altoviti Giovanni Battista', ibid., pp. 575-576).

also provides interesting information about this period. The Salviati were another Florentine banking family, which made their fortune by moving to Rome during the pontificate of Leo X and exploiting their connections with the Pope.[6] Finally, despite having been published more than sixty years ago, Montenovesi's study of the Chigi family is also worth mentioning here. This family of merchant-bankers were from Siena, not Florence, but this research is very interesting as it provides a detailed examination of this family's administration of the contract of the Tolfa alum mines in the very first years of the sixteenth century.[7]

There are two more general works regarding Florentine merchant-bankers in Rome and their activity in relation to the Papal finances, again in the first decades of the sixteenth century, one by the above-mentioned Melissa Bullard and the other by Irene Polverini Fosi. Both underline the continuity of the Florentine companies, respectively during the Medici pontificates and under Paul III, in obtaining the tax-farms (*appalti*) conveyed by the Apostolic Chamber. Neither author, however, does more than provide a list of the tax-farms won by these companies, thus totally neglecting the economic aspects of their administration.[8]

Clearly, the literature is rather limited in scope, almost certainly as a result of the lack of sources suitable for any in-depth analysis. This gap may be filled to some degree by the papers of the Fondo Galli Tassi held in the Archivio di Stato of Florence.[9] These papers document the activities of a single *mercator romanam*

---

6 P. Hurtubise, 'L'implantation d'une famille florentine à Rome au début du XVIe siècle: les Salviati', in S. Gensini (ed.), *Roma capitale (1447-1527)*, pp. 253-271; Id., *Une famille-témoin. Les Salviati* (Vatican City, 1985).

7 O. Montenovesi, 'Agostino Chigi banchiere e appaltatore dell'allume di Tolfa', *Archivio della Società Romana di Storia Patria*, 60 (1937): 107-147. On Chigi see also *Il Magnifico Agostino Chigi* (Rome, 1970).

8 M.M. Bullard, '"Mercatores Florentini Romanam Curiam Sequentes" in the early sixteenth century', *The Journal of Medieval and Renaissance Studies*, 6 (1976): 51-71; I. Polverini Fosi, 'I fiorentini a Roma nel Cinquecento: storia di una presenza', in S. Gensini (ed.), *Roma capitale (1447-1527)*, pp. 389-414.

9 The documents relative to the '*ragione Olivieri*', or Olivieri company, used for this research can be found in: ASF, Galli Tassi 1806-1876, 1912-1962, 2074, 2278-2282, 2294. The complete collection consists of 2311 pieces (some of which today are missing), and it was reorganized in 1790, as documented in Galli Tassi 2310 and Galli Tassi 2311, which contain the inventories of the reorganization. At the beginning of volume 2310 two unnumbered pages describe the criteria used in making the inventory (the documents – originally divided only according to their position in rooms and on shelves – were numbered when they were moved to the Archivio di Stato of Florence); there follow 24 unnumbered pages which recount the history of the Galli family (later the Galli Tassi family) from the end of the fifteenth to the end of the eighteenth century, with information taken from the collection itself. The collection contains above all documents regarding the individual members, the wealth, and the companies of the Galli family (1-1466, 2095-2243), but it also includes *filze* (bundles) and volumes concerning '*li affari mercantili di diverse famiglie*' (the business deals of various families). These last include the already cited Olivieri family as well as many others; in particular, Busini (1732-1733), Strozzi (1976-1978) and Ubaldini (1979-1980). Relative to the Olivieri group (129 pieces), the cataloguing carried out in 1790 appears somewhat haphazard and, particularly with regard to the 54 *filze*, often confused and open to some debate as to their

curiam sequens, Benvenuto Olivieri, thus making it possible to carry out a much more detailed study into the real mechanisms linking these merchant-bankers to the papal finances.

By the beginning of the sixteenth century, the Papacy had almost completely ceased making use of its own salaried functionaries for the collection of taxes. Instead, it normally contracted this task out to private individuals or groups of individuals. During the following hundred years this tendency was, if anything, accentuated. This was clearly indicative of the Papacy's wish, already evident in the last years of the fifteenth century, to obtain a more secure and more consistent temporal income. The most efficient means of ensuring this was by entrusting the collection of taxes to the merchant-banking companies, which had both the capacity and the financial wherewithal to carry out this task and were able to guarantee an increase of the revenue. The traditional taxation system nevertheless remained substantially unaltered, the few modifications made in order to increase efficiency being limited to a restructuring of the provincial offices. Once it had succeeded, within the first twenty years of the century, in almost totally subjugating the lesser powers within its own territory, the Papacy was able to establish a series of general taxes extended to all its subjects and to all the towns and communes. In the sixteenth century, in fact, in particular from the pontificate of Clement VII (1523-34) on, the territories of the Papal State were increasingly used as a source of income, by means of fiscal taxation. This expanding system of taxation culminated in the Triennial Subsidy of 1543, the first real direct State tax (see Chapter 7, pp. 158-160). During the pontificate of Paul III (1534-49), the Papal State's approach to the administration of its finances thus began to undergo a transformation. Nevertheless, this can still be considered a transitory period, because the public debt, created in 1526 with the institution of the *Monte della Fede*, had still to reach the high levels that would characterize it in the successive decades.

Table 1, which lays out the structure of the papal financial organization, is useful as a reference point for the central part of this volume. Where necessary for the discussion, further explanation will, of course, be provided.[10]

In contrast to the lack of historical research into the relationships between private bankers and papal finances, the papal finances in general have been the subject of a great deal of literature, although scholars do not always concur. Most historians, using

---

meaning. Their contents, in fact, are lacking in homogeneity and only part of the documents gathered in each concerns the argument that the title of the *filza* itself would seem to indicate. It has therefore been necessary to repeatedly crosscheck all the sources to ensure that the minimum of information was lost. See, however, the list of the manuscript sources (especially pp. 269-273) for a full inventory of the sources used for this study. The Archivio di Stato of Florence also conserves, in various family collections, other papers relative to the merchant-banking activities of Florentines in Rome in the course of the centuries in which they were protagonists: direct use has been made, for this research, of the documents belonging to the Strozzi Sacrati, Torrigiani, and Lemmo Balducci collections.

10 This summary has been taken from P. Partner, 'Papal financial policy in the Renaissance and Counter-Reformation', *Past and Present*, 88 (1980): 19, where the author notes that the 'assignments to the papal *monti* and to the colleges of papal officers were paid direct by the tax-farmers and tax-commissioners, as well as by the Depositary General'.

Table 1 – The papal financial organization

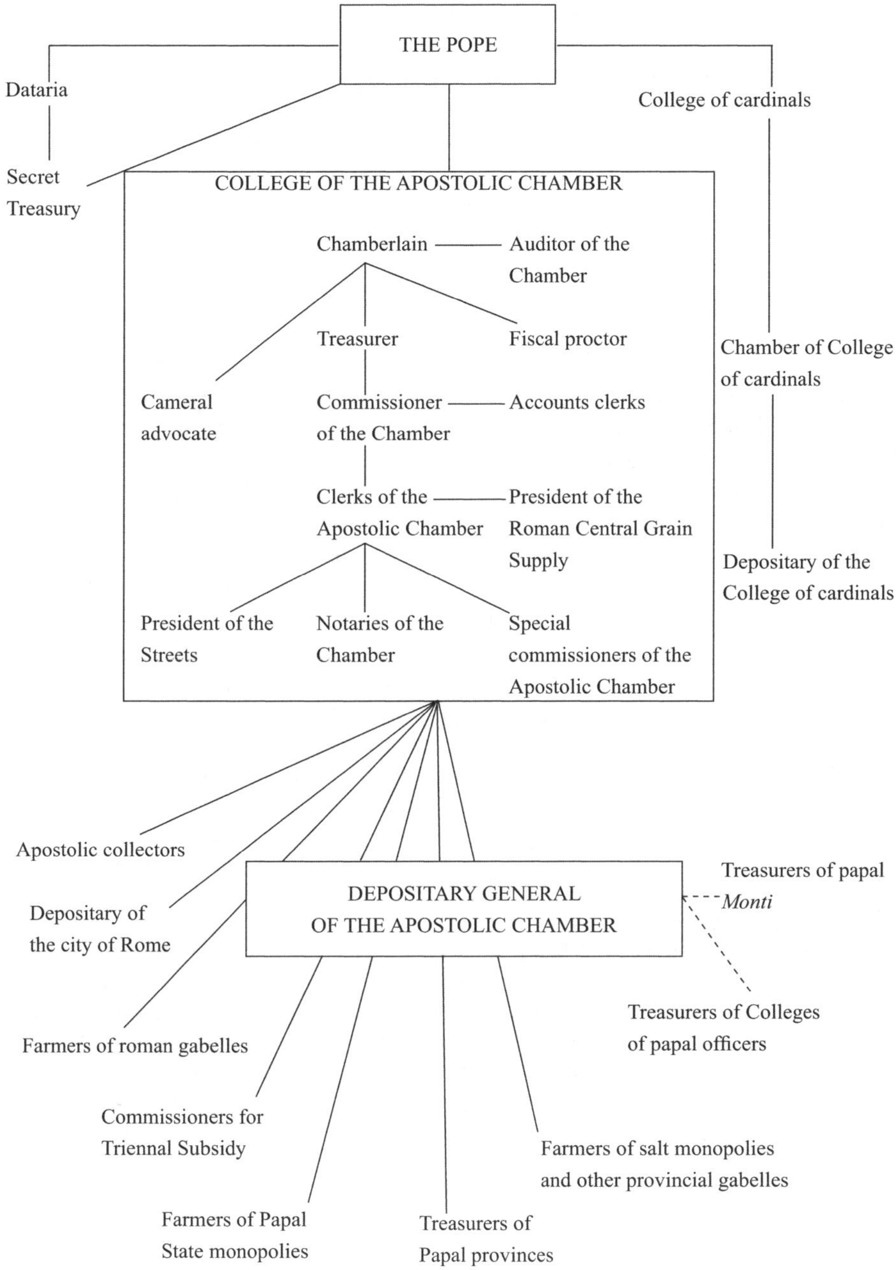

documents originating from the Chamber, have concentrated on the taxation system in general (whether 'temporal' or 'spiritual' or both), and its growing impact together with the increasing centralization of the Papal State, but they have largely neglected the practical aspects of exactly how the private bankers financed the Chamber. While it is well known that at the beginning of the Cinquecento the *appalto* or tax-farm was already the most common means used to obtain financing, its importance has not, perhaps, been given enough weight in the literature. The Papal State relied on the merchant-bankers for almost the entire administration of both direct and indirect forms of taxation, from the Treasuries to the customs.

The papal finances were studied in the nineteenth century by Antonio Coppi and Adolf Gottlob. They were then by and large ignored until the 1920s and 1930s when there was a new upsurge of interest represented by the work of Luigi Nina, William Edward Lunt and, particularly, Clemens Bauer.[11] This upsurge was followed by another short lull until the end of the 1950s when the topic was once again taken up by Michele Monaco. Monaco concentrated particularly on the public debt, seen as a solution to the decrease in revenue arriving from Christendom. More recently, Wolfgang Reinhard has followed the same lines in his work, concentrating particularly on the seventeenth century.[12]

Published in 1957-59, the *Vie économique et sociale de Rome* by Jean Delumeau can be considered a seminal work in this area. Delumeau, in this as in other studies, underlines the progressive centralization of the Papal State and the fact that in the sixteenth century the popes had to rely almost exclusively on the resources that came from the State. It should be pointed out that this work, like the more or less

---

11 C. Bauer, 'Die Epochen der Papstfinanz. Ein Versuch', *Historische Zeitschrift*, 138 (1928): 457-503 (now in Id., *Gesammelte Aufsätze zur Wirtschafts- und Sozialgeschichte*, Freiburg-Basle-Vienna, 1965, pp. 112-147); Id., 'Studi per la storia delle finanze papali durante il pontificato di Sisto IV', *Archivio della Società Romana di Storia Patria*, L (1927): 319-400; A. Coppi, *Discorso sulle finanze dello Stato Pontificio dal secolo XVI al principio del XIX* (Rome, 1855); A. Gottlob, *Aus der Camera apostolica des 15. Jahrhunderts: ein Beitrag zur Geschichte des papstlichen Finanzwesens und des endenden Mittelalters* (Innsbruck, 1889); W.E. Lunt, *Papal Revenues in the Middle Ages* (2 vols, New York, 1934); L. Nina, *Le finanze pontificie nel Medioevo* (3 vols, Milan, 1929-32).

12 M. Monaco, 'Il primo debito pubblico pontificio: il Monte della Fede (1526)', *Studi Romani*, 8 (1960): 553-569; Id., *La situazione della Reverenda Camera Apostolica nell'anno 1525. Ricerche d'archivio (Un contributo alla storia delle finanze pontificie)* (Rome, 1960); Id., 'Le finanze pontificie al tempo di Clemente VII (1523-1534)', *Studi Romani*, 6 (1958): 278-296; Id., *Lo Stato della Chiesa*, I, *Dalla fine del Grande Scisma alla Pace di Cateau-Cambrésis (1417-1559)* (Pescara, 1971); W. Reinhard, 'Finanza ponificia e Stato della Chiesa nel XVI e XVII secolo', in A. De Maddalena-H. Kellenbenz (eds), *Finanze e ragion di Stato in Italia e in Germania nella prima età moderna* (Bologna, 1984), pp. 353-387; Id., 'Finanza pontificia, sistema beneficiale e finanza statale nell'età confessionale', in H. Kellenbenz-P. Prodi (eds), *Fisco religione Stato nell'età confessionale*, Atti della settimana di studio, 21-25 September 1987 (Bologna, 1989), pp. 459-504; Id., 'Papal Power and Family Strategy in the Sixteenth and Seventeenth Centuries', in R.G. Asch-A.M. Birke (eds), *Princes, Patronage and the Nobility. The Court at the Beginning of the Modern Age, c. 1450-1650* (Oxford, 1991), pp. 329-356; Id., *Papstfinanz und Nepotismus unter Paul V (1605-1721). Studien und Quellen zur Struktur und zu quantitativen Aspekten des papstlichen Herrschaftssystem* (2 vols, Stuttgart, 1974).

contemporary volume by Giampiero Carocci (differing from Delumeau's work in that it focuses more on the Papal State than on the city of Rome), considers the situation starting from the second half of the Cinquecento, therefore only covering in a partial manner the period in which Benvenuto Olivieri was active as a merchant-banker.[13]

More recently, Mario Caravale has examined the relationship between State finances and local taxation, while Alberto Caracciolo, Paolo Prodi and other scholars have examined the institutional aspects and the relationships between the various powers existing within the State.[14] The organization of the Papal State has also been discussed by Peter Partner, who, besides studying the history of the temporal dominion of the popes, has dedicated much space to the analysis of the increase of taxation (which increased at a faster pace than prices and salaries) and thus to the public debt, as a necessary means of covering the rising costs.[15]

In a book published in the mid-1980s, Enrico Stumpo continued along the same lines, concentrating on the late sixteenth and early seventeenth centuries. He identifies the extraordinary taxation and the spiritual revenues (those which went into the coffers of the Datary rather than those of the Apostolic Chamber) as the main source of income: in other words, he seeks to show that the Papacy was financially self-sufficient, rather than having to rely on the State (and in doing so he points out some of the limitations of Delumeau's work).[16]

---

13 G. Carocci, *Lo Stato della Chiesa nella seconda metà del secolo XVI* (Milan, 1961); J. Delumeau, *Vie économique et sociale de Rome dans la seconde moitié du XVIe siècle* (2 vols, Paris, 1957-59); and also Id., 'Les progrès de la centralisation dans l'Etat pontifical au XVIe siècle', *Revue Historique*, 226 (1961): 399-410, and Id., *Rome au XVIe siècle* (Paris, 1975).

14 M. Caravale, 'Entrate e uscite dello Stato della Chiesa in un bilancio della metà del Quattrocento', in *Per Francesco Calasso. Studi degli allievi* (Rome, 1978), pp. 167-190; Id., *La finanza pontificia nel Cinquecento: le province del Lazio* (Naples, 1974); Id., 'Le entrate pontificie', in S. Gensini (ed.), *Roma capitale (1447-1527)*, pp. 73-106; M. Caravale-A. Caracciolo, *Lo Stato Pontificio da Martino V a Pio IX*, in G. Galasso (ed.), *Storia d'Italia*, vol. 14 (Turin, 1978); A. Caracciolo, 'I Bilanci dello Stato ecclesiastico tra XVI e XVIII secolo: una fonte e alcune considerazioni', in *Mélanges en l'honneur de Fernand Braudel*, vol. II, *Méthodologie de l'Histoire et des sciences humaines* (Toulouse, 1973), pp. 99-103; Id., 'Sovrano pontefice e sovrani assoluti', *Quaderni storici*, 52 (1983): 279-286; P. Prodi, *The Papal Prince. One Body and Two Souls: the Papal Monarchy in Early Modern Europe* (Cambridge, 1987); Id., *Lo sviluppo dell'assolutismo nello Stato pontificio (secoli XV-XVI)* (Bologna, 1968).

15 P. Partner, 'Camera Papae: Problems of Papal Finance in the Later Middle Ages', *Journal of Ecclesiastical History*, IV (1958): 55-68; Id., 'Papal financial policy': 17-62; Id., 'The 'Budget' of the Roman Church in the Renaissance Period', in E.F. Jacob (ed.), *Italian Renaissance Studies* (London, 1960), pp. 256-278; Id., *The Lands of St. Peter. The Papal State in the Middle Ages and the Early Renaissance* (Berkeley, 1972); Id., *The Papal State under Martin V. The Administration and Government of the Temporal Power in the Early Fifteenth Century* (London, 1958); Id., *The Pope's men. The Papal Civil Service in the Renaissance* (Oxford, 1990).

16 E. Stumpo, *Il capitale finanziario a Roma fra Cinque e Seicento. Contributo alla storia della fiscalità pontificia in età moderna (1570-1660)* (Milan, 1985).

Between the end of the fifteenth and the beginning of the sixteenth century the papal taxation policy underwent some modifications. There is no need to examine these changes here, however, as they have already been widely discussed in the literature. A useful overview of this topic can be found, for example, in the work of Andrea Gardi.[17] The intention of the present study is not in fact to discuss the papal taxation system as such, but rather to examine it from the 'point of view' of the *mercator* in his dealings with it. The following paragraphs therefore serve merely as a brief introduction to the actual substance of the relationships between the bankers and the Chamber. This background is important, as although methods of networking changed slightly over the years, they were essentially the same at the time Benvenuto Olivieri was working with the Apostolic Chamber.

The Chamber documents show that the Apostolic Chamber contracted out the numerous sources of revenue in its power to private individuals, in order to have immediate access to large sums of money. In general, that is, the amount made available to the Chamber was none other than the sum that it was estimated would be earned in the following period from the taxes in question. Sometimes the transactions also included pure and simple loans, with an interest rate that hovered almost always at around 12% per annum and to which at times was added a *donativo*, or premium (3-4%) and a commission (2-3%). What the Chamber documents do not tell us, except in very rare cases, is how the *mercatores* managed to procure such large sums of money and whether it was only the two or three whose names appeared on the contract who managed the transaction or whether there were in reality more bankers involved. The sources from the Fondo Galli Tassi in the Archivio di Stato of Florence, however, have made it possible to examine more deeply exactly how these contracts were managed once they were in the hands of private individuals.

One important fact that emerges is that while the contract between the Chamber and the *mercatores* was signed by at most three bankers, these bankers would then sell shares to other merchant-bankers who remained unnamed in the original contracts. It can be assumed that the sale of some of these shares was agreed on before the contract was made with the Apostolic Chamber; in other cases it is, however, clear that this 'share market' took place after the signing of the contract, and was greatly influenced by the situation of debit and credit that existed between the various merchant-bankers involved. Some of them might therefore have participated for only a fraction of the total period, and their participation might have been a result of or led to their share in other contracts and/or transactions.

Regarding these agreements between bankers, an interesting aspect that emerges clearly from the study of the documents of the Fondo Galli Tassi and which, probably because of the lack of reliable sources, has thus far been ignored, is that in the second quarter of the sixteenth century Florentines and Genoese (and the few others that managed to penetrate these tight-knit communities) did not administer the tax-farms alternately and therefore separately. Rather, it would seem that they often held the reins of the administration in parallel, or even, perhaps, at times worked together. In fact, in the flurry of buying and selling of shares that took place after the contract

17 A. Gardi, 'La fiscalità pontificia tra medioevo ed età moderna', *Società e Storia*, 33 (1986): 509-557.

was signed, it often happened that the Florentines and Genoese found themselves involved in the same deal, and either alternated or shared in its administration. This could be an indication of the growing weakness of the Florentines, who were finding it increasingly difficult to raise on their own the large sums of money necessary to cover important deals. As discussed in greater detail in Chapter 1, this is an element which cannot be ignored; nevertheless, the observation that the Genoese (the Tolfa alum mines, firmly in Grimaldi hands, is a case apart), destined to gain the upper hand only in the second half of the century, were involved to the same degree as the Florentines in these contracts suggests that other factors should also be taken into consideration.[18]

For example, the growing financial outlay of the Papacy meant that it needed advance loans in cash of ever-increasing amounts, impossible for one single bank to provide. Moreover, it can be assumed that the variety of the sources of revenue pushed towards a diversification, making it preferable to have small- to medium-sized shares in a large number of business deals. The fact that the Papal State required increasing amounts of money was literally a golden opportunity for the banks in Rome, as it augmented their possibilities of investment.[19] The Apostolic Chamber continued to assign the bankers future revenues as a guarantee on loans. At the same time, however, it became difficult for the banks to disengage from involvement with the Chamber, as the continual advance loans of money meant that the bankers found themselves accumulating credit upon credit from the Chamber.

The documents that have survived the centuries unfortunately provide scant information about how the signatories of the contracts were chosen. It can be assumed, however, that usually tenders were called for, and the highest bidder was proclaimed victorious,[20] although it is probable that on occasion the Chamber accepted offers made by organized consortia of bankers prior to the signing of the contract. In fact, a single contract was at times financed by such a large number of companies that it would seem impossible for it not to have been organized beforehand; in other words, it might be supposed that a number of banks must have made an agreement with the Chamber without the contract being put on the public market for the highest bidder. Moreover - and this will be clearly seen in the case of the customs (Chapter 5) - the

---

18 Amongst others it should be noted here that, with regard to the *Monti*, i.e. the public debt, F. Piola Caselli claims that in 1585 there was definitely competition between Florentines and Genoese, but the former were still relatively stronger ('La diffusione dei Luoghi di Monte della Camera apostolica alla fine del XVI secolo. Capitali investiti e rendimenti', in *Credito e sviluppo economico in Italia dal Medioevo all'età contemporanea*, Atti del I Convegno nazionale della Società Italiana degli Storici dell'Economia, Verona 4-6 June 1987 (Verona, 1988), p. 212).

19 As Palermo wrote, 'per molto tempo in quasi nessun luogo dell'intera Europa è stato così agevole e conveniente investire in attività finanziarie come a Roma' ('Banchi privati e finanze pubbliche', pp. 436-437).

20 See, for example, Caravale, *La finanza pontificia nel Cinquecento*, in particular pp. 62-63 (note 42); and in the present volume, Chapter 7, p. 147. The result of a '*subhastatio*' carried out as a candle auction, where the winning bid is the last one made before a candle burns out, is also mentioned in ASR, *Notai segretari e cancellieri della R. Camera apostolica 1988*, fols 551v-552v: see also Chapter 6, note 32.

amount agreed on reflected the amount earned in the preceding period: whereas for such sought-after and remunerative contracts, if there had effectively been an open competition the prices would have been pushed to a much higher level. It must be reiterated that these are only conjectures, albeit conjectures solidly supported by a series of documented facts. Not least the already mentioned contemporary presence of Florentines and Genoese: an aspect that must again suggest the exclusion of important power struggles between the two groups, and rather leads us to assume that they had made prior agreements.

Speaking specifically of the tax-farm of the spiritual revenues awarded in 1486 for five years to the Genoese banking house of the Sauli family, but putting forward an argument that could have a more general application, Melissa Bullard notes how ‘the idea behind the *appalto* constituted an important step away from the haphazard, hand-to-mouth money-raising tactics that had heretofore characterized fifteenth-century papal finance and which had made the Vatican such a bountiful hunting ground for eager papal bankers’.[21] It was, in other words, representative of the attempts that since the end of the fifteenth century the popes had been making to reorganize the management of their finances. Tax-farming became increasingly popular and widespread, and, in the period covered by this book, all of the Papal State’s most important sources of revenue were in fact contracted out to private citizens.

As Part Two of this volume will show, the Apostolic Chamber obtained money from the *mercatores romanam curiam sequentes* essentially in three ways. The first was via the normal loan, generally conceded by the bankers at an interest rate of 12%, to which was sometimes added a further remuneration paid either as a percentage or forfeit. The loan could be repaid directly in cash, but more often than not in the cases examined in this book (see in particular Chapter 3, section 3) it was instead repaid with the promise of future revenue: in other words, the Apostolic Chamber, in exchange for the amount loaned plus the interest and the other sums promised, conceded the right to the revenue from the taxes that would be collected in the future months or years.

The second method by which the Chamber obtained money from the *mercatores*, in practice not far removed from the first, was that of the straightforward tax-farm: the Chamber, in other words, gave the papal bankers the administration of determined services for a prearranged period of time. In this case an annual figure was established, which, for a period of three, five or seven years, the *mercatores* would have to pay in advance to the Apostolic Chamber. This sum obviously reflected the predicted actual earnings of the service itself and was therefore based on the income of the preceding years. The contracting bankers in exchange became responsible for the administration of the service in question. The services were administered according to the organizational structure already in place, but all activities were coordinated and supervised by men sent by the banks, while the banker who actually stipulated the contract remained in Rome, or wherever his business affairs took him. The representative was often one of the smaller shareholders in the contract or a minor partner in the company of the main contract-holder. His job was to coordinate

21 Bullard, *Lorenzo il Magnifico*, p. 198.

the affairs in the geographical area in which the operations took place and he was the reference point both for the banker and for the others: on one hand, the members of the papal hierarchy, on the other, the local authorities.[22] Another important figure was the commissioner, who was also connected to the contract-holder or contract-holders, and was responsible for the actual tax-collection, earning his share from a commission on the money collected, or else from a share in the profits.[23] The tax was paid by the community rather than by single individuals, thus facilitating the task of the private contract-holder (or his representative), whose only job was therefore to maintain contacts with the local authority.

Returning to the actual mechanism of the tax-farm, another variation can be noted: a loan with interest could also be included in the agreement. In this case the sum was rendered to the bankers by deducting it from the amount that they had to pay for the contract; and was repaid completely by the end of the contract (the clearest example is the customs of Rome of 1543-49: Chapter 5, pp. 117-125).

The third way by which the Chamber obtained money from the *mercatores*, which, however, did not really come into its own until after the mid-sixteenth century, was that of the *Monti*, that is the public debt (this is discussed in Chapter 4). Essentially this instrument was created as part of the search for new sources of income: with the consolidation of the debt, the way was now opened to an ever greater number of investors; but this was to a large extent possible because 'much of the fundamental groundwork for establishing a funded debt had already been laid'.[24] More precisely, the payment of the interest took place thanks to the assignments that the Colleges, which united the holders of the bonds of the public debt, had on the important services contracted out: the customs, the Treasuries and the salt tax.

This continuous reliance of the Apostolic Chamber on the money of the merchant-bankers created a link between the two bodies that over time became virtually irrevocable: the Chamber continued to need ever greater amounts of money and for this could not do without the bankers; the latter, although their investments could be considered sound, found themselves in the position of having nevertheless to be compliant, because they were always in the position of being creditors and the concession of new loans meant for them an increase in the possibility of repayment. The delays in repayment of the Chamber, moreover, meant that it had to hand over to the bankers constantly increasing shares of future revenues; a process of alienation that would over time spiral completely out of control. Nevertheless, this mechanism meant that the Chamber had immediate (and continuous) access to those sums that otherwise it would have received from its own sources of income only after a longer period of time and in the form of deferred payment. On the other hand, as

22 This can be clearly seen, for example, from the numerous letters or requests scattered through the *filze* relative to the various Treasuries: ASF, Galli Tassi, 1845-1848, 1850-1851, 1980. On 12 December 1545, for example, Benedetto Busini, partner of Benvenuto Olivieri and vice-treasurer of the Romagna, was conceded '*patentes ad exigenda spolia*' (ASV, *Camera apostolica, Diversa Cameralia 141*, fols 80v-81r). The documentation available does not make it possible to investigate in any further depth the relations that developed between the contract-holders and the local bureaucracy; the existing historiography also supplies little information.

23 See, for example, Chapter 6, p. 133 and note 14; Chapter 7, pp. 152-153.

24 Bullard, *Lorenzo il Magnifico*, p. 213.

Partner succinctly sums it up, 'the essential factor was papal inability to meet the extraordinary expenses in any other way than by borrowing'.[25]

A consequence of this commercialization of the money-making offices, deriving from farming out the collection of almost all the taxes, was that the bankers, above all the Florentines and Genoese, came to replace, in the bureaucratic-administrative system, the old Roman aristocracy. In other words, the posts of provincial treasurers, customs officers and even that of the depositary of the Apostolic Chamber disappeared from the ranks of the Curia. In the long term, therefore, particularly from the second half of the sixteenth century, the banking houses that controlled the Depositary, as well as all the other services connected with this body, eventually found themselves in a position of conditioning the papal fiscal policy, which put ever increasing pressure on the territories subject to the papal sovereignty and towards the search for new sources of income that would allow the Pope to honour the debts resulting from increasingly spendthrift policies.

Certainly, as has already been pointed out, for the Apostolic Chamber the delegation of the collection of the taxes carried with it notable advantages in terms of efficiency, both from the point of view of the quantity of money that flowed into the papal coffers, and from the continuity in the payments. On the other hand, there were the merchant-bankers who, thanks to the increasing number of tax-farms, had ample and diversified possibilities of investment, which led to consistent returns in economic terms. The money and collaboration with the Curia also enhanced the prestige of the family, which could thus aspire to a step up the social ladder.

Those who were most damaged by the close ties between the papal hierarchy and the private banking houses were the taxpayers. The alliance between the Curia and the bankers eventually led to a real and proper abdication of the State in favour of the *mercatores*, who administered the tax-collection in the provinces in the name of the former and on its behalf. Over time this led to the birth of a bureaucracy, above all fiscal, linked to the interests of the most important merchant-bankers. Another important consequence was the spreading out of the State's power into the provinces, obtained by the State linking to its own financial interests those of the emerging local social classes (for example, through the institution of the local *Monti*). The clearest manifestation of this can be found in the provincial Treasuries, where the contracting bankers were eventually able to take advantage of all the prerogatives that had formerly belonged to the papal functionaries (see Chapter 6, pp. 129-131); and the placing of these prerogatives in the hands of private bankers was eventually detrimental for the taxpayers.[26]

25 Partner, 'Papal financial policy', p. 29.

26 Moreover, as noted by M.G. Pastura Ruggiero, the taxes were an opportunity not only for the more important bankers but also for those who had influence only at a local level, where, albeit with smaller loans, various tax-farms were offered by the Chamber: *La Reverenda Camera Apostolica e i suoi archivi (secoli XV-XVIII)* (Rome, 1984), pp. 33-34.

PART ONE
Rome, Florence and the Olivieri

CHAPTER 1

Florentines in Rome

Da poi che Costantin fece il presente,
per levarsi la lebbra da le spalle,
non fu più coltivata questa valle,
né venne a Roma mai cotanta gente.
Di Firenze, del papa ognun parente,
e' vengono gridando palle palle,
per istaffetta, in ceste, in mazzi, in balle,
e lasson le lor donne malcontente.
Che pensa aver la barca e chi la rete,
o qualche gran ventura trafficando,
o per un beneficio farsi prete [...]
(Pietro Aretino, *Quando Leon X fu fatto papa*)

Pietro Aretino's sonnet satirizes the large numbers of Florentines who descended on Rome in 1513, the year the first Medici pope, Leo X, was elected, in the hope of obtaining favours and benefices from the papal court. While there was doubtless a basis of truth to this verse, it only captures a part of the nature of a much more complex phenomenon. The story begins, however, rather further back in time...

1. Foreigners in Rome during the fifteenth and sixteenth centuries

The return of the papal seat to Rome from Avignon restored vigour to a city that had become a mere shadow of its former self. The exact number of people living in Rome in the fifteenth and sixteenth centuries can only be guessed at, as the first census of the Roman population was not carried out until the beginning of the sixteenth century, and there are no fiscal data relative to the previous years that provide reliable figures. Consequently, historians have given vague and at times conflicting estimates. In general, however, it is estimated that at the end of the fourteenth century there were 25,000 inhabitants, rising to 30-35,000 around 1450, to approximately 45,000 in 1480, reaching 55-60,000 in the 1520s, 75,000 in 1550, with the population reaching approximately 100,000 in 1600. This spurt in population growth was due in large part to the numerous immigrants who flocked to the city, and who, it should be pointed out, played a very significant role in various sectors of financial and commercial activity.

One important document for anyone wishing to study the demographic aspects of Rome at the beginning of the sixteenth century, despite its occasionally approximate figures, is the census taken a few months before the Sack of 1527:[1] this census indicates that in that year the total population of Rome amounted to 53,689 people.[2] Among historians there is a debate on the place of origin of these inhabitants, and in particular on what could be considered as Roman. According to Delumeau, who bases his estimates on the 3,495 inhabitants (6.5% of the total) who have some reference to their place of origin next to their name, 16.4% of these were from Rome or the surrounding area, 63.6% came from other parts of Italy, while the remaining 20% were from outside Italy.[3] Delumeau's percentages are fairly similar to the figures given by Partner, who calculates that 23.8% of the Eternal City's population were Romans, 57.6% were Italians from outside Rome, and 18.6% were non-Italians.[4] Lee, on the other hand, gives the foreign element slightly less weight, by also including (unlike the others) in the category of 'Romans' those who 'had reached some level of assimilation into Roman society', thus raising the proportion of this group to 68.7%, and at the same time reducing the percentage of non-Roman Italians to 24% and foreigners to 7.3%.[5]

---

1 Published by D. Gnoli, 'Descriptio Urbis o censimento della popolazione di Roma avanti il Sacco Borbonico', *Archivio della Società Romana di Storia Patria*, 17 (1894): 375-520 (also in *Descriptio Urbis. The Roman Census of 1527*, ed. E. Lee (Rome, 1985); this edition contains many indexes).

2 The total given by Gnoli (55,095) was first corrected to 53,897 by J. Delumeau, who noticed several errors of calculation (*Vie économique et sociale de Rome dans la seconde moitié du XVI*[e] *siècle* (2 vols, Paris, 1957-59), I, p. 198); then further adjusted by Lee (*Descriptio Urbis. The Roman Census of 1527*, p. 20), who made his calculations using the figures taken from the original manuscript.

3 Delumeau, *Vie économique et sociale*, I, pp. 198-199 and table. The author considers that the hypothesis of extending these percentages to the whole of the population has '*rien d'invraisemblable*', and in fact adds that the population of Rome, in the XVI century, was essentially fluid and variable, precisely because it included relatively few indigenous members (p. 189). P. Hurtubise makes a similar observation in 'L'implantation d'une famille florentine à Rome au début du XVIe siècle: les Salviati', in S. Gensini (ed.), *Roma capitale (1447-1527)*, Atti del IV Convegno di studio del Centro studi sulla civiltà del tardo Medioevo, San Miniato (Pisa) 27-31 October 1992 (Pisa, 1994), p. 269, where he speaks of a society marked, on the one hand, by its cosmopolitan character, on the other, by its changing character.

4 P. Partner, *Renaissance Rome, 1500-1559. A Portrait of a Society* (Berkeley, 1976), p. 75.

5 E. Lee, 'Foreigners in Quattrocento Rome', *Renaissance and Reformation*, n.s., VII (1983): 137-138 (for the classification of the three categories), 140 (for the figures); the author, nevertheless, underlines the fact that there persisted 'the overriding impression that Rome was a city of non-Romans' (140). These estimates are considered more convincing than those of Delumeau and of Partner also by A. Esposito, 'Note sulla popolazione romana dalla fine del secolo XIV al Sacco (1527)', in Ead., *Un'altra Roma. Minoranze nazionali e comunità ebraiche tra Medioevo e Rinascimento* (Rome, 1995), p. 23. Lee has also proposed much more elastic estimates of the various groups resident in Rome in the third quarter of the fifteenth century: 50-70% Romans (according to the definition given above); 5-10% recent immigrants from the area surrounding Rome, therefore easily assimilated; 20-30% people from other parts of Italy; 5-20% immigrants coming from the rest of Europe ('Foreigners in Quattrocento Rome': 140).

In any case, foreigners predominated to such an extent that only one of the Renaissance popes – Julius III Ciocchi del Monte – was actually born in Rome. Moreover, every non-Roman pope brought in his wake a new wave of immigrants to Rome, as his fellow countrymen followed him. The city's appeal was clearly further heightened by its international character and the constant influx of people, ranging from businessmen to pilgrims. A further magnet for outsiders was the institution peculiar to Rome, the Curia, which had a continuous need for services and for people to work in its administration. It was undoubtedly the cardinals and functionaries of the Curia, together with merchants, bankers and artists, who left the most tangible signs on the city; or, as Lee describes them, 'this dynamic élite of powerful, wealthy, creative and generally interesting foreigners was transforming a delapidated and culturally backward city into Europe's first *cité lumière*'.[6] Nevertheless, it was the general masses, consisting of skilled and unskilled workers, which made Rome one of the most cosmopolitan cities of fifteenth- and sixteenth-century Europe.

Naturally, when a new pope was elected, the national group to which he belonged soared in number (this also happened, albeit to a lesser extent, when a new cardinal was appointed). The new arrivals, who invaded Rome *en masse* eager to take advantage of the privileges that the new pontiff would certainly concede, were, however, generally detested by the local population, and it frequently happened that on the death of the patron, the Romans would give vent to their hatred, unleashing a violent backlash against these foreigners.

Of those who came to Rome from beyond the Alps,[7] the Spanish were, beyond a shadow of a doubt, the largest group. Certainly their numerically strong presence owed much to the fact that in the second half of the previous century there had been two Spanish pontiffs, members of the Borgia family: Callistus III (1455-58) and Alexander VI (1492-1503). The next largest groups were the French and then the Germans. The French were, however, particularly hard hit by the Sack of 1527 and did not begin to increase in number again until the end of the century. The Germans, on the other hand, were at the height of their influence between the fifteenth and sixteenth centuries, holding key positions in the Curia, as well as in various sectors of the economy. Between 1495 and 1523, for example, the Fugger family, with their agents Johannes Zink and Engelhard Sclancz, played a very important part in the administration of the papal finances.[8]

As for the Italians from outside Rome, the most influential, and not only because of their numerical superiority, were the Tuscans; the fulcrum of this group, which was firmly established in Rome by the fourteenth century, was the Florentine colony.

---

6 Lee, 'Foreigners in Quattrocento Rome': 135.

7 P. Hurtubise points out that, despite all the nuances and the ambiguities that this implies in a Europe with borders that were changeable and sometimes uncertain, the tendency at the time was to distinguish between *stranieri*, i.e. the non-Italians, and *forestieri*, i.e. the non-Roman Italians ('La présence des 'étrangers' à la cour de Rome dans la première moitié du XVIe siècle', in *Forestieri e stranieri nelle città basso-medievali*, Atti del Seminario Internazionale di Studio, Bagno a Ripoli 4-8 June 1984 (Florence, 1988), p. 58).

8 Although there is much general information on the bank in Rome in the vast and more recent literature on the Fuggers, the only specific study of its activities remains A. Schulte, *Die Fugger in Rom 1495-1523* (2 vols, Leipzig, 1904).

Relatively large numbers of outsiders also migrated to the city from Lombardy and from Venice and the Venetian hinterland (which at that time included the easternmost part of present-day Lombardy). Rather surprisingly, perhaps, given that three popes – Sixtus IV Della Rovere (1471-84), Innocent VIII Cibo (1484-92) and Julius II Della Rovere (1503-13) – hailed from Genoa, the Genoese colony of Rome was smaller than the above groups. Nevertheless, despite their numerical weakness, the Genoese merchant-bankers were held in high esteem, and in the second half of the sixteenth century they were to become the great financiers of the Papal State. During the Cinquecento, the Italians became increasingly influential not only in the city itself, but also at the papal court.[9] Whereas in 1500 of 35 cardinals only 21 were Italians, by 1598 the number had risen to 46 out of 57.[10] According to Pierre Hurtubise, who has studied the composition of a number of papal and cardinal courts of the first half of the sixteenth century, this marked 'Italianization' reached the 'point of no return' under the pontificate of Paul III (1534-49).[11]

One of the characteristics of all the foreign communities in Rome was the strong sense of separate national identity that they maintained. This sense of identity typically manifested itself in separate hospitals, normally incorporated into churches or chapels, and the financially independent national confraternities, which also had totally autonomous administrations.[12] This 'nationalism' influenced the urban structure of Rome, with streets and entire neighbourhoods taking their names from the national groups that inhabited them.[13] These groups dominated certain areas of the economy, and some of them even formed their own separate artisans' guilds. This being said, however, although geographical endogamy certainly existed, affecting both matrimonial and also certain commercial transactions, its importance should not be overestimated. All the non-Romans, and perhaps particularly the non-Italians, had, in any case, to function in the everyday life of Rome, and therefore to constantly interact with the local reality.[14]

2. The Florentine merchant-bankers and the papal court

'Pope Julius', Cardinal San Giorgio pointed out to the Venetian ambassador, 'used to give about 4,000 ducats per month to the *tinello*; this pope needs 8 or 9,000, because so many Florentines claiming to be his relatives come to the *tinello* to eat'.[15]

---

9 It should be noted that, apart from Alexander VI Borgia, who died in 1503, and Adrian VI Florensz, pontiff for a few short months at the end of 1522 and the beginning of 1523, all the popes of the Cinquecento were Italian.

10 Delumeau, *Vie économique et sociale*, I, p. 219.

11 Hurtubise, 'La présence des "étrangers" à la cour de Rome': 65-68.

12 For more on these associations, see M. Maroni Lumbroso-A. Martini, *Le confraternite romane nelle loro chiese* (Rome, 1963).

13 See F. Castagnoli-C. Cecchelli-G. Giovannoni-M. Zocca, *Topografia e urbanistica di Roma* (Bologna, 1958).

14 Lee, 'Foreigners in Quattrocento Rome': 141-144.

15 '*Papa Giulio soleva dare al tinello quattromila ducati al mese circa; questo Papa ne vuole otto o novemila. La causa è, che vengono molti Fiorentini che si fanno parenti del Papa,*

It was, in other words, believed that Leo X's great extravagance resulted from his having to pander to the wishes of the large numbers of Florentines that, as his fellow countrymen, had flocked to Rome sure of his patronage.

This is the question that will, in fact, be addressed here. Did the presence of the two Medici popes on the papal throne (Leo X from 1513 to 1521 and Clement VII from 1523 to 1534, with the brief interruption of the Fleming, Adrian VI Florensz, 1522-23) really favour the Florentines? And, if so, how? Particularly, therefore, what differences can be found in the situation of the Florentines before 1513, from 1513 to 1534, and after 1534? In seeking to answer this question, I will concentrate above all on the Florentine companies of merchant-bankers active at this time in Rome. There are two reasons for this: first, because they had a pre-eminent role, and, second, because they serve as essential background to the main focus of this book, the Florentine merchant-banker Benvenuto Olivieri.

From the Trecento to the Cinquecento

Much of the research into this period underlines the special relationship that existed between the Florentine merchant-bankers and the Roman Curia from the fourteenth century onwards: this relationship was made even stronger by the papal exile in Avignon (which lasted virtually without interruption from 1309 to 1378) and the financial needs that this situation spawned. It was in this period that the owners of the banking enterprises linked to the Curia became known as '*mercatores romanam curiam sequentes*', a term which, on the one hand, expressed their connection with the papal finances, but, on the other, also their independence from the administration.[16] It is estimated that during these years there were approximately 250 Florentines present at the court, 25 of whom were described as *mercatores*.[17] After the interruption caused by the papal interdict resulting from the war of the Eight Saints (1375-78), the Florentine colony connected to the papacy once again began to grow, its members rapidly recuperating the positions they had held in the past and, in the two decades spanning the end of the fourteenth and the beginning of the fifteenth century, rising to a role of absolute domination.[18] The papacy, having suffered the negative consequences of abruptly detaching itself 'from the best banking network of the world', threw itself anew 'into the arms of the Florentines'.[19]

---

e vanno in tinello a mangiare'; quoted in P. Villari, *Niccolò Machiavelli e i suoi tempi* (3 vols, Florence, 1877-82), II, p. 32.

16 Y. Renouard, *Les relations des Papes d'Avignon et des compagnies commerciales et bancaires de 1316 à 1378* (Paris, 1941), p. 125.

17 A. Esch, 'Florentiner in Rom um 1400. Namensverzeichnis der ersten Quattrocento-generation', *Quellen und Forschungen aus italienischen Archiven und Bibliotheken*, 52 (1972): 477-478, 480 (note 8). According to Y. Renouard, the number of *mercatores* was slightly higher (28): 'Le compagnie commerciali fiorentine del Trecento', *Archivio Storico Italiano*, 96 (1938): 45.

18 M. Cassandro, 'I banchieri pontifici nel XV secolo', in Gensini (ed.) *Roma capitale (1447-1527)*, pp. 218-219.

19 A. Esch, 'Dal Medioevo al Rinascimento: uomini a Roma dal 1350 al 1450', *Archivio della Società Romana di Storia Patria*, 94 (1971), p. 7.

After the return of the popes, and more notably from the fifteenth century onwards, Rome lacked the infrastructure necessary to be completely self-sufficient. Therefore, in order to satisfy both the needs of Roman society and, more particularly, those of the papal and cardinal courts, a considerable quantity of luxury consumer goods were imported into the city.[20] Apart from being a city hungry for luxury goods, Rome was also an important financial market. In both cases, it was non-Romans who acted as intermediaries and who benefited particularly from these transactions; and among the non-Romans it was the Florentines who stood out, holding a virtual monopoly on the ecclesiastical financial movements, and therefore also influencing decisions of a more purely political nature. They used Rome as a market for their own products imported from Florence (the luxury goods industry was sustained by the growing demand on the part of the papal court, as well as the smaller courts of the cardinals),[21] at the same time exporting the whole package of economic and accounting techniques that was part of the Florentine tradition.[22] Florentines were by this time so omnipresent in the various sectors of Rome's economic and cultural life that, according to Esch, 'das Rom der Renaissance ist das Rom nicht der Römer, sondern der Florentiner' ('Renaissance Rome is not the Rome of the Romans, but of the Florentines').[23]

One very singular advantage enjoyed by the papacy at this time was that it received vast amounts of revenue from all over Europe. Clearly these large sums of money had to be transferred somehow, and to this end the popes used the pre-eminent Italian merchant-bankers, who had correspondents and emissaries in the most important

---

20 In the fifteenth century, particularly when ecumenical councils were held, the papal court was transferred outside Rome, sometimes even for several years (as, for example, occurred under Eugene IV, from 1434 to 1443). The papal bankers, who, it should be remembered, were denominated *romanam curiam sequentes*, followed the court in order to meet the rich and varied needs of this large group of people, which included cardinals, other prelates etc.

21 See, for example, the works of H. Hoshino, 'Interessi economici dei lanaiuoli fiorentini nello Stato pontificio e negli Abruzzi nel Quattrocento', *Annuario dell'Istituto Giapponese di cultura*, XI (1973-74): 7-51, which concentrates above all on the amount of goods traded; and of A. Esch, 'Le importazioni nella Roma del primo Rinascimento', in *Aspetti della vita economica e culturale a Roma nel Quattrocento* (Rome, 1981), pp. 7-79 and 'Importe in das Rom der Renaissance. Die Zollregister der Jahre 1470 bis 1480', *Quellen und Forschungen aus italienischen Archiven und Bibliotheken*, 74 (1994): 360-453 (in part.: 378-389), which instead concentrates particularly on the value of the goods traded. By the same author, see also, with regard to the importation of art objects, 'Roman Customs Registers 1470-80: items of interest to historians of art and material culture', *Journal of the Warburg and Courtauld Institutes*, 58 (1995): 72-87.

22 For more on this aspect, see the study by L. Palermo, 'Un aspetto della presenza dei fiorentini a Roma nel '400: le tecniche economiche', in *Forestieri e stranieri*, pp. 81-96. The same author also points out that, from the first years of the fifteenth century, the Florentines had become involved in the management of the port of Ripa, the principal point of entry for imported goods, as well as in the management of various excises (L. Palermo, *Il porto di Roma nel XIV e XV secolo. Strutture socio-economiche e statuti* (Rome, 1979), pp. 37-60).

23 Esch, 'Florentiner in Rom', p. 476.

financial markets of the continent.[24] Given that Rome, as has already been pointed out several times, was mostly a city which dealt with imports, producing little of its own for export, the commerce practised by the banking agents was triangular, using intermediary markets. The banks charged with gathering the sums of money owed to the papacy often 'advanced' an equivalent amount to the Apostolic Chamber. Moreover, the dense network of branches and correspondents created by every great banking house to connect the principal markets of Europe represented an essential support structure for the Curia when it wanted to effect payments abroad.

In the fifteenth century the post of depositary general of the Apostolic Chamber, or, in other words, the first papal banker, who was responsible for the management of the papal finances, was nearly always filled by a Florentine, usually the director of the Roman branch of his particular bank. At the beginning of the century this role was played by the Spini bank, but from 1420 to 1476, with one or two brief interruptions, it was taken over by the directors of the Roman branch of the Medici bank.[25] However, it should be pointed out that not only the Medici, but all the most illustrious family banks of Florence had interests in the city of the pope, and their activity, revolving around the Curia, exercised an influence that extended from the economic to the socio-cultural sphere. Both quantitatively (besides the Medici, there were also, to name but a few, the Cambini, the Pazzi and the Spinelli families) and qualitatively (the importance of the services offered) the Florentines clearly held sway over the city. They were, in short, the main point of reference for the finances of the papal court, and consequently, of Rome: it is generally accepted, in fact, that the Eternal City was an appendix of the papal court, and that Roman finances were, in the final analysis, equivalent to papal finances.

The relationship between the Florentines resident in Rome and the papal court was not always an easy one. In 1478, for example, the excommunication of Sixtus IV brought about a temporary deterioration in relations between the two groups, albeit with not particularly devastating effects.[26] Episodes such as this were not, however, very frequent, because all things considered the papacy was unable to survive without the Florentine bankers and, more to the point, their money.

Thus far, then, two motives that encouraged the Florentines, especially the merchant-bankers, to move to Rome have been identified: the existence of a flourishing local market and the international structure of the papal finances. In the

---

24 As E. Stumpo noted, a fiscal system thus organized was the first to be operated on such a large scale, thanks to the pre-existing ecclesiastical structure. Moreover, it contributed not a little to boosting a monetary economy ('Economia naturale ed economia monetaria: l'imposta', in *Storia d'Italia. Annali, 6, Economia naturale, economia monetaria* (Turin, 1983), p. 546).

25 For a more detailed account of the activities of the Medici as papal bankers, see G. Holmes, 'How the Medici became the Pope's Bankers', in N. Rubinstein (ed.), *Florentine Studies. Politics and Society in Renaissance Florence* (London, 1968), pp. 357-380; see also R. De Roover, *The Rise and Decline of the Medici Bank (1397-1494)* (New York, 1966), pp. 194-224.

26 In fact it was only for two months that no Florentine goods were cleared through customs, as is pointed out by I. Ait, in 'La dogana di terra come fonte per lo studio della presenza di mercanti stranieri a Roma nel XV secolo', in *Forestieri e stranieri*, p. 34 (this work concentrates particularly on the Florentine merchant-bankers on pp. 32-38).

second half of the fifteenth century, and more markedly in the sixteenth, they were also attracted by other factors: first of all, the Tolfa alum mines, which, discovered in 1462, constituted a notable source of profit (see Chapter 8, esp. pp. 167-171); and secondly, the development of the territorial State and the new fiscal organization this necessitated. The papacy's ever increasing financial needs led to a system of more rigorous and efficient taxation, which relied heavily on the collaboration of the bankers: the latter contracted to collect certain levies, advancing to the Apostolic Chamber a previously stipulated amount, which they then recouped directly from the various communes. This relationship between the Apostolic Chamber and the merchant-bankers is, as was mentioned in the introduction, the nucleus of this research.

Organization of the Florentine colony in Rome

The various national colonies in Rome, especially the larger ones, felt the need to create a national association that represented them. In the case of the Florentines, the main expression of this could be found in two confraternities: that of the Pietà and that of S. Giovanni Decollato.

The Florentine nation in Rome quickly became a highly organized group. In 1448, for example, 'it pleased a number of good men then living in Rome to gather together', and these originally informal meetings became the basis for the creation of the national confraternity of the Pietà di S. Giovanni Battista.[27] This confraternity initially came into being as an expression of brotherly solidarity, with the aim of providing mutual aid, when there was an outbreak of a serious epidemic of the plague in Rome, and it became clear that the existing structures were inadequate to deal with the emergency.[28] In 1456 this brotherly impulse was given a formal structure: statutes and rules were laid down, guaranteeing the association's continuity. Its first headquarters were set up in S. Lucia *vecchia* (renamed S. Giovanni in Lucia), but the meetings were held at S. Salvatore in Lauro; then, in 1462, it moved to S. Pantaleo *ad flumen*. Once the danger of the plague had passed, the company of the Pietà broadened its scope, its stated purpose now being to represent the nation (which was already numerous and continuing to expand, but without a consulate until 1515) as the only institution recognized both by Rome and by Florence.[29] From an analysis of the – albeit fragmentary – registers of the national confraternity, the composition of the Florentine colony can be easily deduced. Besides the elitist component of

27 The quotation comes from the preamble of the statutes of 1456 (AASGF, vol. 344, *Ospedale e confraternita*).

28 For a more detailed study of the organizational and charitable aspects of the confraternities, see: I. Polverini Fosi, 'Pietà, devozione e politica: due confraternite fiorentine nella Roma del Rinascimento', *Archivio Storico Italiano*, 149 (1991): 119-161 and E. Rufini, 'L'Archivio di San Giovanni dei Fiorentini in Roma e la Compagnia della Pietà', in Archivio di Stato di Roma, *Scuola di Paleografia Diplomatica e Archivistica, Lezioni speciali*, 1962-63, pp. 108-134.

29 Polverini Fosi, 'Pietà, devozione e politica': 131.

merchant-bankers, various groups of artisans were also fairly well represented: gold- and silversmiths, paper manufacturers and booksellers.[30]

In 1488 the company of the Pietà was flanked by a second Florentine confraternity, S. Giovanni Decollato. The latter's principal aim was to give assistance to those condemned to death and to guarantee that after their death they would be given a dignified burial. This second confraternity enjoyed particular popularity at this time, as the Pietà, in its bid to become a symbol of national unity, had to some degree forgotten its charitable aims. At this point the two confraternities were complementary, with the Pietà acting mostly as an associative symbol of citizens' unity, and S. Giovanni Decollato instead acting mostly as a charitable organization. In the first years of the sixteenth century this was reflected, in a certain sense, in the composition of the two confraternities: the first, which became progressively more hierarchical, was dominated by the merchant-banker families, who increasingly sought to use their charitable activities to further their social affirmation and political recognition; the second was instead dominated by artisans.[31] From 1515 onwards, however, both confraternities lost their authority to the newly instituted consulate.

The position of the Florentine colony of Rome was influenced by the often difficult and quarrelsome relationship between the papacy and Florence. Vulnerable to blackmail by both sides, the *mercatores romanam curiam sequentes* sought to act as mediators in order to avoid any negative backlash resulting from the diplomatic policies of their motherland. As early as the end of the fifteenth century, moreover, they expressed their wish for their nation to be represented by a consul, as already existed elsewhere. However, the pro-Medici tendency of the majority of the Florentine merchants in Rome, who at the dawn of the sixteenth century were already beginning to group themselves around Cardinal Giovanni de' Medici (the future Pope Leo X, and son of Lorenzo *il Magnifico*), was looked upon suspiciously by the current Republican government of Florence, which therefore declined to give them totally unqualified support.

During his pontificate, therefore, Julius II (1503-13) kept the Florentines in a state of uncertainty by exploiting their fear that events might turn against them.[32] Nevertheless, as its ties with the Curia became ever tighter and more intricate, so the nation continued to grow in economic importance. The high point came in September 1512, when the Medici restored their rule over Florence, and the Florentines resident in Rome found that the situation had turned completely in their favour. This change in the wind was underscored the following year when one of their fellow citizens ascended to the papal throne, although it should be pointed out that the election of

30 Polverini Fosi, 'Pietà, devozione e politica': 140-142.

31 Polverini Fosi, 'Pietà, devozione e politica': 133-134, 149. The extent to which the highest levels of the confraternity of the Pietà were by then filled almost exclusively by merchant-bankers is demonstrated by the feast of Candlemas of 1548, when it was the most illustrious *mercatores* who carried the blessed candle to the pope and to the most important ecclesiastics (I. Polverini Fosi, 'I fiorentini a Roma nel Cinquecento: storia di una presenza', in Gensini (ed.), *Roma capitale (1447-1527)*, p. 404).

32 I. Polverini Fosi, 'Il consolato fiorentino a Roma ed il progetto per la chiesa nazionale', *Studi Romani*, 37 (1989): 57.

Leo X in fact served mostly to sanction or to 'institutionalize' the already existing Florentine supremacy.

The heart of the Florentine colony in Rome was in the *rione* Ponte, situated in the loop of the Tiber which lies in front of St Peter's: while this area was home to 16% of the population of Rome overall,[33] the proportion of all Florentines in Rome living there was 34.85%. (Nevertheless, their presence in this area of the city should not be overestimated: although 34.85% is a high percentage, it should be remembered that two-thirds lived elsewhere.)[34] According to Delumeau, of the 3,495 people whose place of origin is expressly indicated in the census of 1526-27, 393 (11.24%) were from Florence, from Lucca and from other parts of Tuscany, and of these 118 (30%) lived in the *rione* Ponte.[35] In the last few decades of the fifteenth century it also included amongst its residents various families belonging to the Florentine aristocracy. Florentine merchant-bankers continued to be identified with this area over the years, as is demonstrated by various episodes: in 1545, for example, Giovan Battista Altoviti was made *caporione* (head of the *rione*).[36]

At the end of the century Julius II Della Rovere began to reorganize the city layout, his first action being to construct Via Giulia and Via della Lungara (previously known as Via Settimiana). The financial connection between the pope and the great Sienese banker Agostino Chigi was reflected in the creation of a geographical connection between St Peter's, Trastevere and the area where the banks were situated (or, in other words, between the religious heart of the city, its port and its financial centre). The same period saw the construction of the *palazzi* that housed the Apostolic Chamber (today the Chancellery), the Mint, the Old Chancellery (today known as the *palazzo* Sforza-Cesarini) and the Lawcourts. During the reign of Leo X construction was begun on S. Giovanni dei Fiorentini, while Paul III's reign saw the inauguration of Via Paola, built to join the church to the Piazza di Ponte, site of the *palazzo* Altoviti. Looking at the maps of that time it is immediately clear that all the main roads converged on Sant'Angelo bridge, the only point of access to the Vatican. The hub was the so-called 'goose's claw' between the streets today known as Via Paola, Via del Banco di S. Spirito and Via di Panico. The axis Via dei Banchi vecchi-Via del Banco di S. Spirito (behind the *palazzo* of the Old Chancellery), destroyed by the construction of Corso Vittorio Emanuele, was called the '*retro Banchi*'. From the Sisto bridge to the Sant'Angelo bridge, 'aristocracy and finance, art, traffic, industry crouch on the left bank of the Tiber, staring at the opposite bank'.[37] The intensity of

33 This was the largest *rione* in terms of population and the third in density (M. Romani, *Pellegrini e viaggiatori nell'economia di Roma dal XIV al XVII* secolo (Milan, 1948), pp. 68-69).

34 E. Lee, 'Gli abitanti del rione Ponte', in Gensini (ed.), *Roma capitale (1447-1527)*, pp. 326-327. The author, while not ignoring the strong Florentine presence, emphasizes the varied origins of the inhabitants of this *rione*.

35 Delumeau, *Vie économique et sociale*, I, pp. 198 (table), 207-211.

36 V. Forcella, *Tornei e giostre, ingressi trionfali e feste carnevalesche in Roma sotto Paolo III* (Rome, 1885, reprinted Bologna, 1971), p. 106.

37 '*Aristocrazia e finanza, arte, traffico, industria si accalcano sulla sponda sinistra del Tevere, coll'occhio fisso sulla sponda opposta*' (E. Rocchi, *Le piante iconografiche e prospettiche di Roma del secolo XVI* (Turin-Rome, 1902), p. 46).

the merchant-banking activities is underlined by an account written after the Sack of 1527: 'When they sacked *Banchi*, they threw from the windows into the street books and other important documents. And from the Castle the streets from Via de' Banchi to the Mint were so covered with paper that it looked like it had been snowing'.[38]

The Medici papacies (1513-21, 1523-34)

The above discussion clearly explains why many authors speak of the 'Florentinization' of Renaissance Rome.[39] The various events described meant that in the course of the fifteenth century the Florentines came to have an increasingly stable and institutionalized role in the management of the affairs of the Apostolic Chamber. The two pontificates of Leo X and of Clement VII, manifest symbols of this 'Florentinization' and holding positions of absolute power, should be understood in this context.

Cardinal Giovanni de' Medici, the future Leo X, had become the focal point of a court which attracted the interest of the major Florentine merchant-banking families resident in Rome, and on whom, in his turn, he bestowed tangible signs of favouritism. When he became pope, his fellow citizens were triumphant, as they were clearly aware that his election was a tangible sanctioning of the Florentine hegemony. Leo X's coronation meant that the requests of the Florentines would be listened to and considered as never before. In fact, by no mere chance did the first years of Leo X's pontificate see the institution of the Florentine consulate and the authorization to build a national church, both of which had for some years been desired by the Florentine colony of Rome. The charter of the consulate was approved by a papal bull issued on 12 June 1515,[40] and the following 30 August, having modified several points, the sea consuls of Florence issued the definitive statute.[41] The Florentine nation in Rome had thus finally achieved autonomy, now being regulated by laws which guaranteed a certain degree of immunity and possessing its own legislative body, who in particular had full jurisdiction in civil cases. Moreover, the consulate was a political institution, which claimed its right to act as principal interlocutor in the relationship between Florence and Rome. The norms laid down in the chapters of the statute were more or less analogous to those established for the

38 '*Quando saccheggiorno Banchi, gittorno per le finestre in la strada li libri et altre scritture de importantia. Et da castello se vedeva la strada de' Banchi fino alla Zecca coperta de scritture che pareva fosse fioccato*'. Quoted in L. Pratesi, *Il rione Ponte* (Rome, 1994), p. 8.

39 Delumeau points out that under Leo X Tuscan became the language of the court. It was normal for every new pope to introduce his own mother-tongue; what was unusual, however, as Delumeau points out, was that in this case the use of the Tuscan language was not lost, even when the Medici popes had disappeared (*Vie économique et sociale*, I, p. 211).

40 *Bullarum Privilegiorum ac Diplomatum Romanorum Pontificum Amplissima Collectio cui accessere pontificum omnium vitae, notae & indices opportuni. Opera et studio Caroli Cocquelines* (6 vols, Rome, 1739-62, reprinted Graz, 1964-67), *Tomus Tertius*, 1743, pp. 469-471.

41 Polverini Fosi, 'Il consolato fiorentino a Roma': 58-59 and note 36 for the inventory number of the existing copies of the statute. For further details on the institution of the consulate see esp. 58-64.

Florentine consulates that already existed in various cities elsewhere,[42] although the rules for electing the consul were far more restrictive. This last was a clear sign that the mercantile élite was now in control of the colony.[43]

The consulate was financed by fixed percentages on the various transactions carried out by the Florentines on the Roman market: 0.025% on bills of exchange, both drawn and remitted, and on insurance, 0.017% on the dispatch of papal bulls and briefs. The money thus raised was intended for the construction of the church and of a *palazzo* to house the consulate.[44]

The members of the Florentine nation of Rome[45] were therefore now exempt from the civil jurisdiction of the Roman lawcourts, in that the consulate proclaimed itself the unique supervisor of all Florentine financial operations; in practice the Florentine nation in Rome became a State within a State. This privilege was confirmed a number of years later by Paul III Farnese, soon after his election as successor to Clement VII.[46]

From 1515 onwards, therefore, a consul and two councillors were elected annually from amongst the Florentine merchants resident in Rome. Running down the list of consuls, the names of the most renowned bankers of the epoch can be found, names which resurface time and again in the rest of this volume: from Filippo Strozzi (1523, 1533) to Francesco Del Nero (1529, 1559), from Bindo Altoviti (1531, 1550) to Benvenuto Olivieri (1534, 1545), from Bastiano da Montauto (1537, 1546) to Luigi Rucellai (1538, 1547).[47]

Even before the papacy of Leo X, however, there were tangible signs of the Florentines' position in Rome. One of the symbols of the increased importance of the Florentines was, for example, the above-mentioned construction of a national church, named S. Giovanni dei Fiorentini, in honour of Florence's patron saint. Its construction was authorized by Julius II, in a decree of 10 September 1508, even if work only began in 1518. The precedence given to the consulate over the church was because, according to Polverini Fosi, Leo X wanted first of all to institutionalize the Florentine nation before sanctifying it. The same author notes that the church was largely financed by those Florentines who were already well established in Rome, while there was a certain coldness towards the whole project from the relative

42 Cf. *Statuti delle colonie fiorentine all'estero (secc. XV-XVI)*, ed. G. Masi (Milan, 1941).

43 Polverini Fosi, 'Il consolato fiorentino a Roma': 59.

44 Delumeau, *Vie économique et sociale*, II, pp. 879-880. See also the *libro azzurro A secondo* of Benvenuto Olivieri & Partners of Rome: ASF, Galli Tassi, 2278, fols 66, 202.

45 It was specifically stated that '*si debba intendere stante et residente in detta Corte et Città di Roma ... tutti quelli che terranno casa aperta a Roma di bancho o fondaco o altro simile exercitio, o che habbino compagni o compagnie ferme per habitare et frequentare in detto luogo di Roma o a Ripa con stare saldamente uno anno o più*' (AASGF, vol. 321, *Statuti del consolato*, ch. XLIII).

46 Rufini, 'L'Archivio di San Giovanni dei Fiorentini', p. 131.

47 A complete list of the consuls between 1515 and 1620, taken from a register of the Archivio di S. Giovanni dei Fiorentini, can be found in Delumeau, *Vie économique et sociale*, I, pp. 209-210 (note 2). M.M. Bullard, *Filippo Strozzi and the Medici. Favor and Finance in Sixteenth-century Florence and Rome* (Cambridge, 1980), p. 94 (note 9) highlights, however, several errors of transcription.

newcomers, those who had arrived in the Eternal City only after the election of their fellow countryman; the Florentine prelates, moreover, remained completely detached, despite the generous contributions made by the pontiff.[48] Consequently, on the death of Leo X work on the church was interrupted. As for the ability of the parish of S. Giovanni dei Fiorentini to unite its flock, it has been noted how in reality the parochial community that already existed maintained their links with a good number of members of the nation, who in any case were assiduous in their frequenting of the national association.[49]

In her research to quantify the Florentine banks in Rome, Melissa Bullard has discovered in the Archivio Segreto of the Vatican two safe-conducts that allowed the companies listed to exercise their business affairs without hindrance.[50] These documents, dated 25 February 1494 and 3 October 1511 (years in which, it should be pointed out, the relationship between the papacy and the government of Florence was anything but easy), list respectively twenty-five and thirty-one companies of Florentine merchant-bankers in Rome; nine of these appear under the same name in both the documents, a further eight suggest a family connection. Altoviti, Della Casa and Strozzi, to name but three of the bankers that will be found frequently in this volume, appear to already have been well established. For the years of Leo X's reign there exist no similar documents but this is because when the papal throne was filled by a Florentine, protection was obviously guaranteed without the need for particular safe-conducts. Bullard estimates at around thirty the number of banks that in the period of the two Medici papacies (1513-34) were designated as belonging to the *mercatores florentini romanam curiam sequentes*; and of these, a good twenty were already active before 1513.[51] As will be examined in more depth in the following, the Florentine bankers continued to wield influence even after the death of Clement VII, during the pontificate of Paul III Farnese.

A clear example of the favours bestowed on the Florentines by the Medici popes is the administration of the Mint. In 1515, two years after his election, Leo X removed it from the Fugger bank, the Germans who had been so influential in Rome until the first years of the sixteenth century, and handed it over to his own fellow citizens. His successor, Adrian VI Florensz (1522-23), interrupted the contract with the Florentines, placing the Mint once again in the hands of an agent of the Fugger bank. But with the arrival of the new Medici pope, Clement VII, the Mint once more

48 Polverini Fosi, 'Il consolato fiorentino a Roma': 67-69. The list of all the contributors in these years can also be found in the small volume AASGF, vol. 431 (*Libro dell'elenco delli benefattori, contribuenti e sottoscritti per sovvenimento della fabrica*); for subsequent contributions, see also the Appendix, doc. 1. For a longer description of the financing of the Church through time, see F. Guidi Bruscoli, 'S. Giovanni dei Fiorentini a Roma. Due secoli di finanziamenti tra pontefici e granduchi, prelati e *mercatanti*', *Quellen und Forschungen aus den italienischen Archiven und Bibliotheken*, 86 (2006): 294-320.

49 Polverini Fosi, 'I fiorentini a Roma', p. 401.

50 M.M. Bullard, '"Mercatores Florentini Romanam Curiam Sequentes" in the early sixteenth century', *The Journal of Medieval and Renaissance Studies*, 6 (1976): 55 (esp. notes 18 and 19).

51 Bullard, 'Mercatores Florentini': 57-59.

changed hands and was again handed over to the 'consuls and councillors of our Florentine nation'.[52]

A good example of how papal favours worked is the case of Jacopo Salviati (1461-1533). Jacopo, who was brother-in-law to Cardinal Giovanni de' Medici, having married the latter's sister Lucrezia, was already living in Rome in 1512, as ambassador of the Florentine Republic. Giovanni de' Medici's ascension to the papal throne as Leo X immediately brought Jacopo notable advantages: by 1514 he had already been assigned the administration of the Treasury of the Romagna, as well as that of the salt of the Papal State, on much better conditions than those which were given to his predecessor, the Genoese banker Giovanni Sauli. From then until 1531 Salviati not only profited financially (an average of 15,000 ducats net per annum), but he also gained great prestige in politico-social terms, becoming, in 1523, the personal secretary of Pope Clement VII. His sons all settled in Rome, acquiring various posts of responsibility, amongst which were the highest honours possible of two cardinalships, bestowed on Giovanni in 1517 and on Bernardo in 1561.[53]

Having enjoyed the great extravagance of Leo X, the bankers were very unhappy at the introduction of Adrian VI's financial constraints and began to quit the city. Not surprisingly, therefore, they rejoiced greatly at his death. History has it that on Adrian's death a piece of paper was attached to his physician's door, singing the latter's praises as saviour of the city.[54] It is true, in fact, that the Florentines, who had made huge loans to Leo X relying solely on the goodwill of their fellow citizen for their repayment, had much to fear.[55] Consequently, they were greatly relieved at the election, in 1523, of Clement VII, who showed himself willing to meet the obligations undertaken by his predecessor, Leo X. The situation thus began to return to one of normality for the Florentines, who once again tightened their grip on the financial reins of the papacy. Of all the pope's bankers, one who stood out head and shoulders above the rest was a man of considerable importance, both political and economic: Filippo Strozzi.[56] He had enthusiastically supported Giovanni de' Medici in his bid to be elected pope, and for this was rewarded with the post of

52 For further details, see Schulte, *Die Fugger in Rom*, I, pp. 205, 209, 219; II, pp. 122, 146. On the Mint, see also Chapter 8, pp. 180-182.

53 P. Hurtubise, 'L'implantation d'une famille florentine', pp. 253-271. For more information about the Salviati family, see, by the same author, *Une famille-témoin. Les Salviati* (Vatican City, 1985).

54 Partner, *Renaissance Rome*, pp. 57-58.

55 As Bullard has noted, the fact of depending on the pledges of the pope increasingly tied the Florentines to the papal debts (*Filippo Strozzi and the Medici*, pp. 22-23).

56 Filippo's wife was Clarice de' Medici, granddaughter of Lorenzo *il Magnifico* and niece of Leo X. To this famous matrimony, which united two such prestigious families and which was to have such importance in determining future events, especially for the Strozzi family, M.M. Bullard has devoted an article: 'Marriage, Politics and the Family in Florence: The Strozzi-Medici Alliance of 1508', *American Historical Review*, 84 (1979): 668-687. On the life and the activities of Strozzi as pope's banker and as a public personality, see also Bullard, *Filippo Strozzi and the Medici*. In this volume, esp. pp. 91-118, 151-178, can be found details of the numerous contracts entered into by Strozzi and by other Florentines during the papacies of Leo X and Clement VII.

depositary general. Filippo Strozzi's first Roman company began its activity in 1515, and its success was certainly favoured by the political influence of its *maggiore*, or senior partner. The company was reorganized several times and Filippo himself was directly involved from 1523 onwards, when he moved to Rome.[57] It would seem that fear of reprisals caused him to dissolve the company immediately after the death of Clement VII, putting the new company in the name of his sons, Giulio and Lorenzo (this is discussed in Chapter 2, p. 49).

The Sack of 1527, when the soldiers of Charles V went on a rampage through the city, is often seen as a turning point for the history of Rome of this period. However, while the bourgeoisie and the poorer part of the population suffered greatly, the same cannot be said for the rich merchant-bankers who, while not passing this unpropitious period completely unscathed, survived by setting themselves up as a lifebelt for a papacy which was navigating in difficult economic waters and which was in need of ever greater revenue. Moreover, according to Polverini Fosi, despite the economic and social upheaval in the wake of the Sack of 1527, the substantial and powerful group of merchant-banking families provided the continuity necessary for the arrival of other professional classes, for example notaries, physicians, spicers and others.[58]

The protection guaranteed by the pope to his fellow countrymen obviously stoked the hatred of the Romans, who felt that what was theirs by right was being usurped by these outsiders. Emblematic of this hatred were the riots that occurred on the death of Clement VII (25 September 1534), as a consequence of a crisis caused by a grain shortage in the years 1533-34.[59] Following the shortage in supplies of the early 1530s, Clement VII authorized the import of Sicilian grain. The man given the responsibility for this was – naturally – Filippo Strozzi, at that time perhaps the richest and most powerful banker in Rome. The marriage between Catherine de' Medici (niece of the pope) and Henry, Duke of Orleans, however, threw Charles V into a rage of fury and pushed him to revoke the agreement he had made with the pope. Strozzi therefore had to resort to French grain, but the delays in the arrival of supplies led to the first mobilization of the population of Rome, threatening, amongst others, Strozzi's agents. In 1533, the fact that the grain had to be procured from ever further away (Flanders), the loss of several ships which were transporting it and the damage sustained by the cargoes of several others, forced the agents of the Florentine banker to sell the little grain which had in fact arrived (there were no reserves from the year before) at double the price originally agreed upon. Shortly afterwards Clement VII died, at which point the fury of the masses was unleashed, with Strozzi their favourite target: his warehouses were sacked, his bank and its agents seriously threatened. According to Bullard, however, 'the riots of 1534 expressed a deep level of resentment, not merely against individual favorites or the

57 R.A. Goldthwaite, *Private Wealth in Renaissance Florence. A Study of Four Families* (Princeton N.J., 1968), pp. 90-93. The father of Filippo, Filippo di Matteo, already active in the financial markets of Florence and Naples, had opened the first branch in Rome in 1482 (p. 57).

58 Polverini Fosi, 'I fiorentini a Roma', p. 410.

59 For an account specifically dedicated to the events of these years, see M.M. Bullard, 'Grain Supply and Urban Unrest in Renaissance Rome: the Crisis of 1533-34', in P.A. Ramsey (ed.), *Rome in the Renaissance. The City and the Myth* (Binghamton N.Y., 1982), pp. 279-292.

specific events of 1533-34, but against Clement VII's government and against the papacy's gradual appropriation of municipal power in progress since the schism';[60] although it should be pointed out that there had always existed a reciprocal contempt between Florentines and Romans. The Roman government decided to sue Strozzi for an exorbitant sum of money (700,000 *scudi*). Later, however, this was reduced to 17,500 *scudi*, and eventually Paul III decided to freeze the amount. Moreover, although the majority of the council was opposed to his decision, he refused to withdraw his own deposit from the Strozzi bank. Evidently, money spoke more loudly than principle.

It has already been mentioned that, basing her research on several Roman and Vatican documents of the period, Bullard has identified thirty Florentine banks that were involved with the Curia between 1513 and 1534 (this therefore does not include other Florentine companies that might have been working in Rome in an exclusively commercial sphere of activity) and whose principals were therefore normally referred to as *mercatores florentini romanam curiam sequentes* or *mercatori di corte*. From the numbers it does not seem that there was a great change in the substance of the Florentine banking agencies between the papacy of Julius II and those of Leo X and Clement VII. If anything, in the last years of Clement VII's reign, the difficulties came from the fact that the banks were at war with their own home town. In 1527 their situation was complicated even further by the Sack of Rome. Nevertheless, while some banks did indeed abandon their activity, others (at least eleven) continued, while yet others (at least ten) began theirs under Pope Paul III Farnese.[61]

Political exiles

At this point it seems opportune to examine the political leanings of the Florentines of Rome and what their position was with regard to Florence and to the papacy, especially considering the rocky relationship that existed between the two.

In 1530, after the fall of the last Republic, Duke Alessandro, a member of the Medici family, had taken power in Florence. From the very beginning he had shown considerable resentment towards Filippo Strozzi, which simmered until the death of Alessandro's uncle, Clement VII, and then exploded into violence. The banker's reaction was to ally himself with those Florentine political exiles who were seeking to rebuild an opposition to the Medici, perhaps himself aspiring to take on an important role. Then, in January 1537, Duke Alessandro was assassinated by Lorenzino de' Medici. From this moment on Strozzi was embroiled even more deeply in the actions of the exiles, who, in August of the same year, suffered military defeat at Montemurlo. Filippo was thrown into prison, where he died the following year, probably, it is believed, by his own hand.[62]

---

60 Bullard, 'Grain Supply', p. 283.

61 Bullard, 'Mercatores Florentini': 58-59.

62 For the events of these years, from the period of Alessandro de' Medici to the defeat of Montemurlo, see R. von Albertini, *Firenze dalla repubblica al principato* (Turin, 1970), pp. 201-224. On the relations of the political exiles, and of Strozzi in particular, with Paul III, see C. Capasso, *Filippo Strozzi, i fuoriusciti e la Corte pontificia* (Camerino, 1901); and the more

By the end of Paul III's reign, the relationship between the papacy and Florence had become very tense and consequently the position of Florentine merchants operating in Rome had become increasingly precarious. It must be said, however, that the essential economic contribution that they made to the finances of the pope, together with close ties of family and patronage, guaranteed them a certain degree of protection: there continued to be, in other words, a reciprocal politico-economic dependence that kept them together.[63]

The anger of the anti-Medici faction of the Florentine colony of Rome exploded again in 1554, when Giovan Battista Altoviti, whose family had traditionally been leaders of the exiles, attacked Averardo Serristori, Cosimo's representative in Rome, who had intercepted a letter from the king of France that urged the Florentine nation of Rome to revolt against the Duke of Florence.[64] It is important to underline the position of the papacy here: it sought to calm the waters, while maintaining a neutral position. It protected Cosimo's representative, but at the same time refrained from making a move against his enemies, on whom it depended financially. In 1554-55 the same Giovan Battista Altoviti, with his father Bindo and with Piero Strozzi, was at the head of an attempt to bring down the Medici regime (the war of Siena).[65] This led to the confiscation both of Bindo's property in Tuscany, and of the property which had come to him as part of the dowry of his wife, Fiammetta Soderini.

Bindo Altoviti (1491-1557), a long-time enemy of the Medici, was protected by and was the recipient of many favours from his patron, Paul III. In 1548 Cosimo I banned Bindo's son, Antonio Altoviti, who had been named archbishop of Florence, from entering Tuscany, and on the death of Paul III Cosimo lost no time in asking his successor, Julius III, to deliver the rebellious Antonio to him. Julius, however, refused.[66]

---

recent essay by P. Costamagna, 'Portraits of Florentine Exiles', in A. Chong-D. Pegazzano-D. Zikos (eds), *Raphael, Cellini & A Renaissance Banker. The Patronage of Bindo Altoviti* (Boston, 2003), pp. 329-350.

63 Polverini Fosi, 'I fiorentini a Roma', p. 395. For relations between the papacy and the Medici during this period, see also M. Lupo Gentile, *La politica di Paolo III nelle sue relazioni colla Corte Medicea* (Sarzana, 1906).

64 For further details about this episode, see Polverini Fosi, 'I fiorentini a Roma', p. 409.

65 It should be noted that the two most illustrious Florentine bankers in Rome, Filippo Strozzi (father of Piero) and Bindo Altoviti, linked by a common anti-Medici sentiment, were also related by marriage: the nephew of the former (the son of Filippo's brother, Lorenzo), Giovan Battista, was in fact the husband of the daughter of the latter, Marietta. In 1551 another marriage further strengthened the union between the two families: that between Clarice Ridolfi (daughter of Lorenzo Ridolfi and of Maria di Filippo Strozzi) and Giovan Battista di Bindo Altoviti (L. Passerini, *Genealogia e storia della famiglia Altoviti* (Florence, 1871), Table II).

66 For further information on Altoviti, see C. Belloni, *Un banchiere del Rinascimento, Bindo Altoviti* (Rome, 1935), esp. pp. 35-39; A. Stella, 'Altoviti Bindo', in *Dizionario Biografico degli Italiani* (Rome, 1960), II, pp. 574-575. And especially Chong-Pegazzano-Zikos (eds), *Raphael, Cellini & A Renaissance Banker*.

With the passage of time, however, the ill-feeling between the Florentine exiles and the Medici regime abated, to the point that in 1570 Cosimo I, on an official visit, was given a triumphal welcome by the Florentine nation of Rome.[67]

Mercatores florentini *in the Rome of Paul III Farnese (1534-49)*

This seems to be a good point at which to look somewhat more closely at what happened after 1534, the year in which Clement VII died, to the relations between the Curia and the Florentine bankers who collaborated with them. Despite the attempts by the Roman citizens, who for some time had been hostile to the Florentines and who with the arrival of a Farnese pope hoped, as has already been mentioned, finally to be rid of them, the position of the *mercatores florentini romanam curiam sequentes* remained strong. At least until the middle of the century, they continued to administer the customs, the provincial Treasuries, and the salt tax, to mention but a few of the services which by this time were virtually a monopoly in the hands of the Florentines. It was difficult to do without their expertise; in fact, the increasing fiscal pressure exercised by Paul III on the Papal State was only possible thanks to the Florentine merchant-bankers who guaranteed the efficient collection of new taxes throughout the territory.[68]

Evidence of the very close relationship between the Florentine bankers and the pontiff is easily found: for example, it is known that not only the renowned Bindo Altoviti, but also Pier Antonio Guasconi and Bartolomeo Bussotti made monetary contributions to the celebration of the funeral-rites of Paul III.[69] Altoviti, moreover, together with other Florentines, also contributed considerable sums to the coronation ceremony of Paul III's successor, the Roman Julius III Ciocchi del Monte.[70]

The clearest proof, however, that the Florentines kept a tight grip on their control of the papal finances comes from an analysis of the money transactions linking them to the Apostolic Chamber. In September 1540, of the 297,000 *scudi* which the Chamber owed to the *mercatores*, 151,000 had come from Florentine purses.[71] On 1 January 1548 a loan of 100,000 *scudi d'oro in oro* to the Apostolic Chamber was registered, with an interest of 12% to which were added 1,000 *scudi* 'for payment before time' and 2,000 *scudi* of premium on the part of the pontiff. As usual a goodly proportion of this money was contributed by the Florentine companies, 62% of the total amount to be precise: Luigi Rucellai contributed 16,000 *scudi*; Tommaso Cavalcanti and Giovanni Giraldi, 15,000; Bastiano da Montauto, 12,000; the heirs of Girolamo Ubaldini, who were succeeded by Benvenuto Olivieri, 7,000; Bindo Altoviti, 6,000; Pier Antonio and Alamanno Bandini, 6,000. The rest of the money

67 Delumeau, *Vie économique et sociale*, I, p. 210.

68 Polverini Fosi, 'I fiorentini a Roma', p. 392.

69 ASR, Camerale I, *Giustificazioni di Tesoreria*, busta 2, regg. 6, 7, 20.

70 ASR, Camerale I, *Giustificazioni di Tesoreria*, busta 2, regg. 9 (the accounts of Alessio Bettini), 14 (the accounts of Bindo Atoviti), 16 (the accounts of Giovan Battista Bonsi), 18 (the accounts of Francesco Scarlatti and Bernardo Acciaiuoli), 20 (the accounts of Bartolomeo Bussotti).

71 ASF, Galli Tassi 1942, fols 189-190; cf. also Chapter 3, p. 83.

was provided by Martino Bernardini, Francesco Cenami and Vincenzo Spada, all three from Lucca (20,000); the Genoese bankers Benedetto Negroni and Girolamo Pallavicini, (12,000); and Baldassarre Olgiatto from Como (6,000).[72]

Another of the more substantial loans which should be noted is that of 128,000 *scudi d'oro in oro* contracted for the period 1549-50, with interest at 12% per annum, to which were added a 2% commission and a 4% premium. The majority of the bankers who underwrote this loan were once again Florentines, contributing altogether 68.4% of the total: Cavalcanti and Giraldi (24,500 *scudi*), Olivieri (19,000), Rucellai (15,000), Montauto (8,000), Ubaldini (8,000), Bandini (7,000), and Altoviti, (6,000); the rest of the loan was put up by Olgiatto (16,000), Bernardini, Cenami and Spada (12,000), Negroni and Pallavicini (9,500), and Francesco Formento (3,000).[73]

The Florentine ascendancy becomes even clearer on examination of the contracts given to the various bankers by the Apostolic Chamber. This element will not be examined in detail here, but in the chapters dedicated to the relations between the Roman company of Benvenuto Olivieri and the Apostolic Chamber (the central part of this study) it will be seen how frequent and varied were the demands made on the *mercatores* by the papacy.

A fundamental role was played by the depositary general: the banker who managed the finances of the Papal State, responsible for both expenditure and the collection of a more or less substantial flow of income.[74] For most of the first half of the century this post remained in the hands of the Florentines: after Bindo Altoviti,[75] the Genoese Ansaldo Grimaldi[76] and the Florentine merchant Paolo Serragli,[77] it was the turn of Benvenuto Olivieri, who, assuming this role in July 1540, kept it until the end of 1542, and then took it on once again in 1543, after a brief period of management by Tobia Pallavicini, and finally for another two years, from 1545 to 1546.[78] After 1546, however, the Genoese bankers began to gain ascendancy.

The Treasuries are another case in point. The papacy often contracted out the administration of the Treasuries to the Florentines: the Treasury of the Romagna, which in the time of Clement VII had been a Tuscan fief, was given first to Salviati, then to Strozzi, followed by Galletti (together with Francesco Tosignani); then, after a brief Genoese interruption it returned into Florentine hands in 1545, when it was

72 For further details on this loan, see Chapter 3, pp. 90-91.

73 Again, for further details, see Chapter 3, pp. 91-93.

74 Numerous examples can be found in ASR, Camerale I, *Mandati Camerali 868-891* (referring to the years of Paul III's pontificate). A detailed overview of all the tax-farms contracted out by the Apostolic Chamber during this period is in F. Guidi Bruscoli, 'Mercanti-banchieri e appalti pontifici nel Cinquecento', in *La papauté, les offices et les charges publiques (XIVe-XVIIe siècle). Économies de l'office* (Rome, forthcoming).

75 Numerous references in ASR, Camerale I, *Mandati Camerali 868*.

76 ASR, Camerale I, *Mandati Camerali 869-872*; Camerale I, *Conti della Depositeria generale 1774-1776*.

77 Various references in ASR, Camerale I, *Mandati Camerali 872*.

78 The numerous sources, both Florentine and Roman, referring to Benvenuto in this period are not listed here. They are discussed in Chapter 3, pp. 72-81 and in the list of manuscript sources (pp. 271, 274-275); for a transcription of the contract relative to 1545-46, see the Appendix, doc. 5.

contracted for seven years to Benvenuto Olivieri, Bastiano da Montauto (who then ceded parts to various fellow citizens) and, with only a share of slightly more than 30%, to the Genoese Pallavicini and Giustiniani.[79] Moreover, the treasurer was more often than not assigned the collection of various local taxes, amongst which stood out, until 1543, the salt tax (Benvenuto Olivieri was responsible for administering the increase of the salt tax of the Romagna from 1540 to 1543);[80] and also the collection of the subsidy that, established in 1543 and originally intended to be triennial, was then prolonged several times (in this case too Olivieri was commissioner in charge of collection).[81] The Treasury of Perugia followed a slightly different path: dominated by the Genoese banker Sauli throughout the 1520s, it then passed decisively into Florentine hands, the treasurers being respectively Ottaviano de' Medici, Francesco Benci, Benvenuto Olivieri, and then, after an extremely brief interruption when the post was held by Curzio Frangipane and Sauli midway through the century, Bindo Altoviti, Bernardo Machiavelli, Roberto Ubaldini and his heirs.[82] Agostino Del Nero and Giovanni degli Albizzi were treasurers of Norcia.[83] Tommaso Cavalcanti and Giovanni Giraldi for a long time held the reins of the Treasury of Parma and Piacenza, succeeding their fellow countryman, Salvestro da Montauto.[84] Of all the Treasuries the richest was probably that of the Marches, which was managed by Filippo Strozzi and Antonio Ugolini (1532-35), Bindo Altoviti (1535-45), Pietro Ugolini and Giuliano Ardinghelli (1546-50). Bindo Altoviti, the most influential banker in the area, from 1536 to 1554 also maintained firm control of the *Salara* and was responsible for the collection of the Triennial Subsidy (1543-49).[85] In the same years Pietro and Niccolò Ugolini (1546-53) were treasurers of Ancona.[86] The Treasury of Ascoli saw the succession of Sinibaldo Gaddi (1538-41), Pietro Ugolini (1545-48) and Bindo Altoviti (1548-50);[87] that of Camerino, Bindo Altoviti (1539-40), Scipione Conti and Bastiano da Montauto (1545-50);[88] Altoviti was also treasurer

---

79 For the Florentine sources, see esp. ASF, Galli Tassi 1850-1851; for the Roman sources, ASR, Camerale I, *Tesoreria provinciale della Romagna*, buste 6-15 (esp. buste 14-15). For further details see Chapter 6, pp. 137-141.

80 Refer to Chapter 7, pp. 150-153, for exact indications as to the sources. Specifically concerning the salt contract are ASF, Galli Tassi, 1863-1866.

81 This is examined in Chapter 7, pp. 158-160.

82 The 'Florentine' share was 65% during the period the Treasury was managed by Benci-Olivieri, but even under the administration of Sauli-Frangipane it was around 30%. Most of the Florentine documents can be found in ASF, Galli Tassi 1845-1848; the Roman ones in ASR, Camerale I, *Tesoreria provinciale di Umbria e Perugia*, buste 29-39 (esp. buste 30-31). For further details, see Chapter 6, pp. 131-137; the contract that assigned the 1541 Treasury to Olivieri and his partners is transcribed in the Appendix, doc. 6.

83 ASF, Diplomatico, *Dono Torrigiani-Appendice*, 7 September 1536; ASV, *Cam. Ap., Div. Cam. 134*, fol. 124r.

84 The sources are indicated in Chapter 6, pp. 141-142.

85 ASR, Camerale I, *Tesoreria provinciale della Marca*, buste 25-27; ASF, Galli Tassi 1977, fols 35, 73; *Torrigiani-Appendice*, filze 1-4.

86 ASR, *Notai segretari e cancellieri della R. Camera apostolica 1988*, fols 692r-696r.

87 ASR, Camerale I, *Tesoreria provinciale di Ascoli*, busta 7, regg. 30, 32-35, 37.

88 For all: ASR, Camerale I, *Tesoreria provinciale di Camerino*, busta 1.

of Fermo (1538).[89] The Treasury of the Patrimonio, finally, was administered in the same years by, among others, Bartolomeo Pucci and Alessandro Del Bene.[90]

The *Salara* of Rome should also be mentioned here: it was held first by Benvenuto Olivieri, Luigi Gaddi and by the Bolognese banker Jacopo Zambeccari between 1539 and 1542, then contracted to Antonio Covoni together with, firstly, the above-mentioned Zambeccari (1542-45) and, secondly, Pier Antonio Bandini (from 1551).[91]

Among the primary sources of income for the Apostolic Chamber were the customs of Ripa and Ripetta (situated on the Tiber), of Merci and of Grascia; these too were controlled by the Florentines. Under the pontificate of Paul III, Giulio and Lorenzo Strozzi, who operated with the Genoese Sauli (1538-42), were succeeded by Benvenuto Olivieri and Bastiano da Montauto (1543-49), who, before the death of the Farnese pope, had already signed the contract for the following seven years; and together with other fellow countrymen had the financial resources to pay 73,000 *scudi* per annum in the first period and 90,000 in the second.[92]

Banking was not, however, the only activity which made for a close relationship between the Florentines and the Apostolic Chamber: many of the bankers were in fact also merchants, exercising the two professions more or less simultaneously, contributing to the needs of the pope's 'family' in particular with goods from the textile industry. Amongst the Florentines who should be mentioned in this context are: Paolo Serragli, Filippo Carducci (head of an *accomandita*, or limited partnership, in which the Olivieri company also participated, see Chapter 2, pp. 60-61), Ludovico Del Palagio and Leonardo and Alessandro Bartoli, whose names reoccur several times in orders of payment for the above-mentioned goods.[93]

To sum up, then, it seems clear that during the first non-Medici pontificate, after twenty years spent under the reign of Leo X and Clement VII (with the negligible interval of Adrian VI), the Florentines suffered no particular ill effects: on the contrary, they maintained the prestigious positions that they had acquired in the preceding years, even if such a period of ascendancy was clearly unlikely to be repeated. Certainly, it cannot be denied that this period of privilege had made a contribution to

89 ASR, Camerale I, *Tesoreria provinciale di Fermo*, busta 1.

90 ASR, Camerale I, *Tesoreria provinciale del Patrimonio*, buste 28-29; cf. also Chapter 6, p. 143, note 73.

91 In this regard, the reader should see Chapter 7, pp. 147-150, as well as, among the Florentine sources, ASF, Galli Tassi 1863-1865.

92 Numerous documents have been traced both in Florence (note especially ASF, Galli Tassi 1831-1834) and in Rome. See Chapter 5 for details on the sources and on the participation of other bankers, almost all Florentines, under the names of those already mentioned: from this it can be seen that the Florentines had 61.25% of the share in the first contract, 87.5% in the second and 70.8% in the third.

93 See, for example: ASR, Camerale I, *Mandati camerali 872*, fols 7v, 10r, *Mandati camerali 874*, fol. 12r and *Giustificazioni di Tesoreria*, busta 1, fasc. 15 for Paolo Serragli; *Mandati camerali 872*, fols 157r, 224v and *Mandati camerali 874*, fols 94v, 100r, 108r, 121r for Filippo Carducci; *Mandati camerali 874*, fol. 18r for Ludovico Del Palagio; *Mandati camerali 872*, fol. 221r, *Mandati camerali 874*, fols 37v, 38r, 93v, 94r, 129r and *Giustificazioni di Tesoreria*, busta 1, fasc. 4-6 for Leonardo and Alessandro Bartoli.

their power, making them essential and ideal interlocutors also subsequently; but it is also true that in the 1530s and 1540s they continued to acquire contracts on merit or because of their expertise, without the – undoubtedly highly favourable – advantage of having a fellow countryman as pontiff. Economic power therefore did not pass from the hands of the Florentines to those of the Genoese until the second half of the century, and the latter's domination became total only towards the end of the sixteenth century. For example, it will be noted that from 1513 to 1546 (the period thus far considered in most detail) Filippo Strozzi, Bartolomeo Lanfredini, Bindo Altoviti, Paolo Serragli and Benvenuto Olivieri held the post of depositary general with few interruptions (the Genoese bankers Grimaldi and Pallavicini-Giustiniani, as has already been mentioned, were depositaries general under Paul III). From the pontificate of the Roman Julius III Ciocchi del Monte this post was then dominated by the Ligurians.[94] Nevertheless, in March 1550, of the 31 banks listed in an edict that proclaimed that Friday was the day ordained for money exchange, at least 12 belonged to Florentines, making them the most numerous group.[95] Perhaps the decisive moment, marking irrevocably the victory of the Genoese bankers, was that of the great construction works promoted by Sixtus V Peretti (1585-90).[96]

What can be noted, for the period that we are more directly interested in, is the striking difference between the Florentine presence and that of the Genoese. Essentially, the Genoese families linked to the Apostolic Chamber were few in number: Sauli, Pallavicini, Giustiniani, Grimaldi (who held a virtual monopoly on the alum mines of Tolfa) and a few others, all of whom possessed considerable financial resources. The Florentine presence, on the other hand, was much more varied and included not only the most powerful bankers of the era, such as Strozzi and Altoviti, but also a large number of other bankers, who, while not becoming quite so influential, managed all the same, singularly or more often in association with others, to create a niche for themselves in relations with the Apostolic Chamber. Ardinghelli, Bandini, Bartoli, Benci, Carducci, Cavalcanti, Covoni, Del Bene, Della Casa, Del Nero, Deti, Gaddi, Giraldi, Mattei, Montauto, Olivieri, Puccini, Rucellai, Ubaldini, Ugolini are only some of the names which recur, more or less frequently, in the Chamber registers of the 1530s and 1540s.[97]

From the documents studied it emerges that relationships were not limited to strictly business, but were often extended to marriage. To cite but a few, besides the above-mentioned Strozzi-Altoviti union: Benvenuto Olivieri and the brothers Girolamo and Roberto Ubaldini married three Ridolfi sisters, while Girolamo Ubaldini's sister married Filippo Carducci.[98]

---

94 Delumeau, *Vie économique et sociale*, II, pp. 880-881: Delumeau provides a list of the depositaries between 1550 and 1621, amongst which the only Florentines were Giovan Battista Altoviti under Pius V (1566-72) and Ubertini under Clement VIII (but only from 1592 to 1594).

95 Delumeau, *Vie économique et sociale*, II, pp. 877-878.

96 Delumeau, *Vie économique et sociale*, I, p. 207.

97 In the Appendix, doc. 1 is a transcription of a list of *mercatanti* who in 1546 probably contributed to the costs of the construction of the church of S. Giovanni dei Fiorentini.

98 Among the more recent publications, see I. Fosi-M.A. Visceglia, 'Marriage and politics at the papal court in the sixteenth and seventeenth centuries', in T. Dean-K.J.P. Lowe

As was already mentioned in the Introduction, the study of the documents of the Fondo Galli Tassi has brought to light the fact that in the second quarter of the sixteenth century the Florentines and the Genoese collaborated or at least worked side by side in administering the tax-farms. This could, as has been suggested, have been an indication of a supervening weakness on the part of the former, who at this point were no longer able to manage on their own. However, such considerations are possible only where the documents of the bankers involved in the contracts are available (in as much as it was the bankers themselves and not the Apostolic Chamber who organized this market of shares); the documentation of the Chamber, given that it contains only the names of the initial contracting parties, can only furnish partial answers. Therefore, in order to be able to make accurate comparisons between the different periods, more complete and detailed sources for periods beyond those studied here must be uncovered. This consideration, however, is not meant to cast any doubt on the fact that the general trend was towards a slow but progressive weakening of the position of the Florentines in the course of the 'century of the Genoese'.

(eds), *Marriage in Italy, 1300-1650* (Cambridge, 1998), pp. 197-224; C. Weber, 'Fünfzig genealogische Tafeln zur Geschichte der römischen Kurie in der frühen Neuzeit', *Quellen und Forschungen aus italienischen Archiven und Bibliotheken*, 73 (1993): 496-571. Further information can be found in the genealogical records held in the Archivio di Stato of Florence such as *Carte Pucci*, *Ceramelli Papiani* and *Raccolta Sebregondi*.

CHAPTER 2

The Ascent of the Olivieri Family

1. The origins of the family

The origins of the Olivieri family can be traced to Sesto Fiorentino, where, according to the *Priorista Mariani*, they were previously known as Benvenuti.[1] Presumably their later surname was acquired from a certain Ulivo, who lived in the first half of the thirteenth century.[2] The family is sometimes referred to as Ulivieri, and sometimes as Olivieri; the second version will be used here and throughout the rest of the book.[3]

From Sesto Fiorentino, the family moved to Florence, settling in the quarter of Santa Maria Novella, *gonfalone* (district) of Lion Bianco. Several architectural traces of the family remain even today: in the basilica of Santa Maria Novella there is a sarcophagus (in the cloister of San Benedetto) and a monument with a coat of arms (in the cemetery of Piazza Nuova, in Via degli Avelli);[4] while in the church of Santa Trinita there are two sepulchral arches.[5] The Olivieri family was at its most powerful at the end of the thirteenth and the beginning of the fourteenth centuries, at which time a large number of family members held public posts. They furnished, for example, the *Signoria* with two priors: Giovanni di Benvenuto (in 1349) and his nephew Giovanni

1 ASF, Manoscritti 250, *Priorista Mariani*, t. 3, fol. 740.

2 Ulivo heads the family tree dedicated to the Olivieri/Ulivieri family in two important genealogical collections held in the Archivio di Stato of Florence (Manoscritti 353, *Carte dell'Ancisa FF*, fol. 586 and Manoscritti 603, *Carte Pucci*, scat XII, 43).

3 The family coat of arms is red '*alla gemella in scaglione d'oro*', accompanied by three stars, again in gold. It is reproduced in colour in ASF, *Ceramelli Papiani*, 4757, famiglia Ulivieri, and in Manoscritti 473 (*Armi di famiglie fiorentine raccolte da Gabbriello Landini piovano di Ripoli*), fols 23.7, 26.8.

4 See ASF, Manoscritti 625, *Sepoltuario fiorentino del Rosselli*, fols 754, 770 and also the copies of the two *Sepoltuari della chiesa di S. Maria Novella di Firenze*: Manoscritti 621, fols 84v, 98v; Manoscritti 812, fols 213 (map at fol. 220), 232 (map at fol. 238).

5 According to ASF, Manoscritti 623, *Sepoltuario della chiesa di S. Trinita di Firenze*, fol. 6v, one of the tombstones of this church was bought from Jacopo Puccetti by Michele Olivieri for 14 *scudi* on 27 October 1554. The Olivieri restored it, 'adding the family arms in marble and the inscription *Sepulcrum de Oliverijs*'. In fact, in his will of 1553, Michele di Paolo Olivieri (born in 1493) requested that on his death a tombstone with the inscription '*Sepulcrum de Oliveriis*' be carved, and if he passed away in Florence (as was evidently the case) that it be erected in Santa Trinita (where it can still be seen today), while if he instead happened to be in Naples at the time of his death that it be erected in San Domenico. According to his will, the tomb was to be used also for descendents and relatives (Galli Tassi 1811, fol. 28v). Foresti is thus in error when he indicates as 1481 the date of the sale of the tomb (Manoscritti 625, *Sepoltuario fiorentino del Rosselli*, fol. 935; *Ceramelli Papiani*, 4757, famiglia Ulivieri).

di Matteo (in 1379 and in 1386), both for the quarter of Santa Maria Novella.[6] Between 1283 and 1380 the family also numbered amongst its members seventeen *signori* and five *gonfalonieri* (the last being Recco di Guido, who held both positions).[7]

The great-grandfather of the Benvenuto di Paolo who is the central figure of this book, Michele di Matteo Olivieri, appears in the *Catasto* of 1427.[8] The assets attributed to Michele therein consisted of several houses in the *popoli* (parishes) of Santa Maria Novella and of San Lorenzo, other houses and farms or small parcels of land in the area surrounding Florence, and several *luoghi* (bonds) of the *Monte Comune*: in total his wealth was estimated at 1,822.4 florins. Once the deductions had been made (a number of debts plus seven mouths to feed), which amounted to 1,663 florins, the remaining total was 159.4 florins.[9] Of Michele's four sons, two (both of whom are named in the *Catasto* of 1480) fathered the principal branches of the family: Benvenuto (born in 1411 or 1413) and Marabottino (born in 1416 or 1418). The younger son, Marabottino,[10] was ancestor to that branch which then adopted the surname Ulivelli and that was recognized as being related to the first in 1614.[11] Benvenuto,[12] on the other hand, was ancestor to that branch of the family which adopted the surname Olivieri, and thus to all the characters whose lives (or at least what little we know of them) will be recounted in this chapter. The latter, therefore, will be briefly discussed below.

6 ASF, Manoscritti 250, *Priorista Mariani*, t. 3, fol. 740.

7 ASF, Manoscritti 603, *Carte Pucci*, scat. XII, 43.

8 The information given in this section is summarized in Table 2. The sources used are the above-mentioned genealogical collections of the Archivio di Stato of Florence: *Ceramelli Papiani*, 4753, famiglia Ulivelli; *Ceramelli Papiani*, 4757, famiglia Ulivieri; Manoscritti 250, *Priorista Mariani*, tomo 3; Manoscritti 351, *Carte dell'Ancisa DD*; Manoscritti 353, *Carte dell'Ancisa FF*; Manoscritti 357, *Carte dell'Ancisa II*; Manoscritti 359, *Carte dell'Ancisa LL*; Manoscritti 360, *Carte dell'Ancisa MM*; Manoscritti 361, *Carte dell'Ancisa NN*; Manoscritti 603, *Carte Pucci*, scat. XII, 43. In addition, in the Biblioteca Nazionale Centrale of Florence the *Poligrafo Gargani*, scat. 2066, 2074-2076, were consulted. In order to avoid a book bottom-heavy in notes, however, specific references have been avoided, except in special cases.

9 ASF, Catasto 77, *Santa Maria Novella, Lion Bianco*, year 1427, fols 115r-116r.

10 ASF, Catasto 1014, *Santa Maria Novella, Lion Bianco*, year 1480, fols 62r-63r. The pages are badly damaged, making them almost impossible to decipher: the only parts which are clearly legible are the '*bocche*' (mouths). Of Marabottino we know only that in 1452 he was recognized as a silk-merchant together with his brother Matteo; the activity was then continued by his son Michele, described as a silk-merchant in 1485 (BNCF, *Poligrafo Gargani*, scat. 2075, fols 189, 199).

11 ASF, Manoscritti 603, *Carte Pucci*, scat. XII, 43.

12 ASF, Castasto 1013, *Santa Maria Novella, Lion Bianco*, year 1480, fol. 175r-v.

Table 2 – Genealogy of the Olivieri family: the branch of Michele di Matteo

- MICHELE (b. 1375) di Matteo = Pippa (b. 1399)
  - Benvenuto (b. 1411/13) = Ginevra Pagagnotti (b. 1426)
    - Michele (b. 1449)
    - Giovanni (b. 1455)
    - Piero (b. 1458) = Maria ...
      - Piero = Maddalena Baldinucci
      - Giovanni (†1574)
        - I = (1538) Ginevra Federighi
          - Maria
          - Tommaso
          - Lorenzo
          - Caterina († 1565) =Filippo Corelli
          - Piero (b. 1543)
          - Benvenuto (b. 1544) = (1578) L. Orlandi
        - II = (1553) Nannina Recchi (†1570)
          - Michele (b. 1558)
      - Ippolita = ... Capponi
      - Leonarda (nun in S. Caterina)
    - PAOLO (b. 1462) — (14 children: cf. Table 3)
    - Lotteringo (b. 1465) – Luigi
    - Caterina (b. 1469) = (1495) Bartolo degli Arrighi
  - Matteo (b. 1415)
  - Marabottino (b. 1416/18) = (1463) Ginevra Del Biada (1446-1531)
    - Nanna (b. 1466)
    - Michele (b. 1467)
    - Serafino (b. 1470)
    - Gio.Franc. (b. 1473) = (1502) Ginevra Mannelli
      - Marabottino Benvenuto (b. 1503) — Antonio (b. 1532)
      - Michele
    - Lucrezia (b. 1474)
    - Camilla (b. 1478)
  - Bice (b. 1417)
  - Niccolò (b. 1425)

Married to Ginevra Pagagnotti, Benvenuto di Michele fathered five sons and one daughter. We know that in 1480 Michele, Giovanni, Paolo and Lotteringo were all 'outside the home with others'; only Piero 'lives in the home and does not work'. The possessions of Benvenuto di Michele Olivieri, resident in the parish of San Lorenzo, consisted of a farm with a building and a parcel of land in the Mugello, for a total value of 257.5 florins. This would seem to be a remarkably small patrimony for a member of this family, but it should not necessarily be accepted at face value. First, in their financial declarations taxpayers tended to conceal the real amount of their wealth, and, second, the statistics contained in the *Catasto* of 1480 are considered to be less accurate than those of 1427. It seems to be fairly certain, however, that in 1484 Benvenuto was working as a goldsmith in the pay of Michele di Antonio Ruote.[13]

Of Benvenuto's five sons, only two are relevant to this research. Piero is of interest inasmuch as he was the father of Giovanni, important in this history because of his role in managing the companies of the Olivieri family. It is Paolo and his descendents, however, who are the real focus of this research, and so their life and activity will be the subject of the following section (see also Table 3).

2. The sons of Paolo di Benvenuto and their companies

How Paolo di Benvenuto Olivieri, born in Florence in 1462, earned his living is unknown. He and his family must, however, have had – or, at some point in his lifetime, developed – interests in the field of merchant-banking, given that several of his sons and grandsons were merchant-bankers in various Italian and European financial markets. Paolo Olivieri had fourteen children: six from his first marriage to Caterina di Jacopo Belcari (who died giving birth to Raffaello, on 25 November 1500) and eight from his second marriage, to the daughter of Salvestro Ceffini,[14] celebrated on 25 November 1501.[15]

Although, as mentioned above, there is no record of this family having had experience in the field of commerce and finance, in the first decades of the sixteenth century virtually an entire generation of Olivieri seems to have followed a very precise strategy of travelling between and working in the principal financial markets of the time: a very particular case, which is worth examining in detail. The various account-books show the close relations that the family companies maintained with each other, particularly when it was a matter of transfers of money or payments in different markets.[16] Moreover, each of the Olivieri companies (as well as individual members of

13 BNCF, *Poligrafo Gargani*, scat. 2076, fol. 84.

14 The Ceffini family, originally from Passignano, lived in the quarter of Santa Croce, *gonfalone* Bue. A certain Salvestro di Giuliano di Salvestro was captain of Volterra for six months from 19 June 1492 (ASF, *Ceramelli Papiani*, 1390, famiglia Ceffini).

15 ASF, Galli Tassi 1806, ins. 1, fol. 2r. The following biographical information has also been taken, in addition to the sources cited in note 8, from Galli Tassi 1806, ins. 1.

16 Relations were frequently maintained by letter, as is shown, for example, by a *copialettere* belonging to Benvenuto Olivieri & Partners of Rome, of 1545-46 (ASF, Galli Tassi 1959).

Table 3 – Genealogy of the Olivieri family: the branch of Paolo di Benvenuto

- PAOLO di Benvenuto
  - Caterina Belcari († 1500) first wife
    - Michele (1493-1554) = (1533) Luisa Cambi
      - Cassandra (b. 1534) = (1553) Piero Corsini
      - Paolo (1536-65)
      - Lorenzo (b. and † 1537)
      - Lucrezia (b. and † 1540)
      - Donato (b. 1543)
    - Alessandro (1494-1562) = (1545) …
    - BENVENUTO (1496-1549) = (1538-39) Isabella Ridolfi
      - Ginevra (1541-59) = (1558) Matteo Morelli
      - Giulio (1542-97) = (1563) Lucrezia Mannelli
        - Camilla = (1598) Tommaso Rinuccini
        - Benvenuto (1574-1615) = (1603) Beatrice Guiducci
        - Ginevra/Gena = (1591) Tommaso Baccelli
      - Maria (b. 1544) = (1563-64) Giovanni Rondinelli
      - Vittoria (b. 1546)
      - Alessandro (1549-97)
    - Aurelia (b. 1497) = (1513) Carlo Paffi
      - Cassandra = (c. 1540) Geri Risaliti
      - Francesco
      - Ginevra (nun in Mater Domini)
    - Jacopo (1498-1524)
      - Girolamo (friar in S. Maria Novella)
      - Lisabetta = (1551) Giovan Battista Del Seta
    - Raffaello (1500-27)
  - second wife =1501 .... Ceffini
    - Salvestro (1503-22) — Giovanni (Giovan Domenico)
    - Caterina (b. 1504) = (1521) Giuliano Ghinetti — Maria = (c. 1541) Simone Guiducci
    - Ginevra (b. and † 1505)
    - Francesco (1506-27)
    - Lorenzo (1507-32)
    - Tommaso (b. and † 1508)
    - Ginevra (1510-27)
    - Marabotto (b. 1514)

the family) naturally had current accounts with the others, so that all the payments and the transfers of money, which were very frequent, could be made more easily.[17]

The Florence company

The family's interests obviously revolved around their hometown, Florence, where a company was set up, with the two cousins Michele di Paolo and Giovanni di Piero at its helm. Michele, Paolo's eldest son, was born on 29 January 1493. Even though he was very involved in the management of the family's affairs (becoming senior partner of companies in Florence, Naples and Nuremberg), he also held public office: he was twice elected one of the twelve *buonuomini* of Florence, in 1539 and in 1540, twice one of the six of *Mercanzia* (1541 and 1546)[18] and once to the Council of the Two Hundred (1550). In 1533 he married Luisa di Lorenzo Cambi, who bore him three sons and two daughters (but one son and one daughter died in infancy). In his will, drawn up in 1553, Michele named his two surviving sons, Paolo (1536-65) and Donato (born in 1543), as his sole heirs, while to his surviving daughter, Cassandra, he left a dowry of 2,000 *scudi d'oro in oro*.[19] He died in October 1554.[20]

The earliest information we have about Giovanni, Michele's cousin, comes instead from the period 1511-14, when he was employed in the *bottega* (workshop) of Paolo and Amadio Del Giocondo & Partners.[21] Later, as we will see, he spent at least several years in Nuremberg. He was married twice: the first time to Ginevra Federighi, in 1538, and the second to Nannina Recchi, in 1553.[22] Of his children it is known that Lorenzo was working in Aquila after 1560; that Piero in 1565-66 found himself 'without goodwill' ('*senza aviamento*');[23] and that Caterina married Filippo Corelli and died in Ravenna in 1565 'giving birth to Siamese twins, who survived'.[24] Giovanni himself died in 1574, probably in Impruneta, and was then buried in the church of San Marco, in the San Giovanni quarter.[25]

---

17 A commission of 0.15% was charged on these accounts: see, for example, ASF, Galli Tassi 2294, fol. 171.

18 In 1548, moreover, he was, like his brother Benvenuto, amongst those elected by the *Arte della Seta* '*per lo squitino della borsa de' signori vj di mercatantia*' (ASF, Galli Tassi 1912, fol. 1).

19 ASF, Galli Tassi 1811, fols 27v-33v.

20 ASF, Galli Tassi 1944, fols 114, 125. On 25 May 1555 a copy of his will was sent to his brother Alessandro in Naples by Giovanni di Piero, their cousin (ASF, Galli Tassi 1811, fol. 27v).

21 ASF, Galli Tassi 1913.

22 ASF, Galli Tassi 1807, ins. 8 for the first marriage; Manoscritti 357, *Carte dell'Ancisa II*, fol. 768 for the second.

23 ASF, Galli Tassi 1960, fols 2, 3, 5: he had in fact been working for Carlo Alagna, but, when the latter found himself without an office, Piero lost his job and in 1566 was in Taranto 'doing nothing'.

24 ASF, Galli Tassi 1960, fols 1, 3.

25 ASF, Galli Tassi 1810, ins. 4, which mentions a number of payments made for the transport of the body and for the burial. Cf. also BNCF, *Poligrafo Gargani*, scat. 2076, fol. 99. The close relationship between Giovanni and his cousin Michele is also demonstrated

The activity of Michele and Giovanni Olivieri & Partners of Florence[26] was largely mercantile, based principally on the trade of coarse and precious woollen and silk cloth. The information available about this company refers to the 1540s, but it is highly likely that it came into being much earlier. On 1 April 1546 it is known that Michele and Giovanni Olivieri set up a new partnership, which followed on from the preceding one without changes and with no new financial contributions. The 1543 balance sheet of the *ragion vecchia* (old company) has survived and this provides an indication of the social capital, which amounted to 3,000 *scudi d'oro* (3,214.1 ducats *di moneta*) equally divided between the two partners, and of the profits, which were around 2,871 *scudi* (3,076.1 ducats *di moneta*).[27] The profits of the new company, calculated on 24 February 1548, amounted, on the other hand, to 507 ducats.[28]

The Olivieri family in Rome

As mentioned in Chapter 1, after Leo X de' Medici ascended to the papal throne in 1513, the city of Rome, which had already in preceding centuries attracted numerous Florentines, became even more alluring to the pope's fellow citizens, who saw the papal court with a Florentine on the throne as offering vast opportunities for making their fortune. Benvenuto moved to Rome in 1516, and, over the span of about thirty years, carved out for himself a brilliant career that saw him reach the most important positions in the service of the Apostolic Chamber (his life and the companies of which he was a partner are discussed in Sections 3-4, while the rest of his business activity constitutes the central nucleus of this volume). He did not go to Rome alone, but was accompanied by four of his brothers, all of whom, however, died at an early age: in 1527, following the Sack, Raffaello (born on 20 February 1500) died of plague while staying in the Gaddi household,[29] and in the same year Francesco (February 1506), on whom had been conferred the title of knight of St John of the Florentine nation, died '*in ... deceptionis urbis*'; in 1532 Lorenzo (23 February 1507) met with the same fate, and was buried in S. Giovanni dei Fiorentini.[30] About Salvestro (1503-22) we

by the fact that on the death of the latter, the former for a great many months gave free accommodation in his own house to the widow Luisa Cambi, the daughter Cassandra (he also organized her wedding, after having maintained her for some time in a nunnery) and several servants: Galli Tassi 1944, fols 114, 125.

26 Relative to this company can be noted the existence of a balance sheet from 1543 (ASF, Galli Tassi 1926) and of a ledger, lacking the first 80 folios, from 1544 to 1547 (Galli Tassi 2294).

27 ASF, Galli Tassi 1926, fols 7v, 9r.

28 ASF, Galli Tassi 2294, fols 329, 332.

29 Raffaello must have been the cashier and book-keeper of the Roman company of Agnolo Gaddi at least from 1523 (ASF, Galli Tassi 1951, fol. 98).

30 For all this information: ASF, Galli Tassi 1806, ins. 1, fols 2r, 3r. In 1531 Lorenzo kept the account-books of the customs of Ripa (Galli Tassi 1942, fol. 347). The young man succumbed to an illness despite the fact that Benvenuto did all in his power to procure the best care for him; on his death, Benvenuto then paid more than 53 *scudi* for the funeral rites (Galli Tassi 1946, fol. 93v). The exact date of the young man's death was 1 December: ASVR,

only know that he was knighted by Pope Leo X[31] and that he had a son, Giovanni (or Giovan Domenico).[32] Although we know practically nothing about what Benvenuto's brothers did, the fact that so many of them moved to Rome would seem to indicate that the family was convinced that success was to be found there.

The companies in the kingdom of Naples

Another area of Italy that attracted large numbers from outside its borders was the kingdom of Naples. Florentines began to frequent the kingdom as early as halfway through the thirteenth century, and the important companies of Florence opened branches there immediately, quickly and easily becoming an intrinsic part of the commercial and financial networks of the kingdom. Moreover, as they did in Rome, the Florentines created a nation in Naples.[33] As elsewhere, these Florentine agents acted on two fronts: on one hand, they dealt in commerce, exporting, for example, consumables and manufactured goods towards Northern Italy, and at the same time importing high-quality Florentine cloth into the kingdom of Naples; on the other, they set up banking services not only for private citizens, but also to carry out financial and fiscal functions for the Neapolitan administration. In the second half of the Quattrocento the Florentine Strozzi family was omnipresent (and indeed the Olivieri would link their fortunes to this family more than once), taking on an organizational role, rationalizing the economic activities of the kingdom and acting as a catalyst for local business.[34] In the first decades of the Cinquecento, however, after Charles V's ascent to the throne, the State of Naples began to spread its economic network to embrace more merchants and bankers. At this point the Genoese merchant-bankers began to threaten the Tuscan supremacy, eventually taking over altogether.

S. Giovanni dei fiorentini. Battesimi, defunti, matrimoni e 'stato delle anime', I (years 1532-1589), fol. 90v.

31 ASF, Manoscritti 603, *Carte Pucci*, scat. XII, 43.

32 Some information exists about the son of Salvestro: in 1523 it was his grandfather Paolo who paid for his wet-nurse's wages, in Rome (ASF, Galli Tassi 1914, fol. 29). Other interesting details emerge from the will of his uncle Michele: Giovanni, having lost his father, went to live in Naples with his uncles, Michele and Alessandro, who, 'to encourage him', remitted a debt of 300 ducats that he owed them and as well as a home gave him work. Giovanni, however, spent a great deal of money 'for his own pleasure' and, fearing that he would ruin them, his uncles paid him the salary owing to him and sent him away. They also added 20 *scudi d'oro* to help him start a new life in Portugal, where he had decided to seek his fortune. In other words, wrote Michele, they treated him 'as though he were their own son' (Galli Tassi 1811, fol. 31v).

33 M. Cassandro, 'L'irradiazione economica fiorentina nell'Italia meridionale tra Medioevo e Rinascimento', in *Fra spazio e tempo. Studi in onore di Luigi De Rosa* (3 vols, Naples, 1995), I, pp. 191-221.

34 M. Del Treppo, 'Il re e il banchiere. Strumenti e processi di razionalizzazione dello Stato aragonese a Napoli', in G. Rossetti (ed.), *Spazio, società e potere nell'Italia dei comuni* (Naples, 1986), p. 267. By the same author, see also 'Stranieri nel regno di Napoli. Le élites finanziarie e la strutturazione dello spazio economico e politico', in G. Rossetti (ed.), *Dentro la città. Stranieri e realtà urbane nell'Europa dei secoli XII-XVI* (Naples, 1989), pp. 179-233.

Around 1520 Alessandro di Paolo Olivieri, born in May 1494, began working in Naples. He was paid 80 ducats *di carlini* per annum by the Neapolitan company of Bartolomeo Ginori and Agnolo Strozzi.[35] In the same period he took part in two *accomandite* (limited partnerships), one drawn up with Domenico di Piero Boninsegni, and the other with Bernardo di Gabriele Strozzi: to the first, Olivieri contributed a share of 315 ducats to the capital, which amounted to 5,000 ducats; to the second, which amounted to 1,750, he contributed 110. In both cases, however, in order to work out the division of the share of the profits, it is necessary to take into consideration also the '*vantaggio*' or '*stima della persona*', that is the capitalization of his service.[36] At the same time, Alessandro Olivieri was also the senior partner of a company in Cosenza, known to be active in 1521.[37] Later, he worked in the family companies with offices in Naples and in Nuremberg, together with his brother Michele. The close relationship between the two brothers is also demonstrated by the fact that Alessandro, unmarried and with no children, gave his own half of certain assets to Michele's children in 1544 (although he subsequently, in June 1545, did, in fact, marry). In the Galli Tassi document in which the two brothers are defined as 'Florentine merchants and Neapolitan citizens', it is stated that 'what belongs to one of them has always belonged to the other, and viceversa'.[38] Alessandro also held political office in Florence: he was one of the twelve *buonuomini* in 1544. He died in Naples in 1562.[39]

By the second quarter of the Cinquecento, Michele and Alessandro Olivieri & Partners of Naples played an important role in the city.[40] A 1545 balance sheet shows that in that year Michele contributed 1,000 ducats to the social capital, and

---

35 ASF, Galli Tassi 1915, fol. 17: the records speak of 18 months lasting until 15 December 1522. At fol. 2 (15 May 1519) he appears in credit in the *libro segreto* (secret book) for 180 ducats for his commission; it could thus be supposed that he had collaborated with them in the preceding two years and three months, that is starting from February 1517.

36 ASF, Galli Tassi 1915, fols 8, 9, 10, 11. A partnership between Bernardo Strozzi and Alessandro Olivieri still existed in 1527: G. Solivetti, *Un conto del banco Altoviti (1526-1530)* (Rome, no date), pp. 9, 24. The fact of becoming partners in a company in virtue of the contribution one made in terms of labour was not new to this period, but went back at least to the Trecento. Examples can be found, among others, in F. Melis, *Aspetti della vita economica medievale (studi nell'archivio Datini di Prato)* (Florence, 1962), vol. I, pp. 148-149 and in M. Spallanzani, 'Una grande azienda fiorentina del Trecento: Carlo Strozzi e compagni', *Ricerche Storiche*, VIII (1978): 422-424, esp. note 30. Sometimes the contribution was only calculated in terms of the evaluation of one's own work; in other cases, the partner's contribution to the capital was made both in cash and by his acting as administrator.

37 See, for example, the records in ASF, Galli Tassi 1914, fol. 115 and in Galli Tassi 1915, fols 8, 9.

38 ASF, Galli Tassi 1807, ins. 14.

39 ASF, Galli Tassi 1944, fol. 113v.

40 References to this company can be found as early as 1532 (ASF, Galli Tassi 1945, fols 320-323). For the 1540s some accounts can be found in Galli Tassi 2294, fols 88, 102, 104, 108, 117, 126, 136, 145, 148,152, 164, 181, 201, 220, 227, 236, 263, 285, 300, 307, 318. We know that Michele and Alessandro traded in wheat and barley in Abruzzo and Basilicata, in the years 1547-48 (G. Coniglio, 'I Medici, i Fiorentini e il Viceregno', in *Napoli nel Cinquecento e la Toscana dei Medici* (Naples, 1980), p. 16).

'*Olivieri proprii*' added a further 7,000.[41] By 1549, however, the capital had reached 25,000 *scudi d'oro*, of which 20,000 belonged to the Olivieri and 5,000 to Francesco Tantucci, who invested in the company '*per via d'acomandita*'. In that moment, moreover, the company found itself in a truly bad state, with 13,833 ducats of losses, and only 2,600 of profits, which, moreover, were actually revenues from the associated company of Cosenza.[42]

In the south of Italy, in fact, there were also other partnerships closely connected to the company of Naples in which members of the Olivieri family were involved: the above-mentioned company in Cosenza (Donato di Michele Olivieri and Francesco di Donato Vecchietti & Partners) and another company in L'Aquila (Paolo di Michele Olivieri and Giandonato di Alessandro Barbadori & Partners).[43] There was also a company in Bari, in which in 1543-45 both the Olivieri of Florence and those of Naples, together with Geri Risaliti, appear to have held shares; in 1549 this company was called Paolo Olivieri and Ippolito Franciotti & Partners, and the Olivieri family had contributed 5,000 *scudi d'oro* to the social capital.[44]

These companies served as reference points for the sister companies above all in the trade of silk.[45] It should be noted, however, that Paolo was born in 1536 and Donato not until 1543. It is very probable, therefore, that these partnerships were actually managed by their father Michele, who used his sons' names in order to remain formally detached, perhaps because he was already head of another company based in the kingdom of Naples and was not allowed to have more than one under his name.

The Olivieri family abroad

The Olivieri family also spread out beyond the Italian peninsula. In the 1520s, for example, members of the family were living and working in Valencia and in Nuremberg. Jacopo Olivieri originally went to Spain to attend to some business affairs at a time when Florentine bankers were beginning to falter in the face of the

41 ASF, Galli Tassi 1944, fols 308-309: on that date the profits exceeded 6,850 ducats. In the same year Tommaso Risaliti also became a partner of the company (Galli Tassi 1962, ins. 3, letter dated 18 June 1545).

42 ASF, Galli Tassi 1944, fol. 287. As can be gleaned from the document, 1,000 *scudi d'oro* were at that time equivalent to 1,100 ducats.

43 Several accounts of these companies can be found in ASF, Galli Tassi 2278, fol. 28 (for the company of L'Aquila); Galli Tassi 2294, fols 122, 209, 219, 254, 269, 287 (L'Aquila) and 154, 195, 284, 309 (Cosenza).

44 Relative to 1543-45 the references are very fragmentary (ASF, Galli Tassi 1926, fols 2r, 7v; Galli Tassi 1962, ins. 3). For 1549, see Galli Tassi 1944, fols 285, 288.

45 For example, a description can be made of one of the operations that shows how the various companies interacted with each other: six bales of silk *crespa* sent to Florence by the company of L'Aquila (value: approx. 1,112 *scudi*), of which half belonged to the Olivieri of Florence, 5/12 to those of Nuremberg and 1/12 to Barbadori, were sent to Frankfurt at the request of the company based in Germany (ASF, Galli Tassi 1926, fol. 9v).

Genoese onslaught. He remained in Spain, where he took minor orders in the Church and where, in 1524, he died.[46]

Nuremberg attracted the Olivieri family in the years in which the German city was becoming a flourishing centre of import and export.[47] The Olivieri who paved the way for the others was Giovanni di Piero, who, in 1521, began working for a Nuremburg-based company belonging to the Florentine family Torrigiani.[48] In August 1526 he became partner of Raffaello and Ridolfo Torrigiani & Partners, which took over the social capital of 4,200 Rheinish florins in silk cloth and cloths of gold and silver that had belonged to the previous company. Giovanni was given a 16.7% share of the profits as capitalization of his service.[49] Five years later, in 1531, the company was dissolved and a new one created, with a social capital in cloth, amounting to 4,000 Rheinish florins '*in moneta di craizze sesanta per fiorino*', and under the new denomination, Luca di Raffaello Torrigiani and Giovanni di Piero Olivieri & Partners. The company's composition had in fact changed somewhat: Ridolfo Torrigiani was no longer with it, while the Florentine merchant-banker Schiatta di Niccolò Ridolfi and the Venetian Francesco di Giorgio Cameli had entered as partners. Raffaello, who continued as senior partner (*maggiore*) even though he had registered the company in his son's name, was entitled to half the

46 ASF, Galli Tassi 1914, fol. 88; Galli Tassi 1806, ins. 1, fol. 2r. To learn more about the relations between the Italians and Valencia in the fifteenth and at the beginning of the sixteenth century, see J. Guiral-Hadziiossif, *Valence. Port méditerranéen au XVe siècle (1410-1525)* (Paris, 1986), pp. 399-408; and the more recent work by D. Igual Luis, *Valencia e Italia en el siglo XV. Rutas, mercados y hombres de negocios en el espacio economico del Mediterraneo occidental* (Valencia, 1998).

47 Nuremberg is known to have acted as a magnet on the Florentines as early as the 1450s: see in this regard H. Kellenbenz, 'Gli operatori economici italiani nell'Europa centrale ed orientale', in *'Aspetti della vita economica medievale'*, Atti del Convegno di Studi nel X Anniversario della morte di Federigo Melis, Florence-Pisa-Prato 10-14 March 1984 (Florence, 1985), pp. 333-358; B. Dini, 'L'economia fiorentina e l'Europa centro-orientale nelle fonti toscane', *Archivio Storico Italiano*, 153 (1995): 633-655; and R. Mazzei, *Itinera mercatorum. Circolazione di uomini e beni nell'Europa centro-orientale, 1550-1650* (Lucca, 1999). For information about other Florentine companies based there in the first part of the sixteenth century, see M. Spallanzani, 'Le compagnie Saliti a Norimberga nella prima metà del Cinquecento (un primo contributo dagli archivi fiorentini)', in *Wirtschaftskräfte und Wirtschaftswege. Festschrift für Hermann Kellenbenz* (5 vols, Nuremberg, 1978), IV, pp. 603-620; Id., 'Tessuti di seta fiorentini per il mercato di Norimberga intorno al 1520', in *Studi in memoria di Giovanni Cassandro* (3 vols, Rome, 1991), III, pp. 995-1016.

48 His earnings grew over the years: 25 Rheinish florins in the first year, 35 the second, 45 the third, 60 the fourth, 70 the fifth; in addition he was paid a further 80 florins (total 315) for the following year, which was, in fact, the first year of the new company of which he was partner (ASF, Galli Tassi 1824, fasc. 10). The activity of Olivieri in Nuremberg and more broadly the trade of cloth between Florence and Germany is analysed in my 'Drappi di seta e tele di lino tra Firenze e Norimberga nella prima metà del Cinquecento', *Archivio Storico Italiano*, CLIX (2001): 359-394 (revised and enriched Italian version of 'Der Handel mit Seidenstoffen und Leinengeweben zwischen Florenz und Nürnberg in der ersten Hälfte des 16. Jahrhunderts', *Mitteilungen des Vereins für Geschichte der Stadt Nürnberg*, 86 (1999): 81-113).

49 ASF, Galli Tassi 1824, fasc. 10.

profits, while the other half was shared equally among the other three. The company dealt in the trade of 'silk cloths from Florence, Lucca, Genoa and elsewhere' – all furnished by Raffaello Torrigiani & Partners of Florence – to Nuremberg, Lubeck (or more generally German territory), Poland and Bohemia. The partnership agreement envisaged a duration of ten years, until August 1541. But after 1536 a number of problems emerged between the partners (concerning in particular unpaid profits) and therefore it is likely that the partnership was dissolved before 1541.[50]

On 9 March 1542, evidently once it had been ascertained that the business was profitable, a new company was created, with a five-year duration: Michele, Alessandro and Giovanni Olivieri & Partners. This company appears to have been the point of reference for the other companies of the family when they had to import precious metals or cloth of medium quality, or when exporting silk cloth or cloth of gold.[51] The social capital, in 1545 (and therefore presumably since the beginning), came to 7,500 ducats (= 10,500 Rheinish florins), of which half were contributed by the Olivieri of Florence and the other half by the Olivieri of Naples; also partners were Schiatta di Niccolò Ridolfi and Cosimo di Piero Bonsi, whose 1/6 (each) share of the profit was presumably calculated as capitalization of their service.[52] At the end of the five years it was decided that the company be dissolved.[53]

Tables 4a-4b summarize the composition of the three companies of Florence, Naples and Nuremberg (in the 1540s), departing from two different points of view: Table 4a lists the partners of each company; Table 4b instead shows the participation of each of the Olivieri in the various companies they were involved in.[54]

---

50 ASF, Galli Tassi 1824, fasc. 11; *Notarile Antecosimiano*, 5424, fol. 366r-v; various unnumbered folios in Galli Tassi 1938 and in *Mercanzia*, 10772. For more details on the Torrigiani companies and on the above-mentiond legal disputes, see my 'Drappi di seta e tele di lino tra Firenze e Norimberga': 361-368.

51 For the Olivieri company of Nuremberg in Galli Tassi 1946, fols 194-195 there is a retrospective balance sheet, drawn up in 1551 (it is also transcribed in my 'Drappi di seta e tele di lino tra Firenze e Norimberga': 392-394); further information can also be gleaned from its accounts in Galli Tassi 2294, fols 80, 121, 157, 161, 173, 183, 196, 222, 232, 250, 271, 290, 298, 308, 315. For example, between February 1545 and March 1546 the Olivieri of Nuremberg sent to Florence almost 4,000 pieces of German cloth (*tele bottane tinte larghe e basse della Magnia*), for a value of approx. 3,432 ducats (fols 163, 228, 232). At the same time, in little more than two years, between 1544 and 1546, the German company bought from Florentine *setaioli* (via the Olivieri of Florence) cloth for a value of almost 13,000 ducats (fol. 183).

52 ASF, Galli Tassi 2294, fols 196, 325, 326; *Notarile antecosimiano*, 9335, fol. 42r. In transferring part of the money to Nuremberg via Lyons, the Olivieri suffered a number of losses, equally divided between the companies of Florence and Naples, at the hands of the agents working in the French market: approximately 80 ducats at the hands of Niccolò, Adriano and Paolo Burlamacchi & Partners and the considerable sum of 592 at the hands of Giovanni and Filippo Balbani & Partners (Galli Tassi 1926, fols 3v, 4r-v, 9r).

53 ASF, *Notarile antecosimiano*, 9335, fols 42v, 44r; *Notarile antecosimiano*, 9338, fol. 9r.

54 This organization recalls that of the *holding* created by the Medici bank in the fifteenth century. In this regard, see: R. De Roover, *The Rise and Decline of the Medici Bank (1397-1494)* (New York, 1966), pp. 60-62, 77, 81; R.A. Goldthwaite, 'The Medici Bank and the World of Florentine Capitalism', *Past and Present*, CXIV (1987): 15. But see also F. Melis, who, in contrast with De Roover and with Sapori, extended the concept to include the Datini companies

Table 4a – The Olivieri companies of Florence, Nuremberg and Naples and their partners

Florence company	Michele
	Giovanni
Nuremberg company	Michele
	Giovanni
	Alessandro
Naples company	Michele
	Alessandro

Table 4b – Michele, Giovanni, Alessandro Olivieri and their companies

Michele	Florence company
	Nuremberg company
	Naples company
Giovanni	Florence company
	Nuremberg company
Alessandro	Nuremberg company
	Naples company

To sum up, it would seem that the Olivieri brothers, while maintaining their headquarters in their hometown, were ready – indeed eager – to move to other cities, whether inside or outside Italy, to take advantage of any favourable opportunities that might present themselves. The systematic way in which they established themselves in these markets suggests that they followed a precise strategy, making the case of this family extremely interesting, especially given that they achieved all this in the course of a single generation. During the 1520s, in the same years in which Raffaello, Francesco, Lorenzo and Salvestro moved to the Eternal City, and Jacopo to Valencia, in search of fortune, Benvenuto and Alessandro began working in two merchant-banking companies belonging to fellow Florentines in, respectively, Rome and Naples. Immediately afterwards, Giovanni di Piero, who had already had experience in a Florentine company, moved to Nuremberg to work for the Torrigiani

of the fourteenth century: 'Le società commerciali a Firenze dalla seconda metà del XIV secolo al XVI secolo', in *Troisième Conférence Internationale d'Histoire économique*, Munich, 1965 (Paris, 1974), pp. 47-62, reprinted in Id., *L'azienda nel medioevo* (Florence, 1991), pp. 161-178 (esp. 168-170); Id., 'Considerazioni su alcuni aspetti della nascita dell'impresa capitalistica', Ibid., pp. 129-160 (esp. p. 157, note 38). A curious case, regarding the legal organization of companies associated with each other can be found in M. Spallanzani, 'Le aziende Pazzi al tempo della congiura del 1478', in *Studi di storia economica toscana nel Medioevo e nel Rinascimento. In memoria di Federigo Melis* (Pisa, 1987), pp. 305-320.

family, later setting up his own firm there with other members of the family. The oldest brother, Michele, whose original business activity is unfortunately not documented, instead remained in Florence; the original Florentine (mother) company acted in the following years as the hub of the system of the Olivieri companies (although the Rome company in fact detached itself from the others), inasmuch as it was the possessor of shares of important capital in both the Nuremberg and the Naples companies. The Naples company, in its turn, was the centre around which circled smaller companies, such as those of Cosenza, L'Aquila and Bari.

As can be seen in the – albeit rather confused – registers of the *Decima Granducale*, of the ten sons fathered by Paolo di Benvenuto in the course of his two marriages, only four were still alive in 1534:[55] curiously enough, the first three (Michele, Alessandro and Benvenuto, born between 1493 and 1496) and the youngest (Marabotto, born in 1514). In 1536 Marabotto moved to Ferrara, where he was still living between 1544 and 1546. While what he actually did there is a mystery, it is known that every year his brothers Michele from Florence and Benvenuto from Rome each sent him 24 *scudi d'oro* 'for his entertainment'.[56] The evidence points to his having been in Naples around 1565, but only for a short period, after which he returned to Florence.[57] Practically nothing is known about another of Paolo di Benvenuto's sons, Tommaso, except that he was born in 1508 and probably died shortly thereafter.

Nor is much known about the four daughters of Paolo di Benvenuto: Aurelia (born in 1497) married Carlo Paffi in 1513, while Caterina (born in 1504) married Giuliano Ghinetti in 1521. The third, Ginevra, died in 1505 shortly after her birth; the same name was therefore given also to the youngest daughter, who, born in 1510, died in the plague of 1527.[58]

3. Benvenuto di Paolo (1496-1549)

Benvenuto Olivieri, the third son of Paolo di Benvenuto's first marriage, was born on Friday 8 January 1496.[59] Unlike his older brothers, Michele and Alessandro, who worked in Florence, Naples and Nuremberg, Benvenuto moved to Rome. No information has come to light as to the exact year he went to the Holy City, but it is certain that he was to be found there from 1516 on.[60] He was part of that multitude of Florentines who, celebrating the election of one of their illustrious fellow citizens to the papal throne,

---

55 ASF, *Decima Granducale*, 3624, fols 29r-30r: in the account of the 'sons of Paolo di Benvenuto Olivieri', the value of the houses and farms came to 121.7 florins, on which the *decima* (tithe) amounted to 10.1 florins.

56 ASF, Galli Tassi 1962, fol. 3; Galli Tassi 2294, fols 137, 165, 194.

57 ASF, Galli Tassi 1960, fol. 6. Paolo di Michele Olivieri wrote from Naples to his uncle Giovanni in Florence: 'I send our Marabotto back to you and I am sorry that he has had the inconvenience and the expenses of coming here, and it gives me displeasure to see him in this sorry state' (28 May 1565).

58 This information can all be found in ASF, Galli Tassi 1806, ins. 1, fols 2r-3r.

59 '*Benvenuto di Paulo Ulivieri nacque di dì 8 di gennaio 1495 ab incarnatione a hora sei sonate d'un pezzetto*' (ASF, Galli Tassi 1806, ins. 1, fol. 1v).

60 Cf. ASF, Galli Tassi 1914.

flocked to Rome in search of fortune. Although there is no record of the exact date of his arrival, Benvenuto Olivieri was working there at least from 1516, having attached himself to one of the most influential Florentine merchant-bankers in the city. He followed the typical path of the young man wishing to embark on a merchant-banking career, who would first of all seek work as a salaried employee of an established company, almost always one belonging to a fellow citizen, then buy himself a share of capital and finally become totally independent, creating his own company. In 1516, in fact, Olivieri was working for Bindo Altoviti (1 November 1516-31 January 1520).[61] He subsequently became his partner, and remained with him throughout the following decade. Towards the end of the 1520s he became increasingly closely attached to the even more powerful merchant-banker Filippo Strozzi, who enjoyed the protection and favour of Pope Clement VII, eventually becoming one of his most trusted collaborators and friends. Evidence of this close relationship can be found in Strozzi's will. In this document,[62] written on 31 December 1537 in the 'Castle of Florence', where he was imprisoned after the failed undertaking of Montemurlo, Strozzi named as his sole heirs his six sons, dividing his wealth into two equal parts: the first was to go to the elder sons; the second part, 'to be divided amongst the younger sons, I wish to be placed in the power and hands of Benvenuto Olivieri. Whom I pray for that love and affection he showed to me in life, not to refuse me in death to act as a second father to these three, and to order my sons' affairs as he thinks best, taking with him immediately Giulio, in whom I have great hope and faith, and instructing him in the business of commerce.'[63] The vast amount of correspondence between Benvenuto Olivieri and Filippo Strozzi as well as the latter's family is further evidence of how highly Strozzi valued the advice of his friend. And, in fact, after Filippo's death Olivieri took it upon himself to manage – as far as he was able – the situation from Rome.[64]

61 Bindo Altoviti, one of the best-known *mercatores* of the period, should be remembered not only for his well-known banking activities, but also for a decided love of patronage (among the artists financed by him it suffices to mention Raffaello, Michelangelo, Cellini and Vasari) and, as we have seen (Chapter 1, p.18), a political and passionate hatred of the Medici. On all these aspects of his life see the recent A. Chong-D. Pegazzano-D. Zikos (eds), *Raphael, Cellini & A Renaissance Banker. The Patronage of Bindo Altoviti* (Boston, 2003).

62 Benvenuto Olivieri, at that time partner of Filippo Strozzi in Rome, was nominated executor of the will together with, amongst others, Neri di Gino Capponi, faithful business partner to Filippo in Lyons, and Francesco di Agostino Dini, his ex-partner in Florence: G.B. Niccolini, *Filippo Strozzi – tragedia* (Florence, 1847), p. 330.

63 Niccolini, *Filippo Strozzi*, pp. 326-327. At the time that Filippo wrote his will, however, Giulio was already dead, but, according to Niccolini, 'perhaps it was his relations' loving solicitude to keep the sorry news quiet' (ibid., p. 527, note 1). On 30 October, 1536, Olivieri had written to his exiled friend in Venice that it seemed to him that 'Giulio enjoys working in business, and I am glad, and as I have already told you I reckon he will succeed, as you wish' (ASF, *Carte Strozziane*, serie III, 95, fol. 57v).

64 Numerous letters can be found in ASF, *Carte Strozziane*, serie III, vols 30, 95, 96, 101, 134. The dates of birth (where known) and death of Filippo Strozzi and his sons are as follows: Filippo (1488-1538), Lorenzo (d. 1571), Piero (d. 1558), Giulio (d. 1537), Roberto (1515-66), Leone (1515-54), Vincenzo (d. 1537), Alessandro (d. 1540).

The 1540s were the years in which Benvenuto reaped the maximum financial benefits for all his efforts: he had by then become senior partner of several companies (cf. pp. 52-56). As will be seen in more precise detail in the following chapters, he was among those *mercatores florentini romanam curiam sequentes* that worked closely with the Apostolic Chamber, providing them with a series of services (from the management of the Depositary to the collection of taxes, from the control of the provincial Treasuries to the customs excises) that brought with them consistent profits, besides guaranteeing a position of prestige. Although he sometimes worked on his own, more often he worked in union with other rich Florentine bankers, who were an important part of the colony that was already well established in Rome. As has been mentioned (pp. 11-12), in 1515 the Florentine nation had been permitted to have a consulate that – and this was of primary importance for anyone working in the area of commerce and banking – guaranteed the right to an autonomous merchant tribunal. Every year a consul was elected, chosen from among the most illustrious *mercatores*. This post was held by Benvenuto Olivieri in 1534 and again in 1545.[65]

That Benvenuto had a special relationship with the papal court is confirmed not only by the verifiable facts, but also by a letter written after his death by Bartolomeo Bettini, administrator of Olivieri's inheritance, to his widow Isabella Ridolfi: 'The pope has been a friend to us and I believe that he truly loved the late Benvenuto and from him we received only good things.'[66]

During his first years in Rome, Olivieri probably lived in the *rione* Ponte, heart of the economic and financial life of the city and above all where, since the Quattrocento, a large part of the Florentine colony was concentrated. Certainly he lived there from 1537 onwards, as for this year there exists the documented purchase of two houses '*sitas in Regione Pontis, una quarum habeabat ab ante viam videlicet viculum qui olim ibat a via Banchorum ad viam Retrobanchus quod est nunc clausum ... altera autem domus, dicte prima contigua et ab ante habet stratam Banchorum et ecclesiam Sancti Celsi et Juliani de urbe in cospectu et a parte posteriori ... viam Retrobancha que dicitur moderno tempore via Paulina.*' These houses were sold to Olivieri by Albertaccio Del Bene and brothers, who in their turn had bought them from the heirs of Ludovico di Gino Capponi, for the sum of approximately 2,500 *scudi d'oro* (1,883 plus 615 '*in melioramentis ... dictarum domorum expositorum que dictus dominus Albertacius voluit in pretium dictarum domorum imputari*').[67] On 24 January 1540

65 J. Delumeau, *Vie économique et sociale de Rome dans la seconde moitié du XVIe siècle* (2 vols, Paris, 1957-59), I, p. 209 (note 2). Olivieri also held several posts in the national confraternity of the Pietà: AASGF, vol. 390, fol. 114; vol. 391, fols 6r, 9r-10r; vol. 392, fols 4r, 7r-9r.

66 Bartolomeo Bettini in Rome to Isabella Ridolfi in Florence, 11 February 1549[=50] (ASF, Galli Tassi 1810, ins. 5, unnumbered folio).

67 The various notarial acts also make mention of a payment of 15 *scudi d'oro in oro* to the Florentine notary, Luigi Rucellai, prior of the venerable society of the Beata Maria Annunziata sopra Minerva, and the *censo* (property tax) of 125 ducats *di carlini* that were to be paid annually, in two instalments (1 May and 1 November) to the same society. All these documents, together with others including the declaration of the payment of the second instalment of the price of the houses in 1546, can be found written in Latin in ASF, Galli Tassi 1812. The vendor, Albertaccio Del Bene, was also *civis et mercator florentinus romanam curiam sequens*.

Olivieri bought a house in the *rione* Ripa for 180 *scudi*, which he then rented out for 36 *scudi* per annum.[68] In his will Benvenuto also mentioned another house in the *rione* Ripa, bought in partnership with the Fossi family, who were entitled to a quarter, and which was rented out for 60 *scudi* per annum (of which 45 thus went to Olivieri).[69] Some years after the death of Benvenuto, in 1558, one of the two houses in the *rione* Ponte together with the house in the *rione* Ripa were sold to Roberto Ubaldini for 1,500 *scudi di moneta*.[70]

Nevertheless, throughout his lifetime Benvenuto maintained close ties with his native city: between 1532 and 1533 he was not only *veduto del Collegio* of the *gonfalone* of the Lion Bianco, but also one of the twelve *buonuomini*, which post he once again held in 1548.[71] In 1548, together with his brother Michele, he was also among the men elected to the *Arte della Seta* '*per lo squitino della borsa de' signori vj di mercatantia*'.[72] In the same period, moreover, he made several property investments in the Florence area. In 1541 he purchased 'the terrain and buildings of the Chiasso' from the Tornabuoni, for the sum of 3,600 *scudi* plus 279 in taxes.[73] Some time before September 1545 he had come into possession of land in the Val di Sieve and Mugello worth about 1,000 *scudi*.[74] On 20 August 1546, for 3,000 *scudi d'oro*, Olivieri purchased from Francesco Corboli four farms with houses 'in the parish of San Piero in the market of Valdelsa, in Florence's *contado*'.[75] In addition, between November 1545 and 1548 he rented a house belonging to Piera, widow of Roberto Nasi, for 50 *scudi di giuli 7 per scudo*.[76] As has been mentioned, he was also part-owner together with his brothers of other possessions. In his will, moreover, Benvenuto instructed

---

68 ASF, Galli Tassi 1806, ins. 2. Years later, in 1556-57, the cellars and the downstairs rooms of the 'large house of Ripa' rendered an annual rent of 35 *scudi di moneta*, while the upstairs rooms were rented out for 10 (Galli Tassi 1928, fols 30, 39).

69 ASF, Galli Tassi 1810, ins. 2, fols 1v-2r.

70 ASF, Galli Tassi 1811, fol. 27r. Ubaldini had already been living for some time in the 'house of via Banchi', for which he paid an annual rent of 160 *scudi d'oro in oro* (Galli Tassi 1928, fols 24, 31, 35). As for the second house, the Olivieri heirs in 1558 sold 'a quarter of the building which presently houses the customs of Ripa, another quarter belonging to the Montauto and the remaining half to the hospital of San Giovanni in Rome' (Galli Tassi 1928, fol. 37).

71 ASF, Manoscritti 603, *Carte Pucci*, scat. XII, 43.

72 ASF, Galli Tassi 1912, fol. 1.

73 ASF, Galli Tassi 1806, ins. 2, unnumbered folio; the same insert gives a detailed inventory of the objects which were in the house. In 1546 Benvenuto had some restoration work done to the *palazzo* and fencing on the farms; the expenses were paid by the Olivieri of the company of Florence, who then deducted the total amount (392.7 ducats *di moneta*) from the account which Benvenuto held with them (Galli Tassi 2294, fols 282, 294).

74 ASF, Galli Tassi 1806, ins. 2, unnumbered folio.

75 ASF, Galli Tassi 1806, ins. 8. A later insert (ins. 10), contains several loose sheets on the administration of this farm in later years (1561-95). The accounts relating to the management of the animals on the Florentine farms after the death of Benvenuto can be found in Galli Tassi 1822: the initial capital, at the end of 1549, was 2,144 *lire* = approx. 306 florins, at the exchange rate of 1 florin = 7 *lire* (fol. 2); in 1553, the livestock provided a profit of 296.4 *lire*, equivalent to c. 42 florins (fol. 153).

76 ASF, Galli Tassi 1807, ins. 3. The payment was once again left in the hands of the Olivieri of Florence (Galli Tassi 2294, fol. 261). An inventory of the goods present in all of these

that more houses be bought: one in Florence for about 2,000 *scudi*, the other one, 'that should be comfortable and not pompous' in Prato or a similar place, for the same value. Not only that: he also expressed his wish that on his death his wife, sons and daughters move back to Florence until the boys were grown up and independent, and until the girls were married.[77] It should be said that this, in fact, was exactly what they did. After the death of Benvenuto his family moved to Florence and went to live, at least for some time, in Via Maggio, in front of Ridolfi's house.[78]

The wife referred to in his will was Isabella di Pagnozzo Ridolfi, who belonged to a notable Florentine family, and whom Benvenuto married at some point between December 1538 and May 1539.[79] Isabella brought Benvenuto a dowry of 2,000 florins *di suggello*, 1,500 from the *Monte delle doti* and 500 in cash and gifts. Five children were born of this marriage, all in Rome:[80] Ginevra (14 June 1541-1559), who in 1558 married Matteo Morelli; Giulio (19 June 1542-13 March 1597),[81] who in March 1562 took as his wife Lucrezia di Niccolò Mannelli; Maria (born on 5 August 1544),[82] who was married to Giovanni di Alessandro Rondinelli; Vittoria (born in June 1546);[83] and, lastly, Alessandro (17 April 1549-1597), who on 8 April 1566 took minor orders in the

houses and farms on the death of Benvenuto can be found in ASF, *Notarile Antecosimiano*, 15123, fols 27r-29v.

77 ASF, Galli Tassi 1810, ins. 2, fols 3r, 4r.

78 This is the address given on a judicial citation (unfortunately undated) which launched a lawsuit against Luisa Cambi, widow of Michele di Paolo Olivieri, probably to do with the inheritance (ASF, Galli Tassi 1810, ins. 18).

79 '*Prese mogle addì vij di dicembre 1538 in m. Isabella di Pagnozzo Ridolphi. Fece le nozze in Roma a 2 di magio 1539*' (ASF, Galli Tassi 1806, ins. 1, fol. 1v). As is well known, the marriage at that time consisted of a series of acts, taking place more or less simultaneously or at least consecutively, that only all together made the union complete. On what happened on 2 May, Benvenuto himself is more exact: '*si contrasse il parentado per verba de presenti et dettili lo anello ... et la sposai la sera medesima*' (Galli Tassi 1807, ins. 7, unnumbered folio). It is interesting to note that the marriage contract was drawn up by Maria di Filippo Strozzi, wife of Lorenzo di Piero Ridolfi.

80 All the information that follows as to the dates of birth and of marriages are taken, unless otherwise specified, from Galli Tassi 1806, ins. 1, fol. 1v.

81 On 27 May 1542, Lorenzo Federighi wrote to his brother-in-law Giovanni Olivieri (cousin to Benvenuto) that Isabella 'was great with child' and that 'Benvenuto I hardly recognized, so happy and fat was he' (ASF, Galli Tassi 1960, fol. 4). For the date of death of Giulio, see Galli Tassi 1962, unnumbered folio.

82 Benvenuto was probably thinking of her rather than of her older sister when on 24 October 1544 he estimated 'how much needs to be deposited in the *Monte di Firenze* today for a dowry' of 1,000 florins: 59.4 florins per year for 15 years, or 81.2 for 12½ years (ASF, Galli Tassi 1824, fol. 32).

83 Of Vittoria we know only the date of her baptism, 14 June: ASVR, *S. Giovanni dei fiorentini. Battesimi, defunti, matrimoni e 'stato delle anime'*, I (1532-1589), fol. 14r. The same source also provides the dates of baptism of Ginevra Bianca (26 June 1541, fol. 9r), of Giulio Giovan Battista Romolo (25 June 1542, fol. 10r) and of Maria (12 August 1544, fol. 12r).

Church.[84] In September of 1549 Benvenuto died, at the age of 53, leaving as his heirs his wife and young children, all of whom were still minors.[85]

In his will,[86] included here in the Appendix (Doc. 2), Olivieri defines himself as a 'Florentine and by privilege also a Roman citizen'.[87] In virtue of this double citizenship, he made arrangements to be buried in San Giovanni dei Fiorentini if he died in Rome (which he did), and in Santa Maria Novella, 'his grave to be marked with a sepulchre or a tombstone', if, instead, death struck him in Florence. The executors named in Benvenuto's will were one of his older brothers, Michele or Alessandro, together with Bartolomeo Bettini and Giovan Battista Acciaiuoli.[88] As for the companies, Olivieri entrusted the task of liquidating them within two years to Benedetto Busini, 'of whom I have always been very fond', his partner since 1537 (see Section 4). His wife would thus be able to recuperate her dowry, as well as having access to a further 1,000 *scudi* and other goods, as indicated in a private deed;[89] to his daughters was to be guaranteed

84 In ASF, Galli Tassi 1811, fol. 35r. In Galli Tassi 1807, ins. 10, there is a petition from Alessandro di Benvenuto to Cosimo I requesting that he be admitted among the knights of Santo Stefano.

85 Perhaps the exact date of death was 13 September 1549, or at least so it would seem from ASF, Galli Tassi 1921, fol. 43, where that day is taken as a watershed for the three customs of Rome, 50% of the administration of which was in the hands of Olivieri. On 14 September, as can be seen in the parochial registers, Benvenuto was buried: ASVR, *S. Giovanni dei fiorentini. Battesimi, defunti, matrimoni e 'stato delle anime'*, I (1532-1589), fol. 111r. On 15 September a solemn high mass was held and Benvenuto's name was recorded at the 'Ufficio dei morti' (AASGF, *Libro del Provveditore*, 1546-52, fol. 78r).

86 ASF, Galli Tassi 1810, ins. 2. In actual fact what has survived is a rough draft, dated 1544; the true will was drawn up by Bartolomeo Cappello in Rome on 14 June 1547, but its substance does not seem to have been very far from the original idea (as is clear in the brief summary made later by the Florentine notary, Niccolò di Filippo di Pratovecchio: ASF, *Notarile Antecosimiano*, 15123, fol. 1r-v). On 9 September 1549 Benvenuto, perhaps foreseeing his imminent death, added to the number of executors of the will also the Very Reverend Guido Ascanio Sforza, Cardinal of Santa Fiora and chamberlain, and confirming his wife Isabella in the custody and in the care of the children (fol. 1v). On 2 November the widow, Isabella Ridolfi, became trustee of the inheritance (Galli Tassi 1810, ins. 3, unnumbered folio).

87 Roman citizenship could be obtained through marriage, or as a favour (Paul III was particularly predisposed towards those who opposed the Medici regime), or if the person concerned had owned property or been a resident for at least ten years. In this period the Florentine merchants were for the most part also Roman citizens (I. Fosi-M.A. Visceglia, *Marriage and politics at the papal court in the sixteenth and seventeenth centuries*, in T. Dean-K.J.P. Lowe (eds), *Marriage in Italy, 1300-1650* (Cambridge, 1998), pp. 207-208).

88 As evidence of Benvenuto's closeness to these two men, it is sufficient to remember that the first was one of the godfathers to Ginevra (ASF, Galli Tassi 1806, ins. 1), the second to Maria (Galli Tassi 1810, ins. 2, fol. 5v). Later also Roberto Ubaldini was added (*Notarile Antecosimiano*, 15123, fol. 1r-v). In the 1550s also Giovan Francesco Ridolfi, Isabella's brother, was asked to stand as procurator for the Olivieri heirs (Galli Tassi 1928, fol. 9).

89 The document alluded to is presumably that contained in ASF, Galli Tassi 1807, ins. 7, in which, further to the amount already stated in the will, Benvenuto requested that Isabella see to the children's education, and that she dress and behave in an appropriate manner. Further, according to this document, at the discretion of the heirs the 1,000 *scudi* to which she had access could be transformed into 90 per annum, for the duration of her natural life.

a dowry of between 2,000 and 2,500 *scudi* if they married and appropriate donations if they entered a nunnery; the remainder, all the other 'real and liquid property', was to go to his sons.[90] While he was still alive, Benvenuto had availed himself of the help of the notary Niccolò di Filippo di Pratovecchio, who received 99 florins for his services, which eventually lasted five and a half years, until 1553.[91] Benvenuto's designated heir was Giulio (who, it should be noted, numbered among his godfathers the very reverend Antonio Pucci, Cardinal of the Santi Quattro Coronati and a great patron of Olivieri).[92]

As with every inheritance, litigation ensued. In the years following Benvenuto's death there were various lawsuits that sought to establish the amount of certain debts or credits and the amount which was due to the various members of the Olivieri household and their relations and heirs. Among the many documents relative to the hereditary procedure that can be found here and there, in no particular order, in a large number of *filze* of the Fondo Galli Tassi,[93] one in particular, dated 16 October 1570, stands out. The contents of this deed, which regards the division between Giulio and Alessandro di Benvenuto,[94] can be laid out as follows:

All the real and liquid property	*scudi*	16.500 –
To the mother for her dowry	*scudi*	3.560 =
Net amount	*scudi*	12.940 –
Expenses incurred by Giulio	*scudi*	2.433 =
	scudi	10.507 /2 = 5.253,5

Each of the two children was therefore entitled to 5,253.5 *scudi*,[95] subdivided thus:

In his will Benvenuto also requested that his sons and brothers forgive Isabella if she decided to remarry, as she was still young (Galli Tassi 1810, ins. 2, fol. 4v). Probably she did indeed remarry, to Zanobi di Jacopo Guasconi: BNCF, *Poligrafo Gargani*, scat. 2075, where 'the widow of Benvenuto di Paolo Olivieri' is named erroneously, first as Lisabetta di Pagnozzo (fol. 150) and then as Giovanna o Nanna di Lorenzo Ridolfi (fol. 151).

90 In actual fact, at the time that this will was written, Alessandro was not yet born; however, the will indicated that the inheritance be divided amongst all the males, including those yet to come, in equal parts.

91 ASF, Galli Tassi 1822, fol. 162. The notarial protocols of Niccolò di Pratovecchio, which contain numerous documents regarding the Olivieri family, are held in the Archivio di Stato of Florence (*Notarile Antecosimiano*, 15121-15125).

92 ASF, Galli Tassi, 1806, ins. 1, fol. 1v. For further information regarding the Florentine Antonio Pucci (1484-1544), made clerk of the Chamber in 1518 by Leo X and cardinal of the Santi Quattro in 1531 by Clement VII, see G. Moroni, *Dizionario di erudizione storico-ecclesiastica* (103 vols, Venice, 1840-61), *ad vocem*; A. Chacon, *Vitae et res gestae pontificum romanorum et cardinalium* (3 vols, Rome, 1677), *ad vocem*.

93 Accounts or records can be found, in inserts or loose folios, in particular in ASF, Galli Tassi 1807, 1808, 1809, 1810, 1811, 1822, 1823, 1928.

94 ASF, Galli Tassi 1807, ins. 17: following Alessandro's complaints that he was being cheated, Giulio on this occasion reworked all the accounts declaring, in truth rather angry with his brother, that he had always acted with honesty.

95 Alessandro found himself, however, owing Giulio 1,187.5 *scudi* and therefore was to have only 4,066 *scudi*: he had remaining to him in assets approximately 3,000 'which … will earn 250 *scudi* net per annum' (ASF, Galli Tassi 1807, ins. 17).

Jewels	*scudi*	350
Furnishings	*scudi*	400
Livestock	*scudi*	250
Goods	*scudi*	4,253.5

It would seem, therefore, that the total inheritance Benvenuto Olivieri bequeathed to his heirs came to 14,067 *scudi*: this figure has been calculated by subtracting the expenses incurred by Giulio (2,433 *scudi*) from the value of all the real and liquid property (16,500 *scudi*).

This document, it must be pointed out, was written at a relatively late date: twenty years had passed since the death of Benvenuto and much might have happened in the meantime. More convincing proof of the actual wealth he had accumulated in the course of his working life can be found in a brief memorandum, signed by him, dated 3 September 1545, the contents of which can be considered to be accurate, given that it was a document for personal use. According to what Benvenuto wrote in this memorandum, his *substantie* (possessions) amounted to approximately 40,000 *scudi*: of these, approximately 7,500 were in real estate, more than 28,000 derived from the business transactions of his companies, and the rest came from other sources of income.[96] Between the date of this document and his death a further four years passed, during which Olivieri continued to stipulate contracts with the Apostolic Chamber; consequently this sum must have undergone some modifications, which it is impossible to calculate. Nevertheless, it gives us a picture of the state of affairs at a moment in which Benvenuto was at the height of his activity.

4. Benvenuto Olivieri in Rome and his companies

Initial activity (1516-20)

In 1516, therefore, Benvenuto di Paolo Olivieri was living and working in Rome. At the age of twenty or thereabouts he began his career as an employee of the company belonging to the Altoviti family. What exactly his job was has proved impossible to establish; what can be assumed, however, is that Benvenuto acquired increasing responsibility in the course of time, if it is true that between 1 November 1516 and 30 June 1518 he received 60 gold ducats (an average of 36 per annum), while between 1 July 1518 and 31 January 1520 this had increased to 87.1 (an average of 55 per annum). In total, for a period of 39 months, Benvenuto earned 147.1 gold cameral ducats.[97] Bindo Altoviti must have been satisfied with Olivieri's collaboration, given that he subsequently promoted him, making him a partner in his company.

96 ASF, Galli Tassi 1806, ins. 2, unnumbered folio: the document is transcribed in the Appendix (doc. 3). For a comparison with other personal patrimonies between the fifteenth and the seventeenth centuries, see R.A. Goldthwaite, *Wealth and the Demand for Art in Italy 1300-1600* (Baltimore and London, 1993), pp. 54-62.

97 ASF, Galli Tassi 1914, fol. 1.

Bindo Altoviti & Partners (1 February 1520-31 January 1531)

From 1 February 1520 (the partnership agreement is dated 26 January), therefore, the company of Bindo Altoviti & Partners was set up, destined to last three years plus one (if notice was not given within the six months preceding the end).[98] Probably at this point the company belonging to Bindo's father, Antonio (which, as always provided for in the institutive agreement, was interrupted by the death of the senior partner) had already undergone the closing of the accounts and the liquidation of the debts and credits, and therefore Bindo was able to set up a company under his own name. Altoviti's partner was Giovan Battista di Bernardo Puccini: of the 20% share that he possessed,[99] 8.3% was conceded to Benvenuto Olivieri.

As it often happened, the partnership was extended several times. But on 29 July 1530 Olivieri sent a letter to Puccini giving notice that he wished to leave the company and it would therefore have to be dissolved. In this letter, although he described Altoviti as 'my patron' ('*el mio patrone*'), he made it clear that he no longer wished to manage his company in Rome, which therefore should not last longer than 31 July and for the following six months would exist only until all the accounts had been settled.[100]

Olivieri's decision to withdraw from the partnership was, however, met with dismay on the part of Bindo Altoviti. Benvenuto found it necessary to send a further letter (in July 1531) explaining, but also reiterating, his decision, reconfirming their personal friendship but unswayable in his wish to leave by the following All Saints' Day. In fact, as he had already explained to Altoviti in the course of an earlier conversation, Olivieri felt the need to become wholly independent. Or, otherwise, rather than continuing with a limited participation, he wrote, he preferred to return to Florence to his brothers 'and enjoy that which through you I have acquired'.[101] It was often included in partnership agreements that disputes should be brought before the consulate of the Florentine nation, which had the competence to make judgements with regard to its own citizens, and in fact it was to this body that the two turned in order to settle the question. The sentence (31 July 1531) was handed down in favour of Olivieri and it was ordered that the company be dissolved.[102]

On 24 March 1531 the final balance was drawn up, resulting in a profit for the company, covering its entire duration (from 1520), of 42,476.3 ducats. Olivieri's 8.3% share made him a profit of 3,539.7 ducats. Several months then passed, the time necessary to close the accounts, liquidate the debts and credits, and probably also

98 ASF, Galli Tassi 1914, fol. 186.

99 According to ASF, Galli Tassi 1824, fasc. 15, the share was 23.3%; however, Galli Tassi 1914, fol. 186, which holds the accounting records and provides the subdivision of the profits, is more credible.

100 ASF, Galli Tassi 1824, fasc. 15.

101 Ibid.

102 In the document relative to the lawsuit of Benvenuto Olivieri against Battista Puccini and Bindo Altoviti, which was drawn up by Bartolomeo Cappello, notary and chancellor of the Florentine nation, several passages of the letter requesting that the company be dissolved sent by Olivieri to Puccini (described in more detail above) are cited and it is decreed that 'in no way can ignorance be considered an excuse'. However, while Puccini accepted this, Altoviti refused in no uncertain terms (ASF, Galli Tassi 1824, fasc. 15).

to resolve the problems mentioned above. Finally, on 16 January 1532 Olivieri was credited with his share of the profits, and the same day he was paid approximately half (1,791.7 ducats) of these.[103]

It is also possible to calculate the amount earned by Olivieri in the years in which he was an employee and then partner of the Altoviti company. The balance between profits and losses, including the profits cited above, can be estimated at 6,188.6 ducats.[104] Between 1531 and 1532, in fact, Benvenuto had received other proceeds from various investments that he had made in partnership with Bindo: in particular, 756 ducats from the customs of Rome and more than 1,400 from an office of apostolic secretary. Adding to the 6,188.6 ducats the 434.9 ducats from Benvenuto's personal account (147.1 of his employee's salary, 37.8 of profit in the first years and 250 of gifts from Altoviti), a total of 6,623.5 ducats is obtained.[105] During this period, it would seem that Olivieri was mostly involved in commercial activity regarding above all the trading of silk cloth and cloth of gold; but he also made profits from money-changing and, especially in the final years, from a number of investments made with the Apostolic Chamber.

Soon after terminating his partnership with Altoviti, Benvenuto appears to have found those suitable conditions of which he had spoken in the letter sent to Bindo: he entered into partnership with Filippo Strozzi, with a 16.7% share. It is in fact more likely that he and Strozzi had already agreed to form a company together, and that Olivieri had chosen this new option (at the expense of the old) because it offered him better prospects for the future. Strozzi was at that time the most powerful and influential banker working in Rome, closely linked to the pontiff by a relationship that was both personal and financial. Partnership with him was therefore a golden opportunity for Benvenuto. It should be said, however, that it was probably also an advantageous move for Strozzi, as his new partner had in the preceding years shown an astute business capacity appreciated by the other Florentine bankers. Filippo Strozzi, increasingly involved in politics, did not administer his company himself; instead, he delegated this position to Francesco Del Nero and Benvenuto Olivieri, who must therefore have enjoyed the complete trust of the senior partner.[106]

As we will see in the following sections, the companies almost always lasted longer than had been initially established: in other words it was common practice to renew them by mutual agreement. However, in most cases, even when a continuity is clearly present, some modifications were made (in the trading name, in each partner's share, etc.). Therefore, for reasons of clarity, I have chosen to highlight these changes, each time creating a different section.

---

103 ASF, Galli Tassi 1914, fol. 186. Slightly dissimilar is a 'Balance sheet of the *libro rosso A* of Benvenuto Olivieri', again of 24 March 1531, according to which Olivieri was entitled to 3,582.9 ducats of the 42,995.4 total profit of the company (Galli Tassi 1912, fol. 2).

104 ASF, Galli Tassi 1914, fols 66, 176. Virtually identical is the result of Galli Tassi 1946, fols 317-319, balance sheet of Benvenuto Olivieri's personal accounts until 16 January 1532, dated 23 August 1545.

105 ASF, Galli Tassi 1914, fols 1, 10. Of the 250 ducats, 150 were a reward 'for having been diligent in procuring him [Altoviti] the 2,500 ducats from the loan for the annates' (fol. 1).

106 The close relationship between Olivieri and Strozzi has already been mentioned (p. 39).

Filippo Strozzi & Partners (1 January 1532-31 December 1534)

In September 1531 Filippo Strozzi and Benvenuto Olivieri made an agreement to establish a company based in Rome that would follow the papal court in its travels, under the name of Filippo Strozzi & Partners of Rome.[107] This company, which started up on 1 January 1532, was to last three years, after which, if neither of the two partners had given notice within the six months preceding the expiry date, it would continue for a further two years. It would be automatically dissolved, however, in the case of the death of one of the two partners. The social capital, which amounted to 36,000 gold cameral ducats, was divided thus:

Filippo Strozzi	30,000	
Benvenuto Olivieri	6,000	(4,000 in cash, 2,000 for the capitalization of his service)[108]

The first half of the capital was to be deposited three months after the beginning of the company's activity and the second half after a further three months, with a 15% annual interest applied to those who failed to pay. Both partners were named as managers and administrators, but while Strozzi could absent himself when and as he wished, Olivieri could not, and was also obliged to draw up a balance sheet at the end of each year and send it to Strozzi. The company's business activities included 'trade, exchange, dispatches, farms of alum mines, customs, depositaries and others'. Neither of the two partners would be allowed to have business dealings in Rome independent of the company without the permission of the other; however, whereas Benvenuto could not do so elsewhere either, outside Rome Filippo would be free to carry out his own business transactions independently.[109] Furthermore, neither of the two could withdraw anything, either from the capital or from the profits, until the company had been dissolved, unless they repaid the amount together with an added interest of 15% per annum. It was up to Strozzi to choose, albeit with the consensus of Benvenuto, the young men to be taken on as employees. When the partnership was dissolved, Olivieri would be obliged to take care of the liquidation of the debts and credits for at least six months; he would be paid the expenses but no salary. Firstly all the creditors would have to be paid, but if Strozzi needed money, 'for the preservation of his name and honour', he would be free to borrow as he pleased. Profits and losses would be shared according to each partner's contribution to the social capital – to Filippo Strozzi 5/6 (=83.3%) and to Benvenuto Olivieri 1/6 (=16.7%) – and 5% of the profits would be given to charity.[110] It was established that on the dissolution of the company the

107 Copies of the partnership agreement, of the subsequent participation of Del Nero into the company, and of the extension can be found in ASF, Galli Tassi 1810, ins. 16; Galli Tassi 1826, fols 1r-3r; Galli Tassi 1939, fols 50v-53v.

108 For the '*stima della persona*', or capitalization of the service, see note 36.

109 In fact, Strozzi had other companies in Florence, Venice and Lyons.

110 This donation of part of the profits to charity was by that time a well-established custom among the merchant-banking companies (see A. Sapori, 'La beneficenza delle compagnie mercantili del Trecento', *Archivio Storico Italiano*, 83 (1925): 251-272, reprinted in Id., *Studi di storia economica. Secoli XIII-XIV-XV* (3 vols, Florence, 1982), II, pp. 839-858).

account-books would remain the property of Filippo Strozzi, although Benvenuto Olivieri could obtain a copy on request. Every failure to comply with what was laid down in the contract would be punished with a fine of 300 gold cameral ducats and any disputes would be settled before the *Mercanzia* of Florence.

According to the contract signed in Florence on 26 March 1532, Francesco Del Nero was also taken on as a silent partner, with a share of one-third of Strozzi's quota (equivalent to 10,000 ducats). Consequently, the capital, expressed in gold ducats, and the profits were subdivided thus:

Filippo Strozzi	20,000	share of profits	55.55%
Francesco Del Nero	10,000	share of profits	27.78%
Benvenuto Olivieri	6,000	share of profits	16.67%

Giulio and Lorenzo Strozzi & Partners (1 January 1535-31 December 1536)

Towards the end of the three years, the partners declared that the company would be discontinued, but then renewed for another two years, with the same agreements, albeit in the name of Filippo's sons, Giulio and Lorenzo.[111]

This modification of the company's name should not come as a surprise. The death of Clement VII Medici, on 25 September 1534, was a blow to the fortunes of Filippo Strozzi and consequently, at least in part, also to those of his associates, including Benvenuto Olivieri. While Paul III Farnese's ascension to the papal throne did not mark the end of Strozzi's business dealings, it did mean that the loans and the investments were not as frequent or as substantial as they had been under the Medici pontiff. This, together with the ever increasing political difficulties that Filippo was also encountering in his dealings with Florence, therefore led him to withdraw his name from the company and substitute it with, as mentioned above, those of his sons, Giulio and Lorenzo.[112]

111 ASF, Galli Tassi 1826, fol. 3r; Galli Tassi 1810, ins. 16, fol. 3v. Elsewhere a Strozzi/Olivieri partnership with *libro bianco* is mentioned as having begun on 1 January 1532 and terminated on 12 July 1536, even though 'it should have lasted until the end of December 1536' (Galli Tassi 1824, fol. 14; Galli Tassi 1939, fol. 59r).

112 Another case is even more significant: in 1532 Filippo, already an exile and warring against the Medici Signoria, wishing to operate in Spain (which was a Medici ally) but not being able, for obvious political reasons, to appear openly among the names of the partners, created an *accomandita* (limited partnership) registered only in Francesco Lapi's name ('Francesco di Giovanni Lapi & Partners in Seville and in Cadiz'): F. Melis, *Documenti per la storia economica dei secoli XIII-XVI* (Florence, 1972), doc. 105, pp. 348-351. Olivieri also ran into problems because of his collaboration with Strozzi, fallen into disgrace in the eyes of the Florentine government. This can be seen in a request for pardon that he presented to the *Otto di Balìa* in 1547, in which, admitting that he had been a partner of Filippo and then of his sons, he asked on the one hand '*absolutione ex gratia*' for the past, and on the other permission to liquidate all the business deals resulting from those companies (ASF, Galli Tassi 1978, fol. 6).

Giulio and Lorenzo Strozzi & Partners (1 July 1537-18 December 1538)

After the end of the preceding company (31 December 1536), several months passed before Filippo Strozzi and Benvenuto Olivieri signed a formal agreement to set up a new partnership in Rome or wherever the Roman court was in residence. Strozzi signed the new contract in Venice on 20 June 1537, and Olivieri in Rome on 28 July 1537. They were joined this time by Benedetto Busini and Simone Guiducci, who signed together with Olivieri. The social capital, which amounted to 40,000 gold cameral ducats,[113] was divided thus:

Filippo Strozzi	26,666.67	in cash
Benvenuto Olivieri	8,333.33	(6,833.33 in cash, 1,500 for the capitalization of his service)
Benedetto Busini	3,000	(2,250 in cash, 750 for the capitalization of his service)
Simone Guiducci	2,000	(1,250 cash, 750 for the capitalization of his service)

The profits, consequently, would be distributed in the following proportions:

Filippo Strozzi	share of profits	66.67%
Benvenuto Olivieri	share of profits	20.83%
Benedetto Busini	share of profits	7.50%
Simone Guiducci	share of profits	5.00%

The agreements, obligations and rights for the administrators (Olivieri, with the help of Busini and Guiducci) and the principal partner (Strozzi) were standard. Half of the social capital was to be deposited immediately, the rest by the end of December, with an interest of 10% to be paid by anyone who defaulted. Once again, Francesco Del Nero participated in the company as a silent partner; it is not known, however, what his financial contribution was this time.[114]

The partnership, supposed to last four years from 1 July 1537, instead came to an end little more than a year after its creation because of the death of Filippo Strozzi on 18 December 1538. From that date the usual six months were allowed for the closing of the books, as is mentioned in a document signed, on 16 April 1539, by Roberto Strozzi (Filippo's son and administrator of the inheritance in his own name and in that of his brothers), Benvenuto Olivieri, Benedetto Busini and Simone Guiducci.[115]

113 ASF, Galli Tassi 1824, fol. 4. This partnership is also remembered by Filippo Strozzi in the will he wrote on 31 December 1537: 'and I wish for [Benvenuto Olivieri] to continue to manage the company of Rome, still in the name of Giulio and Lorenzo, with conditions that seem honest to him' (Niccolini, *Filippo Strozzi*, p. 527). In actual fact, as has been mentioned (note 63), Giulio was already dead, but Filippo was unaware of this.

114 ASF, Galli Tassi 1810, ins. 16, fols 4v-5r.

115 ASF, Galli Tassi 1978, fol. 1; according to an unnumbered folio in the same *filza*, the liquidation actually lasted until the end of October.

Table 5 – The companies with Benvenuto Olivieri (the social capital is in gold cameral ducats)

COMPANY NAME	DURATION	PARTNERS	CAPITAL	SHARE OF PROFITS (%)	NOTES
Bindo Altoviti & Partners	1/2/1520-31/1/1531	B. Altoviti	?	80.0	
		G.B. Puccini	?	11.7	
		B. Olivieri	?	8.3	behind Puccini
Filippo Strozzi & Partners, then	1/1/1532-31/12/1534	F. Strozzi	20,000	55.5	
Giulio and Lorenzo Strozzi & Partners	1/1/1535-31/12/1536	F. Del Nero	10,000	27.8	behind Strozzi
		B. Olivieri	6,000	16.7	
Giulio and Lorenzo Strozzi & Partners	1/7/1537-18/12/1538	F. Strozzi }	26,666.7	66.7	
		F. Del Nero }			behind Strozzi
		B. Olivieri	8,333.3	20.8	
		B. Busini	3,000	7.5	
		S. Guiducci	2,000	5.0	
Benvenuto Olivieri & Partners	1/7/1539-16/9/1543	R. Strozzi	12,000	50.0	behind Olivieri
		B. Olivieri	7,000	29.2	
		B. Busini	3,000	12.5	
		S. Guiducci	2,000	8.3	
Benvenuto Olivieri & Partners *	25/3/1543-end 1545	R. Strozzi	25,000	50.0	behind Olivieri
		B. Olivieri	17,500	35.0	
		B. Busini	7,500	15.0	
Benvenuto Olivieri & Partners	15/12/1545-end 1549	B. Olivieri	16,000	66.7	
		B. Busini	8,000	33.3	until 16/3/1549

* There are doubts concerning the existence of this company (cf. pp. 54-55).

Table 5 summarizes the situation of the companies in which Benvenuto Olivieri participated: both those in the name of others (Altoviti and Strozzi), which have been discussed above, and those of which he was the senior partner, and which therefore were under his name. These will be examined in the following sections.

Benvenuto Olivieri & Partners (1 July 1539-16 September 1543)

On 1 July 1539 Benvenuto Olivieri, Benedetto Busini and Simone Guiducci 'agreed to set up a company in Rome or wherever the Roman court was in residence' under the name Benvenuto Olivieri & Partners of Rome.[116] The social capital, equal to 24,000 ducats, was divided thus:

Benvenuto Olivieri	19,000	(17,000 in cash, 2,000 'at his wish')
Benedetto Busini	3,000	(2,000 in cash, 1,000 for the capitalization of his service)
Simone Guiducci	2,000	(1,000 in cash, 1,000 for the capitalization of his service)

The contributions in cash were to be deposited after two months; any of the partners who failed to do so would be in debt to the company with an added interest of 15% per annum. The profits would be divided proportionally: to Benvenuto Olivieri 79.17%, to Benedetto Busini 12.5% and to Simone Guiducci 8.33%.

On 18 July 1539, Roberto Strozzi also joined the company as a silent partner, contributing 12,000 ducats of Benvenuto Olivieri's share in cash.[117] Consequently, the social capital (expressed in gold cameral ducats) and profits were eventually divided as follows:

Roberto Strozzi	12,000	share of profits	50.00%
Benvenuto Olivieri	7,000	share of profits	29.17%
Benedetto Busini	3,000	share of profits	12.50%
Simone Guiducci	2,000	share of profits	8.33%

Several employees were taken on: Giovan Francesco di Pagnozzo Ridolfi, Benvenuto's brother-in-law, being his wife's brother (with a remuneration of 10 ducats a month),

116 ASF, Galli Tassi 1826, fols 3v-5r; Galli Tassi 1810, ins. 16, fols 5r-6v. A transcription of the partnership agreement can be found in the Appendix, doc. 4.

117 ASF, Galli Tassi 1826, fol. 5r; Galli Tassi 1824, fol. 14. Regarding the link between Roberto Strozzi and Benvenuto Olivieri, natural if one considers the relationship of the latter with the father of the former, it can be mentioned that in April 1539 Roberto Strozzi and Benvenuto Olivieri agreed with Mariotto Della Palla (from 1 October for five years) to run livestock on the land of Lunghezza. This land, which belonged to Roberto Strozzi, was worth approximately 13,000 *scudi* calculating 'livestock, debtors, furnishings and others'. The farm was rented out for 1,000 *scudi di sole* and its management entrusted principally to Della Palla, who was rewarded for this with 1/5 of the profits. The participation of Olivieri was instead limited to 8.33%, in that his share of the capital amounted to 1,083.3 *scudi* (Galli Tassi 1824, fol. 6). Some days before this new agreement, the same participants had cancelled a preceding one (fol. 14).

and Francesco di Giulio Del Riccio (with a remuneration of 2 ducats a month);[118] another employee was Guglielmo Dei, who, initially earning 4 ducats a month, then saw both his responsibilities and salary grow (to 5 ducats): on 9 October 1542 he was made chief cashier, a position which until then had been held by Simone Guiducci.[119]

This company, which existed during Benvenuto Olivieri's most prolific years, is well documented by an enormous ledger, the so-called *Libro azzuro segnato A secondo*, which covers the period 1 January 1542 to 31 January 1544.[120]

On 17 March 1543 the 'consul and councillors of the Florentine nation in Rome' were advised formally that the company would be dissolved by mutual agreement. From that date on, therefore, none of the partners could act in the name of the company but only in their own names.[121]

In the partnership agreement there is some confusion over dates (1542 and 1543 are used interchangeably even though the same year is clearly being referred to). This confusion is heightened by the use of the double calendar (*a nativitate / ab incarnatione*) in the period 1-24 March of every year, where it is not specified which system is being chosen.[122] A number of elements make 1543 more probable. First of all, in the large ledger mentioned above, the 20,000 ducats of capital deposited are credited to the three partners on 30 June 1543, or, in other words, exactly four years after the creation of the company.[123] Moreover, the last registrations of this ledger, which cross-reference to a subsequent volume (*azzuro segnato A terzo*), carry the date of 31 January 1544.[124]

In another *filza*, dedicated to the Busini family, there exists a partnership agreement drawn up by Benedetto Busini and Benvenuto Olivieri referring to a company which was to begin in December 1545 (this partnership will be discussed in more detail shortly). In a number of accounts listed at the foot of this agreement bearing the date 16 March 1548 *ab incarnatione* (therefore 1549) there is mention of money owed to Busini by Olivieri: 'for money owed to him for the time spent in the service of Benvenuto

---

118 Ridolfi received 180 gold cameral ducats for the period 1 January 1542-30 June 1543; Del Riccio received 30 ducats for the 15 months from 1 April 1542 to 30 June 1543 (ASF, Galli Tassi, 2278, fol. 362). Francesco Boni must also have worked for the Olivieri bank in some capacity between 1541 and 1543 (fol. 311).

119 ASF, Galli Tassi 2278, fols 87, 227: Dei was given 24 ducats for the period 1 January-30 June 1542 and 60 ducats for the 12 months running from 1 July 1542 to 30 June 1543. On 9 May 1542 he also made an investment, buying an '*ufficio di portione*' for 465 *scudi d'oro in oro*, for which he then received the profits, equivalent to almost 70 *scudi*, between May 1542 and August 1543 (fols 87, 376).

120 ASF, Galli Tassi 2278. For an analysis of the balance sheet drawn from this book see Chapter 9.

121 ASF, Galli Tassi 1826, fol. 5v. The date on the document is in fact 1542; however, as will be seen, 1543 is the more probable date.

122 As is well known, in Florence but also amongst the Florentines abroad the calendar *ab incarnatione* was used, according to which the year began on 25 March: this means that a year needs to be added to the dates between 1 January and 24 March inclusive to obtain the modern dating system.

123 ASF, Galli Tassi 2278, fol. 2.

124 This date is in no doubt, as it says explicitly '*e addì xxxj di gennaio 1543 ab incarnatione*' (ASF, Galli Tassi 2278, fol. 380).

Olivieri and Benvenuto Olivieri & Partners after the end of the activity of the company of the *libro azzurro*, that is 5 years and 6 months'.[125] A rapid calculation gives us the date 16 September 1543.[126] But on 25 March 1543 it would seem that another company was set up, including the same partners with the exception of Guiducci.

Benvenuto Olivieri & Partners (25 March 1543-end of 1545)

Even as to the existence of this company, however, there are more doubts than certainties. The circumstances surrounding the various partnerships stipulated between the Olivieri and Strozzi families are covered in a document relative to a lawsuit between the heirs of Benvenuto Olivieri and those of Roberto Strozzi. A notation in the margins of the paragraph relating to this particular company runs thus: 'it is not true. We made the agreement but with no effect, so that they will have to demonstrate that there was a contribution to the social capital; but the effort will be in vain.'[127]

At the time the partnership agreement was signed, on 25 March 1542, it was, however, stated that this new activity was to last three years 'from the 25th of March 1543 or before, if this is convenient for the partners'.[128]

To the social capital, which consisted of 50,000 gold cameral ducats 'of the old coin', the partners were to contribute in the following proportions:

Benvenuto Olivieri	42,500[129]
Benedetto Busini	7,500 (5,500 in cash, 2,000 for the capitalization of his service)

125 ASF, Galli Tassi 1731, ins. 7.

126 Increasing, if possible, the confusion there is also another document which, referring to this company, speaks of 'the last day of May 1547, when the accounts were balanced between the partners' (ASF, Galli Tassi 1833, fol. 3). Moreover, according to this note, Busini's share would seem to be 10%, while it has been seen that in fact it amounted to 12.5%; here the confusion might have been caused by the fact that the actual cash deposits amounted to 20,000 ducats, of which 2,000 (therefore 10%) came from Busini, to whom 1,000 more were attributed as capitalization of his service. In any case, for this share Benedetto received profits of 842.3 ducats (Galli Tassi 1833, fol. 3): from this it can be deduced that the profits of the company in total came to 8,422.6 ducats. Nevertheless, on 31 January 1544 the net profit was 23,001 ducats (cf. Table 15, p. 189). According to Galli Tassi 1920, fol. 26, undated, the *Libro azzurro terzo* [the last of this company] had a positive balance of 21,545.3 ducats in the profit and loss account.

127 ASF, Galli Tassi 1810, ins. 16, fol. 6v.

128 ASF, Galli Tassi 1826, fols 6r-7r. With regard to the duration, an article of the partnership agreement states that, given 'the dangers of war, death of the pope and other travails that hourly threaten Italy and Rome', Benvenuto could close the company before the end of the three years, provided he gave Benedetto three months' notice (fol. 7r). See also Galli Tassi 1810, ins. 16, fols 6v-7v.

129 Of which 39,500 ducats in cash and 3,000 'when it is convenient for him, and he cannot be obliged to contribute them until the end of the company'.

On 18 April 1542, Roberto Strozzi also entered into the company, contributing 25,000 ducats in cash as a silent partner. Consequently, the social capital and the profits were eventually divided thus:

Roberto Strozzi	25,000	share of profits	50%
Benvenuto Olivieri	17,500	share of profits	35%
Benedetto Busini	7,500	share of profits	15%

According to the original agreement, the company was to be dissolved on 24 March 1546. However – and this would seem to confirm the theory that this partnership never actually existed – in December 1545 yet another company in the name of Benvenuto Olivieri & Partners of Rome was set up.

Benvenuto Olivieri & Partners (15 December 1545-end of 1549)

According to the partnership agreement of 15 December 1545, this company, dealing under the name of Benvenuto Olivieri & Partners of Rome (although Olivieri reserved the right to be able to change the denomination to Giulio Olivieri and Benedetto Busini & Partners if he so desired), was to last seven years from the date of the signing. The social capital amounted to 24,000 gold cameral ducats ('*a sc. 102 d'oro per cento*', as specified) and was divided thus:

Benvenuto Olivieri	16,000[130]
Benedetto Busini	8,000 (6,000 in cash, 2,000 for the capitalization of his service)

The articles of the agreement followed the usual formula and the profits were divided as follows: Benvenuto 66.7% and Benedetto 33.3%. Francesco Del Riccio was chosen as a cashier, at least for 1549.[131] The partnership would be dissolved in the event of the death of either of the two partners; but in the case of Benedetto's death the contracts obtained in the meantime would be kept by Benvenuto (as would the account-books).[132]

Finally, 'they agreed that Benvenuto being in Rome with his wife, servants and children, for the expenses sustained had to refund the company one hundred and fifty *scudi* per annum, the rest being considered capitalization of the service of said Benvenuto; and when he is in Rome without his wife, servants and children, for the time that he remains he will have from the company one hundred and fifty ducats per annum in recognition of the capitalization of his service'.[133]

130 Of which 4,000 immediately, 4,000 at Christmas, 4,000 at the end of January and 4,000 at the end of February. Busini also had to deposit his own share in cash on the same dates: 1,000 immediately, 2,000 at Christmas, 2,000 at the end of January and 1,000 at the end of February (ASF, Galli Tassi 1979, ins. 33).

131 ASF, Galli Tassi 1959, various unnumbered folios.

132 ASF, Galli Tassi 1979, ins. 33.

133 ASF, Galli Tassi 1979, ins. 33.

As will be seen in more detail shortly, in the following December this company took over the share of 6,000 ducats that Benvenuto, in the name of his son Giulio, had invested in the Ubaldini company (and the sum was subtracted from the amount Olivieri had still to deposit with his own company). Since the figure due to Giulio in the Ubaldini company then diminished by 2,000 ducats (the share of the 6,000 which became Busini's, partner in Olivieri's company for ⅓), the same sum was credited to him in the Olivieri–Busini partnership.[134]

The company did not, however, develop as originally planned. By 16 March 1549 Benedetto Busini, whose contribution to the social capital should have been 6,000 ducats, did not appear to have paid; nor did he appear able to pay the sum stipulated plus the interest of 15% owed by whoever defaulted on payment within the time agreed on (calculating three years and three months' delay, Busini should thus at this point have paid 9,467 ducats). At Olivieri's behest, however, the following agreement was reached: Benvenuto took over all the company affairs from Benedetto. Moreover, Benvenuto released Benedetto from his legal obligations, recognizing all the work he had done up to that moment. Additionally Benedetto accepted the decision to forego 300 ducats for each of the past years and declared himself to be 'very content and satisfied with the agreement'.[135]

It is not known, however, how much Busini owed 'Benvenuto & Partners or Benvenuto personally' in the time which passed between the end of the preceding company and the beginning of this one. From the data available it would seem that at the moment of the above agreement Busini owed 5,256 ducats and had owing to him 2,691; the final balance, negative for him, was therefore of 2,565 ducats. Benedetto, however, promised to pay over the next five years (one-fifth every year) everything he owed or might owe in the future, using as surety 'all his real and liquid property, present and future'. By 28 November 1561, however, the debt had still not been paid. On that date, in fact, Isabella Ridolfi, Olivieri's widow, requested the entire amount owed by Benedetto according to an agreement made between the two men dated 16 March 1549 and signed 'in his [Busini's] own hand'.[136]

As well as these companies in which Benvenuto was directly involved, there were also others in which he was a sleeping partner, contributing capital only, without taking part in their administration. The money sometimes came from Benvenuto's own pockets, sometimes from the coffers of his companies.

Investments of Olivieri and his companies in the Ubaldini companies

Benvenuto nurtured a number of close relationships with the other *mercatores florentini romanam curiam sequentes*, one of the most important being that with the Ubaldini family. Two of them, Girolamo and Roberto, were in fact related by marriage

134 ASF, Galli Tassi 1979, ins. 33. For further details, see pp. 57-58.

135 ASF, Galli Tassi 1732, ins. 7; Galli Tassi 1824, fol. 5 (the two documents are virtually identical).

136 ASF, Galli Tassi 1810, ins. 10, fol. 1v. The request includes other sums, for a total of 8,273 ducats owed by Busini, and 7,136 owed to him (fols 1v-4v).

to the Olivieri family, in that they too had married into the Ridolfi family: the first was married to Fiammetta, the second to Maddalena.

On 15 July 1542 an *accomandita* (limited partnership), destined to last five years, was set up between Antonio di Nofri Mellini, Girolamo di Raffaello Ubaldini and Salvestro Gerini for 'exchange, dispatches, farms, alum and customs', and was called Girolamo Ubaldini & Partners. The first two contributed 6,000 ducats a head, while to the third were attributed 1,000 ducats for the capitalization of his service, given that he administered the firm together with Ubaldini. As a silent partner, behind the name of Mellini, Benvenuto Olivieri also participated in this business deal, contributing 2,000 ducats.[137] Therefore, social capital (in ducats) and profits were divided as follows:

Girolamo Ubaldini	6,000	share of profits	46.1%
Antonio Mellini	4,000	share of profits	30.8%
Benvenuto Olivieri	2,000	share of profits	15.4%
Salvestro Gerini	1,000	share of profits	7.7%

Three years later, however, Olivieri and Ubaldini created a new partnership. Given that the simultaneous existence on the Rome market of two companies called 'Girolamo Ubaldini & Partners' is extremely unlikely, it can be assumed that the second, in which Ubaldini was formally associated with Benvenuto's son, Giulio, was in some way a continuation of the first. It was called Girolamo di Raffaello Ubaldini and Giulio di Benvenuto Olivieri & Partners, the first contributing 12,000 gold cameral ducats, and the second 6,000. Benvenuto would act on behalf of his son Giulio, at the time still a minor (he was four years old), until he reached the age of 20. The managers were Giovan Francesco di Pagnozzo Ridolfi (Benvenuto's brother-in-law) and Giovan Maria di Raffaello Ubaldini (Girolamo's brother), who, 'for the capitalization of their service but without any salary', held shares in the company corresponding to 1,000 ducats each. The articles of the partnership agreement followed the usual formula and no one was permitted to undertake business negotiations independently of the company. However, Girolamo Ubaldini was allowed to manage the custom of Terra and get for himself (and not for the company) the remuneration deriving from it. Moreover, every year he would be credited with 700 ducats from the social capital for household furnishings and 100 for their wear and tear. Capital (in ducats) and profits were to be divided as follows:[138]

Girolamo Ubaldini	12,000	share of profits	60%
Giulio Olivieri	6,000	share of profits	30%
Giovan Francesco Ridolfi	1,000	share of profits	5%
Giovan Maria Ubaldini	1,000	share of profits	5%

137 ASF, Galli Tassi 1824, fol. 14, 29; Galli Tassi 1945, fol. 249. In Galli Tassi 2278 (ledger of Benvenuto Olivieri & Partners) on 16 July Benvenuto transferred 2,000 ducats from his own current account to that of Antonio Mellini (fols 131, 173); and then on the same day he transferred from Mellini's account to that of Girolamo Ubaldini & Partners those 2,000 plus the 4,000 of Antonio (fols 173, 180). In this case it was Benvenuto himself and not his company who was a partner.

138 ASF, Galli Tassi 1824, fasc. 22; Galli Tassi 1979, ins. 33.

Article XV states: 'Item, even though said Benvenuto has a company in Rome and other business affairs, he deposited 6,000 ducats as capital for the said Giulio merely in his role as father (*in peculio profettizio et non altrimenti*), and therefore they declare that neither said Benvenuto nor his company are partners of said Girolamo and Giulio and that therefore said Benvenuto can continue his activity in Rome in his name and in the name of others.' Also significant is a final addition to the partnership agreement: 'Item, they agree that for now the company begins with the name of Girolamo Ubaldini & Partners and the name of Giulio will be added when the time appears right.'[139] Benvenuto, who already was senior partner of another company, was seeking, in other words, to appear formally as little as possible: it has already been mentioned in fact how in general the partnership agreements forbade the partners to undertake individual business affairs in the same city (in this case Rome) as the company in question.

Several months later things changed yet again. In December, as has already been noted, Benvenuto, together with Benedetto Busini, formed a new partnership, which he then decided should replace him as shareholder in the Ubaldini company. In other words, Benvenuto Olivieri & Partners, and no longer Benvenuto as a private party, were now hidden behind Giulio Olivieri's name. Giulio was compensated with 2,000 ducats in his father's company, the equivalent of Busini's share in the Ubaldini company.[140]

On 22 March 1547 Girolamo Ubaldini died but, as stipulated in his will and in agreement with the other partners, he was replaced by his brother Roberto, and the company continued under the name of the Heir of Girolamo Ubaldini & Partners. The shares in the social capital, which from 20,000 ducats were raised to 27,500, were modified thus:

Heir of Girolamo Ubaldini	11,000	share of profits	40.0%
Giulio Olivieri	7,500	share of profits	27.3%
Roberto Ubaldini	6,500	share of profits	23.6%
Giovan Francesco Ridolfi	1,500	share of profits	5.5%
Giovan Maria Ubaldini	1,000	share of profits	3.6%

Of the total sum, the capitalization of the partners' service passed from the 2,000 ducats of the shares of Giovan Francesco Ridolfi and of Giovan Maria Ubaldini to 4,000 ducats, because a further 500 of Ridolfi and 1,500 of Roberto Ubaldini were added. In other words, while the social capital increased by 37.5%, the real increase in the contribution in cash was limited to 30.6%. In this new contract, signed on 2 June 1547, the agreements remained the same (including the above-quoted article XV). Moreover, it was established that Roberto would be in charge of the management and for this would receive 50 ducats annually; in addition, he could avail himself of the right to take out interest-free loans of up to 150 ducats a year.[141]

It would seem that the company was dissolved before the end of the five years, in 1550, or that at least there was a separation from the Olivieri. Benvenuto died in September 1549, when Giulio was only seven years old, and it is therefore probable that the administrators of his inheritance decided to evaluate the situation carefully before

139 Ibid.

140 ASF, Galli Tassi 1979, ins. 33.

141 ASF, Galli Tassi 1979, ins. 34.

making any new moves.[142] In the following years the final balances were calculated: on 26 July 1551 almost 11,500 gold cameral ducats were credited to Olivieri 'as an advance payment … for his share of social capital and of profits of this company'.[143] Between 1555 and 1556 profits for 4,252 *scudi* were divided up, 1,198 going to Olivieri.[144] In the meanwhile, Giovan Francesco Ridolfi had also passed away (the exact date of his death is not known) and his share had been transferred to Roberto Ubaldini.[145]

Table 6 shows the shares held by Benvenuto in the various companies of which he was a partner. What should be noted is the continual increase, in proportional terms, of the weight that he had in these companies; this followed increasing financial contributions also in absolute terms (it should be remembered that in the first two cases 2,000 and 1,500 ducats respectively were given as the equivalent of the capitalization of his service).

Table 6 – Investments of Benvenuto Olivieri (in gold cameral ducats)

YEARS	COMPANY	OLIVIERI'S INVESTMENT	%	YEARS	COMPANY	OLIVIERI'S INVESTMENT	%
1520-31	Altoviti	?	8.3				
1532-36	Strozzi	6,000	16.7				
1537-38	Strozzi	8,333.3	20.8				
1539-43	Olivieri	7,000	29.2				
				1542-?	Ubaldini	2,000	15.4
1543-45	Olivieri	17,500	35.0				
				1545	Ubaldini*	6,000	30.0
1545-49	Olivieri	16,000	66.7				

* The Ubaldini company continued until 1547; but from December 1545 the investment in the social capital was not made by Benvenuto, but by his company (cf. Table 7).

Investments of the Olivieri companies in other companies

In 1542 the company of Benvenuto Olivieri held shares for 8,500 *scudi d'oro in oro* (equivalent to 8,292.7 gold cameral ducats) in that of Antonio Covoni & Partners of Rome. Unfortunately both the date of the beginning of this company and the exact composition of its capital are unknown; the only certainty is that it was dissolved on 31 March 1543.[146] On 30 June of the same year Benvenuto Olivieri & Partners were

142 Regarding the Olivieri companies, Benvenuto, in his will, instructed Benedetto Busini to liquidate them within the two years following Benvenuto's death (cf. p. 43).

143 ASF, Galli Tassi 1953, fol. 143. In 1548 a contribution to the social capital of 7,500 ducats is mentioned (Galli Tassi 1923, fol. 5; Galli Tassi 1921, fol. 28).

144 ASF, Galli Tassi 1953, fol. 143.

145 ASF, Galli Tassi 1979, ins. 13.

146 ASF, Galli Tassi 2278, fols 195, 199, 274.

credited with 1,127.7 *scudi d'oro in oro* (=1,100.2 gold cameral ducats) for the share of profits due to them: this implied a profit, though not yet calculated in a definitive way, equal to 13.27% of the capital initially deposited.[147]

On 29 August 1543 the company of Benvenuto Olivieri invested 5,000 gold cameral ducats in another company called Antonio Covoni & Partners of Rome. Underwritten on 1 April, this numbered amongst its partners Luigi Del Riccio and Niccolò Busini (the latter with a share of 1,800 ducats). The social capital must have amounted to 30,000 ducats, since Benvenuto participated for one-sixth.[148]

Absolutely nothing, on the other hand, is known of the company of Bartolomeo Bettini, in which the Olivieri seem to have had some interest between the years 1545 and 1549. In the document that ratified the transfer of all the shares of the company into the hands of Benvenuto when Busini left the partnership, it is in fact recalled that these shares also included those held in other businesses by Bartolmeo Bettini & Partners, as well as of Benvenuto Olivieri & Partners.[149]

Another company in which the Olivieri had continuing business interests, at least from the last months of the Strozzi company, was that of Filippo Carducci. The partnership lasted at least ten years, as there were various renewals: the social capital always remained 6,000 *scudi di giuli 10 per scudo* after the first year, even though each partner's share varied in time. When the *accomandita* (limited partnership) called Filippo Carducci & Partners was set up on 1 November 1538, Giulio and Lorenzo Strozzi & Partners invested 3,000 *scudi di giuli 10 per scudo* as silent partners behind the name of Benedetto Busini. Carducci contributed 1,000 *scudi* as well as his own labour, valued at a further 500, while the other partner, Banco Neroni, contributed to the social capital only 500 *scudi* as capitalization of his service. The profits must therefore have been divided as follows: to Busini 60%; to Carducci 30%; to Neroni 10%. After a year Busini, still acting on behalf of the Strozzi, added a further 1,000 *scudi*, thus taking the capital to 6,000 *scudi* and the division of the profits to the following proportions:[150]

Strozzi & Partners behind Busini	4,000	share of profits	66.7%
Filippo Carducci	1,500	share of profits	25.0%
Banco Neroni	500	share of profits	8.3%

After three years the partnership was dissolved,[151] but another was immediately set up which was active from 1 November 1541 and continued dealing under the name of Filippo Carducci & Partners, taking upon itself the debts of the preceding company.[152]

147 ASF, Galli Tassi 2278, fols 274, 311. Confirmed also by Galli Tassi 1952, fol. 33.

148 ASF, Galli Tassi 1824, fol. 14; Galli Tassi 1949, fols 99-100, 183; Galli Tassi 1952, fols 33, 39. Luigi Del Riccio, a close friend of Buonarroti, was in these years procurator of Roberto Strozzi and acted as intermediary between Strozzi, exiled in Lyons, and the Olivieri bank (E. Rufini, *Michelangelo e la colonia fiorentina a Roma* (Naples, 1965), pp. 8, 10).

149 ASF, Galli Tassi 1732, ins. 7; Galli Tassi 1824, fol. 5.

150 For this information see: ASF, Galli Tassi 1824, fasc. 8, fol. 14.

151 ASF, Galli Tassi 1824, fol. 14. An indication in this sense was given to Busini by Benvenuto Olivieri on 5 August (fol. 26). Cf. also Galli Tassi 1946, fol. 22r.

152 At the end of 1539 the profits of the company amounted to 1,307.8 ducats, at the end of the second year to 2,171.6, and on 1 November 1541 to 3,674.6, at the moment when the

The declared aim of this new firm was to 'sell and buy silk and woollen cloths and other merchandise'. The capital was contributed by Benedetto Busini (3,200 *scudi*, guaranteeing him a share in the profits equal to 53.3%) and by Filippo Carducci (1,700 *scudi* in cash plus 1,100 *scudi* as capitalization of his service, for a total of 2,800 and a share in the profits equal to 46.7%); any loss would be shouldered proportionately, but in Busini's case with a limit, given by his contribution to the social capital. Whereas in the preceding case it was the Strozzi company which was acting behind the name of Busini, now it was the company of Benvenuto Olivieri, natural successor to the former, which was doing so.[153] The table below shows contributions (in *scudi di giuli 10 per scudo*) and profits:

Olivieri & Partners behind Busini	3,200	share of profits	53.3%
Filippo Carducci	2,800	share of profits	46.7%

On 25 March 1546 the balance sheet showed profits of 4,698.8 ducats: Busini was entitled to 2,506 and Carducci to 2,192.8.[154] On the same day the partners changed yet again: Luigi Del Riccio and Benedetto Busini invested 3,000 *scudi* (1,500 each), of which 1,600 in goods and 1,400 in cash; Filippo Carducci contributed 1,500 *scudi* (900 in goods and 600 in cash) to which were added another 600 for the capitalization of his service; Giovanni Barducci contributed 300 *scudi* in cash plus his labour, this too valued at 600 *scudi*.[155] In other words:

Filippo Carducci	2,100	share of profits	35%
Luigi Del Riccio	1,500	share of profits	25%
Benedetto Busini	1,500	share of profits	25%
Giovanni Barducci	900	share of profits	15%

The fact that Benvenuto Olivieri acted as Busini's procurator would seem to suggest that in this case, as in previous cases, the latter was not acting on his own, but in the name of his company. At Luigi Del Riccio's death, on 16 October 1546, with the agreement of the other partners Filippo Carducci took over the former's quota, thus raising his share of profits to 60% and his part of the capital to 3,600 *scudi*.[156]

Table 7 compares the companies in which Benvenuto Olivieri was partner, and their social capital, with those companies in which the first ones had bought shares.[157]

new company was created (ASF, Galli Tassi 1941, fols 443r, 438r, 457r, 472v).

153 ASF, Galli Tassi 1824, fol. 3, 14. It should, in fact, be remembered that the partners of Giulio and Lorenzo Strozzi & Partners, active until December 1538, were now reunited (with Roberto Strozzi having taken the place of his deceased father Filippo) under the name of Benvenuto Olivieri & Partners. See also ASF, *Mercanzia*, 10832, fols 23v-24r, 28r, 36r-v.

154 ASF, Galli Tassi 1941, fol. 394r.

155 ASF, Galli Tassi 1824, fol. 7. See also ASF, *Mercanzia*, 10832, fols 61v, 80v.

156 ASF, Galli Tassi 1824, fol. 7. On 28 July 1548 the profit and loss account showed a positive balance of 2,092.3 ducats (Galli Tassi 1941, fol. 462r).

157 As can be seen, the companies of Benvenuto Olivieri had investments in a considerable number of other companies; but the case seems to prefigure something different to that of the *holding* (which was spoken of in note 54).

Table 7 – Investments of Benvenuto Olivieri's companies in other companies

YEARS	PARTNERS	SOCIAL CAPITAL	INVESTMENT	COMPANY	YEARS
1537 - 38	F. Strozzi F. Del Nero B. Olivieri B. Busini S. Guiducci	40,000 gold ducats	→ 3,000 subsequently: 4,000 *scudi di moneta*	F. Carducci & Partners	1538 - 41
1539 - 43	R. Strozzi B. Olivieri B. Busini S. Guiducci	24,000 gold ducats	→ 3,200 *scudi di moneta* → 8,500 *scudi d'oro*	F. Carducci & Partners A. Covoni & Partners	1541 - ? ? - 1543
1543 - 45	R. Strozzi B. Olivieri B. Busini	50,000 gold ducats	→ 5,000 gold ducats	A. Covoni & Partners	1543 - ?
1543 - 49	B. Olivieri B. Busini	24,000 gold ducats	→ 1,500 *scudi di moneta* → 6,000 gold ducats → 7,500 gold ducats → ?	F. Carducci & Partners G. Ubaldini & Partners Ubaldini heirs and Partners B. Bettini & Partners	1546 - ? 1546 - 47 1547 - 49 ? - 1549

This chapter has thus far recounted the internal history of the companies in which Benvenuto Olivieri participated. It should, at this point, be clear how important the personal relationships between the partners were: these relationships were often family ties – as in the case of Giovan Francesco Ridolfi, brother of Benvenuto's wife, or of Girolamo Ubaldini, who had married Benvenuto's wife's sister – but not always. The Florentine community in Rome, as was mentioned in Chapter 1, was very powerful and united; it is not surprising, therefore, that Florentine merchant-bankers were also very united. They often set up companies together or worked together on single financial operations (always of considerable importance). It can be seen as very natural, therefore, that Benvenuto, who moved to Rome at a young age, had sought to build up relationships with the most illustrious of his fellow countrymen who had been working there for some time: first Bindo Altoviti, then Filippo Strozzi. Olivieri was certainly appreciated for his capacity: Altoviti, in fact, did all he could to keep him, while Strozzi bestowed on him not only very wide powers as his procurator, but also entrusted him with the guardianship of his children. Having achieved independent wealth and authority, Benvenuto Olivieri disassociated himself (albeit never completely) from Strozzi, becoming senior partner of new companies and in turn acting as a point of reference for other young Florentines in Rome. With the passing of the years, as is shown in Table 6, Olivieri acquired an increasingly large share in the companies of which he became partner.

5. Benvenuto's sons and legal disputes over his business affairs

Neither of his sons continued the activity which had taken Benvenuto, as will be seen in the rest of this book, to work at the highest levels with the Apostolic Chamber. There are many possible reasons for this: from the fact that at the moment of their father's death they were both very young, to the ever diminishing influence that the Florentines had at the papal court. But certainly there were also other reasons: one of these is probably to be found in the series of trials and lawsuits that Giulio and Alessandro were subjected to in the years following the death of their father.

Among the various persecutors of the Olivieri heirs, the first that should be mentioned is Bartolomeo Bettini, who, despite being their guardian, behaved in what could be described as a rather reprehensible manner. A lawsuit of 1553, in which Benvenuto's sons were represented by their uncle Giovan Francesco Ridolfi, explains, for example, that Bettini had collected 12,000 *scudi* in the name of Olivieri from Pallavicini and Giustiniani for operations concerning the customs, which he had used as if they belonged to his own company. This clearly was to the great detriment of the Olivieri heirs, who were still very young. Ridolfi then requested that Bettini give the Olivieri more than 10,000 *scudi* and that more than 25,000 in debt be cancelled.[158]

But the person who, more than any other, subjected the heirs of Benvenuto to lengthy lawsuits was certainly Francesco di Piero Del Nero.[159] From 1515 he had been the right-hand man of Strozzi, collaborating closely with him in the care of

158 ASF, Galli Tassi 1938, fasc. 14.

159 M.M. Bullard defines Francesco Del Nero (1487-1563) as 'one of the more picaresque personalities with whom Filippo associated for both business and pleasure' and

his interests and of his financial affairs, to the point that he assumed the role of senior partner in his absence. This activity brought him such wealth and power that in 1529 he was even named treasurer general, a virtually unheard of privilege for a layman.[160] Later, however, around 1537, Del Nero was involved in various lawsuits brought against the Apostolic Chamber, which led to his spending some time in prison. Olivieri, during his partner's incarceration, had taken it upon himself to keep him informed of all that was going on and had also done all he could to extrapolate him from this unpleasant situation. It was, moreover, to Benvenuto that Del Nero turned on 28 August 1537, when he needed someone to post his bail in order to secure his release from prison. On that date, as Francesco wrote, the figure that 'I agreed to pay to His Holiness for the clearing of all my debts and my release from imprisonment' amounted to the enormous sum of 40,000 *scudi*.[161]

Benvenuto and Francesco worked together for a long time as partners in the company of Filippo Strozzi, who had with both of them a relationship not only of collaboration but also of close friendship. In the 1540s, however, a series of problems, which until then had more or less remained buried (in fact, as has been seen, Olivieri had done everything in his power to help Del Nero), surfaced with a vengeance. Francesco, despite being in trouble with the Apostolic Chamber, must nevertheless have maintained strong ties with the ecclesiastical hierarchy. Evidently he availed himself of these contacts to put pressure on the ecclesiastical tribunals, as is revealed by a mournful letter of 26 March 1546 that Benvenuto Olivieri wrote to Pope Paul III. In the letter Olivieri recalls that in the past Del Nero had had problems with the law in Florence, in Naples and in Rome. Despite this Del Nero now saw Olivieri as an enemy, and not only did he demand payment of personal debts, but also payment of debts owed to the fiscal authorities, as well as casting aspersions on his reputation before the pope.[162]

Evidence of discord between the two can be found as early as 1544, when Benvenuto and Francesco decided to refer any disagreement to the judgement of Cardinals Gambara and Pucci.[163] In April 1546 Bastiano da Montauto, Giovan Battista Acciaiuoli and Leonardo Sauli, merchant-bankers (Florentines the first two,

---

'by nature impatient and quick to temper' (*Filippo Strozzi and the Medici. Favor and Finance in Sixteenth-century Florence and Rome* (Cambridge, 1980), p. 89, note 91).

160 In virtue of this, in 1533 he was also made commissioner general of the Romagna, the Marches, Perugia, Umbria, Patrimonio, Campagna, Marittima, the duchy of Urbino, Parma, Piacenza and Bologna. The commissioner general's duty was to collect the tithes and other taxes, with wide powers to inspect and revise the activity of treasuries, depostaries, etc. (ASF, Diplomatico, *Dono Torrigiani-Appendice*, 29 October 1533). In 1534, moreover, he was renewed in the post of treasurer general (*Dono Torrigiani-Appendice*, 3 August 1534).

161 ASF, Galli Tassi 1939, fols 22, 74r-93r, 103 ff. Again in 1544, however, Del Nero, then resident in Naples, would be recalled to Rome to explain several matters that occurred in the period of his administration of the General Treasury (ASF, Diplomatico, *Dono Torrigiani-Appendice*, 13 March 1544).

162 ASF, Galli Tassi 1938, unnumbered sheet. The letter begins in the third person, but at the foot bears Olivieri's signature.

163 ASF, Galli Tassi 1939, fol. 58r-v: given the delicacy of the question, the deadlines were then extended until the following year.

Genoese the third) in Rome and common friends of the two opposing parties, were given the task of examining a list of 'differences' and requests that Del Nero had presented, accusing Olivieri both in his own name and as partner of Strozzi. The two defendants were obliged to obey the arbitrators' decision, or face a penalty of 10,000 *scudi*, to be given to the Apostolic Chamber, and 'the disgrace of Our Lord'.

The list submitted by Del Nero consisted of twenty-six items that the plaintiff demanded be reimbursed to him by Olivieri. In total, Francesco asked that he be given the sum of 17,621 *scudi*, that debts for a total of 1,374 *scudi* be removed and that he be paid further revenue and interests (to be calculated). After having made use of the month-long extension consented, because while quick action was necessary, careful consideration was needed in order to reach the fairest result possible, and having analysed, one by one, the twenty-six requests, Montauto, Acciaiuoli and Sauli communicated their decision. Some of the deliberations were in favour of Del Nero, others in favour of Olivieri. But overall it was the plaintiff who came out as the winner: first of all, 2,000 ducats were to be credited to him; moreover, he had to be paid 3,000 *scudi* as an account within four days; finally, within fifteen days of the sentence, the balance of the remaining money owed him had to be calculated, and would have to be paid to him within six months, in three instalments.[164]

The question, however, must still have been far from being resolved. In fact, Francesco Del Nero was not at all softened by the death of Benvenuto, and after his demise he did not hesitate to take out proceedings against his heirs. As we can read in a letter written on 15 January 1551 by Bartolomeo Bettini, at the time trustee of the inheritance of Benvenuto Olivieri, to Cardinal Crescenzi,

> Francesco Del Nero has brought civil and criminal suits [against Benvenuto Olivieri]; and since the latter's death he has been persecuting his heirs instead of the revenue authorities concerning the accounts between Benvenuto and the Apostolic Chamber ... But I ask you, most reverend and illustrious sir, as protector of justice, to embrace and protect the two sons and three daughters of Benvenuto, the eldest being only 8 years of age, from persecution by Francesco Del Nero, fierce enemy of their father.[165]

Del Nero, who was clearly not yet satisfied, made further demands, acting both for himself and – without any formal authority to do so – for the tax authorities, thus dealing as harsh a blow as possible to the heirs of Benvenuto.[166] Unfortunately we do not know if and how the various questions were eventually resolved; but it is

---

164 ASF, Galli Tassi 1826, fols 8r-13v, 18r-19v (fols 14r-16v are a copy of part of the same document). Moreover, article VI of the deliberation stated that Benvenuto should be condemned if he did not produce the 'secret book', which detailed the profits of the three partners (fol. 9r). Regarding this lawsuit there is also an unnumbered *fascicolo* in Galli Tassi 1938.

165 ASF, Galli Tassi 1839, fol. 7; Galli Tassi 1844, fols 1, 9.

166 Among other things, we know that in 1554 Francesco and his brother Agostino lived in a house in Florence in Borgo SS. Apostoli which previously belonged to Olivieri's sons, because they declared that the property had passed to them in payment of a debt. The house had been assigned to Giulio and Alessandro in lieu of 2,500 *scudi* that they were owed by their uncle Michele, the house's previous owner (ASF, Galli Tassi 1810, ins. 14); for these debts the latter had also been imprisoned (Galli Tassi 1944, fols 114, 125). On 24 May 1555 Paolo di Michele Olivieri, declaring through his procurator, Giandonato Barbadori (the former's partner in the

certain that all these facts must have strongly influenced the future of the young sons of Olivieri, depriving them of the necessary strength to successfully continue their father's business.[167]

L'Aquila company), that he refused his father's inheritance, asked instead to be reintegrated into possession of the house (ASF, Diplomatico, *Legato Torrigiani*, 24 May 1555).

167 Giulio must, however, have maintained some interests in Rome, as can be seen by the various letters, mostly private, of which he was author or recipient between the 1560s and 1590s (ASF, Galli Tassi 1960-1962). At least between 1561 and 1564 he had a minority share in the company of his uncle, Giovan Francesco Ridolfi (Galli Tassi 1955, fasc. 1, fol. 4). In 1561 he was *camerlengo* of the fraternity of the Pietà (AASGF, vol. 390, fol. 72; vol. 391, fol. 22v).

PART TWO
Benvenuto Olivieri and the Apostolic Chamber

CHAPTER 3

The Depositary and Loans to the Pontiff

1. The Depositary of the Apostolic Chamber

Of all the banking appointments of the Apostolic Chamber the role of depositary general was regarded as the most prestigious; in other words, the man who held this post was considered the first, or most important, papal banker. In general, although there was undoubtedly a financial profit to be made, the benefits were probably indirect rather than direct. The depositary was obliged to advance (and consequently to risk) huge sums of money in the banking transactions in which he was involved:[1] tardy repayment on the part of the Chamber (which, as will be seen, was the norm) carried with it more costs than benefits. Clearly, however, no private individual would have assumed such a position purely for the prestige that it bestowed, without there being the opportunity for profit, even though this clearly also implied the risk of loss. There was one benefit in particular that made this post very attractive – the banker acting as depositary general had access to the multiple sources of income which fed into the papal finances. It was for this reason, therefore, that in May 1515 the Florentine Benedetto Buondelmonti sought to convince a hesitant Filippo Strozzi to accept this position, promising to administer it in his name and to share the profits.[2] From various sources, Melissa Bullard has estimated that in the 1520s the commission collected by the depositary amounted to 4-5% of the payments he carried out on behalf of the Apostolic Chamber; in the 1540s, however, it dropped, seldom rising above 3%, except in the case of the extraordinary expenditure.[3] The

1 On 15 April 1517 Filippo Strozzi wrote to Francesco Del Nero: 'I will not mention here how much money the Rome company has provided the pope, nor for how much we are his creditors in the Depository of Rome. Both accounts are very substantial, but at the moment I do not know exactly how big they are' (M.M. Bullard, *Filippo Strozzi and the Medici: Favor and Finance in Sixteenth-century Florence and Rome* (Cambridge, 1980), pp. 127-128. Source: ASF, *Carte Strozziane*, serie III, 110, fol. 31r). It is clear that the privileges bestowed on the depositary also included several customs exemptions: in 1543, for example, an order was given to the '*datiariis, gabellariis, dohanariis et passageriis portuum, passium et pontium*' to allow free passage to goods belonging to Benvenuto Olivieri, depositary general (ASV, *Cam. Ap., Div. Cam. 127*, fol. 203r). In the text it should be noted that a distinction has been made between depositary, which refers to the person holding the post, and Depositary, which refers to the post itself (the same applies to datary/Datary).

2 Bullard, *Filippo Strozzi and the Medici*, p. 97.

3 For the first period, see Bullard, *Filippo Strozzi and the Medici*, pp. 113-115; for the second, see below, p. 77.

main source of earnings, given their substance, were the salaries of the officials of the Curia and of Rome, of the papal guards and of the mercenaries.

Before the beginning of the fifteenth century the papal finances were administered by the general treasurer, who was normally an ecclesiast or a high-ranking dignitary. From that time on, however, this task was entrusted to the depositary general of the Apostolic Chamber, who was chosen from among the *mercatores romanam curiam sequentes*. Precisely because of its constant need to borrow money, and because its first point of reference was the depositary, the papacy entrusted this post to a bank that it considered reliable. The Apostolic Chamber kept its accounts in the depositary's name, a situation which De Roover has likened to the United States Treasury's account with one of the Federal Reserve banks:[4] all the sums that the depositary received were credited to this account, and all the payments that he carried out on the mandate of the Chamber or of one of its officials were debited to it. Although most papal money passed through it, a number of large sums followed alternative paths: some went directly from the Datary to the Secret Treasury of the pope; the income of the provincial Treasuries was spent locally; other sums were paid to holders of offices and to shareholders of the public debt.[5]

It should, however, be pointed out that, despite being considered the first papal banker, the depositary was not the highest functionary of papal finances. This role in fact belonged to the chamberlain (*camerlengo*), the head administrator of the Apostolic Chamber, and immediately subordinate to him was the treasurer, responsible for the finances of the Papal State and for the various tax-collectors' offices. Thus, while the depositary had the undoubted advantage of being able to intervene quickly (and thus of being able to make a profit more easily) when new sources of income were created, and, after 1526, when the *Monte della Fede* was instituted, in practice he had little power to decide, but acted above all on orders from the pope or one of the two above-mentioned functionaries. Further limiting the depositary's power was the fact that the bank that administered the Depositary was not the only entity responsible for the papal finances: not only did other banks also have dealings with the pope, but there were also various other offices that administered financial matters and kept their own accounts. The Datary, for example, which dealt with the sales of venal offices, was growing in importance at this time. Then there was the *penitenziario*, who administered the income deriving from the sales of indulgences; the *camerario segreto* of the pope, who administered the Secret Treasury; and the *maestro di casa*, who was in charge of the daily expenses of the

4 R. De Roover, *The Rise and Decline of the Medici Bank (1397-1494)*, New York, 1966, p. 197.

5 A document of 1545 is relevant here: in that year the estimated income for the Holy Seat amounted to 871,900 *scudi*. Of these 225,500 were allotted to functionaries: there remained therefore 646,400, 'from which were paid the salaries of the guards and other officials. The remainder is thus 400,000 … from which will be paid the military expenses and a number of debts still owed to the bankers, leaving almost nothing for the present year' (ASF, Galli Tassi 1837, fol. 4). Therefore, in this case 45.9% of the total income of the papacy passed through the hands of the depositary. This is confirmed by P. Partner, according to whom the flow of money that the depositary handled was slightly less than half of the tax revenue ('Papal financial policy in the Renaissance and Counter-Reformation', *Past and Present*, 88 (1980): 38).

palace. Finally, separate accounts were also held by the various colleges, provincial treasurers, and tax-collectors' offices.

As has already been mentioned, (Chapter 1, p. 7), the banks chosen by the papacy to manage the Depositary in the fifteenth century reflect yet again the Florentine ascendancy in Rome in that period. The Depositary was first conceded to the director of the Spini bank, until 1420,[6] after which it was assigned to whoever was head of the Roman branch of the Medici bank, with only a few interruptions until 1476.[7] After this date, because of the disagreements which had arisen between the Medici family and Pope Sixtus IV (1471-84), the Depositary was taken from them and handed over to the Genoese Cigala and Usodimare families, and then, between 1493 and 1503, to the Spannocchi family from Siena. When Julius II came to power he too naturally favoured his fellow Genoese, and, more specifically, the Sauli family. The Florentines returned to their position of power when Leo X, shortly after his election in 1515, nominated Filippo Strozzi to the post of depositary general; the Depositary remained in Strozzi's hands until 1527, year of the Sack of Rome. On Clement VII's return to Rome in October 1528, Strozzi, as was to be expected, was offered the position once again. However, his administrators in Rome, Migliore Covoni and Francesco Del Nero, did not consider the offer to be an advantageous one, and following their advice Strozzi refused. The post of depositary general was therefore offered to and accepted by another *mercator florentinus*, Bartolomeo Lanfredini.[8] Throughout the first half of the 1530s the Florentines continued to hold sway: among the holders of this prestigious position were Bindo Altoviti and, during the vacant papal see after the death of Clement VII, Amerigo Antinori.[9]

In the second half of the 1530s, until September 1539, the position of depositary was held by the powerful company of the Genoese banker Ansaldo Grimaldi, which already had total control over the alum mines of Tolfa, although in the last months the Grimaldi company alternated with (or perhaps worked in association with) that of the Florentine banker Paolo Serragli.[10] The following depositaries were once again Genoese, Tobia Pallavicini & Partners, although they retained the post for

---

6 M.G. Pastura Ruggiero, in *La Reverenda Camera Apostolica e i suoi archivi (secoli XV-XVIII)* (Rome, 1984), p. 193 and note 54, states that the first depositary was, from 1 December 1417, Carlo Geri, *mercator florentinus romanam curiam sequens*. However the sources seem to show that previously this post was held by Jacopo Del Bene and Francesco de' Boscoli, *civibus et mercatoribus florentinis*; the contract of March 1411 envisaged a duration of two years, with the possibility of a further three-year extension (ASF, *Mediceo Avanti Principato*, filza 99, n. 42, fols 149r-154r).

7 De Roover, *The Rise and Decline*, p. 198. Between 1443 and 1447 the Depositary was administered by Tommaso Spinelli; under Pius II (1458-64) it was the turn of Ambrogio Spannocchi of Siena; between 1465 and 1471, finally, the depositary was Giovanni Condulmer, a Venetian related to Pope Paul II.

8 Bullard, *Filippo Strozzi and the Medici*, p. 151 and note 1.

9 Numerous references to Altoviti can be found in ASR, Camerale I, *Mandati Camerali 868*; to Antinori in Camerale I, *Conti della Depositeria generale 1773*, fol. 117v.

10 ASR, Camerale I, *Conti della Depositeria generale 1774*, fol. 176r; *Conti della Depositeria generale 1775*, fols 93, 113, 130, 134, 149; Camerale I, *Mandati Camerali 872*, fols 2r, 29r, 35r, 48r-v, 56r.

only a few months.[11] From July of the following year, in fact, it was once again the turn of a Florentine company: that of Benvenuto Olivieri.

2. Benvenuto Olivieri, depositary

The merchant-banker who was awarded the administration of a tax farm, apart from agreeing to cover the expenses and to collect the revenues, was also obliged to lend a more or less substantial sum that would be repaid with or without interest during the course of his administration or at the end of it. Sometimes not even the depositary general himself was exempt from this rule.

In July 1540, when they were awarded the Depositary contract for the first time, Benvenuto Olivieri & Partners handed over to the Chamber 15,000 *scudi di moneta*, which would be used 'without interest by the Apostolic Chamber for the term of the Depositary'; on the other loans, however, Olivieri would, as was usual, receive a 12% interest '*ratione lucri cessantis*'.[12] The 15,000 *scudi* in practice constituted a kind of *corpo*, that is an initial capital, which was registered in a '*conto a parte*' (a separate account used solely for the handling of debts and credits relative to specific transactions) at the beginning of the period, and which then became a collectable credit on 17 March 1543, '*per essere finita la Depositeria*', or, in other words, at the end of the contract.[13]

For the whole of 1541, the *introitus* of the Depositary amounted to more than 571,000 *scudi d'oro*, while the *exitus*, including the expenditure for the *popolo romano*, came to 650,000 *scudi*: this meant a difference of 79,000 *scudi*, which was credited to the Olivieri company.[14] The trend was reversed in 1542: between January and September the *introitus* was more than 313,000 *scudi*, while the *exitus* was limited to 290,000 (to which 7,000 were added for the *popolo romano*). The initial sum was evidently being reimbursed very gradually; for example, between October 1542 and January 1543 the expenditure did not rise above 42,000 *scudi*, compared with the more than 71,000 *scudi* of income. By the beginning of 1543 the Genoese banker Pallavicini had taken over the role of depositary, leaving the Olivieri company with only a marginal involvement.[15] Table 8 shows the movement of the accounts of the Depositary, held by Benvenuto Olivieri, between 1 January 1541 and the first days of February 1543.

---

11 See ASR, Camerale I, *Mandati Camerali 872*, fol. 67r.

12 ASF, Galli Tassi 1851, fol. 11.

13 ASF, Galli Tassi 2278, fol. 7. The 'end' of the Depositary will be discussed further on (p. 76). For the entire period Olivieri's employee (or cashier) at the Depositary was Giovanni di Zaccaria Strozzi (fols 11, 360).

14 ASR, Camerale I, *Conti della Depositeria generale 1778*, fols 63-64, 101-102, 133-134, 187-188.

15 ASR, Camerale I, *Conti della Depositeria generale 1779*, fols 69, 98, 124, 136. On the administration of the Depositary in the last months of 1542 and the first months of 1543 see below, pp. 76-77.

Table 8 – *Introitus* and *exitus* of the Chamber in the accounts kept by Benvenuto Olivieri & Partners, depositaries (January 1541-February 1543). Values in *scudi d'oro*

MONTH AND YEAR	*INTROITUS*	*EXITUS*	DIFFERENCE	ACCUMULATED DIFFERENCE
Jan-Mar 1541	145,669.62	189,634.25	– 43,964.63	– 43,964.63
Apr-Jun 1541	178,554.89	214,618.42	– 36,063.53	– 80,028.16
Jul-Sep 1541	155,292.37	145,603.66	9,688.71	– 70,339.45
Oct-Dec 1541	91,950.09	100,469.12	– 8,519.03	– 78,858.48
total Jan-Dec 1541	**571,466.97**	**650,325.45**	**– 78,858.48**	
Jan-Mar 1542	78,407.94	69,465.58	8,942.36	– 69,916.12
Apr-Jun 1542	128,178.09	114,398.51	13,779.58	– 56,136.54
Jul-Sep 1542	107,168.47	114,120.96	– 6,952.49	– 63,089.03
Oct 1542-Feb 1543	71,577.14	41,966.68	29,610.46	– 33,478.57
tot. Jan 1542-Feb 1543	**385,331.64**	**339,951.73**	**45,379.91**	
tot. Jan 1541-Feb 1543	**956,798.61**	**990,277.18**		**– 33,478.57**

Source: ASR, Camerale I, *Conti della Depositeria generale 1777, 1778, 1779*

On 7 February 1543 Benvenuto and his partners were owed a sum of almost 35,000 *scudi d'oro*; the repayment included 12% interest, calculated on the same day, with the guarantee of all the goods and assets and the present and future revenue of the Chamber if the sum was not repaid.[16]

As already mentioned, the *mercatores* who had business dealings with the Apostolic Chamber were referred to as *romanam curiam sequentes*: the meaning of this term becomes quite clear if we look at what happened when the pontiff moved with his court (with all the financial needs that this entailed) for longer or shorter periods.[17] For example, when, between 12 September and 19 October 1541, Paul III sojourned in Lucca and Bologna, he was accompanied by Benedetto Busini, an envoy sent by the depositaries Benvenuto Olivieri & Partners.[18] When the books

16 ASF, Galli Tassi 1851, fol. 11. See also Galli Tassi 2278, fol. 294.

17 For information about the travels of the pontiff, see A.M. Corbo, 'La serie Viaggi di Pontefici e Sovrani del Camerale I', *Rassegna degli Archivi di Stato*, 25 (1965): 406-420; A. Bertolotti, 'Speserie segrete e pubbliche di Paolo III', *Atti e memorie delle Deputazioni di Storia Patria per le Province dell'Emilia*, n.s., 3, fasc. 1 (1878): 175-176.

18 The aim of the trip was a meeting with Charles V in order to discuss the religious situation in Germany, the outcome of the Diet of Regensburg and the eventual convocation of a Council. At the end of August, moreover, the Turks had taken Buda: consequently the discussion revolved around this and around Charles V's preparations to attack Algiers.

were balanced in the December following this journey, the depositary had paid more than 21,000 ducats *di giuli* 10 per ducat, while he had received 5,000 gold ducats from the treasurer general (6 October), and calculated a profit of 476.7 (3 December). Once again, according to the account book of the depositary, the Chamber was in debt. On this occasion it owed approximately 15,000 ducats, plus interest calculated in the month and a half following its return, which came to 205 ducats.[19]

In 1543, when the pontiff and his court transferred temporarily to Bologna and Busseto, they were once again accompanied by Benvenuto Olivieri's representative, Busini.[20] Paul III left Rome on 26 February with the double aim of being closer to the seat of the Council (Trent) and, in view of a meeting with Charles V, of favouring the peace process. He arrived in Bologna on 17 March, and on 21 June (after a series of negotiations over where the meeting would take place) he met with Charles V in Busseto; on the 25th the two parted company and the pontiff, after a brief stay in Parma, arrived back in Bologna on 1 July. He left on the 11th, and reached Rome on 19 August (during the trip he stopped at Ancona, Perugia and Viterbo).[21] It was only years later – to be exact on 1 February 1549 – that Benedetto Busini, and therefore the Olivieri company, was credited with 700 *scudi di moneta* for the profits and 2,100 *scudi d'oro in oro* for the interest which had matured in the meantime.[22]

The Chamber's tardiness in paying its debts clearly never ceased to be a problem, and it is worth quoting here an exemplary illustration of this: a letter from Bartolomeo Bettini, administrator of Benvenuto Olivieri's inheritance, addressed to Cardinal Crescenzi on 15 January 1551, regarding a problem over the remuneration of money owed by the Chamber to Benvenuto, depositary for ten months during the period referred to. This long document – of which a brief summary is given below – shows clearly how lengthy and controversial the procedures for the assessment of the accounts with the Apostolic Chamber were. Complicating this specific case, moreover, was the involvement of Benvenuto's ex-partner, Francesco Del Nero, who, as mentioned in Chapter 2, had become an '*odiosissimo nemico*' (detested enemy) and persecutor of Benvenuto's children, preventing the latter from enjoying the rights bestowed on their father by the Apostolic Chamber.

The letter recalls that when Paul III journeyed to Bologna and Busseto to meet Charles V, the Depositary was placed in the hands of Benvenuto Olivieri (without, however, 'any written convention'), who sent a representative (Busini) with the papal court. For the ten months that he was depositary, Benvenuto claimed 1,855 *scudi di giuli 10 per scudo* from the revenue of the Chamber as commission on payments

---

According to L. von Pastor, Paul III left Rome on 27 August and reached Lucca on 8 September; he left Lucca on the 20th and, after a brief stay in Bologna, Loreto and Camerino, returned to the Eternal City only at the end of October (*The History of the Popes from the close of the Middle Ages* (40 vols, London, 1949-53), vol. XII, 1950, ed. R.F. Kerr, pp. 126-127). The dates quoted above in the text come from the accounts concerning the trip.

19 ASF, Galli Tassi 1855, fols 1r-2r, 18r-24r; Galli Tassi 1917, fol. 79; ASR, Camerale I, *Conti della Depositeria generale 1777 bis*, fols 2r-v, 25.

20 ASF, Galli Tassi 2278, fol. 310. On the expenses pertaining to this trip, see also ASR, Camerale I, *Viaggi di Pontefici e Sovrani*, busta 1-2, fols 1-245.

21 von Pastor, *The History of the Popes*, vol. XII, pp. 169-182.

22 ASF, Galli Tassi 1918, fol. 28.

made and 2,000 as his remuneration for the work of ten months, at 200 *scudi* a month. But 'someone who wished Benvenuto ill', or, in other words Francesco Del Nero, pointed out that Olivieri should be paid one or the other amount. Asked for a decision, the pope ruled that there should be uniformity with the treatment of the former depositaries, the Pallavicini, who for two and a half months had earned a commission of 900 *scudi*. Benvenuto accepted the payment of the 1,855 *scudi* only. This was not, however, the end of the matter – in fact, in 1551 the sum had still not been paid. Nevertheless, wrote Bettini, the Cardinals de' Grandi and Camei would certainly be able to advise Pope Julius III of Paul III's decision taken years before, which the pope would certainly act on, thus finally resolving the question and treating Olivieri similarly to the way in which the Pallavicini had previously been treated.[23]

The requests of the administrators of Benvenuto's inheritance must eventually have fallen on fertile ground: when Giulio de' Grandi, president of the Chamber from 1544, was called on to provide written evidence, he recalled that he had discussed the question with the general treasurer and the pope. At the time, in fact, the chamberlain, whom Olivieri had asked to intervene regarding the payment of the commission he was owed, refused to do so without the express order of the pope. Paul III had decided that Olivieri should be paid the amount he requested, as it was the same as that of the earlier administrators, 'and thus it seemed to him to be reasonable'.[24]

This case has been described in some detail, because it is a perfect example of the complications that always emerged when the time came to settle the accounts. It is also, as mentioned, a demonstration of how lengthy the procedures were: eight years after the events described above, in fact, although Benvenuto was already dead and the amounts involved were not particularly substantial, the question had still not been settled.[25]

As has already been pointed out several times, the depositary general made substantial advance loans to the Apostolic Chamber, so substantial that the bankers, even though making a profit from the interest at a rate of 12%, were always in the position of being owed considerable sums of money. Again in February 1543, for example, the Genoese bankers Pallavicini and Giustiniani (who, in their role as depositaries, had created a sort of fund of 40,000 *scudi* in favour of the Chamber), were instructed in a Chamber mandate to pay to Olivieri 20,000 *scudi d'oro in oro* as

---

23 ASF, Galli Tassi 1839, fol. 7; Galli Tassi 1844, fol. 1. Of similar content, even if probably written some time earlier, is Galli Tassi 1864, fol. 1, in which advice was asked of a magnificent '*messer Antonio*'. For the relations between Benvenuto and his heirs with Francesco Del Nero, see Chapter 2, pp. 63-66.

24 ASF, Galli Tassi 1844, fol. 3.

25 This also makes it difficult to calculate with any precision the profits that the company of Benvenuto Olivieri was able to make from the various operations. Consequently, in the present chapter and in those following the figures will at times necessarily be vague or imprecise. Nevertheless, those available to us are indicative of the general situation: for example, at the end of 1553 it was declared that the Olivieri company was still owed 7,955 *scudi d'oro in oro* by the Apostolic Chamber (ASF, Galli Tassi 1844, fol. 18), and it is improbable that this was in settlement of all the outstanding accounts.

a partial repayment of his credit, as well as to give him a diamond ring worth 3,000 *scudi*, a ruby ring worth 4,000 and several other jewels as a pledge.[26]

On 17 March 1543 Benvenuto Olivieri & Partners registered in their ledger a profit of 14,530 *scudi* paid by the depositary, which was in debt to them;[27] these were the profits deriving from their 32-month administration of the Depositary. In addition, on the same day the Olivieri company was also credited with the 15,000 *scudi* that they had lent to the Chamber free of interest.

It is not clear who exactly was in charge of the Depositary at this time: while on one hand (according to the contents of the document quoted above) the Olivieri company would appear to have again assumed the role of depositary general on 1 March 1543 after two and a half months in which it was in the hands of Tobia Pallavicini & Partners, on the other (on the basis of various accounts) they seem to have maintained it without interruption until 17 March 1543. There is a ledger of Benvenuto Olivieri & Partners in their role as depositaries that contains records from 1 January 1542 to 16 March 1543, thus seeming to confirm the date of 17 March as the end of the contract. From 14 December onwards, however, the records are interrupted, to reappear only on the final date, giving weight to the theory that the Pallavicini held the Depositary for this brief period (from mid-December 1542 to March 1543).[28] The probable explanation is that a new administration was established specifically for Paul III's journey (even if there was no written agreement), which did not invalidate the preceding contract. Moreover, the fact that the date 17 March 1543 was also the date that the pontiff arrived in Bologna, where he established his court temporarily, but for an undefined length of time, is unlikely to be a mere coincidence; this would therefore have meant that the preceding contract would be annulled, given that it was stipulated dependent on a connection of the papal court with Rome.

---

26 ASR, Camerale I, *Mandati Camerali 874*, fol. 133r-v. Precious jewels were frequently used as a pledge by the Apostolic Chamber: in 1542 various *mercatores* had in their possession jewels to a value of 135,000 *scudi*; the depositary Benvenuto Olivieri had 'the beautiful ruby' (value: 10,000 *scudi*), '2 balases' (2,000) and even 'the precious mitre' (16,500), for a total sum of 28,500 *scudi* (ASF, Galli Tassi 1917, fol. 70v). For the repayment of the 20,000 *scudi* see also ASR, Camerale I, *Conti della Depositeria generale 1780*, fol. 29v.

27 ASF, Galli Tassi 2278, fol. 11.

28 ASF, Galli Tassi 1817. ASR, Camerale I, *Mandati Camerali 874*, provides the following information: Benvenuto Olivieri is indicated as depositary until 7 December 1542 (fol. 102r); there follow several records in which the '*depositarius*' is mentioned without specifying the name; finally, from 13 January to 28 February 1543, Tobia Pallavicini and Luca Giustiniani are mentioned as those to whom '*pecuniis Camere apostolice ad eorum manus delatis et deferentis*' (fols 108v-153r). *Mandati Camerali 878* provides similar information: the presence of the two Genoese (who, it should be pointed out, are never indicated explicitly as depositaries, but again as the bankers with whom the money of the Apostolic Chamber is '*existentis seu ad eorum manus perventuris*') is recorded between 11 January and 10 March 1543 (fols 20v-54r), followed by Olivieri from 12 March (fol. 54v). It is evident in *Mandati Camerali 875* that the compiler of the registers was also somewhat confused: he first wrote the name Olivieri, then crossed it out and replaced it with those of Pallavicini and Giustiniani (fol. 237r).

The expenses relative to the pope's travels were therefore considered as something separate. Further evidence of this can be seen in the documents referring to the papal journey to Lucca in 1541, when Olivieri, in his role as depositary, kept separate two accounting records: one contained the normal records of the *introito et exito* of the Depositary, the other those relative to the transfer, the sojourn and the return of the papal court.[29] The trip of 1543, however, was a case apart, because it was known that the court would be absent from Rome for several months, thus presumably necessitating two separate agreements. It would seem therefore that, at least for a certain period, there were two different administrations for the Depositary. Roman documents explicitly mention an 'administration … of Tobia Pallavicini and Luca Giustiniani … begun on 26 October 1542 and ended on 17 October 1543, in addition to another administration of Benvenuto Olivieri'.[30]

Complicating the situation of the accounts regarding the papal trip even further, as mentioned above, was also the lack of precise written agreements. Normally the contracts relative to the book-keeping of the Depositary were extremely precise (an example covering the two-year period 1545-46 will later be examined): they listed in detail the estimated expenses and the income of the Depositary, and also noted exactly the commission fees that the depositary could make on the actual expenditure.

In 1543, and probably also in the years immediately preceding, the usual commission fee was 3%, with only a few exceptions: 2.5% for the papal guards and the construction of the palace (*fabbrica di palazzo*); 2% for the papal chapel; while no commission fee was applied to the expenses of the household and the *conservatori del popolo romano* (the commission fee on all the other administrative expenses of the city of Rome was 3%). Regarding the extraordinary expenses, the same document of 1543 states that the decision on the commission to be paid on the costs for the war against Ascanio Colonna had been delegated to the Chamber, which had decided to pay the depositary two-thirds per cent (=0.66%). The commission was not however calculated for the extraordinary wages of the soldiers in the Papal State and in Hungary; even though it was admitted that the depositary 'deserves a higher commission, because it is more difficult to pay them [the soldiers] on time and to transfer the money where they are based'. No commission – as was the usual practice – was due on money paid directly to the pope.[31] Thus, although the depositary had to make large advance loans in favour of the Chamber, it could also make a considerable profit from the commission fee that it collected on the huge sums of money that it paid out on behalf of and on the mandate of the Chamber.

After Benvenuto Olivieri & Partners, the role of depositary of the Apostolic Chamber was once again assumed by the Genoese bankers Tobia Pallavicini and Luca Giustiniani & Partners, who maintained this position until the end of 1544; Tobia had already been depositary in 1540, and then, in the period 1542-43, the two Genoese once again held this position, either alternating with or working contemporaneously with Olivieri.

29 ASF, Galli Tassi 1917, fols 78-79.

30 ASR, Camerale I, *Conti della Depositeria generale 1780*, fol. 72.

31 ASF, Galli Tassi 1835, ins. 2, fols 4r-5v.

Presumably this was a planned alternation between the Florentines and the Genoese, and in fact, on 1 January 1545 the Apostolic Chamber conceded the Depositary for two years to Benvenuto Olivieri, who 'as usual promptly accepted this burden to do service to His Holiness'. In exchange for the ordinary expenditure that they would carry out on behalf of the Chamber they were promised the following revenues, 'which cannot be either diverted or assigned elsewhere and if not paid within the time prescribed the Chamber will pay immediately in cash' (see Table 9).

Table 9 – Assignments to the depositary for 1545-46 (values in *scudi d'oro in oro*)

Quarto dei frutti of the regular monastic congregations	21,000
Feudal *censi* of Naples, Ferrara, Urbino, Pesaro, Senigallia and the others paid in June	17,000
Vigesima of the Jews of the Papal State, including Avignon and Comtat Venaissin	8,000
Tithes of the whole Papal State with the *quarto dei frutti* of the *benefici regolari extra congregationes*	8,000
Third year of the Triennial Subsidy of Parma and Piacenza	6,000
Income from criminal offences of Rome, or other assignment until the due sum	4,000
TOTAL	64,000

Source: ASF, Galli Tassi 1851, fasc. 10, cc. 1v-2r

Formally this situation differed from the preceding one. In this case, in fact, 'it has been decided to no longer assign the Depositary, but instead all the payments of the Chamber [separately]', so that although Olivieri was depositary, he was responsible 'only for the abovementioned assignments'.[32]

The sum of 64,000 *scudi d'oro*[33] came close to the estimated expenses: a maximum of 68,000 *scudi* ('*insino a la soma de cinque millia settecento scudi in circa ogni mese*') that the depositary undertook to pay on the mandate of the chamberlain and of the treasurer general and that consisted in various types of payments. The largest sums were the almost 16,000 *scudi* per annum destined to the papal guards, 8,200 for the *castellano* and the *bombardieri* of Sant'Angelo, 4,300 for the nuncio to France

32 ASF, Galli Tassi 1851, fasc. 10, fols 1r-2r. For a complete transcription of the contract (fols 1r-4v) see the Appendix, doc. 5. A copy can also be found in ASR, *Notai segretari e cancellieri della R. Camera apostolica 1988*, fols 420v-425v.

33 Several months earlier, in 1544, presumably in a first draft of the contract, it was envisaged that 20,800 *scudi* instead of 21,000 would be collected from the monastic congregations, and, above all, 27,000 *scudi 'sopra l'impositione de l'Umbria et di Campagna, cominciando al quarto di maggio proximo 1545'* in the place of the 10,000 of the last two items of the list, making a total of 80,800 *scudi*, much more than the total of 64,000 that was in fact established in the actual contract; even then, however, doubts were expressed as to the real possibility of obtaining this last payment (ASF, Galli Tassi 1942, fol. 44r). The draft, moreover, envisaged 1 December 1544 as the initial day of the contract's validity.

and the same amount for the pope's chapel, 3,800 destined to the *bargello*, 3,500 necessary for the payment of other officials, as well as several expenses relative to the *popolo romano*.[34]

If Benvenuto did not receive the payments owed to him, the contract would be declared null and void, and the Chamber would have to reimburse him with the costs incurred, plus an annual interest of 12%. As compensation for his '*faticha*' (work) Olivieri could avail himself of the usual commission.[35] In general, as has already been mentioned, the depositary collected a commission fee of between 2% and 3% (more often the second than the first) on the payments made.[36] Certain costs were, however, exempt, while for others forfeit amounts were calculated: in this case, 100 *scudi* a month 'for the costs of the Archive, secretaries, cubiculars and scutifers, presents for the very reverend chamberlain, the clerks of the Chamber and others, expenses and salaries of the *sollecitatore*, the salary of a young employee'.[37] This last figure, which provided the depositary with an annual revenue of 1,200 *scudi*, was a considerable part of the total, which could be calculated at 3,000-3,500 *scudi*.[38]

Another interesting note is: 'if the papal court journeys further than 40 miles out of Rome, then [Olivieri] will receive 5% of all payments made outside the city as well as all expenses for himself, 4 others, 4 horses and 2 carriages, as usual':[39] if such an agreement had been made in 1543, many problems would have been avoided.

In fact, by September 1545 the Chamber had already failed to make several payments to Olivieri by the due dates, so that at the end of the month the total interest (referring to three months, given that the end of June was the due date for almost all the payments in question) had reached 782 *scudi di moneta*.[40] Shortly afterwards, Benvenuto Olivieri & Partners asked the Apostolic Chamber to credit to them the 12% interest on the 21,000 *scudi* of the monastic congregations that had not been

34 The complete list can be found in ASF, Galli Tassi 1851, fasc. 10, fols 3r-4r and here in the Appendix, doc. 5, pp. 229-232. The payments were made by Vincenzo Romoli and several others, to whom the Olivieri company allocated large sums so that these, over time, could make the payments (the account of Romoli occupies many pages in Galli Tassi 2280, starting from fol. 2).

35 ASF, Galli Tassi 1851, fasc. 10, fol. 2r.

36 For an example of this, see the case of the contract of 1543 analysed above (p. 77).

37 ASF, Galli Tassi 1942, fol. 44v.

38 The figures given here have been calculated from the draft of the contract (ASF, Galli Tassi 1942, fols 46r-v, 47v-48r), even if the annual costs provided in the draft differ slightly from those in the final contract (Galli Tassi 1851, fasc. 10, fols 3r-4r); given that the former is incomplete and details expenses for not even 54,000 *scudi*, against the more than 69,000 of the latter, the sum of the commission fees has been increased proportionally, albeit leaving an ample margin for the possible oscillation of the percentages and for the possible exemptions. In 1544, making an approximate estimation, for the commission it was calculated that at least 200 *scudi* per month would be received, i.e. 2,400 a year (Galli Tassi 1836, fasc. 3, fol. 2r).

39 ASF, Galli Tassi 1942, fol. 44v.

40 ASF, Galli Tassi 1824, fol. 24; Galli Tassi 1839, fol. 2. In Galli Tassi 2280, fol. 36, the interests are credited to the profit account as follows: 833 *scudi* on 30 September 1545; 368 on 24 December; 26 and 776 respectively on 11 and 30 December of the following year. The collection of the assignments began on 5 May 1545 (fol. 25).

paid by the established date of 24 June;[41] they also requested that the interest on the 4,000 *scudi* of the criminal offences (*malefici*), for which they had only received partial payment, be paid in full, as well as the interest on the 6,000 *scudi* of the Triennial Subsidy of Parma and Piacenza, of which they had as yet seen nothing; and finally the interests on the money which still had to be received from the tithes and the *vigesime* of the Jews.[42] By 16 June 1546 the Olivieri company was owed 23,544 *scudi*, despite having already collected commission fees for 2,811 *scudi* and being credited with profits for 952 and commissions for 217 (total 3,980 *scudi*).[43]

In practice, as should by now be clear, the Chamber almost always failed to meet its commitments within the time stipulated, and the sums of money that it owed to the bankers thus continued to increase. This had the effect of binding the bankers ever more closely to the papal finances, on which they continued to receive assignments, but rarely a complete repayment.

A closer look at the years 1545 and 1546 provide a clear picture of the general trend with regard to the debts owed to the depositaries by the Chamber. In March 1545 the Chamber owed the depositary almost 15,000 *scudi* and in the balance sheets of the successive quarters (30 June and 30 September) this figure remained steady (apart from a slight reduction when the depositary began to collect taxes).[44] By 31 December the Chamber's debt had been reduced to approximately 4,500 *scudi*, thanks to the 14,300 *scudi* coming from the tithes of Naples.[45] By 31 March 1546, however, the Chamber's debts had once again climbed to almost 22,000 *scudi*; in the course of the following quarter they increased further, to then fall to 15,000, thanks mostly to the feudal *censi* that on 28 June guaranteed the depositary an income of approximately 28,000 *scudi*, bringing back to within acceptable limits a figure that had been swelling dangerously.[46] Unlike the other items, which were paid with continuity over time, the feudal *censi* were collected once a year (on the eve of Sts Peter and Paul), drastically reducing the money owed to the depositary. In the following quarter (July-September 1546) the debt, which had by then exceeded 35,000 *scudi*, dropped quickly to less than 8,000 because of the liquidation of several

41 The payments on the part of the congregations were actually made as follows: on 30 June 1545 2,733 *scudi d'oro in oro*; 30 September 12,341; 31 December 3,005.6 (total for the year 18,079.6); 31 March 1546 2,435.9; 30 September 16,296.8 (total for two years 36,812.3); 4 March 1547 4,713.7. This almost completed the assignment, which, as will be remembered, amounted in the two-year period to 42,000 *scudi* (ASF, Galli Tassi 2280, fol. 28).

42 ASF, Galli Tassi 1824, fol. 16.

43 ASF, Galli Tassi 1839, fol. 1.

44 ASF, Galli Tassi 2280, fols 21, 46, 60. The maximum amount was reached, however, at the end of May, at which time Olivieri was owed 24,470 ducats (ASR, Camerale I, *Conti della Depositeria generale 1781*, fol. 75).

45 ASF, Galli Tassi 2280, fols 82, 97. For the accounts of 1545, see also ASR, Camerale I, *Conti della Depositeria generale 1781*, especially fols 54, 75, 94, 119.

46 ASF, Galli Tassi 2280, fols 101, 124. Among the *censi* stand out the 7,892 *scudi* paid by Ercole d'Este for the investiture of the duchy of Ferrara, a similar sum paid by Charles V for the investiture of the Kingdom of Naples, the 2,626 of Guidobaldo Feltro Della Rovere for Urbino, Pesaro e Senigallia and the huge sum of 10,791 paid by Pier Luigi Farnese, duke of Parma and Piacenza (fol. 123).

assignments and because of a further 10,000 *scudi* that were paid to the depositary for the 'advance payment of the Treasury of Camerino'.[47] Towards the end of the year, that is at the end of the term stipulated in the contract, the Chamber still owed approximately 10,000 *scudi*; this sum decreased slowly until by 1 February 1548 the account had been virtually settled.[48] The withholding tax exercised by Benvenuto Olivieri & Partners on behalf of the Depositary brought in, in the period January 1545-January 1548, a profit of approximately 4,500 *scudi di moneta*, plus commissions (generally 3%, but for some services also 1 or 5%) for a further 616 *scudi*.[49] Nevertheless, the positive balance of the profit and loss account amounted to only 336 *scudi*, as a result of the almost 3,900 *scudi* of losses on exchange operations ('*cambi patiti per conto di questo partito*').[50]

At the end of 1546, when the two-year contract with Benvenuto Olivieri & Partners expired, it was the turn of another Tuscan banker, Vincenzo Spada from Lucca, to be nominated depositary.[51] In 1548 the same banker, together with his fellow citizen Martino Bernardini, once again took the reins of the Depositary for a further two-year period.[52] In 1549, however, he renegotiated the contract for a further three years (expiry date 30 April 1552). In exchange for agreeing to cover the costs requested of them, the two Tuscans were given a commission of 500 *scudi* per month as well as the usual commission fees and the pledge of jewels for 15,000 *scudi*; they were obliged, however, to make a loan of 15,000 *scudi* free of interest (although interest would be calculated for every figure over and above this sum).[53] In 1550, the Chamber contracted the office of depositary to the Bolognese banker Cornelio Malvasia, who managed to reduce the interest-free loan to 10,000 *scudi*, and also managed to obtain the monopoly of the supply of cloth to the Chamber. Having won these favourable terms, Malvasia then made an agreement with the previous contract-holders, leaving the administration of the office to them.[54]

In 1554 the Genoese banker Tommaso Marini agreed to cover the monthly expenses of 16,000 *scudi* (with an advance loan of 30,000 *scudi* free of interest). In December 1555 he obtained a nine-year contract, confirmed after the vacant papal see, for which he would cover the expenses for 17,500 *scudi* per month, in exchange for a commission of 1,560 per month, 3% on all the payments made and 12% on all the loans, and the right to be the exclusive supplier of cloth. By the time he left the post in 1561 (having requested a revision of the contract in 1559), he had

47 ASF, Galli Tassi 2280, fols 147, 175.

48 ASF, Galli Tassi 2280, fols 173, 176, 178, 179, 183. As usual, it took several months to settle the accounts, because of the delays in the payments.

49 ASF, Galli Tassi 2280, fols 6, 36, 50, 88.

50 ASF, Galli Tassi 2280, fol. 36; in the *Dare* (loss) of the account there are 6,777 *scudi* and in the *Avere* (profit) 7,113.

51 ASV, *Cam. Ap., Div. Cam. 147*, fols 80v-81r; ASR, Camerale I, *Mandati Camerali 877*, fol. 245r, *Mandati Camerali 883*, fols 104r-end; *Mandati Camerali 884*, fols 55r-108r.

52 ASV, *Cam. Ap., Div. Cam. 157*, fols 30r-31r; ASR, Camerale I, *Conti della Depositeria generale 1782*; *Mandati Camerali 884*, fols 108v-124r.

53 Pastura Ruggiero, *La Reverenda Camera Apostolica*, pp. 196-197.

54 Pastura Ruggiero, *La Reverenda Camera Apostolica*, p. 198; see also *Mandati Camerali 884*, fols 124r-134v.

accumulated an enormous amount of credit, including 50,000 *scudi*, which were restored to him in 500 bonds of the *Monte della Farina*.[55]

His fellow countrymen and successors, Tommaso, Agostino, Tobia and Giovan Battista Pallavicini, contracted to pay a monthly figure of 18,000 *scudi*, obtaining in exchange for the following year the entire Triennial Subsidy of 400,000 *scudi* '*nuovamente imposto*'.[56]

This brief digression has shown how over time the Apostolic Chamber's need for money to cover the ordinary expenditure grew disproportionately (from 5,700 *scudi* per month in 1545 to 16,000 in 1554), while at the same time the assignments on which the depositary could recover his money grew increasingly vague and uncertain, with the consequence that the latter accumulated vast amounts of credit. In partial compensation, the Apostolic Chamber either bestowed on the depositary new sources of income, or requested that certain sums be paid by other bankers. Although this obviously did nothing to change the amount of money the Chamber owed, it did make it possible for it to postpone its repayments.

3. Loans to the pontiff

This section makes no claims to being exhaustive regarding all the money transactions that bound Benvenuto Olivieri and his company to the Apostolic Chamber. Rather, it seeks to highlight their continuity, focusing on the transactions involving the greatest sums of money, often carried out by consortia of bankers rather than individuals. Reference has already been made in the introduction to the complicated mechanisms of repayment, whereby the Chamber guaranteed its own future revenue from taxes to those who lent it money; other times precise farming contracts regarding the administration of determined services were stipulated between the pope and the *mercatores*, who in return paid an annual sum and at the same time often an additional loan. The discussion that follows is therefore intrinsically linked to the following chapters, which are dedicated to the business activity of Benvenuto Olivieri; in particular, some sections of Chapter 7 (4, 5 and 6) necessarily refer back to this one. The more important contracts, deserving a discussion and a space of their own, have instead been treated separately in order to underline more clearly the commitment that they demanded and the complicated mechanisms concerning the sale of the shares and the reimbursement that they involved. Lastly, it should be pointed out that, because they were discussed in the section above, the numerous advance loans that Benvenuto Olivieri & Partners made in their role as depositaries, in their continuous covering of the ordinary expenditure of the Apostolic Chamber,

55 Pastura Ruggiero, *La Reverenda Camera Apostolica*, pp. 198-199. At least for some of this period, Pier Antonio Pannilani from Siena collaborated with Marini (ASR, *Mandati Camerali 884*, fols 137v-138r; *Mandati Camerali 893*, fol. 35v).

56 Pastura Ruggiero, *La Reverenda Camera Apostolica*, pp. 200-201. Only under the pontificate of Pius V (1566-72) would the Depositary be newly contracted to a Florentine, Giovan Battista Altoviti (BAV, *Vat. Lat.* 6190, fol. 530v); then again, but for a short period only (from 1592 to 1594) it would be the turn of Ubertini (J. Delumeau, *Vie économique et sociale de Rome dans la seconde moitié du XVIe siècle* (2 vols., Paris, 1957-59), II, p. 881).

have been ignored here; nor is there any discussion of the loans effected by other bankers that saw Olivieri involved only as administrator of the papal money and not directly as 'actor'.

To give yet another example of the large amounts of money involved in the transactions between the Chamber and the bankers, on 24 September 1540 the former found itself in debt to the latter for the substantial amount of 297,000 *scudi*: 22,000 owed to the Olivieri company (on the increase of the salt tax of Rome, the Romagna and Bologna), 21,000 to the Olivieri and the Cavalcanti companies (tithes of the Papal State), 17,000 to the Cavalcanti-Giraldi company (Treasury of Parma and Piacenza), 50,000 to the Grimaldi company (30,000 for the alum mines, 20,000 for the Spanish revenues, *spoglie di Spagna*), 20,000 to the Pallavicini company (tithes of Florence and Milan), 20,000 to the Pallavicini and the Giustiniani companies (tithes of Naples), 45,000 to the farmers of the customs of Rome (who at that time were a group of *mercatores* headed by Giulio and Lorenzo Strozzi, Luca Giustiniani and Salvestro da Montauto), 36,000 to Bindo Altoviti (Treasury and increase of the salt tax of the Marches), 30,000 to the Sauli company (Treasury of the Romagna), 20,000 to Alessandro Del Bene (*dogana delle pecore,* customs on sheep) and 16,000 for other mandates or surplus payments. Nevertheless, despite their enormity, these advance loans were still not sufficient to satisfy the Chamber. In fact it found itself in the position of having to request further loans totalling 60,000 *scudi* in order to meet its needs until Christmas: 15,000 from the Treasury and the increase of the salt tax of Parma and Piacenza, 25,000 from the Treasury and the increase of the salt tax of the Marches and a further 20,000 which would be provided by the depositary, or, in other words, Benvenuto Olivieri & Partners.[57] It was these enormous figures that, while providing the *mercatores romanam curiam sequentes* with ample opportunity for eventual profit, also chained them to the papal finances: in fact, they almost never obtained total repayment, but only the promise of future income.

The following loan operations have been grouped in chronological order. Unfortunately, due to the nature of manuscript sources, which provide incomplete information, it has not been possible to group them in other ways. For example, categorizing the loans according to purpose was not an option, because it is underlined only in a few cases (e.g. war against the Turks) whereas in general there was no specific purpose mentioned. An alternative would have been to group these operations by source of restitution, but as we shall see most loans were paid back from a number of different sources.

57 ASF, Galli Tassi 1942, fols 189-190. The credits were in practice divided in half between the Florentines and the Genoese: in fact 151,000 *scudi* (50.84%) came from the former and 146,000 (49.16%) from the latter. An analogous calculation of 1 August 1542 saw the Chamber in debt for 253,000 *scudi* to more or less the same merchants: among these they owed 68,000 *scudi* to the depositaries, that is Benvenuto Olivieri & Partners, and a further 40,000 for the *imposizione delle galere* (for the financing of the pontifical fleet) again to the Olivieri company, together with those of Altoviti and Cavalcanti-Giraldi; other large debts were owed to Tobia Pallavicini and others for the *imposizione dei mezzi frutti* (25,000 *scudi*) and to Cavalcanti and Giraldi on the Treasury of Parma and Piacenza (11,250); with regard to the customs of Rome, the Chamber estimated a debit of 60,000 *scudi* (ASF, Galli Tassi 1917, fols 65v-66r). In this last case the Florentines were more heavily involved.

In March 1538 the companies of Rome of the Florentine bankers Cavalcanti-Giraldi and Strozzi (in the proportions of 3/5 and 2/5 respectively) lent 58,760 *scudi d'oro di sole*, thus acquiring the right to collect the 0.5% impost on the ecclesiastical property (*mezzo ducato per cento*) in the provinces of the Marches, the Romagna and Bologna. The repayment was to be made within a year with a remuneration of 5%; as a guarantee the Florentine bankers were given in pledge 28 knighthoods of St Peter and some jewels. A few months later, the same companies made a further loan of 11,800 *scudi*, with the same agreements and conditions.[58] It should be remembered that at that time Olivieri was a partner, as well as administrator, of the company of Giulio and Lorenzo Strozzi, and that from 1 July 1539 he would be, with a company registered in his own name, the successor.

In the same year, 1539, Benvenuto Olivieri & Partners made 15,000 *scudi* available to the Apostolic Chamber, which they used to carry out several payments on the Chamber's behalf. In return for this service they were entitled to the tithes of Urbino, those of Perugia and Umbria and those of Bologna. Shortly afterwards they made a further loan of 2,000 *scudi* (they actually paid this sum directly to Paolo Serragli, another Florentine merchant, to whom the Chamber was in debt) on the same conditions as the preceding agreement: an interest of 13%, a remuneration of 5% and the guarantee of '*iocalia*' (jewels, precious gems, rings) that were in the hands of Cavalcanti-Giraldi and Strozzi as a pledge for the earlier loan.[59]

In 1540, as was noted above, the Olivieri and Cavalcanti companies loaned 21,000 *scudi* to the Chamber, which sum they were then entitled to recuperate from the tithes of the Papal State.

On 23 October 1541 the Chamber asked Benvenuto Olivieri & Partners as depositaries to draw a bill of exchange for 20,000 *scudi a grossi 20 per scudo* to be paid in Augsburg (10,000 on 10 December, 10,000 on 10 January), to the reverend monsignor Girolamo Varaldo, apostolic nuncio to the 'king of the Romans'. This sum was to be considered as part of the 28,000 *scudi* promised to the Chamber by a consortium of bankers based in Rome: 10,000 from the company of the heirs of Pandolfo Della Casa, 9,000 from the Olivieri themselves, 5,000 from Cavalcanti and Giraldi, and 4,000 from the Genoese bankers Damiano and Tobia Pallavicini. Of this loan, 10,000 *scudi* had already been paid, again in Augsburg, to Giovan Battista Savelli; the total, therefore, which came to 30,000, exceeded the sum initially agreed on. The Chamber, however, promised to reimburse everything, with interest, considering that 'in Augsburg it might not be necessary to pay these 20,000 *scudi*'.[60]

Very similar – so similar in fact that it might well be the same operation, which could have been renegotiated or deferred – was the loan of 28,000 *scudi d'oro in oro* contracted in May 1542 to finance the army fighting in Hungary against the Turks. The bankers involved were, as above, the heirs of Pandolfo Della Casa

58 ASF, Galli Tassi 1868, fasc. 2, fols 1r-8v, 11r-15v; AASGF, vol. 393, fols 1r-3r. The subsidy referred to here consisted in half a ducat to be paid for every 100 of value of real estate.

59 ASF, Galli Tassi 1867, fol. 5-6; ASR, *Mandati Camerali 872*, fols 4r, 10r, 17r, 17v, 18r.

60 ASF, Galli Tassi 1844, fol. 12. A subsequent arrangement was made for the bills of exchange to be drawn instead by Baldassarre Olgiatto (fol. 19).

(10,000 *scudi*), Benvenuto Olivieri (9,000), the Cavalcanti and Giraldi (5,000), and Damiano and Tobia Pallavicini (4,000). They were given the mandate that '*per una vel plures cedulas bancarias* [more precisely 12,000 *scudi* on 15 June, 12,000 on 20 July, 4,000 on 25 August] *remittatis in Germaniam solvenda et numeranda in civitatem viennensem*' again to monsignor Varaldo.[61]

At the end of 1541 the Apostolic Chamber was loaned 60,000 *scudi d'oro in oro* (12,000 by each company) by a consortium of bankers based in Rome: the Florentines, Bindo Altoviti & Partners, Benvenuto Olivieri & Partners, Tommaso Cavalcanti and Giovanni Giraldi & Partners (the *institor* [62] of which was Bartolomeo Bettini), and the Genoese bankers Damiano and Tobia Pallavicini and Agostino Lomellini & Partners, and Luca Giustiniani & Partners. In return the bankers were given the right to recoup their money from '*subsidio medietatis fructum congregationum et locorum regularium nuper imposito*' for 1542. Apart from the reimbursement of the sum, this would guarantee them interest of 12% and a commission of 2%.[63] In December 1542 the Olivieri company acquired the Giustiniani company's share of 12,000 *scudi*, presumably as compensation for debts and credits that existed between the two companies.[64] Under the name of Olivieri, Antonio Covoni & Partners also participated, contributing 4,000 *scudi* and receiving profits of 508 *scudi*.[65] The total, which can be calculated at 7,620 *scudi*, corresponds to a profit of 12.7% on the investment.

In March 1542 the Olivieri company loaned to the Chamber 4,500 *scudi d'oro in oro*, as a guarantee for which they were given an office of apostolic secretary: if the money was not repaid within a year, the Florentine partnership could sell the office for the price that it was able to retrieve. This last operation was actually part of a larger transaction: the Olivieri and Cavalcanti-Giraldi companies had promised Ercole Varano of Camerino and his heirs that they would pay them an annual revenue of 600 gold ducats (plus a single payment of other goods) when the duchy was ceded to the Chamber and to Ottavio Farnese on 1 April; if they failed to do so, the Florentine bankers would pay Varano 10,000 ducats at the Chamber's request. In exchange they would receive 5,500 ducats of the revenue and proceeds of the Treasury of Parma and Piacenza (of which the Cavalcanti-Giraldi company were contract-holders and the Olivieri company participants) and of the increase of the salt tax of the Romagna (the exaction of which was in fact administered by

61 ASR, Camerale I, *Mandati Camerali 874*, fols 49v-50r.

62 *Institor* is a legal term which indicates the *fattore*, thus denominating someone who does business in the name of and on behalf of another person. In the sixteenth century this figure, who previously had already had wide responsibilities, assumed an increasingly important role and acquired executive powers at a very high level, both political and financial.

63 ASF, Galli Tassi 1825, fol. 5v. ASR, Camerale I, *Mandati Camerali 874*, fols 30r-31r; at fol. 223v, several congregations were instructed by mandate to provide for the payment of 20,000 *scudi* in two instalments (February 1542). See also ASF, Galli Tassi 1835, ins. 1, fol. 12; Galli Tassi 1844, fol. 8.

64 ASF, Galli Tassi 1835, ins. 1, fol. 11. Galli Tassi 1942, fol. 198r claims that Olivieri's share is 2/5.

65 ASF, Galli Tassi 2278, fol. 329.

Benvenuto's company, together with others); moreover, for the remaining 4,500, Olivieri was, as mentioned, awarded the office of apostolic secretary.[66]

On 13 May 1542 Olivieri loaned to the Chamber 20,000 *scudi d'oro in oro*, to be repaid after a year with 12% interest (2,400 *scudi*).[67] In exchange, he was awarded the assignment on the *imposizione delle galere* of the provinces of Patrimonio, Campagna and Marittima, Umbria, the duchy of Spoleto, the Romagna, the city and *contado* of Bologna, acquiring the right to a commission of 5% (1,000 *scudi*); furthermore, he kept as guarantee several jewels that he already had in pledge.[68] Under the name of Olivieri, investments were also made by other bankers: 5,000 *scudi* were contributed by the heirs of Carlo Cattani & Partners of Bologna; a further 5,000 *scudi* were deposited on behalf of Roberto Strozzi (under the name of Benedetto Busini, partner in the Olivieri company) and 4,000 by Luca Giustiniani; for the remaining quarter (again 5,000 *scudi*), finally, Antonio Covoni & Partners also joined in, making a profit of 825 *scudi* by 30 June 1543. In total, therefore, the profits must have come to 3,300 *scudi*, which corresponds roughly to the sum of the interest and of the commission.[69] In other words, the shares were divided as follows:

Heirs of Carlo Cattani & Partners	5,000
Antonio Covoni & Partners	5,000
Roberto Strozzi (under the name of Benedetto Busini)	5,000
Luca Giustiniani & Partners	4,000
Benvenuto Olivieri & Partners	1,000

On 31 July 1542 an even larger loan was agreed on: 55,000 *scudi d'oro in oro* with the usual 12% interest (6,600 *scudi* per annum) and a 5% commission (2,750 *scudi*).[70] The assignments on which Olivieri and his partners could recoup their money were:

66 ASF, Galli Tassi 1837, fols 6, 10. The 4,500 *scudi* were credited to the Chamber as follows: 1,500 in cash and the remaining 3,000 in the form of 30 bonds of the *Monte* (Galli Tassi 2278, fol. 295).

67 In ASF, Galli Tassi 1844, fol. 16 a mandate was given to Benvenuto Olivieri's company to pay the 20,000 *scudi* to Benvenuto Olivieri & Partners, depositaries: Olivieri thus played a double role.

68 ASF, Galli Tassi 2278, fol. 197; Galli Tassi 1859, fol. 1; ASR, Camerale I, *Conti della Depositeria generale 1779*, fol. 10r. In actual fact, as mentioned in Galli Tassi 1942, fol. 197v, only 3% of commission was due to the assignees, given that the 2% was destined to the commissioner for the tax collection. With regard to this loan, and the successive one of 55,000 *scudi*, in 1542 it was Benvenuto Olivieri & Partners who were the commissioners for the collection of the *imposizione delle galere*, of the income from communes, of the tithes and of the *mezzi frutti* of the entire Papal State (Galli Tassi 1867, fol. 4).

69 ASF, Galli Tassi 1942, fol. 197r; Galli Tassi 2278, fols 195, 200, 329.

70 The loan was paid in three instalments (ASF, Galli Tassi 1859, fol. 15): 25,000 *scudi* in August (in those same days Olivieri loaned a further 8,900 *scudi d'oro in oro* '*ad civitatem Ancone pro conficiendi tormentis bellicis*', acquiring the right to recoup his money on the subsidy of the Jews of the Romagna and Bologna: ASR, Camerale I, *Mandati Camerali 874*, fols 72v, 75v), 12,500 on 7 September, 17,500 on 6 February. For the calculation of the commissions, ASF, Galli Tassi 2278, fol. 197 indicates 5% on the tithes of the Papal State and the income from communes, 10% on the tithes of Milan and 3% on the tax on the clergy of Rome.

the tax on the clergy of Rome (20,000 *scudi*), the income on communes of the Papal State except for the province of the Marches (12,000), and the tithes of the State of Milan (8,000).[71] As a guarantee the *mercatores* kept in pledge several jewels and above all they had the Treasury of Perugia and the increase on the salt tax of the Romagna, Bologna and Rome.[72] On 26 August 1544, the accounts relative to the last two operations (that of 20,000 and that of 55,000 *scudi*), which are often combined in the sources, showed that Benvenuto Olivieri & Partners still had 17,682 *scudi* of credit: 3,519 coming from their commission, 9,540 from the interest of 12%, the rest (more than 4,500) as a share of capital not yet reimbursed.[73] On 19 March 1548 the Olivieri company was still owed more than 9,800 *scudi*, although the debt had been partially repaid: 6,000 *scudi* from the Spanish revenues in July 1545 (see below) and 7,500 *scudi* from the Cavalcanti-Giraldi and Ubaldini companies. The latter, in a contract dated December 1545, had promised to loan 16,000 *scudi* to the Chamber, which they would be able to recoup from the Spanish revenues. Moreover, in the same period 1544-45, a further 4,500 *scudi* (approximately) had arrived as part of the outstanding payments (*imposizione delle galere*, *mezzi frutti*, etc.). This was still not sufficient, however, to liquidate the initial debt, which continued to increase over time because of the annual interest of 12%.[74]

In this transaction of 55,000 *scudi*, however, Olivieri did not act alone, but, as has been seen in almost all the cases in which large sums were being dealt with, he nominated as co-participants other bankers operating on the market of Rome. The Genoese bankers Luca Giustiniani and Cristoforo Sauli contributed 12,500 *scudi* and acquired rights on the income from communes, *imposizione delle galere* and the tithes of the Romagna, to be shared (50% each) with Olivieri: the first under the name of the Genoese company, the others under that of the Florentine company.[75] Antonio Covoni & Partners contributed 8,000 *scudi*, which they would recoup on the tithes and the income from communes.[76] Another Florentine company, that of Girolamo Ubaldini, contributed 6,000 *scudi*, to be recouped on the *imposizione delle galere*, the income from communes and the tithes of Patrimonio (contracted with the Apostolic Chamber in September 1542); under the name of the Ubaldini company, Benvenuto Olivieri & Partners again participated for 50%.[77]

71 ASF, Galli Tassi 1859, fol. 1. The figures in Galli Tassi 1942, fol. 197v differ somewhat: 19,300 *scudi* from the tithes of the ecclesiastic State, 10,000 from that of Milan, 25,000 from the income from communes, 10,000 from the clergy of Rome.

72 ASF, Galli Tassi 2278, fol. 197.

73 ASF, Galli Tassi 1859, fol. 15; Galli Tassi 1862, fol. 1.

74 ASF, Galli Tassi 1862, fol. 1, 4: on 15 March 1548 the interests came to 5,170 *scudi*.

75 ASF, Galli Tassi 2278, fols 197, 238: in the Olivieri ledger there are two accounts of Luca Giustiniani, in which he is credited with the profits on the transactions carried out behind Olivieri's name and debited with Olivieri's fees for the collections carried out by Giustiniani.

76 ASF, Galli Tassi 2278, fol. 312. If Olivieri had failed to reimburse this sum to Covoni within nine months, he would have had to pay him an additional interest of 15% (Galli Tassi 1867, fol. 9).

77 ASF, Galli Tassi 2278, fol. 197; Galli Tassi 1942, fol. 199v. The relationship that existed between Olivieri (and his company) and the Covoni and Ubaldini partnerships should not be forgotten: cf. Chapter 2, pp. 56-60. Several accounts relative to this part of the loan

Olivieri, together with other bankers, also made numerous smaller loans in 1542, including 4,000 ducats to Giovanni Gaddi, president of the clerks of the Chamber, in the following proportions: Altoviti 1,000, Cavalcanti and Giraldi 1,000, Bandini 800, Olivieri 700 and Pallavicini 500.[78]

In December 1542 Olivieri, together with Pallavicini, loaned 7,000 *scudi d'oro in oro* as an advance on the *vigesima* of the Jews of the Romagna and Bologna, as part of a loan of 10,000 *scudi* stipulated with the Apostolic Chamber.[79] Olivieri's share, as stated in the contract of 16 December, amounted to 3,500 *scudi*: under the name of the two signatories, however, the company of the Genoese banker Luca Giustiniani entered immediately into the business deal, acquiring 1/3 of the total.[80] The bankers, to each of whom therefore was attributed a share of 33.3%, would receive 8,460 *scudi* (meaning a profit of 20.86%) in two instalments, one after six months and the other after a year, from the *vigesima* of the Jews of Bologna (2,700 *scudi*), the Marches (2,500), the Romagna (1,000), Comtat Venaissin (800), Patrimonio (300), Rome (?) (360), Umbria (250), Avignon (200), Campagna and Marittima (200), Città di Castello (100), Benevento (50).[81]

In February 1543 Benvenuto Olivieri became the assignee – unfortunately there is no record of how much money was involved – of the collection of the tithes '*monasteriorum et locorum congregationis lateranensis canonicorum reguliarum Italie*'. Little more information, although in this case the actual amount is known, is available of a loan of 20,000 *scudi*, given by Benvenuto's company in May 1543 '*pro triremibus*'.[82]

On 27 July 1543 Benvenuto Olivieri's company loaned to the Apostolic Chamber 6,000 *scudi di moneta* which were to be repaid within eight months or a year; in exchange they obtained bonds of the *Monte della Concordia* for a value of 8,000 *scudi* (they were entitled to the interest on 6,000 of the 8,000 *scudi*) and a *donativo* (premium) of 480 *scudi*.[83]

Again in 1543 a loan of 26,000 *scudi* for the defence of the coasts from Turkish attacks was made by a consortium of Florentine bankers: Giovan Battista Puccini,

can be found in Galli Tassi 1857, fols 1-36: the communes must have been encumbered with approximately 6,800 *scudi*, or, in other words, the initial figure plus interest. As for the shares of the '*partito*' of 55,000 *scudi*, Galli Tassi 1942, fol. 197r differs slightly, attributing to the Olivieri company 43,500 *scudi*, to that of Giustiniani 8,500 ('*sopra le cose di Romagna*') and to the Ubaldini company 3,000 ('*sopra le cose del Patrimonio*'); this difference is probably, however, due to the slight amount of time that elapsed between the various registrations. In March 1543 Olivieri was reimbursed 1,600 *scudi*: 500 from the *galere*, 950 from the income from communes, 150 from the tithes (Galli Tassi 2278, fol. 200).

78 ASR, Camerale I, *Mandati Camerali 874*, fols 96v-97r.

79 ASF, Galli Tassi 2278, fol. 281; ASR, Camerale I, *Mandati Camerali 874*, fol. 32r. Camerale I, *Conti della Depositeria generale 1778*, fol. 33r specifies that the Genoese company involved was that of Pallavicini and Lomellini. On the *vigesima* of the Jews, see Chapter 7, note 65.

80 ASF, Galli Tassi 1825, fol. 6r; Galli Tassi 2278, fol. 102.

81 ASF, Galli Tassi 1942, fol. 198r.

82 ASR, Camerale I, *Mandati Camerali 874*, fols 47v, 141r-v.

83 ASF, Galli Tassi 2074, fasc. 4, fols 2r, 5r, 6r-v.

consul of the Florentine nation, contributed the most substantial amount of 10,000 *scudi*; followed by Alessandro Deti with 8,000; Bindo Altoviti and Luigi Del Riccio, 1,400 each; while Pier Antonio Bandini, Bartolomeo Bussotti, Benvenuto Olivieri and Luigi Rucellai each contributed 1,300 *scudi*.[84]

Between 1543 and 1544, 40,000 ducats were guaranteed from the Spanish revenues to the company of Benvenuto Olivieri, who had evidently loaned a sum of that amount. Under Olivieri's name Cavalcanti and Giraldi held a share of 2,000 ducats.[85]

In March 1544 the Olivieri company and that of the German merchant, Michele Incuria, loaned the Chamber respectively 10,000 and 15,000 *scudi d'oro*, receiving as repayment the right to collect the '*contributione*', that is the Triennial Subsidy of Bologna.[86]

On 5 August of the same year, Benvenuto Olivieri, collector of the *quarto dei frutti* from the monastic congregations in Italy and of the *vigesima* of the Jews in Bologna and the province of the Marches, was given the mandate to pay 5,000 gold ducats to the Pallavicini-Giustiniani company, depositary general, following an agreement signed two months earlier.[87] At the beginning of June, in fact, Olivieri had promised the Chamber a certain sum (that he would then have to pay on behalf of and on the mandate of the latter), receiving in exchange a corresponding assignment on the revenue mentioned above.[88]

As has been seen (p. 78), the same revenue was guaranteed to him, together with others, for the following two years, as repayment for the expenditure during his time as depositary.

In April 1545 the companies of the Florentines Olivieri and Cavalcanti-Giraldi and that of Olgiatto from Como undertook to send to Germany the enormous amount of 100,000 *scudi d'oro* (=140,000 Rheinish florins) for the 'subsidy of the faith'. This was not, however, a loan, but rather a service provided by the banking companies through their correspondents.[89]

On 14 and 15 July 1545 Benvenuto Olivieri stipulated with the pontiff two contracts for loans amounting to 6,000 *scudi d'oro in oro* each (total: 12,000).[90] To obtain the repayment of the sum, plus the usual 12% annual interest and the 2% commission on the tax collection, the Florentine banker could recoup 6,000 *scudi* from the '*entrate dello Stato nuovo*', recovered from the Chamber after the war against Ascanio Colonna, the tithes of Siena and the Spanish revenues. The other

84 ASR, Camerale I, *Mandati Camerali 877*, fol. 99r-v.

85 ASF, Galli Tassi 1844, fol. 7.

86 ASR, *Notai segretari e cancellieri della R. Camera apostolica 1988*, fol. 265r-v.

87 ASF, Galli Tassi 2074, fol. 9.

88 ASR, *Notai segretari e cancellieri della R. Camera apostolica 1988*, fols 339r-342r.

89 Among the correspondents in Germany were representatives of the illustrious banking houses Fugger and Welser (ASR, *Notai segretari e cancellieri della R. Camera apostolica 1988*, fols 477r-482r). This substantial consignment of money is also alluded to in the document granting the extension of the Triennial Subsidy for a further three years (Chapter 7, p. 159).

90 Of the first 6,000 *scudi*, more than half (3,500) were destined to the *maestro di casa* (steward of the household) and 909 to Cardinal Farnese (ASF, Galli Tassi 1953, fol. 212fv).

6,000, which again gave the right to the Spanish revenues, were not in fact paid out by Olivieri; the agreement instead stipulated that that sum would be subtracted from what was still owing to him in the transaction of 55,000 *scudi* spoken of above.[91] However, half of these assignments would go to Luigi Del Riccio (or to one of his associates), who had deposited 3,000 *scudi* in cash and had 'made good' to Olivieri a further 3,000 through Antonio Covoni, on behalf of Neri Capponi.[92]

A few months later, in December, Olivieri, in his role as depositary, administered another loan transaction with the Chamber that amounted to 16,000 *scudi*, of which 8,000 under the name of Cavalcanti and Giraldi and 8,000 under that of Ubaldini (a company in which, it should be remembered, the Olivieri company held a share). The contracting parties could recoup 10,000 *scudi* from the Spanish revenues, 5,000 from the Triennial Subsidy of the Romagna and 1,000 from the 'spoils' and the tithes of Ferrara; in addition to this they earned 12% interest and 3% commission.[93]

On 30 October 1546 a group of Florentine companies loaned the Chamber 20,700 *scudi d'oro in oro*: Benvenuto Olivieri contributed 7,000, Girolamo Ubaldini 5,000, Luigi Rucellai 4,700, Pier Antonio and Alamanno Bandini 4,000. In order to recoup this money they were entitled to the tithes of Milan, Bologna, the Marches, Umbria and Urbino and the *vigesima* of the Jews of the Romagna, Bologna, Umbria and Avignon; in addition they earned an annual interest of 12% and a commission of 4% on the tithes of Milan, 3% on the other tithes and 2% on the *vigesima*. In total the commissions placed in the pockets of the bankers were approximately 620 *scudi*.[94]

In 1547 another larger consortium of merchant-bankers underwrote a loan of 100,000 *scudi d'oro in oro* to be made on 1 January 1548, and repaid within the year with an interest of 12% and a commission of 1%, as well as 1,000 *scudi* for the anticipated payment and a premium of 2,000.[95] The shares were subdivided as follows (the origin of those *mercatores* who were not Florentine is noted in brackets):

M. Bernardini, F. Cenami and V. Spada & Partners (Lucca)	20,000
Luigi Rucellai & Partners	16,000
T. Cavalcanti and G. Giraldi & Partners	15,000
B. Negroni and G. Pallavicini & Partners (Genoa)	12,000
Bastiano da Montauto & Partners	12,000

91 See, for the two contracts of July, ASF, Galli Tassi 1828, fasc. 3, fols 1r-2v, 5r-7r; Galli Tassi 1829, fol. 7; Galli Tassi 1953, fol. 212a-f; ASR, *Notai segretari e cancellieri della R. Camera apostolica 1988*, fols 558r-561r, 571r-574r. See also Galli Tassi 1862, fol. 1 for the record of the Chamber mandate of 14 July 1545 which allotted the Spanish revenues to Olivieri. On 12 August 1546 the interest amounted to 1,547 *scudi* (Galli Tassi 1953, fol. 212fv).

92 ASF, Galli Tassi 1829, fol. 7.

93 ASF, Galli Tassi 1829, fol. 8. At least 5,000 *scudi* (of this or the preceding loan) of the Spanish revenues, however, were not collected, and consequently the Chamber declared itself to be in debt to Benvenuto Olivieri & Partners (Galli Tassi 2280, fol. 175).

94 ASF, Galli Tassi 1843, fasc. 10. It is probable that, under the name of Olivieri, Cornelio Malvasia also entered into the business deal with 1,000 *scudi* (Galli Tassi 1951, fol. 56).

95 ASF, Galli Tassi 1951, fol. 217r-v; ASR, Camerale I, *Giustificazioni di Tesoreria*, busta 2, reg. 2 (this contains the accounts of the collectors of the loan, the Florentine bankers Andrea Boni and Roberto Ubaldini); Camerale I, *Mandati Camerali 883*, fols 238r-244r.

Heirs of Girolamo Ubaldini & Partners	7,000
Bindo Altoviti & Partners	6,000
Pier Antonio and Alamanno Baldini & Partners	6,000
Baldassarre Olgiatto (Como)	6,000
Total	100,000

Benvenuto Olivieri's company, which initially had not entered into the business deal, did so very soon under the name of their fellow countrymen, the Ubaldini, acquiring thus a share of 7,000 *scudi*.[96]

For the 3,000 *scudi* (1,000 for having started to pay before 1 January and the premium of 2,000) to which they had the right at the beginning, the bankers could recoup their money from the *gabella della farina* (tax on flour). The loan would be repaid from the following:[97]

Vacant offices	30,000
Gabella della farina (tax on flour)	25,000
Commune of Bologna	25,000
Spanish revenues	19,283

Shortly afterwards there was another loan of notable size that involved yet again a large consortium of *mercatores romanam curiam sequentes*: a loan of 128,000 *scudi d'oro in oro*, according to the contract of 8 June 1548. As well as the usual interest of 12% '*occasione lucri cessantis et damni emergenti*', there was also a premium of 4% and a 2% commission on the money spent.[98] Given below is the list of bankers who participated (only for the non-Florentines is their origin noted) and the amount, expressed in *scudi d'oro in oro*, that each undertook to contribute, in quarterly instalments:

T. Cavalcanti and G. Giraldi & Partners	24,500
Benvenuto Olivieri & Partners[99]	19,000
Baldassarre Olgiatto (Como)	16,000
Luigi Rucellai & Partners	15,000

96 ASR, Camerale I, *Giustificazioni di Tesoreria*, busta 2, reg. 23.

97 ASF, Galli Tassi 1951, fols 218r-223r. Vincenzo Spada was the *doganiere* of the tax on flour and Luigi Rucellai collector for the vacant offices (fols 220r, 221r).

98 ASF, Galli Tassi 1828, fasc. 4, fols 3r-5v; ASR, Camerale I, *Giustificazioni di Tesoreria*, busta 2, reg. 15. The sums were not paid all at once, but detailed records were kept (by Pier Antonio and Alamanno Bandini) and the percentages calculated on each sum on the date of its actual payment: in May 1550 the interests of 12% amounted to 10,537.9 *scudi*, the premium of 4% to 4,425.8, the commission of 2% to 2,212.9. The agreements are also briefly mentioned in Camerale I, *Mandati Camerali 891*, fol. 81r. In January and in June 1549 the premium was credited in two instalments of 2,560 *scudi* (2% each time), as was stipulated in the contract: ASF, Galli Tassi 1861, fols 1, 15. As well as in the sources cited here and in the notes below, a list of the merchants with their deposits can be found in Galli Tassi 1837, fol. 9.

99 But 6,000 of the 19,000 *scudi* underwritten belonged to Cornelio Malvasia (ASF, Galli Tassi 1923, fol. 1).

M. Bernardini, F. Cenami, V. Spada & Partners (Lucca)	12,000
B. Negroni and G. Pallavicini (Genoa)	9,500
Bastiano da Montauto & Partners	8,000
Heirs of Girolamo Ubaldini & Partners	8,000
Pier Antonio and Alamanno Bandini & Partners	7,000
Bindo Altoviti & Partners	6,000
Francesco Formento	3,000
Total	128,000

For the repayment of this sum, the merchant-bankers could avail themselves of the Triennial Subsidy of 1549 and part of 1550 (beginning on 1 February 1549 and terminating at the end of April 1550) for 106,000 *scudi*, subdivided by province:

Marches	30,000
Bologna	25,000
Ravenna	20,000
Umbria and Perugia	20,000
Patrimonio and Civitavecchia	6,000
Campagna and Marittima	5,000

The remaining 12,000 *scudi* would be contributed by the Grimaldi, contract-holders of the Tolfa alum mines. The bankers were also entitled to the taxes of Spoleto, and the *livelli*, and would eventually be given the remainder in cash. Subsequently the details of the repayment were more clearly defined and the new assignments, which included the interests, were:

Tolfa alum mines	16,363
'*Estinzione del censo e dei livelli*' of the Florentine State	22,000
Taxes from Spoleto	12,000

If the bankers were unable to collect the revenue from the last two sources, they would be exempted from the payment of a corresponding sum. They also requested that the jewels and gems that had been given as a pledge for the above-mentioned loan of 100,000 *scudi* be confirmed also for this new loan.[100]

As the *mercatores* did not pay the entire sum agreed on immediately,[101] some time passed between the signing of the contract and the beginning of the collection of the taxes. In fact, at the moment in which the reimbursement of this loan of 128,000

100 ASF, Galli Tassi 1828, fasc. 4, fols 2r-4r, Galli Tassi 1830, fol. 1; Galli Tassi 1850, fol. 14.

101 By 26 August 1549 the Chamber had received 'only' 99,797 *scudi* (ASF, Galli Tassi 1861, fols 1, 15; fols 2-8 list the sums paid by the individual bankers). By 30 May 1550 the sum of 120,705 had been reached (ASR, Camerale I, *Giustificazioni di Tesoreria*, busta 2, reg. 15). According to M.G. Pastura Ruggiero, on 11 January 1549 C. Sauli, B. da Montauto and L. Rucellai made an additional loan of 18,000 *scudi*, guaranteed by the same revenue (*La Reverenda Camera Apostolica*, p. 30).

scudi should have begun, the previous 100,000 *scudi* had not yet been repaid in full: this was contrary to what was laid down in the contract of June 1548, according to which in February 1549 the bankers should have been free from the obligations of the loan of 100,000 *scudi* on the tax on flour of Rome, the Spanish revenues and the vacant offices.[102] Consequently several new assignments were conceded that served to repay both the first and the second loan, replacing in each case some pre-existing assignments. To be more precise, according to a Chamber mandate of 31 January 1549, these new sources of income (except for the Tolfa alum mines, which remained unchanged) were:[103]

Subsidy from the commune of Bologna	37,500
Vacant offices of Rome	35,000
Gabella della farina (tax on flour)	35,000
Tolfa alum mines	16,363
Spanish revenues	14,137
'*Alienazione dei livelli*' of Florence (B. Olivieri & Partners)[104]	12,000
Total	150,000

Despite the death of Benvenuto Olivieri in September 1549, this particular business deal continued: on 30 July 1550 a new contract for 64,000 *scudi* must have been stipulated with the Apostolic Chamber in order to repay the *mercatores* the remainder of the 128,000 *scudi* loan. In this contract (and perhaps already in the first) Olivieri's heirs possessed 5/8 of the share of the Ubaldini company, in other words 2,500 of the 4,000 *scudi* that the latter were still owed by the Chamber.[105]

These pages have concentrated only on those business deals that involved Benvenuto Olivieri. Obviously the number of deals and the amount of money that linked the Apostolic Chamber to the *mercatores romanam curiam sequentes*, mostly Florentines and Genoese, was much greater. As has often been noted, the papacy needed to be able to have access to very large sums in a very short space of time in order to cover its expenditure; in fact, its own sources of income would have guaranteed an adequate flow of money only over much longer periods of time. None of the banking companies working in Rome was able to provide on its own the enormous sums requested; only by collaborating were they able to provide the Chamber with timely (and regular) sums. In the following chapters, which discuss the most sought after of the contracts linked to the finances of the Papal State, we will see how the *mercatores* followed a strategy of close collaboration with each

102 ASF, Galli Tassi 1828, fasc. 4, fols 4v-5r.

103 ASF, Galli Tassi 1850, fol. 14; Galli Tassi 1861, fols 9-14.

104 The proceeds of the '*alienatione et estintione de' livelli*' of the Florentine State, of which Piero di Gino Capponi & Partners were depositaries, had been conceded the same year to Benvenuto Olivieri & Partners in repayment for a loan of 20,000 *scudi d'oro in oro*. In actual fact, the contract, signed on 26 April, was stipulated for a sum of 27,777.77 *scudi*, which included 7,777.77 *scudi* of commission fees (that is, 28% of the total): ASF, Galli Tassi 1951, fols 100, 162; Galli Tassi 1953, fol. 204.

105 ASF, Galli Tassi 1928, fol. 26. The books would not be balanced before September 1553 (fol. 27).

other. The Florentine banks in particular, which were generally of medium size, worked very closely together on the various transactions. As further proof of these relationships, several companies (the Olivieri companies are discussed in Chapter 2) even acquired shares in the capital of the others.

CHAPTER 4

The Papal Public Debt: Venal Offices and *Monti*

From the late Middle Ages, the more advanced cities of central and northern Italy began to institute the so-called *Monti* (funded debt), in order to acquire the money necessary to meet their expenses. While these institutions were usually forced loans, there also existed relatively successful voluntary ones, obviously with higher interest rates. The latter, moreover, implicated a redistribution of resources from the poor towards the rich: in order to pay the interests to those who had the means to speculate on the public debt, the taxes, above all the indirect taxes, were applied more rigorously, and the hardest hit were the least well-to-do classes. In the sixteenth century the increasingly powerful European monarchies found that they were able to gather together enormous sums by placing the bonds of the public debt directly on the market, in the large fairs. Their success was at least in part due to the support of consortia of bankers that managed these affairs for them.

The growing political strength of the nation States, however, had already begun to affect the papal finances in the fifteenth century. The former became increasingly reluctant to send money to Rome, and the papacy's income from these sources was therefore reduced. 'It was no accident – Braudel has observed – that during the last years of the fifteenth century and the first years of the sixteenth, the Supreme Pontiffs resembled temporal rulers rather than spiritual leaders' and sought to fight as much as possible against the financial immunities.[1] The papacy used various methods to obtain money, one of the most often practised being the recourse to loans. Short- or mid-term loans, which were generally guaranteed by smaller or larger groups of bankers (as was discussed in Chapter 3), could be taken out for single operations; long-term loans, on the other hand, could be obtained through the sales of the so-called venal offices, which will be discussed shortly, and, from 1526, through the institution of the *Monti*.

In the second quarter of the sixteenth century the Papal State was facing serious financial difficulties. Clement VII's reaction was to increase taxes and to institute a public debt, the *Monte della Fede*.[2] As has been mentioned, however, a precedent already existed, consisting of more or less honorary offices, from the sales of which the Papal State obtained a large sum in a single payment, but on which it also had to pay interest: the venal offices.

---

1 F. Braudel, *The Mediterranean and the Mediterranean World in the Age of Philip II* (2 vols, London, 1972), II, p. 697.

2 The problems of this period are examined in detail by M. Monaco, 'Le finanze pontificie al tempo di Clemente VII (1523-1534)', *Studi Romani*, 6 (1958): 278-296.

1. Venal offices

These were offices that were offered for sale at varying prices (according to their prestige and the privileges that they carried with them) and that, while they generally returned to the Datary in the case of the death of the holder, could sometimes also be transferred to the holder's heirs, or be sold.[3] Over time, three types of offices evolved:[4]

1. A very restricted number (approximately 1%) of very expensive offices, accessible only to those who were already part of the curial hierarchy, useful as the first step on the way to becoming a cardinal. This became a vicious circle: on one hand, high prelates bought the office in the hope of one day wearing a cardinal's hat; on the other, the pope created new cardinals with the declared aim of liberating ('vacating') posts that could be put anew on sale at often higher prices. Examples of this category were the offices of chamberlain, auditor of the Chamber, treasurer general and clerk of the Chamber.[5]
2. A larger number (15%) of less expensive offices, which could also be bought by laymen and which had half real and half honorary functions (in these cases the title-holder often used a proxy to fulfil the few functions he was called on to carry out). There were about 600 offices of these two types by the end of the sixteenth century.
3. The largest number of offices (some 84%, or well over 3,000, by the end of the sixteenth century) at the most accessible price. These were purely nominal offices,[6] which granted some privileges but remained outside the curial hierarchy. Physically, the titles consisted of a nominal letter patent, but could fairly easily be sold to other people or left to the holder's heirs.[7] This third

3 The venality of the offices has been described by R. Mousnier as a '*phenomène mondial qui designe un stade de civilisation*', having interested practically the whole of Europe ('Le trafic des offices à Venise', *Revue historique du droit français et étranger*, 1952: 552).

4 This classification was first used by G.B. De Luca, *Tractatus de officiis venalibus vacabilibus Romanae Curiae* (Rome, 1682), ch. II, and since then has been adopted by all the historiography.

5 Under Gregory XIII (1572-85) the offices of vice-chancellor and chamberlain were valued at 100,000 *scudi*, a figure which it was hoped could also be applied to the office of auditor of the Chamber, until that time sold for 60,000; a post of clerk of the Chamber was worth 36,000 *scudi*, while 50,000 was requested for the office of treasurer general, until then sold for 15,000 (ASF, Galli Tassi 1954, fols 38r-39r).

6 As De Luca wrote, '*illorum sunt capaces etiam idiotae et infantes*' (*Tractatus de officiis venalibus*, p. 8).

7 Nevertheless, J. Delumeau calculates that on average they were all vacated in the space of 15 years, and that under the pontificate of Paul III, which lasted 14 years, all were vacated (*Vie économique et sociale de Rome dans la seconde moitié du XVIe siècle* (2 vols, Paris, 1957-59), II, p. 775). Other historians have noted that even between the fifteenth and sixteenth centuries considerable use was made of the '*rassegna*', that is of the transfer of titles involving a vacancy, but only because two separate acts were made: first, the title-holder renounced the office and second the office was conferred to others, on the payment of a sum for the stipulation of the acts (S. Levati, 'La venalità delle cariche nello Stato pontificio

category included the Colleges of knights, which will be discussed below.

Although the sale of the offices brought in fresh revenue, it was insufficient to cover the cost of the annuities, making it necessary to choose between either diminishing considerably the number of the offices themselves, or increasing them in continuation to obtain, even if only temporarily, large sums: the latter was the most frequent choice. The need to sell an ever increasing number of offices, moreover, meant that the pontiffs gradually began to accept the *societates officiorum*, groups of people who united to buy a single office on which they had rights proportional to their contribution. This system, while it obviously gave rise to numerous speculations, also made it possible for the papacy to continue to resort to these forms of credit.[8]

The venality of the offices developed in the course of the second half of the fifteenth century in order to side-step the anti-usury provisions that forbade interest rates on capital.[9] But while this method allowed the papacy to procure substantial and immediate income, at the same time it brought with it, as already mentioned, a heavy burden of interests to be paid in future years. The annuities of the offices, which around 1500 were approximately 12%, fell to 10% towards halfway through the century, to stabilize at 8% for all of the seventeenth century.[10] This system developed enormously in the sixteenth century; in fact from the 300 offices sold up until 1471 (the beginning of the pontificate of Sixtus IV),[11] the number had shot up to 4,000 by 1590 (the end of the pontificate of Sixtus V). This increase was due in particular to Leo X (1513-20), who gave a notable push to the growth in the number. He founded more than 1,200 venal offices, which, while they allowed him to gather almost 900,000 ducats, also meant a huge increase in the expenditure for interests:

---

tra XVI e XVII secolo', *Ricerche Storiche*, XXVI (1996): 535). Eventually this became the established way of doing things, so that by the mid-seventeenth century only 3% of the offices returned to the Datary (F. Piola Caselli, 'Aspetti del debito pubblico nello Stato Pontificio: gli uffici vacabili', *Annali della Facoltà di Scienze Politiche, Università degli Studi di Perugia*, 11 (1970-72): 117, 154).

8 Delumeau, *Vie économique et sociale*, II, pp. 775-776: it was Leo X, in 1514, who was the first to recognize these as juridical persons.

9 General complaints about the existence of this phenomenon which were referred to the Council of Costance (1414-18) would nevertheless date the origins to the years around 1400, even if at this time with regard to commerce of offices between individuals (Levati, 'La venalità delle cariche': 527).

10 F. Piola Caselli, 'Gerarchie curiali e compravendita degli uffici a Roma tra il XVI ed il XVII secolo', *Archivio della Società Romana di Storia Patria*, CXIV (1991): 122-123. P. Partner, noting how the price of the purchase was paid in gold while the annuities were paid in silver and considering the net loss of value of the latter with respect to the former, puts the real cost of the offices, for the papacy, at around 5-6% a year ('Papal financial policy in the Renaissance and Counter-Reformation', *Past and Present*, 88 (1980): 22-23).

11 This pope, as L. von Ranke said, '*vendait tout: ... il poussa les choses si loin qu'on le regarda comme l'inventeur de ce système, quand il n'avait fait que le dèvelopper, il est vrai, très largement*' (*Histoire de la papauté pendant les XVI*[e] *et XVII*[e] *siècles* (4 vols, Paris, 1848), II, p. 24); during his pontificate the offices placed on sale went from 300 to 625 (F. Litva, 'L'attività finanziaria della Dataria durante il periodo Tridentino', *Archivum Historiae Pontificiae*, V (1967): 133).

during his pontificate the number of 2,150 offices was reached, which meant an annual cost of interests equal to approximately 320,000 ducats.[12] Among the new offices that he created should be remembered the 612 portioneers of the port taxes (*porzionari di Ripa*, 1513) and the 200 cubiculars and scutifers (1520). Subsequently other similar Colleges were instituted, which, however, gathered together honorary titles only: the first of these, still under Leo X, was the College of the 401 knights of St Peter (1520);[13] following this example, other new Colleges, a list of which is given below, were then instituted under Paul III:[14]

Year	Office	Number	Unit price	Total income	Annual interest
1540	Knights of St Paul	200	1,000	200,000	24,000
1545	Knights *lauretani*	151	500	75,500	9,060
1546	Knights of St George	150	500	75,000	9,000
1546	Knights of the Red Fleur-de-lis	50	500	25,000	3,000
		551		375,500	45,060

The holders of the offices tended from the very beginning to be grouped into large Colleges, the first of which was instituted by Sixtus IV. Sixtus's successor, Innocent VIII (1484-92), created the first completely honorary offices, a necessary innovation given that those with administrative functions had been exhausted by the impetus given by his predecessor. In this second phase single offices were no longer instituted, but were all grouped into Colleges – further proof, if any were needed, that they closely resembled bonds of public debt. Moreover, this made it possible for the papacy to obtain large sums in a very short space of time, something which was not possible with the sale *ad personam*, and which facilitated greatly the payment of the annuities to the holders.

Those who held the administrative offices profited from the taxes that the population paid for the services they offered; the holders of the honorary offices profited instead from the interests, paid from assignments on other income or papal monopolies. Between 1531 and 1541, for example, the contract-holders of the Tolfa alum mines had to make an annual payment of 7,920 ducats *di giuli* 10 per ducat to the knights of St Peter;[15] between 1553 and 1565 this figure had increased to 9,440 *scudi* per annum.[16] In the 1540s the income coming from the customs of

12 Monaco, 'Le finanze pontificie': 287-288. Cf. also ASF, Galli Tassi 1954, fol. 35.

13 Comparing these to the offices which might in appearance be part of the curial bureaucracy (for example the *sollecitatores*) and to those that were in part curial and in part honorary (as the cubiculars), P. Partner defines the knights of St Peter as 'frankly snobbish': *Renaissance Rome 1500-1559. A Portrait of a Society* (Berkeley, 1976), p. 60.

14 ASF, Galli Tassi 1954, fol. 35r. The knights *lauretani*, in reality, were initially 101, but they became 151 scarcely a year after their institution: M.G. Pancaldi, 'Militi lauretani', in *La Marca e le sue istituzioni al tempo di Sisto V* (Macerata, 1991), p. 318.

15 ASF, Galli Tassi 1830, loose unnumbered folios.

16 J. Delumeau, *L'alun de Rome XV-XIX siècle* (Paris, 1962), p. 158.

Rome served for the most part to pay the interest on the public debt: a large amount (24,000 *scudi di moneta* per annum, which then increased to 36,000), was destined, as will be seen, to the stockholders of the *Monte della Fede* (p. 105), while another considerable portion was allotted to the knights of St Paul (14,600 *scudi* per annum) and the knights of St Peter (8,000).[17] The College of the knights of St Peter was, moreover, allotted 2,458 *scudi di moneta*, which then decreased to 2,200-2,300, from the revenue of the *Salara* of Rome;[18] as well as a further 828 *scudi* per annum from the Treasury of Perugia.[19]

Of the few Florentine merchants who bought an office of knight of St Paul, as well as members of illustrious families such as the Altoviti and the Strozzi, was also Benvenuto Olivieri.[20] It should also be noted that some years later his son Giulio, defined by the sources as '*scholaris romanus*', was numbered among the knights of the Fleur-de-lis, who, in exchange for nobility for themselves and for their descendants and an annual pension of 200 ducats, had been created to defend the security of the province of Patrimonio.[21]

The knighthoods were often used by the Chamber to guarantee the loans received: they were, in other words, given in pledge to the *mercatores* to whom it was in debt. The latter, if repayment was not made within the terms established, could then do as they pleased with these knighthoods; in other words, they could either sell them or collect the relative revenue. For example, in 1538 the Roman companies of Cavalcanti-Giraldi and Strozzi, in return for a loan of 58,760 *scudi d'oro di sole*, were pledged 28 knighthoods of St Peter and several valuables.[22] In 1540 the Chamber, finding itself unable to pay its debt (12,000 *scudi* of a loan and the interest which had matured on this amount) to Olivieri and his partners, contract-holders for the collection of the increase of the salt tax of Bologna and the Romagna (see Chapter 7, pp. 150-153), assigned them 12 knighthoods of St Paul. These would

17 Examples in Chapter 5, in particular Table 11, p. 122. For the sources, see those already mentioned, and also ASF, Galli Tassi 2278, fols 4, 287, 302, 366. In the 1540s Alessandro Deti was depositary of the College of the knights of St Paul and Giovan Pietro Crivello of the College of the knights of St Peter.

18 ASF, Galli Tassi 1863, fasc. 4-5; Galli Tassi 1864, fasc. 9, fol. 2; Galli Tassi 2278, fols 3, 4, 57, 75, 226; ASR, Camerale I, *Mandati camerali* 874, fols 27v, 70v, 71r. Cf. also Chapter 7, p. 148.

19 ASF, Galli Tassi 2278, fols 4, 226.

20 I. Polverini Fosi, 'I fiorentini a Roma nel Cinquecento: storia di una presenza', in S. Gensini (ed.), *Roma capitale (1447-1527)*, Atti del IV Convegno di studio del Centro studi sulla civiltà del tardo Medioevo, San Miniato (Pisa) 27-31 October 1992 (Pisa, 1994), p. 398; ASF, Galli Tassi 1954, fols 238, 242.

21 Polverini Fosi, 'I fiorentini a Roma', p. 398. According to the sources used here (ASF, Galli Tassi 1954, fol. 35r), however, the revenue amounted instead to a more reasonable figure of 60 ducats per annum.

22 ASF, Galli Tassi 1868, fasc. 2, fols 1r-8v. Cf also Chapter 3, p. 84; it should again be recalled that from 1539 the Olivieri company was the continuation of the Strozzi company.

remain in their possession (meaning that they would have the right to the relative revenue) until the complete repayment of the debt.[23]

Again in 1540, the year of their institution, a group of 70 knights of St Paul were pledged to redeem the '*annate*' from Grimaldi and Strozzi: in practice, Benvenuto Olivieri & Partners, depositaries general, on behalf of the Apostolic Chamber paid 61,500 *scudi d'oro in oro* to the Grimaldi and Strozzi companies, each of which had the right to 30,750 on the '*annate*'; for this operation they obtained in pledge the 70 knighthoods.[24] On 6 August Benvenuto Olivieri began to assign them to various people, although he kept 11 in his own name (of these one each went to his employees, Giovan Francesco Ridolfi and Guglielmo Dei, and one to Niccolò Busini) and 11 in the name of his partner, Benedetto Busini. Subsequently he was able to sell others, so that by the following year he had only 26 (of which 7 in his name and 3 in the name of Busini) of the original 70. In 1542 the number of offices had dropped to 6 in the name of Busini and 3 in that of Bandini (as will be seen shortly), besides the 2 bought by Olivieri and by Busini himself.[25]

On 26 March 1541 the Chamber gave a further 35 knighthoods of St Paul to the Olivieri company as a pledge for a loan. If the debt was not reimbursed within a year, these knighthoods could be alienated by Olivieri. Since 1,900 *scudi d'oro in oro* had been loaned by Bartolomeo Angiolini, Olivieri promised to repay this sum after a year or, alternatively, give him two offices and the corresponding revenue;[26] the same agreement was made with Benedetto Busini, who had paid 19,950 *scudi d'oro in oro*, giving him the right to 21 knighthoods.[27] In actual fact Benvenuto kept the 35 offices in his name until February 1542, thus earning the corresponding revenue.[28] In March, however, evidently because the money had not been repaid to him, he began to sell these offices, and by August none remained in his name.[29] However, between

23 ASF, Galli Tassi 1865, fol. 9 (confirmed also in Galli Tassi 1864, fasc. 13). On 5 June 1542, for their share of five knighthoods of St Paul (the remaining seven had been divided proportionally amongst the other partners) included in the deal of the increase of the salt tax of the Romagna, the Olivieri company received 781.5 *scudi di moneta* (Galli Tassi 2278, fols 54, 151).

24 ASF, Galli Tassi 1954, fol. 270; ASR, Camerale I, *Conti della Depositeria generale 1777*, fol. 107v.

25 ASF, Galli Tassi 1954, fol. 238r, 244-245, 256r, 276, 281; for the knighthood of Olivieri see also note 20.

26 ASF, Galli Tassi 1835, ins. 1, fol. 1.

27 ASF, Galli Tassi 1836, fol. 7. Galli Tassi 1942, fol. 207r speaks of 35 offices of knights given in pledge and 12 sold in 1542.

28 To be precise he received 315 ducats *di moneta* (9 for every knighthood) for January 1542 and 507.5 (14.5) for February (ASF, Galli Tassi 1817, fols 3r, 4r).

29 For the 34 knighthoods possessed in March he received an annuity of 357 ducats, for the 30 of April, 396, for the 26 (of which in reality he had only 13 remaining to him) of May, 297.5, for the 7 (of which only 4 were his) of June, 84 (ASF, Galli Tassi 1817, fols 7r, 8v, 12v, 17r). Presumably relative to the two deals were the 47 offices kept in pledge that Olivieri managed to sell, for 47,000 *scudi* (7,000 of which went to Busini), between 20 March and 29 June 1542 (Galli Tassi 1954, fol. 235). Cf. also Galli Tassi 2278, fol. 162 for other offices of knights of St Paul held in pledge in 1543; and ASV, *Cam. Ap., Div. Cam. 147*, fols 94v-95r for other offices held in 1546.

September and December 1542, several knighthoods, oscillating between 3 and 7 in number, were in the possession of Busini (who usually acted as representative of Benvenuto Olivieri & Partners), who was thus entitled to the revenue.[30]

On 4 July 1542 Benvenuto Olivieri's company gave 3,000 *scudi d'oro* to Bandini's company in order to obtain the right to receive the revenue of 3 knights of St Paul that the latter possessed in pledge from the preceding year. At the end of January 1543 the revenue amounted to 97 *scudi d'oro*, which was paid to the cashier, Guglielmo Dei.[31] These offices, however, had in fact been bought by the Cavalcanti-Giraldi, on whose behalf the Olivieri company administered them.[32]

Between 1546 and 1549 Benvenuto Olivieri was '*pecuniarius proventium ex venditionibus officiorum militum Sancti Georgii*'; he dealt, in other words, with the sale, for 500 *scudi* each, of the new knighthoods of St George.[33] Until October 1547, of the 45,000 *scudi* that the Chamber had earned from the sale of 90 offices, more than 23,000 were 'made good' to Olivieri, who clearly had been the intermediary for the sale of at least half of these.[34]

As mentioned at the beginning of the section, it was not only the offices of knight that were put up for sale. The commerce also included less prestigious offices as well as more prestigious positions both within the Apostolic Chamber and beyond it. In any case the model of commercialization seems to have been the same for all of them: in other words, while the offices could also be a sign of honour, they were above all used as simple objects of speculation or as a guarantee on loans. On 11 November 1537 Benvenuto Olivieri was granted an office of apostolic secretary, from which he was entitled to the corresponding revenue.[35] In March 1542 he obtained another office of secretary as a guarantee on a loan of 4,500 *scudi d'oro in oro* made by his company: if the money was not reimbursed within a year, the Florentine company would be able to sell the office for whatever price that it managed to obtain.[36] This last agreement was part of a larger deal relative to the transfer of the Duchy of Camerino, in which the Cavalcanti-Giraldi company was also involved, and which was worth a total sum of 10,000 ducats (see, for more detail, Chapter 3, pp. 85-86).

30 ASF, Galli Tassi 1817, fols 20v, 22r, 23r, 23v, 24r. Busini appears as holder of two offices also in June (Galli Tassi 1917, fol. 49v). Throughout the year, moreover, a knighthood remained under the name of another of Benvenuto's employees, Giovanni Strozzi.

31 ASF, Galli Tassi 1844, fol. 17.

32 ASF, Galli Tassi 2278, fol. 162.

33 ASF, Galli Tassi 1850, various unnumbered folios.

34 ASF, Galli Tassi 1946, fol. 274.

35 ASF, Galli Tassi 1867, fol. 1: this is a parchment that confirms the bestowal of the title. The College of the 24 apostolic secretaries was founded in 1487 by Innocent VIII (G. Moroni, *Dizionario di erudizione storico-ecclesiastica* (103 vols, Venice, 1840-1861), vol. 7, p. 182). In 1531-32 Benvenuto was already part-owner (1/3) of the office of a secretary with Bindo Altoviti (see Chapter 2, p. 47).

36 ASF, Galli Tassi 1837, fol. 6. In reality the office of secretary, which in the period 1 March 1542-31 January 1543 provided a revenue of 599 gold cameral ducats, was held on behalf of Luigi de Torres, to whom, in March 1543 (therefore a year from the date of the loan), it was credited together with the revenue which had accumulated: Galli Tassi 2278, fol. 130.

On 26 February 1542 Benvenuto Olivieri held in pledge, in the name of Roberto Strozzi, three portioneers of the port taxes for 1,440 *scudi*. He must, however, already have held another of these offices, which in the period 1 September 1537 to 30 April 1543 earned him 330.5 *scudi*.[37]

In September 1542 Benvenuto Olivieri bought, for 1,500 *scudi d'oro*, also an office of abbreviator:[38] this office was *non vacabile*, and would therefore be passed on to his heirs in the case of Benvenuto's death. However, 1,000 *scudi* were contributed by Niccolò Del Riccio, who therefore would have earned 2/3 of the revenue; this is a clear example of one of the *societates officiorum* mentioned above.[39]

To sum up, while there was, as is pointed out by the literature,[40] a very strong desire on the part of the bankers to become noblemen or to link themselves and identify themselves with the politics of the pontiff, purely economic-financial interests must also be given their due weight (as has been suggested above). In the cases looked at here, in particular, this second aspect was clearly very important: a considerable number of these offices were granted or given in pledge as compensation or guarantee for other business deals.[41] Certainly those offices that have been indicated here as of the first or second type were a launching pad for the acquisition of more important roles by the families of merchant-bankers that aimed, as a final reward, at the purple. For the offices of type 3, that is those which were exclusively honorary, often organized in Colleges, which on paper guaranteed the title of knight and some privileges to those who bought them, however, this argument would seem to be rather forced:[42] in the circumstances that I have been able to analyse, where this type of office was most common, one notes above all the speculative aspect. Moreover, whereas for the first transferable offices the authorization of the Datary

37 ASF, Galli Tassi 1833, fol. 5, 13. For this office see Moroni, *Dizionario di erudizione storico-ecclesiastica*, vol. 7, pp. 184-185.

38 Pius II had instituted the 12 *abbreviatori* of the Parco Maggiore, high-ranking prelates who were aiming at even higher offices, and the 60 of the Parco Minore, who could be either clerics or laypersons: to rise to these offices the former had to pay approximately 10,000 *scudi*, and the latter approximately 2,000 (Moroni, *Dizionario di erudizione storico-ecclesiastica*, vol. 7, p. 181).

39 ASF, Galli Tassi 1824, fol. 33; see also Galli Tassi 1918, fol. 17. For other examples of *societates officiorum* see the Appendix, doc. 8, p. 267.

40 In addition to the classic work by P. Prodi, *The Papal Prince. One Body and Two Souls: the Papal Monarchy in Early Modern Europe* (Cambridge, 1987), should also be mentioned M. Rosa, 'La "scarsella di Nostro Signore": aspetti della fiscalità spirituale pontificia nell'età moderna', *Società e Storia*, 38 (1987): 818-845; P. Partner, *The Pope's Men. The Papal Civil Service in the Renaissance* (Oxford, 1990); and, amongst the more recent contributors, M. Pellegrini, 'Corte di Roma e aristocrazie italiane in età moderna. Per una lettura storico-sociale della curia romana', *Rivista di Storia e Letteratura Religiosa*, 19 (1994): 543-603.

41 See also M.M. Bullard, *Filippo Strozzi and the Medici: Favor and Finance in Sixteenth-century Florence and Rome* (Cambridge, 1980), p. 152 and note 7, where the author points out the high number of offices that Filippo Strozzi obtained from Clement VII in exchange for loans. The fact that these offices could also be held by women (and moreover by children) makes it even more difficult to think of them as a stepping stone to a future career.

42 Polverini Fosi nevertheless gives great weight to this, to indicate the increasingly close ties between the *mercatores* and the pope ('I fiorentini a Roma', pp. 395-399).

had been necessary, this was no longer the case, reinforcing once again the idea that they were very similar to the bonds of the public debt. Certainly there existed those *mercatores* with little financial backing whose highest aspiration was to enter into one of these Colleges, but it would seem that amongst the merchant-bankers the prevailing idea was that of a good investment. The *mercatores* in fact tended to use these offices almost as a means of exchange: sometimes they accepted them as a pledge or guarantee for loans they had made; other times they undertook to place a certain number on the market (and to speculate on the difference between the buying and the selling price), acting in other words as intermediaries.[43] This was exactly the same, as shall be seen in the next section, as what happened with regard to the bonds of the *Monte*; and this renders even more convincing the interpretation that most of the venal offices can in fact be compared to the bonds of the public debt and thus considered as the legal and financial precedent to the *Monti*.[44]

2. Papal *Monti*

Against a background that already included both normal loans with interest and the sale of offices which provided income for at least the owner's lifetime if not beyond, the *Monte della Fede* was instituted with the bull *Romanum Pontificem* of 15 November 1526:[45] the first true papal funded debt, created on the model which

43 Litva, 'L'attività finanziaria della Dataria': 139-140 speaks of the role of the banks as intermediaries for the sale of the offices.

44 As is underlined by, among other authors, F. Piola Caselli, who notes that for the entire sixteenth century the interests of the bonds of the *Monti vacabili* coincided with those of the offices ('La diffusione dei Luoghi di Monte della Camera apostolica alla fine del XVI secolo. Capitali investiti e rendimenti', in *Credito e sviluppo economico in Italia dal Medioevo all'età contemporanea*, Atti del I Convegno nazionale della Società Italiana degli Storici dell'Economia, Verona 4-6 June 1987 (Verona, 1988), p. 198). P. Partner is also convinced that the holders of these offices 'were in effect share-holders in the papal debt' ('The "Budget" of the Roman Church in the Renaissance Period', in E.F. Jacob (ed.), *Italian Renaissance Studies* (London, 1960), p. 258). Similarly, W. Reinhard affirms that these were no longer authentic offices but merely instruments of credit ('*si tratta appunto non più di uffici autentici bensì ormai solo di strumenti di credito!*') ('Finanza pontificia e Stato della Chiesa nel XVI e XVII secolo', in A. De Maddalena-H. Kellenbenz (eds), *Finanze e ragion di Stato in Italia e in Germania nella prima età moderna* (Bologna, 1984), p. 374).

45 The *Monte della Fede* was extinguished in 1587, but was then immediately reopened with fresh capital, reaching, through successive additions, the value of 5 million *scudi* in 1682; however, like the other *Monti*, it gradually lost its administrative autonomy. Immediately after the first *Monte*, it would seem that between 1526 and 1527 a further two were instituted, the *Monte del Sale e Oro* (284,800 ducats) and the *Monte del Macinato* (290,000), both of which, however, would seem to have almost immediately undergone rapid transformation: these last two *Monti* are, however, first mentioned only in works published in the nineteenth century, lending weight to the doubts about their existence expressed by Delumeau (*Vie économique et sociale*, II, p. 793) and M. Monaco ('Il primo debito pubblico pontificio: il Monte della Fede (1526), *Studi Romani*, 8 (1960): 565-568).

had already existed for some time in many Italian cities.[46] The threat Vienna was facing from the Turks and the need to help Charles V push them back (from whence the name 'Faith' given to the *Monte*) were decisive in this sense;[47] before that, in order to procure the money necessary for the crusades or for the wars against the infidels, the popes had used the tithes, the proceeds from the sale of towns or castles belonging to the State and the venal offices. Between 1526 and the end of the century the Apostolic Chamber instituted approximately forty *Monti*. This system relied on the collaboration of groups of bankers: the latter purchased the bonds from the Apostolic Chamber, and then more often than not placed them on the market, obtaining a commission equal to at least 1%. It seems nevertheless that only after the mid-sixteenth century did private financial operators begin to underwrite in block all the bonds of a single *Monte*.[48] Previously the bonds were probably seen as a guarantee of past credits: in 1530, for example, almost half of the bonds of the *Monte della Fede* were in the hands of Filippo Strozzi and Jacopo Salviati, Florentine bankers both related to the pontiff.[49]

There existed two types of *Monti*: *non vacabili*, the bonds of which could be passed on either via acts between living persons or via hereditary succession; and *vacabili*, which in contrast conferred rights on the shareholder (*montista*) that were only valid until his death, when the bonds returned to the possession of the Apostolic Chamber. To compensate for this, the *Monti* of this second type normally earned interests that were on average 2% higher.

The initial fund of the *Monte della Fede* (*non vacabile*) was 200,000 gold ducats (2,000 bonds of 100 ducats each) with interests of 10% (20,000 per annum) to be paid from the revenue of the customs of Merci or St Eustace. The *Monti*, in general, could in time be modified, extinguished or reconstituted: to the 200,000 gold ducats of the first *Monte della Fede* were added 120,000 relative to the first increase, which took

46 It is probable that the fact that Clement VII Medici was a Florentine, and had had the opportunity to observe the success with which the *Monte Comune*, erected in 1345, had met and still met, contributed in no small way to the decision to create an analogous institution in Rome.

47 Even though, according to L. Palermo, the anti-Turkish crusade tended towards becoming a myth which could be usefully called upon every time there was a need for money ('Ricchezza privata e debito pubblico nello Stato della Chiesa durante il XVI secolo', *Studi Romani*, 22 (1974): 301). The original aims of the *Monte della Fede* were, however, at least in part, respected: between 28 February and 13 October 1542, in fact, various Chamber mandates obliged Benvenuto Olivieri, depositary of the increase of the College of the *Monte della Fede*, to give to Francesco Benci, treasurer of the apostolic army, 37,340 *scudi di moneta* (ASR, Camerale I, *Mandati Camerali 872*, fols 87v, 90v, 94r, 102r, 145v, 148v, 150v-151r, 185v).

48 Delumeau, *Vie économique et sociale*, II, pp. 784-785, 857-859; F. Piola Caselli, 'Banchi privati e debito pubblico pontificio a Roma tra Cinquecento e Seicento', in *Banchi pubblici, banchi privati e monti di pietà nell'Europa pre-industriale. Amministrazione, tecniche operative e ruoli economici*, Atti del Convegno, Genoa 1-6 October (2 vols, Genoa, 1991), I, p. 476.

49 Bullard, *Filippo Strozzi and the Medici*, p. 151; Ead., 'Grain Supply and Urban Unrest in Renaissance Rome: the Crisis of 1533-34', in P.A. Ramsey (ed.), *Rome in the Renaissance. The City and the Myth* (Binghamton N.Y., 1982), p. 287 (note 8).

place in February 1541, and 160,000, finally, after the second increase of December 1542, thus bringing the total to 480,000 ducats.[50]

Like the holders of the venal offices, the shareholders of the *Monti* also formed Colleges, thus assuming a more direct control of the administration of the revenue necessary to guarantee the payment of the interests. As mentioned, the underwriters of the original *Monte* had the right, according to the institutional bull, to an annual interest of 10% to be paid bimonthly on the proceeds of the customs of Merci; however, because of the Sack, only part of that sum was received, and in the following years only 15,000 *scudi* were paid, with an interest that had therefore dropped to 7.5%.[51] The same income was guaranteed with the first increase, which therefore brought to the College of the *Monte della Fede* an additional 9,000 *scudi* per annum, coming from the three customs of Ripa, Merci and Grascia ('*solvendis ex redditibus Dohanarum Urbis, aliisque iuribus Camerae cum facultate redimendi*'[52]), and the total to 24,000;[53] the second increase guaranteed a further 12,000 *scudi*, taking the total income to 36,000 – this money came from the customs, the *Salara* of Rome and from the increase of the salt tax of Rome (later replaced by the Triennial Subsidy).[54]

Every *Monte* had a depositary (who after the mid-sixteenth century was often someone who bought bonds in block to place them on the market) and a 'patron-cardinal', who acted as an intermediary between the apostolic authority and the shareholders.[55] In the years covered by this study, Benvenuto Olivieri was depositary, while the very reverend cardinal of the Santi Quattro Coronati was the 'patron-cardinal'.[56] The role of depositary of the single *Monte*, while not bestowing great prestige, was nevertheless a sought-after post, because of the flow of money that passed through his hands as well as the possibility of creating relationships with private investors.[57] Olivieri, in his role as depositary of the *Monte*, found himself in the advantageous position of being able to buy bonds as soon as they were placed on the market in order to resell them, thereby profiting from the difference between the price of the sale and the price of the purchase.[58] Between 1543 and 1549 the Olivieri company played the double role of depositary of the *Monte della Fede* (a post that

---

50 ASF, Galli Tassi 2281, fols 5, 6.

51 ASF, Galli Tassi 2281, fol. 6.

52 A. Lodolini, 'I "Monti Camerali" nel sistema della finanza pontificia', in *Archivi Storici delle Aziende di Credito* (2 vols, Rome, 1956), I, p. 267.

53 ASF, Galli Tassi 1833, fasc. 11, fol. 5r, which makes separate mention of the 15,000 *scudi* of the first assignment and the 8,250 earned from the first 11 months following the increase. See also Galli Tassi 2278, fols 259, 305, 361.

54 ASF, Galli Tassi 2281, fol. 6.

55 Delumeau, *Vie économique et sociale*, II, p. 789.

56 ASF, Galli Tassi 1836, fol. 8. In the 1540s the cardinals of the Santi Quattro were: until 1544 Antonio Pucci (see Chapter 2, note 92), followed by his uncle, Roberto (A. Eubel-G. Van Gulik, *Hierarchia Catholica Medii et Recentioris Aevi sive Summorum Pontificum, S.R.E. Cardinalium, Ecclesiarum Antistitum Series* (Regensburg, 1923), vol. 3, p. 62).

57 Piola Caselli, 'Banchi privati e debito pubblico', p. 474.

58 Various references to such business transactions can be found scattered throughout ASF, Galli Tassi 1835, 1836, 1837, 1838, 1839, 2074.

it held at least from 1541) and of farmer of the customs of Rome.[59] As depositaries, Benvenuto Olivieri & Partners kept the records of the sale of bonds, both when they acted as intermediaries (buying the bonds and then selling them on) and when the bonds were transferred directly from one person to another.[60]

In February 1541, therefore, the first increase of 120,000 ducats was instituted, although – as was normal practice – it was not immediately underwritten. The number of stockholders grew from 32 in February with little more than 54,000 ducats, to 43 in April with 60,700, to 81 in June with 100,200.[61] By 1542 the entire 320,000 ducats (of which 20,000 of the *Monte de' Medici*[62]) plus an annual interest of 7.5% paid bimonthly had been underwritten.[63] In January 1542 there were 281 stockholders (of which 36 of the *Monte de' Medici*), 12 of whom held shares for more than 5,000 ducats.[64] Between 1542 and 1543 there was the above-mentioned increase of 160,000 ducats, which therefore placed a further 2,000 ducats in the pockets of the stockholders every two months. In that period there were as many as 465 holders of bonds of the *Monte*, with shares oscillating between a few dozen ducats and the 31,293 held by Girolamo Conte, abbot of St Gregory. In total, 18 (or 3.9%) of the stockholders owned shares of 5,000 ducats or more, the sum of which was almost 163,000 (34% of the total).[65] Not even the conveyance of these bonds took place immediately, so that in the first two months of 1543 12,638 ducats were held by only 12 stockholders; this increased then to 22 with 45,680 between March and June; to 34 with 65,680 in July and August; to 55 with 152,280 in September and October; and to 67 with 139,350 ducats in the last two months of the year.

---

59 See, for example, ASF, Galli Tassi 2278, fols 11, 259, 305, 361; see also Chapter 5, pp. 117-125. Olivieri must, however, have also been depositary earlier, in the 1530s, since, in a request for compensation, Francesco Del Nero, partner of Filippo Strozzi on the same level as Benvenuto, complained: 'I could ask for the entire share of the Depositary of the Monte della Fede, because pope Clement VII entrusted it to me with the provision that I did not give it to Strozzi; and instead I gave it to Benvenuto' (Galli Tassi 1826, fol. 9v).

60 See in particular ASF, Galli Tassi 2281, fols 106, 146, 152, 162, 175, 182, 188, 191, 198, 202, 207, 227.

61 ASF, Galli Tassi 1840, fols 1r-v, 2r-v, 3r-4r. Benvenuto Olivieri, depositary of the *Monte*, received 47,874 ducats on 31 March; 18,011 on 28 May; 39,240 on 30 June; 14,875 on 2 July (Galli Tassi 1836, fasc. 4, fol. 3).

62 This was a *Monte* relative to the creditors of the deceased Cardinal Ippolito de' Medici.

63 In reality only a 7.2% interest (=3,840 ducats instead of 4,000) was attributed every two months and only later, after certain expenses had been paid, was a part of the remainder distributed, which amounted each time to 90-95 or even 100 or more ducats (ASF, Galli Tassi 1841, fols 11r, 19r, 27v, 35v, 43r, 51r, 59r, 67r, 75v, 85r, 95r, 105r). In fact, it was calculated that 20 ducats of every 1,000 of income, that is 720 on 36,000 of assignment, would be used for expenses (notary, chaplain, secretary, depositary and so on) every year: in 1543 the real costs were 617 ducats, the following year 621 (Galli Tassi 1836, fol. 1).

64 The underwriters of shares changed little at this time, as can be seen, for example, if we compare the data referring to the first two-month period of 1542 with those of the last of 1543 (ASF, Galli Tassi 1841, fols 5r-11r, 97r-103v); this impression is confirmed also by data from 1549 (Galli Tassi 2074, fol. 1).

65 ASF, Galli Tassi 2281, fols 1-5.

For this increase in particular, many of the bankers already mentioned participated: Roberto Strozzi held 25,000 ducats from the beginning; between September and October the Genoese Pallavicini and Giustiniani acquired 24,000 and the Olgiatto of Como 30,000.[66] The bonds of this '*Monte Nuovo*' seem to have been used by the Chamber as a means of compensating the bankers who made them loans: in July and August, Bartolomeo Bussotti (on behalf of Bindo Altoviti) acquired 2,800 ducats; Alessandro Deti, Benvenuto Olivieri, Bastiano da Montauto, Luigi Del Riccio (for Antonio Covoni), Luigi Rucellai, Pier Antonio Bandini took 2,600 each and Battista Puccini 1,600; all this came to a total of 20,000 ducats, which would seem to indicate one of the usual loans by a consortium.[67]

Turning now more specifically to Benvenuto Olivieri, on 31 December 1542 his company possessed shares of the *Monte della Fede* for the equivalent of 3,425 *scudi d'oro in oro*, 300 of which were in the name of Benvenuto himself and the rest (3,125) in the name of Busini.[68] For all of 1542 Benvenuto held between 201 and 301 ducats of the first *Monte* as well as the 427 of the *Monte de' Medici*: a total which oscillated therefore between 628 and 728, guaranteeing him an interest of 7.5-9 ducats every two months.[69] At the same time he, in his role as depositary, received a further 25 ducats.[70] With the creation of the '*Monte Nuovo*' (or, it might be said, of the increase of the *Monte della Fede*) Olivieri, while maintaining more or less constant his share in the *Monte de' Medici*, reduced the one he held in '*Monte*

66 ASF, Galli Tassi 1841, fols 59v, 67v, 76r, 84r-v, 94r-95r, 104r-105r. According to a document dated 11 April 1543, the 25,000 of Roberto Strozzi were in actual fact a pledge for the credit that Benvenuto Olivieri & Partners had with the Chamber; consequently he should have returned them after four months, and would be fined (a fine that obviously the Olivieri company would have paid) if he failed to pay on time (Galli Tassi 1835, ins. 1, fol. 6). We do not know what happened after this; perhaps the agreements were modified given that Strozzi was still in possession of these 25,000 ducats after August.

67 ASF, Galli Tassi 1841, fol. 84r.

68 By July 1543 many of these bonds would however be sold, giving a profit of 44 *scudi* (ASF, Galli Tassi 2278, fol. 73).

69 ASF, Galli Tassi 1841, fols 6v, 10r, 14v, 18r, 22v, 26v, 30v, 34v, 38v, 42r, 46v, 50r. In the *Monte de' Medici* his participation must probably be understood as the participation of the company. This *Monte* was a particular favourite of the Florentine bankers, amongst whom stood out Bindo Altoviti (5,925), Benedetto Busini (2,598), perhaps as representative of the Olivieri company of which he was partner, and Bastiano da Montauto (1,183): these three bankers in fact held almost half of the titles (fol. 10r-v). But already at the beginning of 1540 Olivieri had 328 ducats, Altoviti 4,632, the heirs of Pandolfo Della Casa 1,366 and the others the shares that they would then maintain (Galli Tassi 1836, fasc. 6, fol. 3v); in July-August 1541, while Olivieri kept the 328 ducats, the others acquired the shares they would have in 1542-43 (fasc. 5, fol. 3v) and in the first months of 1544 (Galli Tassi 1839, fasc. 5, fol. 6r; Galli Tassi 1953, fol. 199fr; Galli Tassi 1837, fasc. 3, fol. 6v). In 1549 the shares of Olivieri and Montauto remained the same, while that of Altoviti increased to almost 6,400 and there was also a participation of Roberto Strozzi and brothers, with 2,692 ducats (Galli Tassi 2074, fol. 1).

70 ASF, Galli Tassi 1841, fols 11r, 19r, 27v, 35r, 43r, 51r. These were part of the 90-100 ducats of above-mentioned expenses (note 63); also the following year he maintained the same right, to which were added, in December, a further 6 ducats 'for a calf given to the depositary as gratuity for the new year' (fol. 103r).

Vecchio', but at the same time purchased with his company important shares in the '*Nuovo*'. From the approximately 650 ducats of March-June 1543, he reached over 2,600 in July-August and almost 11,000 in September-October, to then drop again to approximately 3,160 at the end of the year.[71] These large oscillations were presumably, as has been mentioned, due to various business transactions with the Apostolic Chamber. In total, the available data allow us to estimate at about 608 ducats the profit of Olivieri and his company in the two-year period: approximately 302 ducats were the interests, 306 were his recompense as depositary. The following year, however, Benvenuto was still owed a 'notable sum'.[72]

The bonds of the *Monte*, as mentioned, were at times also used to appease or repay creditors of the Chamber, who obtained thus a guarantee for the money loaned or a repayment in shares of the public debt. In 1543, for example, being in debt to the contract-holders of the customs of Rome of the period 1538-42 (the companies of Giulio and Lorenzo Strozzi, Salvestro da Montauto and Luca Giustiniani), the Apostolic Chamber transferred to them 8,000 ducats of shares of the *Monte della Fede*, of which they could enjoy the revenue.[73] In May 1545 the Cavalcanti-Giraldi, Olivieri and Olgiatto companies became creditors of the *Monte della Fede* for 12,983 *scudi* (1/3 each), very probably as a guarantee of a loan; their rights to foreclose on the bonds were also established. On 20 July 1546, by a Chamber mandate, Olivieri paid 1,500 *scudi d'oro in oro* to Girolamo Ubaldini and 4,000 to Baldassarre Olgiatto, to whom the Chamber was in debt; in exchange he himself became creditor of the *Monte della Fede* for 5,500 *scudi*.[74]

The Strozzi company was succeeded by Benvenuto Olivieri & Partners, which maintained the Depositary of the *Monte della Fede* until Benvenuto's death (September 1549), and was succeeded in turn by the Montauto until 1571 and then by the Altoviti.[75] All Florentines, therefore, for a *Monte* that was born thanks to a Florentine pope.

Olivieri did not limit himself to working only in Rome, but also expanded into other territories of the Papal State: Bologna and the Romagna were the areas to which he dedicated the most attention and this was true for the Treasury (see Chapter 6, pp. 137-141), for the salt tax (Chapter 7, pp. 150-153), for the Triennial Subsidy (Chapter 7, p.160), for various other taxes (Chapter 3, pp. 82-94) and also for the *Monti*.

Between December 1542 and January 1543 Benedetto Busini and Benvenuto Olivieri, paying respectively 1,600 and 1,400 *scudi d'oro in oro*, purchased 30 bonds

71 ASF, Galli Tassi 1841, fols 67v, 76r, 84r, 94r, 104r. The last share remained unchanged also at the beginning of the following year (Galli Tassi 1839, fasc. 5, fol. 7r), dropping only very slightly between March and April (Galli Tassi 1953, fol. 199gr).

72 ASF, Galli Tassi 2074, fol. 3.

73 ASF, Galli Tassi 1864, fasc. 2. The revenue from 1 February to 31 August 1543 came to 336 ducats (Galli Tassi 1835, fasc. 1, fol. 9).

74 ASF, Galli Tassi 1837, fols 8, 11.

75 ASF, Galli Tassi 2074, fol. 2; this *filza* contains several documents addressed to the depositaries of the *Monte della Fede* from 1539 to 1549. Relative to the bonds of the *Monte* there is also a journal of Benvenuto Olivieri & Partners of 1549 (Galli Tassi 1933, fols 1r-11r).

of the *Monte del Dazio del Vino* of Bologna, previously the property of Ercole Cessa.[76] On 21 September 1548 Benvenuto put the bonds he still held in this *Monte* for 200 *scudi d'oro* in the name of his daughter Ginevra;[77] on 16 July 1552 she received revenue for 133 *lire di moneta bolognese*, equivalent to almost 18 *scudi d'oro*.[78]

On 27 July 1543 the company of Benvenuto Olivieri loaned 6,000 *scudi di moneta* to the Apostolic Chamber to be reimbursed in eight months or a year; in exchange it was given 8,000 *scudi* in bonds of the *Monte della Concordia* (on 6,000 of which they could collect the revenue) and a premium of 480 *scudi*.[79] These are probably part of those bonds of the *Monte della Concordia* that Benvenuto Olivieri and his company sold, for a total of 11,542 *scudi*, with individual shares varying between 90 and 2,500 *scudi*, between 28 July and 20 October 1543.[80] This means that it is likely that they were also depositaries of this *Monte*, or that at least they had acquired a large stock that they then administered, as is demonstrated by the numerous sums that were 'made good' to them in this period.[81]

Benvenuto's daughter, Ginevra, possessed a number of shares not only in the *Monte del Dazio del Vino*, but also in the above-mentioned *Monte della Concordia*: on 23 February 1553 she received proceeds for 217 *lire di moneta bolognese*, equal to approximately 29 *scudi d'oro*.[82] In 1555 Ginevra was paid a dividend of 146 *lire*.[83] Presumably she owned this share since 21 September 1548, when Olivieri consigned 294 ducats and 1 *lira di moneta bolognese a giuli* 10 per ducat to Busini, in order that these be invested in the *Monte della Concordia* in the name of his daughter.[84] It is

---

76 ASF, Galli Tassi 1837, fol. 7. This *Monte* was erected with 250 bonds of 100 ducats each on 5 November 1526 by Clement VII, again '*pro fidei defensione*' (Monaco, 'Il primo debito pubblico': 569; M. Carboni, *Il debito della città. Mercato del credito, fisco e società a Bologna fra Cinque e Seicento* (Bologna, 1995), p. 92). The Medici pope, therefore, founded both the *Monte* of Rome (with 200,000 ducats and 15,000 of assignment) and of Bologna (with 25,000 and 2,000 of assignment). Paul III increased both of them: the first by 280,000 (and 21,000 of assignment), the second by 10,000 (and 800): see ASF, Galli Tassi 1954, fol. 36r.

77 ASF, *Notarile Antecosimiano 15122*, fols 6r-7v.

78 ASF, Galli Tassi 1822, fol. 119. It is not known with any certainty over what period of time these proceeds matured: it is probable that they were relative to a year, with a consequent profit of 9%, in line with all the other *Monti*, the interests on which were almost always between 7.5 and 10%.

79 ASF, Galli Tassi 2074, fasc. 4. The *Monte della Concordia* was instituted as *francabile* (it could therefore be retracted) in 1542 with the usual aim of the defence of the Papal State, a capital of 52,395 gold ducats and an interest of 8%; it would then be made perpetual in 1587, with a capital increased to 70,000 ducats and an interest lowered to 6% (Carboni, *Il debito della città*, p. 87).

80 ASF, Galli Tassi 1824, fol. 23.

81 ASF, Galli Tassi 1953, fol. 137.

82 ASF, Galli Tassi 1822, fol. 119.

83 Carboni, *Il debito della città*, p. 208. If it is true that the annual interest amounted to 8% (ibid., p. 87), then the share held in 1555 by Olivieri's daughter must have amounted to 1,825 *lire*, or, in other words, about 244 *scudi d'oro*.

84 ASF, *Notarile Antecosimiano 15122*, fols 5r-6r.

also possible that this sum included the 158 gold cameral ducats that Benvenuto had bought for his daughter from Cornelio Malvasia on 10 December 1548.[85]

At the end of the 1540s other creditors of this *Monte* were Benedetto Busini (perhaps on behalf of the Olivieri company) for 5,000 ducats, the Genoese Tobia Pallavicini for 3,342, and the Florentines Cavalcanti and Giraldi for 2,451.[86]

Little space has been dedicated here to a general discussion on the *Monti* in Rome for two reasons: first, much has already been written on this subject in the literature, and, second, at the time in which the Olivieri company was active there the recourse to the public debt had not yet assumed overwhelming importance in Rome. In fact Paul III was extremely cautious in his use of the method of public loans[87] and it was only from the mid-sixteenth century that the popes wholeheartedly adopted this system.[88]

The papal bankers, as we have seen, acted as intermediaries and placed the bonds of the public debt with a large number of small investors, speculating on the difference between the price of purchase and price of sale; this fact, among others, contributed to bind them even more tightly with the papacy. In the Papal State, where the most active speculators came from outside Rome, the main beneficiaries of the redistribution of wealth through the public debt were not Romans. Therefore, while elsewhere (for example in Venice) it was the local ruling classes who became richer, in the Papal State it was the merchant-bankers from the northern Italian cities.[89]

85 ASF, Galli Tassi 1918, fol. 19.

86 ASF, Galli Tassi 1839, fol. 4.

87 In addition to increasing the *Monte della Fede* twice, Paul III instituted only a *Monte vacabile*, which for a year from the initial date (1548) would, however, be *non vacabile*: the *Monte di S. Spirito*, with a capital of 77,000 ducats and an annual revenue of 9,240 (F. Piola Caselli, 'La disciplina amministrativa ed il trattamento fiscale dei luoghi di monte della Camera apostolica tra il XVI ed il XVII secolo', in *Historia economica y de las instituciones financieras en Europa. Trabajos en homenaje a Ferran Valls I Taberner* (Barcelona, 1989), vol. XII, p. 3538; ASF, Galli Tassi 1954, fol. 36v).

88 '*Les Papes se convertirent définitivement au système des monti*' (Delumeau, *Vie économique et sociale*, II, p. 784).

89 Palermo, 'Ricchezza privata e debito pubblico': 310-311.

CHAPTER 5

The Customs of Rome

It might seem a strange decision to discuss the customs of Rome here, rather than in Chapter 7, which deals with the other indirect taxes characterizing the papal finances. While this choice is certainly debatable, it has been made because the administration of the customs was of immense importance and held a central position in the relations between the *mercatores* and the Apostolic Chamber. For the latter the revenues originating from the customs constituted one of their main sources of income; moreover, a large part of it served to pay the annuities of the venal offices or of the bonds of the public debt (discussed in Chapter 4). For the merchant-bankers, on the other hand, this contract represented a notable financial effort, and, in fact, to be able to deal with it they used those techniques and mechanisms that can be considered 'exemplary' for their administration of contracts in general.

Although the period we are mainly interested in here is the sixteenth century, the following brief introduction will concentrate primarily on the fifteenth century. This is because the absolute lack of customs records relative to the sixteenth century has meant that the studies in this subject are limited to the earlier periods, about which, on the contrary, the archives of Rome are rich in information.

1. Ripa and Ripetta, Terra and Grascia

A system of custom duties on the import or export of merchandises, or on their trade, came into being in the last three decades of the twelfth century.[1] The administration of the customs, like the other tax revenues of the city,[2] fell under the jurisdiction of the *Camera Urbis*. This body was originally autonomous, but then increasingly came under the influence of the Apostolic Chamber: by halfway through the fifteenth century the proceeds of the customs were in fact deposited in the coffers of the latter body.[3] The increasing influence of the Chamber is also demonstrated by the fact that, while until the end of the fourteenth century the officers assigned to the customs were elected with the same criteria used for the other magistrates of the town, by

1 S. Malatesta (ed.), *Statuti delle gabelle di Roma* (Rome, 1885), p. 23.

2 M.L. Lombardo, *La Camera Urbis. Premesse per uno studio sull'organizzazione amministrativa della città di Roma durante il pontificato di Martino V* (Rome, 1970), p. 39, recalls the contract of the *gabella*, the *dogana minuta*, the *dogana del terzo vino*, the customs of Ripa e Ripetta, the salt monopoly and the salt and hearth (*focatico*) tax.

3 See I. Ait, 'La dogana di Sant'Eustachio nel XV secolo', in *Aspetti della vita economica e culturale a Roma nel Quattrocento* (Rome, 1981), pp. 86-87, for evidence of these changes with regard to the customs of Terra (or of St Eustace).

the first part of the fifteenth century they were generally nominated by papal bull.[4] Between the fifteenth and the sixteenth centuries the post of president of the Ripe (assigned annually to a clerk of the Chamber) was created: this was a legal office that took from the communal authority administrative and judicial powers over the two city ports situated on the Tiber river, Ripagrande and Ripetta.

The collection of the port customs toll had begun to be contracted out to private citizens in the fourteenth century. This system had two advantages for the State: on the one hand, lacking the administrative structures necessary for efficient control and tax collection, by using those of others it was thus able to obtain a larger quantity of money; on the other, there was the guarantee of an immediate large amount of money, which could be used to meet the demands of the city. Moreover, the merchant class thus had direct influence on the port activity, avoiding the necessity for mediation by the city council.[5] In 1369, for example, the toll collection of Ripa was contracted out for a year to three Roman citizens, who paid 820 gold florins for this right.[6] At that time, the tax was 4% of the value of the merchandise unloaded directly in the port of Ripa or which arrived there by land after having been unloaded in any of the ports between Argentario and Circeo. The tax was waived only for the pontiff, the emperor, the cardinals and their functionaries. The contract-holders were protected by the *Curia Capitolii*, to which they had the right to appeal: this right was in fact one of the best guarantees for an efficient provisioning.

Before 1390 a duty was also introduced for the customs of Ripetta, separate from the customs of Ripa. In the statute of 1416 this was laid down as 2.5% of the value of the goods, to be added to the 4% of Ripa for all those goods that, unloaded in the ports between Civitavecchia and Astura, were then transported to the '*portum fluminis Riperomee*', or, in other words, the port of Rome. By the statute of 1463, however, although on paper the denomination '*Ripa et Ripecta*' continued to be used, any real distinction between the two customs seems to have disappeared and a duty of 6.5% was applied to all goods except for wine, which was subject to a separate sliding scale of taxes. By the sixteenth century, perhaps after several adjustments made in the time of Clement VII, the tax imposed by the customs of Ripa had risen to 10.5%.[7] All the imports and exports that were transported via the Tiber river passed through the customs of Ripa and Ripetta; the customs of Ripa, which were situated on the Tiber at the port of Ripa Romea, also imposed import duties on the goods unloaded on the coast between Civitavecchia and Terracina.

The statute of 1416 (*Capitula et Ordinamenta Ripe et Ripecte portus Riperomee Urbis*) placed at the head of the customs a *camerarius*, or chamberlain, who was responsible for administration and security (he also had the powers of an administrative

4 Ait, 'La dogana di Sant'Eustachio', pp. 88-89.

5 L. Palermo, *Il porto di Roma nel XIV e XV secolo. Strutture socio-economiche e statuti* (Rome, 1979), p. 143.

6 M.L. Lombardo, 'La dogana di Ripa e Ripetta nel sistema dell'ordinamento tributario a Roma dal Medio Evo al sec. XV', *Archivi e cultura*, XII (1978): 21-26, 53-56. According to Palermo they were 2,800 florins, but he cites Lombardo as his source (*Il porto di Roma*, p. 145).

7 J. Delumeau, *Vie économique et sociale de Rome dans la seconde moitié du XVI*e *siècle* (2 vols, Paris, 1957-59), I, p. 129.

judge, with the ability to make quick decisions in order to guarantee that trade was able to be carried out smoothly). When a private citizen won the contract, he obtained the powers of collection, but remained nevertheless subordinate to the statutory rules. The increasing amount of traffic both to and from Rome made it necessary to reorganize the administration of the customs. This reorganization was also carried out in order to increase the economic power of the popes, who were constantly searching for fresh sources of income (the revenues of Ripa in fact ended up in the coffers of the Apostolic Chamber). Thus, the statute of 1463 included the figure of the *doganiere*. This figure was actually created half a century before, in 1416, but his function in 1463 was quite different from that of the earlier customs officer: his responsibilities now included keeping the books and calculating and collecting the taxes, or, in other words, dealing with all the financial operations. The *camerarius* maintained the jurisdictional and security functions: these duties clearly were of far greater importance when the customs officer was not a salaried functionary, but a private contract-holder who might have had illegitimate or exorbitant pretensions. A last office, existing from at least 1445, was the *castellano* (lord of the castle) of Ostia, who was employed by the Apostolic Chamber to ensure the security of the merchandise passing through the customs.

The merchandise that was most frequently unloaded in the port of Rome was Latin, Corsican or Greek wine (in decreasing order of quantity and increasing order of price), the quantity of which increased enormously in the holy years.[8]

It can be assumed that the boats coming from the upriver areas probably – at least in the sixteenth century – docked at the customs house of the Grascia, situated on the Tiber river between Via della Scrofa and the new Via di Ripetta. This establishment included the customs of Ripetta (which must at this time have been considered separately from the customs of Ripa) and three small complementary customs: Pescaria, Borgo and Camigliano.[9]

All goods which were transported by land – whether directed to Rome or in transit – passed through the customs of Merci or Terra (also known as St Eustace, because of its vicinity to the church of the same name), the only exceptions being basic foodstuffs such as wine and cereals. The tax rate was initially 5% of the value of the merchandise; in the first decades of the sixteenth century, however, it rose to 7.5%.[10] Unfortunately, it is difficult to calculate the total amount of imports as this customs,

8 For further information on the impact of the holy year on the imports, see, for example: I. Ait-A. Esch, 'Aspettando l'Anno Santo. Fornitura di vino e gestione di taverne nella Roma del 1475', *Quellen und Forschungen aus italienischen Archiven und Bibliotheken*, 73 (1993): 387-417; A. Esch, 'Im heiligen Jahr am römischen Zoll. Importe nach Rom um 1475', in J. Helmrath-H. Muller-H. Wolff (eds), *Studien zum 15. Jahrhundert. Festschrift für Erich Meuthen* (2 vols, Munich, 1994), II, pp. 869-901; A. Esch, 'Roma come centro d'importazioni nella seconda metà del Quattrocento ed il peso economico del Papato', in S. Gensini (ed.), *Roma capitale (1447-1527)*, Atti del IV Convegno di studio del Centro Studi sulla Civiltà del tardo Medioevo, San Miniato (Pisa) 27-31 October 1992 (Pisa, 1994), pp. 107-143 (especially pp. 122-143).

9 P. Pecchiai, *Roma nel Cinquecento*, Storia di Roma, vol. XIII (Bologna, 1948), p. 274; Delumeau, *Vie économique et sociale*, I, p. 127.

10 Delumeau, *Vie économique et sociale*, I, p. 129.

unlike the customs of Ripa, did not keep a record of the goods '*in franchigia*' (that is, those exempt from taxes because they were destined for the pope, the clergy and other members of the ruling classes).[11] For both the customs, official values were generally inferior to market values.[12] The statutes that regulated the transport of the merchandise over land can be traced back to 1398. The goods that passed through these customs came above all from areas close to the city: the poor state of the roads and the consequent high cost of transport discouraged long journeys over land and made the journey by water preferable for goods of low value.[13]

Interestingly, the records show that there were very few goods leaving or in transit through Rome. For both the port customs and for that of Terra, consumer goods or finished products dominated over primary or unfinished products, proof that fifteenth-century Rome had a poorly developed industrial sector.[14]

Almost from the beginning, the administration of the revenues and expenditure of the customs were farmed out to private citizens. In general, in order to obtain this right, the contract-holders paid a fixed annual sum to the Apostolic Chamber. Moreover, they often made an advance loan of a further sum, which would be gradually reimbursed to them with interest over the time they held the contract, until the debt was completely extinguished on the final date.

As mentioned, the customs registers referring to the sixteenth century have, unfortunately, been lost. A certain amount of information has been traced by various historians, but this is necessarily fragmentary. Our overall knowledge of the period is therefore enriched by the discovery of the Fondo Galli Tassi, even though it too is incomplete and refers to a limited number of years.

As early as 1516 the customs, or at least the customs of Ripa, were in Tuscan hands. In 1518 Pandolfo Della Casa (with a 20% share), Francesco Della Fonte (23.3%), the heir of Alessio Boccamassi (23.3%) and Baldassarre and the heir of Giovanni Balducci (33.3%) earned profits which amounted to the substantial sum of 7,770 gold cameral ducats.[15] Subsequently, until 30 June 1526, it was Bartolomeo Della Valle & Partners who administered the customs, for an annual figure of 58,600 gold cameral ducats.[16] In 1528 the contract was awarded to the Roman banker Ciriaco Mattei, to the Genoese banker Sebastiano Sauli and to Bernardo Bracci, who in return paid 36,000 *scudi* per annum.[17]

---

11 Esch, 'Roma come centro d'importazioni', p. 114.

12 A. Esch shows how marked these differences were above all for textiles, while for the other goods it rarely reached 15% ('Le importazioni nella Roma del primo Rinascimento', in *Aspetti della vita economica e culturale*, pp. 64-66).

13 Ait, 'La dogana di Sant'Eustachio', p. 92.

14 Esch, 'Roma come centro d'importazioni', p. 128. By the same author there is an interesting study specifically on art objects: 'Roman Customs Registers 1470-80: items of interest to historians of art and material culture', *Journal of the Warburg and Courtauld Institutes*, 58 (1995): 72-87.

15 ASF, *Eredità Lemmo Balducci*, 74, fol. 159.

16 M. Monaco, *La situazione della Reverenda Camera Apostolica nell'anno 1525. Ricerche d'archivio (Un contributo alla storia delle finanze pontificie)* (Rome, 1960), p. 77.

17 ASF, Galli Tassi 1843, fol. 8.

2. The contracts of 1530-1533 and of 1534-1537

In 1530 the customs of Rome were farmed out to three illustrious bankers: the Florentines, Filippo Strozzi and Bindo Altoviti, and the Roman, Ciriaco Mattei. Benvenuto Olivieri, at that time a partner in the Altoviti company, took part in the contract under its name with a 5% share. For the four years of the duration of the contract, the sum loaned by the *mercatores* amounted to 40,000 gold cameral ducats per annum, 2,000 of which were supplied by Olivieri. The first year, the contract-holders made a profit of 9,129 ducats: proportionally, Olivieri was therefore entitled to 456 ducats.[18]

There is no precise information available with regard to the period 1534-1537, although it can be assumed that the customs continued to be administered by other Florentine bankers. In 1537, and therefore presumably for the entire four-year period, the contract was held for 1/3 by Francesco Del Nero and for 2/3 by Ciriaco da Montauto.[19] In the meantime, as we know, Benvenuto had left Bindo Altoviti and had become partner of Filippo Strozzi, in a company registered first in the name of Strozzi himself, and then of the latter's sons, Giulio and Lorenzo.

3. The contract of 1538-1542

From 1 January 1538 the customs were administered by the company of the Genoese banker Girolamo Sauli, together with the company of Giulio and Lorenzo Strozzi, who took part '*in personam domini Benvenuti Oliverii eorum institoris*'. The contract envisaged a duration of five years, for a sum of 48,000 gold cameral ducats per annum, as well as a loan of 40,000 ducats to the Apostolic Chamber, which would be paid back during the period of the contract, with an annual interest of 12%.[20] On 24 September 1538 it was established that on the following 15 October the first part of the loan – 20,000 ducats – would be deposited, 12,000 by Girolamo Sauli and 8,000 by the Strozzi company. As a guarantee, the contracting bankers received the following objects in pledge: a 13-carat diamond ring (worth 15,000 gold ducats); a large ruby ring (worth 4,000 ducats); a diamond ring '*a faccetta in garbo di barca*' (worth 3,000 ducats). The total value of these jewels therefore came to 22,000 gold ducats.[21] The request for the remaining 20,000 ducats was made by a mandate from the Apostolic Chamber to the *doganieri* on 11 May 1541.[22]

Often the contracts with the Apostolic Chamber were signed officially only by two or three bankers. Subsequently, however, these bankers would often sell a part of their shares to other bankers, who in turn might divide these shares even

18 ASF, Galli Tassi 1914, fol. 174. It is probable that the Genoese banker Sebastiano Sauli, who had already held the post of *doganiere* in the past, also had a share in the contract (Galli Tassi 1843, fol. 8).

19 ASF, Galli Tassi 1952, fol. 117.

20 ASF, Galli Tassi 1833, fasc. 11, fol. 1r; Galli Tassi 1831, fol. 8; Galli Tassi 1977, fol. 79. For more details on this type of combined loan operation, see the Introduction, pp. xxiv-xxv.

21 ASF, Galli Tassi 1831, fol. 8; AASGF, vol. 393, fols 3r-8r.

22 ASR, Camerale I, *Mandati Camerali 872*, fol. 116r-v.

further. In other words, the participations did not necessarily remain invariable; on the contrary, more often than not the number of participants increased several times throughout the duration of a single contract. It is not surprising, therefore, that during this particular contract Sauli and Strozzi transferred fractions of their shares to other bankers. Although the division is not clear, it is however certain that the company of Luca Giustiniani, Genoese, also became involved (as assignee of Girolamo Sauli), as did the company of Salvestro da Montauto, Florentine.[23] Another certainty is that the Strozzi company transferred a 2.5% share to Bartolomeo Angiolini, governor of the customs of Terra. On the death of the latter, on 14 August 1541, Girolamo Ubaldini took over this role. For the profits of the period from that date to 31 December 1542, Ubaldini received 672 *scudi d'oro in oro*.[24] This sum can be attributed to a share of 2.5% for a period of sixteen and a half months: the same share in a year therefore earned 489 *scudi*. If this is true, then the profits distributed in the period amounted to the substantial sum of approximately 19,550 *scudi* per annum; in a period of five years, this would therefore mean almost 100,000 *scudi*, that is a profit of 35.7%, calculating that the investment (anticipation plus loan) was of 280,000 *scudi*.

According to the sources, the shares of the contract in the name of Giulio and Lorenzo Strozzi, Luca Giustiniani and Salvestro da Montauto must have been as follows:[25]

Luca Giustiniani & Partners	38.75%
Giulio and Lorenzo Strozzi & Partners	21.25%
Salvestro da Montauto & Partners	17.50%
Luigi Rucellai & Partners or heirs of Della Casa & Partners	12.50%
Giovan Battista Puccini	7.50%
Bartolomeo Angiolini (followed by Girolamo Ubaldini)	2.50%

23 ASF, Galli Tassi 1833, fasc. 11. In ASR, Camerale I, *Mandati Camerali 872*, fols 59v, 116r-v, the companies of Giulio and Lorenzo Strozzi, Luca Giustiniani, Salvestro da Montauto are referred to as modern *doganieri* '*dohanarum ac gabellarum grassie ac ripe et ripette alme urbis*', as early as 1539.

24 ASF, Galli Tassi 1832, fol. 8.

25 ASF, Galli Tassi 1921, fol. 47; Galli Tassi 1825, fol. 4r; Galli Tassi 1942, fol. 196r; Galli Tassi 1952, fol. 55. This information is taken from documents of the Strozzi family, shareholders with 55%; of the 45% belonging to Giustiniani it is known only that 6.25% belonged to Puccini, who, moreover, already owned shares for 1.25% under the Strozzi. In 1543 the *doganieri*, still owed money by the Chamber, received 8,000 ducats in bonds of the *Monte della Fede*, which sum was divided in the following proportions: Della Casa 1,800 (500 for L. Giustiniani, 1,300 for the Strozzi) = 22.5%; Strozzi 1,620 = 20.25%; Bastiano da Montauto 1,580 (1,100 for S. da Montauto himself, 480 for S. da Montauto & Partners) = 19.75%; Benvenuto Olivieri 930 (for the Strozzi) = 11.63%; Bandinello and Giorgio Sauli 700 (for L. Giustiniani) = 8.75%; Giovan Battista Puccini 650 (for L. Giustiniani) = 8.12%; Giovanni Berlinghieri(?) 480 (for S. da Montauto) = 6%; Luigi Del Riccio 240 (for S. da Montauto) = 3%. Clearly further changes had been made, most probably as a result of the continual paying off of debts and granting of loans by one banker to another: Galli Tassi 1864, fasc. 2.

In the company of Giulio and Lorenzo Strozzi, Olivieri was partner with a share of 20.83%; consequently, if the share of the Strozzi in the contract was of 21.25%, Olivieri must have received profits for a share of approximately 4.4%. This would have meant for him, in the entire duration of the contract, a profit of 4,400 *scudi d'oro*. As mentioned (Chapter 2, p. 50), however, the company of Giulio and Lorenzo Strozzi was terminated on 18 December 1538 and the accounts balanced on the following 16 April; on 1 July the company of Benvenuto Olivieri came into being. It is unfortunately not known how, in these circumstances, the contract was dealt with.

As usually happened (and this will be examined in more detail later on), the revenues of the customs were then distributed to Colleges or individuals that had rights over them: for example, the Colleges of the knights of St Peter, of the knights of St Paul, of the *Monte della Fede* and of the clerks of the Chamber had assignments on the income of the customs; also various individuals, amongst whom stood out the Reverend Alessandro Guidicciono, *maestro di casa* (house steward) of Paul III, responsible for the expenses of the *familia*.[26]

4. The contract of 1543-1549

The contract of 1543 was awarded to the companies of Benvenuto Olivieri and of Bastiano da Montauto, who divided it in half. The customs charges were 3% on Ripa and 2% on Merci.[27] The contract, signed on 3 May 1541, envisaged a duration of seven years on payment of 73,000 *scudi di giuli 10 per scudo* per annum. At the moment of the stipulation of the contract a loan of 10,000 *scudi* (free of interest until 1 January 1543 and then at 12%) was made to the pope, through the depositary general – who at the time was Benvenuto Olivieri – and a further loan of 2,000 *scudi* to Monsignor Sebastiano d'Ancona (vice-chamberlain and president of the clerks of the Chamber), free of interest, but to be reimbursed at the end of the first year of administration.[28]

Moreover, at the beginning of the farm (1 January 1543), the previous *doganieri* were paid 40,000 *scudi* with the agreement that this sum would be repaid to the new contract-holders together with the above-mentioned 10,000 in seven years, at an interest rate of 12% per annum, according to a plan that provided for the reimbursement of one-seventh every year, plus the interest calculated each time on the remainder. Benvenuto Olivieri had therefore to pay 10,000 *scudi* to Giulio and Lorenzo Strozzi and 10,000 to Salvestro da Montauto; Bastiano da Montauto, correspondingly, had to pay an analogous sum to Luca Giustiniani. The reason, as is specified, was '*anticipata solutione eadem Camera tempore appaltus eorum predicti exbursatarum*'; or, in other words, a kind of 'golden handshake'. At the same time, however, the new contract-holders must have received from the former *doganieri* the jewels given in pledge, which, as mentioned above, consisted in rings with rubies and diamonds, for a total

---

26 ASF, Galli Tassi 1833, fasc. 11, fols 4r-6r; ASR, Camerale I, *Mandati Camerali 872*, fols 59v, 79v, 116r-v; *Mandati Camerali 874*, fols 60v-61r.

27 This perhaps refers to the goods '*in franchigia*' (toll-free), on which, at least in this period, a customs duty had to be paid, albeit reduced: 3% instead of the 10.5% on Ripa; 2% instead of the 7.5% elsewhere (Delumeau, *Vie économique et sociale*, I, p. 129).

28 ASF, Galli Tassi 1832, fasc. 5; ASR, Camerale I, *Mandati camerali 874*, fol. 26r.

value of 22,000 *scudi*.[29] Moreover, the new contract-holders were obliged to repay to the previous ones the credits they were owed by the Chamber; this sum would be deducted from the sum of 73,000 *scudi* that they had to pay for the first year. If, after the first year, the entire amount had not been repaid, the Chamber would owe the current contract-holders 12% interest on the remainder.[30]

In this case, therefore, there were two connected operations: the price paid for the farm, the profits of which came from the difference between actual and presumed income (the 73,000 *scudi* paid annually); and an actual loan, to be repaid with interest from the revenue of the customs themselves.

Therefore, the total loan was 52,000 *scudi*: the 2,000 conceded to the president of the clerks of the Chamber would be repaid within the first year; the remaining 50,000 according to the following plan (Table 10) that provided for an annual reimbursement of approximately 7,143 *scudi* and of the interest on the remaining amount. In the seven years this interest came to a total of 24,000 *scudi*.

Table 10 – Repayment of loan and interest (1 January 1543-31 December 1549); in *scudi di moneta*

1543	Annual repayment	7142.17. 1
	Interest on 50000	6000
	To the clerks of the Chamber	2000
	TOTAL	15142.17. 1
1544	Annual repayment	7142.17. 1
	Interest on 42857.2.11	5142.17
	TOTAL	12285.14. 1
1545	Annual repayment	7142.17. 1
	Interest on 35714.5.10	4285.13
	TOTAL	11428.10. 1
1546	Annual repayment	7142.17. 1
	Interest on 28571.8.9	3428. 6
	TOTAL	10571. 3. 1
1547	Annual repayment	7142.17. 1

29 In addition they must have received other jewels, if it is true that in 1543 Bastiano da Montauto had in his possession jewels worth some 14,000 *scudi* as a pledge for half of the amount (ASF, Galli Tassi 1832, ins. 6). The consignment of the jewels from the old to the new *doganieri* is also mentioned in ASR, *Notai segretari e cancellieri della R. Camera apostolica 1988*, fols 1r-2r.

30 ASR, Camerale I, *Mandati camerali 874*, fols 105v-106v; ASV, *Cam. Ap., Div. Cam. 127*, fol. 156r-v. See also ASF, Galli Tassi 1947, fol. 469. In Galli Tassi 1834, fols 1r-4v these figures are inserted in the accounts of the first year of administration.

	Interest on 21428.11.8	2571. 7
	TOTAL	9714. 4. 1
1548	Annual repayment	7142.17. 1
	Interest on 14285.14.7	1714. 5
	TOTAL	8857. 2. 1
1549	Annual repayment	7142.17. 1
	Interest on 7142.17.6	857. 2.11
	TOTAL	8000

Source: ASF, Galli Tassi 1832, ins. 4

From the share of Bastiano da Montauto, 15% went to the company of his brother Salvestro (agreement dated 21 February 1542). For this share the latter paid 7,800 *scudi*: 1,800 at the moment of the payment of the 12,000 *scudi* to the pope and to the president of the clerks of the Chamber; 6,000 at the moment the 40,000 were deposited, at the beginning of the administration. Salvestro's share was in turn divided between himself (2/5 = 6%), Giovanni Berlinghieri (2/5 = 6%) and Luigi Del Riccio (1/5 = 3%). On the death of Salvestro, as shown by a declaration signed by Bastiano on 5 October 1543, the latter was given his brother's share, while the others continued to have the right to receive the profits in proportion to their participation.[31] The Ubaldini company then took over Luigi Del Riccio's share, Giovanni Berlinghieri sold all his share to Roberto Strozzi, and Bastiano da Montauto 5% (part of his share) to the heirs of Alessandro Deti.[32] Lastly, from at least 1544 Agostino Del Nero obtained a share of 10% under the name of Montauto.[33]

At this point, Bastiano had a 26% share; by 1548, however, his share was reduced to 10%, but virtually nothing is known of how the rest was distributed.[34] The situation regarding his half can therefore be laid out as follows:

Unknown persons behind Bastiano da Montauto & Partners	16%
Bastiano da Montauto & Partners	10%
Agostino Del Nero & Partners	10%
Roberto Strozzi	6%
Heirs of Alessandro Deti & Partners	5%
Ubaldini & Partners	3%

31 ASF, Galli Tassi 1832, fasc. 6.

32 ASF, Galli Tassi 1921, fol. 42.

33 ASF, Galli Tassi 1833, fol. 9.

34 ASF, Galli Tassi 1833, fol. 4. An unspecified share, but certainly less than 5%, belonged to Antonio Del Riccio (Galli Tassi 1951, fols 109, 176).

With regard to the half in the hands of the Olivieri company, the situation was initially as follows:[35]

Benvenuto Olivieri & Partners	12.5%
Luca Giustiniani & Partners	12.5%
Tommaso Cavalcanti and Giovanni Giraldi & Partners	12.5%
Alessandro and Giovan Battista Del Bene & Partners	7.5%
Ciriaco Mattei and sons	5.0%

However, the Olivieri conveyed most of their share (10%) to Antonio Covoni & Partners, to whom they were in debt (but of whom they were also partners, see Chapter 2, pp. 59-60): the conveyance took place in two instalments, of 2.5% (on 4 April 1543) and of 7.5% (on 5 July 1543), for a total of 5,200 *scudi di moneta*. For the following three years Benvenuto Olivieri continued to hold 2.5%. In 1547 he conveyed a 1% share to Simone Guiducci, thus leaving his company with a 1.5% share.[36] However, as shown below, Olivieri must, in the same year, have come back into possession of part of this.

In the meantime, on 22 June 1542, Alessandro and Giovan Battista Del Bene had sold a third of their share (2.5%) to Girolamo Ubaldini for 1,500 *scudi*.[37] To arrive at the situation laid out below, relative to 1547, there must also have been other transactions, which however can only be guessed at, as no records have come down to us: the remaining 5% of the Del Bene company was probably conveyed to Antonio Covoni, who, however, must have in turn transferred it to Agostino Del Nero;[38] of the 10% remaining in Covoni's possession, 2.9% must have been transferred to Mariotto Guiducci and a further 2.9% to Benvenuto Olivieri, who perhaps had extinguished all or a part of his debt with Covoni (who remained a participant on his own and no longer as a company), to whom years before he had transferred a share of his own participation as guarantee. To sum up, in the fifth year (1547) the participants under the name of the Olivieri company held shares divided thus:[39]

Tobia Pallavicini and Luca Giustiniani & Partners	12.5%
Tommaso Cavalcanti and Giovanni Giraldi & Partners	12.5%
Agostino Del Nero & Partners	5.0%
Ciriaco Mattei and sons	5.0%
Benvenuto Olivieri & Partners	4.4%

35 ASF, Galli Tassi 2278, fols 102-103. Galli Tassi 1942, fol. 194r provides slightly different figures, attributing to the Del Bene company 6.25% and to the Olivieri company 13.75% (but this refers to a period preceding the beginning of the contract: the situation might therefore subsequently have changed). See Galli Tassi 1833, fol. 10 for the contract detailing the participation of the Cavalcanti and Giraldi company in the customs of Rome, under the name of Benvenuto Olivieri (30 May 1541).

36 ASF, Galli Tassi 1833, fol. 3; Galli Tassi 2278, fols 312, 339.

37 ASF, Galli Tassi 2278, fols 296, 337.

38 ASF, Galli Tassi 1833, fol. 9: this is an account of Del Nero, shareholder of 5% on the 15% of Covoni, from 1544 to 1552. See also Galli Tassi 1952, fol. 9.

39 ASF, Galli Tassi 1832, fasc. 5; Galli Tassi 1921, fol. 42; Galli Tassi 1952, fol. 207.

Antonio Covoni	4.2%
Mariotto Guiducci under Strozzi's name	2.9%
Ubaldini & Partners	2.5%
Simone Guiducci	1.0%

It has been said that the price paid by the *doganieri* for the customs was in practice an advance to the Apostolic Chamber of the presumed revenue for every year. These enormous sums of money generally had a fixed destination, serving for the most part to pay the interests on the public debt or the annuities on the venal offices (items that, as seen in Chapter 4, can in practice be assimilated). The situation is laid out in Table 11, which shows an account of the two *doganieri* of Rome: the *Dare* side includes the price paid for the customs (or, it could be said, the presumed income) and other minor items; the *Avere* side, the destinations of these sums of money. The assignments that the Colleges of the knights of St Paul, of the knights of St Peter and of the *Monte della Fede* had on the revenue of the customs were very substantial. Another item that stands out, as has already been mentioned, is that concerning the repayment of the loan that the contract-holders had made to the Chamber at the beginning of their administration; in addition there are the sums necessary for the payment of the interests, even though these are not complete here except for the first year (cf. Table 10). The final item that should be highlighted concerns the *gabella dei contratti* from 1544 on: the original agreement established that it should be considered together with the three customs; but, from the second year of their administration, Olivieri and Montauto accepted that it '*separatim exigi et exercere possit*', in exchange for an annual indemnity of 1,000 *scudi*.[40]

Table 11 – Account of Bastiano da Montauto and Benvenuto Olivieri *doganieri* (1543-49), in *scudi di moneta*, rounded to the nearest *scudo*

DARE: Expected revenues of the three customs							
	1543	**1544**	**1545**	**1546**	**1547**	**1548**	**1549**
Price of the three customs	73,000	73,000	73,000	73,000	73,000	73,000	73,000
Frauds	82	80	80	80	80	80	80
1,422 butts (*botti*) '*date mancho*'	1,422						
Remainder of first year (incl. interest)		4,400					
DARE - AVERE (previous year)			5,293	8,593	13,076	16,045	22,118
Interest on *scudi* 1,569					186		
'*Cambi*'						1,602	2,490

40 ASR, *Notai segretari e cancellieri della R. Camera apostolica 1988*, fol 209v. The *gabella dei contratti* will be treated further in Chapter 7, p. 157.

AVERE: Destination of the expected revenues							
	1543	**1544**	**1545**	**1546**	**1547**	**1548**	**1549**
College of the knights of St Peter	8,000	8,000	8,000	8,000	8,000	8,000	8,000
College of the knights of St Paul	14,600	14,600	14,600	14,600	14,600	14,600	14,600
College of the *Monte della Fede*	33,000	36,000	36,000	36,000	36,000	36,000	36,000
President of the clerks of the Chamber	2,000						
Maestro di casa (3% on the wine)	150	465	723	442	783	996	2,777
G. Laverolo, warden of the gates	105	60	60	60	60	60	60
Gabella dei contratti		1,000	1,000	1,000	3,128	1,000	3,673
Clerks of the Chamber and others		264	264	264	264	264	264
Bastiano d'Ancona, vice-chamberlain	2,000						
Earl Anguillara (for iron)			55	33	17	48	70
Fabbrica of St Peter's		573					
Monastery of Conv‹…›te (for wine)	40	40	40				
Referendari (their exemptions)		36	56	40	114	142	127
Annual repayment	7,143	7,143	7,143	7,143	7,143	7,143	7,143
Interest (12% per annum)	6,000	3,757	1,669	897			
Hospital of Consolazione (butts)	40	40	40	40	40	40	40
Castellano (butts)	27	209	131	83	109	240	189
Hospital of the Holy Spirit (butts)					40	40	
Hospital of St James (butts)						37	83
G.A. Perini for Ap. Chamber							500
'*Quello possiamo domandare*'							800
Others							111
DARE - *AVERE* (*Dare* the following year)		5,293	8,593	13,078	16,045	[22,118]	23,254

Source: ASF, Galli Tassi 1947, fols 469v-476r

So far only presumed income has been spoken of. Now, however, actual income will be discussed in order to be able to calculate the profit made by the contract-holders.[41] This was in fact calculated as the difference between the actual income, that is the customs duties collected, and the presumed income, that is the price of the contract established at the time of its stipulation. Generally the calculation was based on the actual figures of the preceding years, and it should be pointed out that the *doganieri* easily managed to exceed this sum; in fact, the customs were considered one of the most profitable business affairs by those bankers who had dealings with the Apostolic Chamber.

In Table 12 the revenues of the three customs for the period 1543-49 are listed in detail. The expenses of 1549 are unfortunately missing in all the documents consulted, but it has been possible to insert estimates by calculating the average of the preceding years.[42] It has thus been possible to give an overall picture, albeit not a perfectly exact one.

Table 12 – Income received by the three customs of Rome (1 January 1543-31 December 1549), in *scudi di moneta*

Year	Customs	Revenues (R)	Frauds +exemptions (F)	(R+F)	Expenses (E)	(R+F) - E
1543	Ripa	29782.17			1334.17	
	Terra	28171.30			692.84	
	Grascia	19404.25			2040.14	
	TOTAL	77357.72	274.00	77631.27	4067.15	73564.57
1544	Ripa	26634.79			1290.00	
	Terra	28936.37			686.75	
	Grascia	23647.43			1850.46	
	TOTAL	79218.59	2477.00	81695.59	3827.21	77868.38
1545	Ripa	26985.47			1286.00	
	Terra	38753.81			756.84	

41 It is interesting to note that in 1543 a request was made to the Chamber for 5,000 *scudi* as compensation for the fact that the pope had been absent from Rome for six months because he had been to Bologna and Busseto to meet Charles V (ASF, Galli Tassi 1834, fol. 4). Clearly the transfer of the papal court meant a large drop in the imports and consequently less income for the *doganieri*.

42 In the first six years there is no correlation between income and expenditure: for this reason the expenditure of 1549 has been calculated without taking into account the enormous increase in income recorded during that year. This increase, which mostly concerned the customs of Ripa and, to a lesser extent, Terra, was caused by the need to import more wine than usual, first because of poor local production and second because of the Jubilee year (ASF, Galli Tassi 1833, fol. 8). The cashiers were: for Ripa, Paolo Ponte; for Terra, Ludovico Deti; and for Grascia, Leonardo Del Caccia.

	Grascia	24607.63			1740.48	
	TOTAL	90346.91	2141.00	92487.91	3783.32	88704.59
1546	Ripa	30792.47			1290.30	
	Terra	33777.84			710.58	
	Grascia	24319.33			1682.32	
	TOTAL	88889.64	1704.00	90593.64	3683.20	86910.44
1547	Ripa	30132.96			1454.18	
	Terra	35175.78			779.25	
	Grascia	23717.52			2004.72	
	TOTAL	89026.26	4527.00	93553.26	4238.15	89315.11
1548	Ripa	34644.93			1382.00	
	Terra	34698.76			737.32	
	Grascia	24340.54			1677.30	
	TOTAL	93684.23	2712.00	96396.23	3796.62	92599.61
1543-48	**TOTAL**	518523.35	13835.00	532358.35	23395.65	508962.70
1549	Ripa	55470.52			?	
	Terra	40222.53			?	
	Grascia	23588.33			?	
	TOTAL	119281.38	7974.00	127255.38	[c. 4000.00]	[123255.38]
1543-49	**TOTAL**	637804.73	21809.00	659613.73	[27395.65]	[632218.08]
1543-49	AVERAGE	91114.96	3155.57	94230.53	3913.66	90316.87

Source: ASF, Galli Tassi 1833, fols 2, 8; Galli Tassi 1921, fol. 18

In the whole period the customs yielded (5th column: revenues + frauds and exemptions) almost 660,000 *scudi*, that is, every year, almost 94,300 *scudi*;[43] subtracting the expenses, there remains a figure close to 90,400 *scudi* per annum. In the calculations made later by the *doganieri* themselves, who had perhaps balanced the accounts, the income of the customs after the expenses had been deducted was approximately 88,000 *scudi*, with an average difference of 15,000 *scudi* a year between the real income and the advance (roughly 20% of the sum originally paid).[44] The revenues were considerably higher in 1549, a pre-Jubilee year, especially as far

43 A Chamber mandate of October 1542 ordered that the revenue coming from the customs be paid by the tax collectors to the depositary general of the Apostolic Chamber (in that year Benvenuto Olivieri) and only subsequently was the latter to credit it to the *doganieri* (ASR, Camerale I, *Mandati Camerali 874*, fol. 85v).

44 ASF, Galli Tassi 1833, fol. 8. The percentage of earnings is in line with that sustained by Delumeau, *Vie économique et sociale*, I, p. 128.

as Ripa was concerned. Overall the customs yielded almost 130,000 *scudi* compared with the average of 89,000 for the six previous years.

In total, therefore, considering all the participants, several calculations can be made regarding the profits:

- the total interests on the loan of 50,000 *scudi* came to 24,000 *scudi*;
- the difference between real income and the price paid came to approximately 105,000 *scudi*;
- the total must therefore have been somewhere in the vicinity of 130,000 *scudi*.

If this sum is compared with the total investment, which is equal to 563,000 *scudi* (the 50,000 of the loan at interest + the 2,000 of the loan without interest + the 511,000 in yearly payments of 73,000 for seven years), the resulting profit is 23.1%.

5. The extension of 1550-1552

From 1 January 1550 to 31 December 1552 the customs was yet again contracted out to Olivieri and Montauto. A Chamber mandate of May 1546 in fact enjoined them to pay more than 21,000 *scudi di paoli 10 per scudo* in order to obtain the '*extensione appaltus dohanarum ad tres annos pro postfinitam presentem locationem* [that is, the period 1550-52]'; of this sum they would have had to pay immediately 8,000 *scudi d'oro*, which amount would then be subtracted from the remainder.[45] A *Motu proprio* of 24 November 1548 then confirmed the three-year extension for a price equal to that which had already been paid: 73,000 *scudi* (with the usual indemnity for the *gabella dei contratti*).[46]

For the same period Francesco Del Nero acquired a share under the name of Benvenuto Olivieri.[47] It is also known that the Ubaldini company held for the whole period a 10% share, and that for the first seven months of 1550 the Pallavicini and Giustiniani companies, which until 1549 had possessed a 12.5% share, held a further 10%, for a total of 22.5%.[48] As in the case discussed below, however, there is no information available on what happened after Benvenuto's death, which occurred in September 1549.

45 ASR, Camerale I, *Mandati Camerali 882*, fols 112v-113r; ASV, *Cam. Ap., Div. Cam. 153*, fol. 8r-v; *Cam. Ap., Div. Cam.* 157, fol. 69v. The *doganieri* distributed the sum as follows: 8,800 *scudi di paoli* (i.e. 8,000 *scudi d'oro*) to the pontiff; the remainder to various merchant companies, above all Florentine, '*per l'abundantia*', that is for the importation of wheat (ASF, Galli Tassi 2280, fol. 156). It can, incidentally, be noted how much in advance the Apostolic Chamber, always in need of money, requested the payment of figures relative to a contract that was to begin three and a half years later.

46 ASV, *Cam. Ap., Div. Cam. 157*, fols 54v-55r.

47 ASF, Galli Tassi 1809, ins. 4.

48 ASF, Galli Tassi 1979, ins. 34; Galli Tassi 1811, fol. 9v.

6. The contract of 1553-1560

Before the contract of 1543-49 had expired, a new contract was stipulated for the conveyance of the customs of Rome to the companies of Benvenuto Olivieri and Bastiano da Montauto: the duration of the contract was to be seven years, starting on 1 January 1553. At that time the period of management spoken of above was drawing to a close and it was therefore logical to think about the future; moreover, it was normal practice for contracts to be signed several years in advance. To guarantee the contract, in any case, Olivieri and Montauto paid an '*anticipazione*' (in the form of a loan) of 24,000 *scudi*.[49]

The price agreed on for the new seven-year period was 90,000 *scudi* per annum.[50] This is hardly surprising given, as we have seen (p. 124), that the income for the period 1543-49, having deducted the expenses, had reached the average sum of 88,000 *scudi* per annum. This is a clear demonstration of the fact that the actual amount collected in a given period was used as a starting point for the negotiations regarding the contract of the successive period. The customs were, as has already been mentioned, considered one of the most profitable investments and consequently were certainly much sought after. Nevertheless, the merchant-bankers, who advanced substantial amounts of money, naturally wished to protect their interests and reserve for themselves large margins of profit: they therefore had to be sure that it would be easy to obtain – if not surpass – the same results as those reached in the preceding period. However, another point which should not be ignored, among the factors influencing the price of the contract, was the monetary problems and the widespread increase in prices that occurred throughout the sixteenth century.[51]

Bandinello di Agostino Sauli was also named as a partner in the administration which was to begin in 1553, acquiring a share of 29.2%.[52] At the same time Olivieri conveyed 2.5% to Bartolomeo Bettini & Partners.[53] To sum up, therefore, the shares of participation were as follows:

Bastiano da Montauto & Partners	35.4%
Benvenuto Olivieri & Partners	32.9%
Bandinello Sauli	29.2%
Bartolomeo Bettini & Partners	2.5%

At some unspecified later date, which must nevertheless have been before the beginning of the contract, the distribution of the shares had changed:[54]

49 ASF, Galli Tassi 1831, fol. 9; Galli Tassi 1832, fol. 7.

50 ASF, Galli Tassi 1833, fol. 8.

51 For more details, see Delumeau, *Vie économique et sociale*, II, pp. 653-750.

52 ASF, Galli Tassi 1831, fol. 9.

53 ASF, Galli Tassi 1832, fol. 7 (contract of 28 November 1548, signed on 1 April 1549).

54 ASF, Galli Tassi 1921, fol. 47. Of the 16.2% share belonging to Olivieri, the Ubaldini claimed 7.5%; if this is true, Benvenuto's share must have been reduced to 8.7%.

Bastiano da Montauto & Partners	29.2%
Bandinello Sauli	29.2%
Benvenuto Olivieri & Partners	16.2%
Cavalcanti & Partners	10.4%
Bandini & Partners	7.5%
Bartolomeo Bettini & Partners	5.0%
Guiducci	2.5%

It is probable that there were further transfers and individual participations were of similar amounts to those already seen for the contract of 1543-49. However, in the documentation of the Fondo Galli Tassi no trace has remained of how the situation was modified. Similarly, there is no trace of any document relative to the revenue of the customs, nor of the distribution, even partial, of the profits. The most likely explanation for this is the death of Benvenuto Olivieri, which occurred well before the beginning of the new period of contract. The absence of direct documentation is due to the winding-up of Benvenuto's company immediately following the death of its senior partner.

The Florentines continued to hold numerous contracts as *doganieri* until the beginning of the following century: Marcello Del Nero, Giovan Battista Bufalini and Matteo Morelli (1558-67); Pier Antonio Bandini together with the Bernardo Olgiatto of Como (1576-85); Francesco and Niccolò Capponi, Giovan Battista Ubertini and Aurelio Ridolfi (1594-1603); Filippo Guicciardini with another Olgiatto, Settimio (1603-12).[55] In the same period, the annual price paid by the contract-holders was as follows: in 1564, 114,500 *scudi*; in 1576, 133,000 *scudi*; in 1590, 180,000 *scudi*; in 1604, 186,000 *scudi*.[56]

55 Delumeau, *Vie économique et sociale*, II, p. 861.
56 Delumeau, *Vie économique et sociale*, I, p. 126.

CHAPTER 6

The Provincial Treasuries

1. The Treasuries and papal finances

One of the results of the strengthening of the temporal power of the popes was the creation of the provincial Treasuries towards the end of the thirteenth century (the first was the Treasury of the Marches, created in 1272). Originally the treasurer was no more than an official who was answerable to the *rettore* (rector), and it was not until the beginning of the fourteenth century that he was entrusted with the actual administration of the collection of taxes. During this century he became increasingly autonomous, thanks to a series of papal interventions. A precise regulation on the office of the treasurer was included in the *Costituzioni egidiane* in 1356. Among other things, these established that it was his responsibility to keep a record of the accounts, which would then be authenticated by a notary of the Apostolic Chamber. The regulation stated that several original copies of the books had to be kept, one of which had to be submitted to the audit of the clerks of the Chamber.[1] With these new powers of collection the treasurer, who was already responsible for administering the assets of the Church of Rome, became representative of the Church in all financial transactions, although he was not permitted to alienate the assets of the Church itself.[2] On stepping down from office he would formally recognize his successor, provide him with all the necessary information about the current state of the business affairs, and hand over his powers.

The provincial treasurers were responsible in the provinces both for the collecting of all revenue directed towards Rome and for all payments on behalf of the Apostolic Chamber. The two virtually balanced each other out, with the payments absorbing most of the revenue collected. The revenue of the Treasury was used by the treasurer to pay the administrative costs of the province, as well as the alms, and it was also occasionally used for extraordinary expenses, on the mandate of the pontiff or his delegates.[3]

---

1 See M. Cristofori Mancia (ed.), *Il primo registro della Tesoreria di Ascoli (20 agosto 1426-30 aprile 1427)* (Rome, 1974), p. 23 (note 1); E. Lodolini, 'I registri delle Tesorerie provinciali dello Stato Pontificio (1397-1816) nell'Archivio di Stato di Roma', in *Studi in memoria di Federigo Melis* (5 vols, Naples, 1978), II, pp. 432-433; L. Fumi, *Inventario e spoglio dei registri della tesoreria apostolica di Perugia e Umbria dal R. Archivio di Stato di Roma* (Perugia, 1901), pp. XII-XIX.

2 C. Reydellet-Guttinger, *L'administration pontificale dans le Duché de Spolete (1305-1352)* (Florence, 1975), p. 61.

3 To give an example from a later date, in October 1546 Benvenuto Olivieri, while he was treasurer of the Romagna, was given the task of collecting the tithes imposed to sustain the costs of the War of Germany (ASF, Galli Tassi 2282, fol. 16).

Throughout the fifteenth century the provincial treasurer remained – as he had been originally – a functionary of the local papal administration; from the beginning of the sixteenth century, however, the Treasury was contracted out. From this point on the treasurer was almost without exception a merchant-banker. Another important change also took place at this time: alongside the traditional system of revenue, used in almost all the cases for the payment of the provincial costs, a new system of taxation was introduced with the purpose of filling the State coffers. The ever increasing financial needs of the Papal State required first of all a constant and regular tax revenue; a revenue, in other words, the size of which could be counted on with certainty. The way these contracts worked has already been explained in the introduction. To recap, however, they guaranteed to the Apostolic Chamber a secure revenue, both constant and paid in advance. Moreover, they made it possible for the Chamber to request further services or loans from the contract-holder, the repayment of which was guaranteed by the revenue from the office in question. The banker, for his part, obviously sought to render the office as efficient as possible, in order to maximize his margin of profit. The consequence was that the taxpayers were under a fiscal pressure much greater and more organized than in the past and at the same time papal temporal power increased.[4]

Rather than taking money directly from the citizens, the Papal State instead relied on a hierarchical system. The citizens paid town dues and taxes to the communal authorities, who in turn paid taxes to the Apostolic Chamber. In other words, the communes themselves were responsible for collecting taxes, meaning that there was no direct contact between the Papal State and the taxpayers. This served two purposes: first, the State thus minimized the costs of tax collection, its expenses being limited to the annuity of the treasurer; second, it ensured itself of a secure and punctual income, as eventual delays were punished with fines imposed by the treasurer.[5] During the last years of the pontificate of Clement VII this tendency to place responsibility on the shoulders of the treasurer became increasingly more marked. After a brief hiatus, this fiscal policy was reaffirmed under Paul III, when it was easier to put it into practice, largely thanks to the bankers who contracted these offices, the only ones with the capacity and networks to collect the new taxes in such a detailed and widespread way. It should, however, be pointed out that every commune then made individual agreements with the Apostolic Chamber, by which it could obtain privileges or immunity; moreover, certain social groups or economic sectors were also given special treatment.[6]

---

4 M. Caravale, *La finanza pontificia nel Cinquecento: le province del Lazio* (Naples, 1974), p. 11.

5 C. Rotelli, 'La finanza locale pontificia nel Cinquecento: il caso di Imola', *Studi Storici*, IX (1968): 132-133 (and notes 138-139). On the relations between local and State finance see also M. Carboni, 'Camere delle città e Camera apostolica: l'evoluzione dei rapporti finanziari fra centro e periferia nello Stato della Chiesa in età moderna', *Studi Storici Luigi Simeoni*, L (2000): 9-22.

6 From the correspondence between the communes (whose requests, however, often met with negative answers) and the representatives of the Papal State, it emerges that each commune had its own protector cardinal, to whom it could appeal (Rotelli, 'La finanza locale pontificia': 133).

The Treasuries were therefore the offices in charge of the collection of the sums of money owed by the communes; at the local level other offices also collaborated, for example the *Salare* (the offices in charge of collecting the sum owed by each commune for the quantity of salt given to it by the Chamber, which held the monopoly; see Chapter 7, pp. 146-147), or the *dogana dei pascoli* (which was in charge of issuing grazing rights); further tax burdens borne by the communes were the *bargello*, the tax of 0.5%, the tax on dead horses and the hearth tax. In the sixteenth century these other offices were also often farmed out, usually to the same people who were already involved in the administration of the Treasury: it came naturally to entrust the administration of these revenues to those who were already responsible for the collection at the local level. Thus it was common practice for the same men to deal with both the existing taxes and the new ones, such as the increase of the salt tax and the Triennial Subsidy of 300,000 *scudi*. The latter, which was instituted in 1543 and then prolonged, can be seen as the symbol of this new taxation push (see Chapter 7, pp. 158-160).

The taxes collected at the local level, often by the treasurer of the province himself, are, however, mentioned only in passing here as they are discussed in more depth in Chapter 7. The present chapter instead concentrates on the figure of the treasurer, and more specifically on Olivieri's activities as treasurer. It must be pointed out that, unfortunately, no complete studies on the provincial Treasuries exist; the only sources available are limited to inventories or lists of the various archives, some studies on local finance[7] and obviously more general, but always useful, research into the finances of the Papal State.[8]

2. The Treasury of Perugia and Umbria

The Treasury of Perugia and Umbria was farmed out to both Genoese and Florentine bankers, alternating between the two. In some cases enough documents have survived to make it possible to trace all the merchants who were involved, and not only those who actually signed the contract with the Apostolic Chamber. In fact, not

7 In particular see Rotelli, 'La finanza locale pontificia': 107-144; Carboni, 'Camere delle città e Camera apostolica': 9-22; G. Berti, 'Lineamenti di politica economica farnesiana nei ducati di Parma e Piacenza', *Archivio Storico per le Province Parmensi*, s. IV, 11 (1959): 65-88; G. Contini, 'Contributo documentario per uno studio delle condizioni finanziarie del Comune di Perugia alla vigilia della "guerra del sale"', *Rassegna degli Archivi di Stato*, 30 (1970): 365-376; the introduction of Fumi, *Inventario e spoglio*, pp. I-LXVIII. The volume *La Marca e le sue istituzioni al tempo di Sisto V* (Macerata, 1991) includes two articles of general interest by E. Stumpo ('La gestione delle tesorerie provinciali nello Stato della Chiesa fra Cinque e Seicento', pp. 49-62) and M.G. Pastura Ruggiero ('Tesorerie e depositerie', pp. 191-198). Although it refers to an earlier moment, *Il primo registro della Tesoreria di Ascoli* has a useful introduction concerning a longer period; again regarding the fifteenth century is E. Lodolini, 'I libri di conti di Antonio Fatati tesoriere generale della Marca (1449-1453) nell'Archivio di Stato di Roma', *Atti e memorie della Deputazione di Storia Patria per le Marche*, s. VIII, IV (1966): 137-176. On the Treasuries of the provinces of Lazio (Patrimonio, Campagna and Marittima), see Caravale, *La finanza pontificia nel Cinquecento*.

8 For the bibliographical references, see the Introduction, notes 11-17.

necessarily did the signatories represent both national groups, but where the sources are complete they show that behind the scenes the financial burden of a contract was always shared between the two. As has already been pointed out in the Introduction, such detailed information is not to be found in the documentation of the Chamber, but only in the papers of the bankers themselves. Here, naturally, the focus will be on those contracts in which Olivieri was involved.

In the 1520s the Treasury was administered by the Genoese bankers Giovanni, Agostino and Sebastiano Sauli. From the beginning of the 1530s until the mid-1540s it was administered by various Florentines: Ottaviano de' Medici (1531-36) was succeeded by Francesco Benci, who was soon supported by Benvenuto Olivieri (1539-45). It was then briefly once again the turn of the Genoese Sauli family, this time Girolamo and Bartolomeo, who relied on support from the Roman banker Curzio Frangipane (1546-52). After 1553 the Treasury of Perugia and Umbria once again returned into Florentine hands: first, Bindo Altoviti (1553) and then, for almost two decades, Bernardo Machiavelli and Roberto Ubaldini and his heirs, who alternated the post for almost all of the 1550s and 1560s.[9]

On 1 May 1539 Francesco Benci was nominated treasurer of Perugia for seven years (the contract was drawn up by Niccolò Casulano, notary of the Chamber). He immediately conveyed half of the contract to Benvenuto Olivieri & Partners.[10] But then the situation changed, as a rebellion that had been simmering for some time exploded in 1540, when the salt tax was increased. This insurrection was, however, very quickly repressed.[11]

A new agreement was therefore made, this time, however, in the name of Benvenuto Olivieri & Partners; the duration laid down in the contract was of five years, from 1 January 1541. It was decided that 40% of the profits should go to Francesco Benci and 10% to the administrators ('and if not given to the administrators it will be shared between said Benvenuto and Francesco'); the latter job was given to

9 ASR, Camerale I, *Tesoreria provinciale di Umbria e Perugia*, buste 29-39. See also the numerous references in Camerale I, *Mandati Camerali 871-874* (for Francesco Benci). Bindo Altoviti had also been involved in Ottaviano de' Medici's farm, exercising the Treasury on his behalf: M.M. Bullard, 'Bindo Altoviti, Renaissance Banker and Papal Financier', in A. Chong-D. Pegazzano-D. Zikos (eds), *Raphael, Cellini & A Renaissance Banker. The Patronage of Bindo Altoviti* (Boston, 2003), p. 35. On the period of Benvenuto Olivieri's administration see the notes below.

10 ASF, Galli Tassi 1846, fasc. 1, fol. 13r; Galli Tassi 1845, fasc. 3, fol. 13r; Galli Tassi 1848, fol. 12 (these are three identical documents, the second of which is rather damaged).

11 For further details see R. Chiacchella, 'Per una reinterpretazione della "guerra del sale" e della costruzione della Rocca Paolina in Perugia', *Archivio Storico Italiano*, 145 (1987): 3-60; G. Frollière, 'La guerra del sale sostenuta dai Perugini contro Paolo III nel 1540', ed. F. Bonaini-A. Fabritti-F.L. Polidori, *Archivio Storico Italiano*, series I, 16, parts 1-2 (1850-1851): 405-476; L. Fumi, 'Ragguaglio della ribellione di Perugia (Nota dall'Archivio di Stato di Milano)', *Bollettino della R. Deputazione di Storia Patria per l'Umbria*, XIV (1908): 69-81; and above all G. Contini, 'Contributo documentario', which publishes the entire register of *exitus* of the Treasury of Perugia and Umbria of 1538-1539, discovered in the Fondo Magliabechiano of the Biblioteca Nazionale of Florence (inventory number at p. 366).

Francesco Iacobello from Foligno. Of Olivieri's 50% share, 25% was then conveyed to the company of the Genoese banker Luca Giustiniani.[12] After 1 January 1543, then, the Olivieri company, in exchange for 200 *scudi di moneta*, conveyed 5% to Antonio Covoni & Partners.[13]

The Treasury of Perugia and Umbria therefore, halfway through the duration of the contract, was divided thus:

Francesco Benci	40%
Luca Giustiniani & Partners	25%
Benvenuto Olivieri & Partners	20%
Francesco Iacobello[14]	10%
Antonio Covoni & Partners	5%

The vice-treasurer was initially Benedetto di Jacopantonio Busini, Olivieri's partner in the company of Rome.[15]

The agreements stated that the profits would be distributed at the end of the year, and, like the losses, would be calculated on the basis of the respective shares: if the contractors delayed payment they would have to pay additional interest of 12% per annum.[16] For the new contract, which included '*omnibus et singulis privilegiis, indultis, facultatibus, membris, honoribus et oneribus ac emolumentis solitis et consuetis*', the treasurer had to pay an annual 58,898 florins of Perugia, equivalent to approximately 33,130 *scudi di giuli 10 per scudo*.[17] Of these, 19,000 *scudi* (that is 33,778 florins of Perugia) served for the annual *rente* of the Treasury of Perugia and Umbria, *Salara* and increase of the salt tax of Perugia, Città di Castello, Castel

12 ASF, Galli Tassi 1846, fasc. 1, fol. 13v; Galli Tassi 1845, fasc. 3, fol. 13r; Galli Tassi 1848, fol. 12.

13 ASF, Galli Tassi 2278, fol. 312.

14 After the first three years Iacobello was replaced by Bernardo di Niccolò Machiavelli who, however, at the end of his term (31 December 1545), wished to be paid a commission of 300 *scudi* per annum. The contract-holders, instead, were prepared to give Machiavelli his share of the profits, even though he would first have to reimburse Benvenuto Olivieri the 500 *scudi* which he had borrowed from the cash account that had been in his hands for personal expenses ('*e più paghi le spese che ha dato a detta Texaureria oltre al solyto nelle spese di casa, per avervi tenuto la moglie, figlioli, fantesche e cognyati*'). That Machiavelli was not paid on commission as he wished, since the Chamber had cut the bankers' profits 'by many thousands of *scudi*', is demonstrated by the fact that nothing of the sort was contemplated in the annual end-of-year accounts (ASF, Galli Tassi 1810, ins. 2, unnumbered folio).

15 Nominated on 28 March 1542 (ASF, Galli Tassi 1848, fol. 16). Busini was entitled to 1/8 of the share of Olivieri, that is 3.12% (Galli Tassi 1810, ins. 10, fol. 7v). The cashier of the Treasury was a member of an illustrious family of *mercatores florentini romanam curiam sequentes*: Lorenzo Altoviti, who received 132 *scudi* as a salary for the period 1 November 1543-15 March 1545 (Galli Tassi 1953, fol. 203).

16 ASF, Galli Tassi 1846, fasc. 1, fol. 13r; Galli Tassi 1845, fasc. 3, fol. 13r; Galli Tassi 1848, fol. 12.

17 Of the contract, which is given in full in the Appendix (doc. 6), the inventory number is: ASR, Camerale I, *Tesoreria provinciale di Umbria e Perugia*, busta 30, reg. 129, fols 1quattor r-10r; quotation at fol. 2r.

della Pieve, Citerna and Montone. They were, in other words, the price that the treasurers had to pay to purchase the right to administer the revenues of the province. An additional sum, of approximately 14,130 *scudi* (=25,120 florins), was necessary for salaries of officials of Rome, the Treasury and the University: in other words, the treasurer had to pay this amount every year to cover all the salaries, expenses, commissions and assignments of various officials.[18]

The *rente* was paid in three instalments, every four months; but it would be reduced if there were '*aliquam gratiam, concessionem et seu reintegrationem officiorum et aliarum rerum et bonorum*'.[19] Among the other provisions, it can be noted that the sums relative to the *malefici* (the administration of justice) exceeding 3,000 ducats, and those relative to the *focolaribus civitatis* superior to 5,000, were to be divided between the Chamber and Olivieri, 2/3 to the former and 1/3 to the latter.

The revenues and expenses of the Treasury were listed in detail.[20] The accounts were kept just as carefully: in 1541, against a revenue of 22,096.6 *scudi*, there were expenses of 20,109.9 *scudi* (balance +1,986.7); in the same year the treasurer received from the depositary 46,615.1 *scudi* for the payment of the guards, but had to pay out for the same item 46,018.6 *scudi* (balance +596.5); the following year, the 26,973.2 *scudi* in the revenue column was counterbalanced by 27,659.2 *scudi* in the expenses column (balance –686). For the first two years, therefore, income exceeded expenditure by 1,897.2 *scudi*, meaning that the treasurer owed this sum to the depositary. In 1543, instead, the balance was negative by 3,703.6 *scudi*: the income came to 22,673.9 *scudi* and the expenditure to 26,377.5. A similar trend could be seen in 1544, with 22,693.4 *scudi* of revenue and 25,031.6 *scudi* of expenses (balance –2,338.2); however, 4,272.8 *scudi* were added to the revenue column from the subsidy for the four-year period just passed, resulting in a total positive balance, for the four years, of 128.2 *scudi* to be carried over to 1545. In that year the expenditure greatly exceeded the income: 27,969.2 *scudi* against 20,184.2 (balance –7,785); other transactions and corrections, however, brought the negative difference down to 3,220.3, with a general total, therefore, of 3,092.1.[21]

It is difficult to decide exactly how much weight should be given to these figures in estimating Olivieri's possible profits. As Stumpo has pointed out, it is difficult to calculate the exact revenue of the Treasury, contracted out for 20-30,000 *scudi* per

---

18 ASR, Camerale I, *Tesoreria provinciale di Umbria e Perugia*, busta 30, reg. 129, fol. 97; this sum, here given precisely as 14,130.25 *scudi di giuli 10 per scudo*, was divided into the various items in busta 30, reg. 129, fol. 23 for 1541-42; in busta 31, reg. 133, fol. 17 for 1543; in busta 31, reg. 136, fol. 55 for 1544; in busta 31, reg. 137, fol. 41 for 1545. The contract differs somewhat, however, listing also in a detailed manner the destination of this money, and giving the amount as 13,239.75 *scudi* (Camerale I, *Tesoreria provinciale di Umbria e Perugia*, busta 30, reg. 129, fols 8v-10r; here, Appendix, doc. 6, pp. 241-242). See also ASF, Galli Tassi 1941, fols 215-216.

19 ASR, Camerale I, *Tesoreria provinciale di Umbria e Perugia*, busta 30, reg. 129, fol. 3r (here, p. 237).

20 For the ordinary payments that the treasurer had to effect, see table at the end of doc. 6 in the Appendix, pp. 241-242.

21 ASR, Camerale I, *Tesoreria provinciale di Umbria e Perugia*, busta 30, reg. 129, fol. 97; busta 31, reg. 133, fol. 47; busta 31, reg. 136, fols 62, 77.

annum, because it came from the collection of a series of local taxes, not specified in the sources, but which nevertheless must have been quite profitable for the contract-holder.[22]

When the contract came to an end, there must – as often happened – have been some kind of dispute, as legal proceedings were taken against Benvenuto Olivieri & Partners. The sentence was proclaimed on 4 March 1547. With regard to most of the 73 complaints brought against Olivieri and his partners by the tax authorities (represented by Niccolò Farfani), the Florentine banker was however cleared.[23]

At the end of the five years, in 1546, the Olivieri company found itself creditor of roughly 15,500 *scudi di giuli 10 per scudo*, an amount that increased to approximately 24,500 at the beginning of 1550 thanks to other operations, which included annual interests of 12%. The 15,500 *scudi* consisted of 5,000 advanced to Luca Giustiniani, 5,000 for a promise made on behalf of Benci, 4,000 of which Benci was again debtor, and 1,500 borrowed by Iacobello. This confusion and the missing payment occurred because in 1544 Benci and Iacobello had been imprisoned (in the gaol of 'Turris nove') 'for their action in these matters of the Treasury'. Benci was accused of having failed to pay 5,000 *scudi* he owed the Chamber, while Iacobello was relieved of the administration.[24] The books were sent to the Chamber administration, but matters were not resolved quickly, and eventually a payment of 5,000 or more *scudi* was made in order to settle the question. Just as in the first years, because of the delays in balancing the books, the profits were not distributed. Benvenuto took money from his own pocket to pay the interests on the Treasury affairs of Perugia to the 'stingy' ('*tanto tirati*') Genoese bankers, complaining, however, 'and this is an unjust thing'. 5,000 *scudi* were then paid in order to set Benci free. In the end, because of the money already paid to the Chamber, there remained almost nothing of the profits.[25] As Olivieri's procurators then commented bitterly, 'if these associates of Benvenuto had not taken profits which either did not exist or had not been collected, we would not now be speaking of interest'.[26]

Given all the troubles and disputes, it was therefore decided that from that time on, for all expenses that were not ordinary expenses, a separate agreement would have to be made each time between the contract-holder and the Apostolic Chamber.[27]

Among the other things, it seems that Benci had leased 'the lake of Perugia' for 8,000 florins of Perugia to several local merchants. The Chamber, however, declared that 2/3 of the lease (5,333.3 florins) should be paid to Benvenuto Olivieri and established that the profits should be divided in the proportion of 2/3 to the

---

22 E. Stumpo, *Il capitale finanziario a Roma fra Cinque e Seicento. Contributo alla storia della fiscalità pontificia in età moderna (1570-1650)* (Milan, 1985), p. 109.

23 ASR, Camerale I, *Tesoreria provinciale di Umbria e Perugia*, busta 31, reg. 137, fols 79r-82r.

24 On 24 March 1544 Benci admitted his debt and the additional interest of 300 *scudi* (ASF, Galli Tassi 1846, fasc. 5).

25 ASF, Galli Tassi 1846, fasc. 1, fols 14r-15r; ins. 4, fols 1r-2r; Galli Tassi 1848, fol. 13 (these are three copies, the first of which badly damaged).

26 ASF, Galli Tassi 1927, fol. 7r.

27 ASF, Galli Tassi 1846, fasc. 7.

treasurer and 1/3 to the administrators.[28] A legal dispute then arose between Olivieri and Iacobello: in November 1552 the latter was hoping that the court case still in progress between him and the heirs of the former would finish 'as quickly as possible and in a friendly manner'.[29]

Years later it was claimed that the profits arising from the administration of this particular Treasury had amounted to 11,324 *scudi*, of which 2,831 were owed to Benvenuto Olivieri & Partners.[30] Not all of this amount, however, would go to the partners: in 1564, in fact, the Treasury was still owed money by Francesco Benci, who was by that time dead and bankrupt ('*morto et fallito*'). A large part of this sum was therefore detracted from the profits of the survivors (from Olivieri 631 *scudi*), while a smaller share (316) was frozen until such time as all debts were paid.[31] In the end, if this last amount was also truly lost, Benvenuto Olivieri & Partners must have made a profit of only 1,884 *scudi*.

From 1 January 1546 the Treasury of Perugia and Umbria was farmed out to the Roman banker Curzio Frangipane, who thus undertook to pay, for seven years, the same sum as his predecessors: 58,898 florins of Perugia (= approximately 33,130 *scudi*) a year.[32] Moreover, he agreed to loan 15,000 *scudi* a year to be repaid, without interest, within three years;[33] he was also under contract to make a further loan of 12,000, with the usual interest of 12%. As '*segurtà*' (guarantee) the treasurer would use all the income of the Chamber as collateral, and in particular the collection of the Triennial Subsidy and of the increase of the salt tax in the territories of Perugia and Umbria. Frangipane was also named tax farmer of the same Triennial Subsidy with a commission of 1% on the money collected.[34] Clearly, no Roman banker had

28 ASF, Galli Tassi 1846, fol. 8; Galli Tassi 1939, fol. 2. At the head of this group of merchants was the Roman, Curzio Frangipane, who would be given the contract of the Treasury of Perugia and Umbria in 1546 (the 8,000 florins to be given to Benvenuto are also mentioned in the new contract: Galli Tassi 1847, fasc. 1). Further details on this contract are in Galli Tassi 1848, fol. 7, where it is specified that its duration would be of three years, from 1 May 1543. Among the names on the contract were Urbano Lioncini and Michelangelo Ranieri; there is also mention of another merchant from Perugia, Orazio Delle Cornie, who took a 5% share under the name of Olivieri.

29 ASF, Galli Tassi 1938, fol. 1. In the same period a court case was in progress between the Olivieri heirs and Giustiniani (fol. 14).

30 More optimistic was the forecast made in September 1545, which estimated Benvenuto's profits at around 5,000 *scudi* (ASF, Galli Tassi 1806, ins. 2, unnumbered folio; see also the Appendix, doc. 3, p. 221).

31 ASF, Galli Tassi 1810, ins. 10, fasc. 2.

32 This contract was won by a certain Decio Alberio (acting in the name of Curzio Frangipane), who made an offer slightly higher than those of Lorenzo Altoviti and Giovan Battista Puccini (*ASR, Notai segretari e cancellieri della R. Camera apostolica 1988*, fols 551r-552v).

33 ASV, *Cam. Ap., Div. Cam. 142*, fol. 45r-v. This contradicts an earlier document, dated 1544, in which the Chamber, in agreement with Olivieri, declared its intention to once again farm out the Treasury: among the 'inviolable' norms was the request to make an advance deposit of 20,000 *scudi* to be repaid in four years (ASF, Galli Tassi 1848, fasc. 2, fol. 1r).

34 ASF, Galli Tassi 1847, fasc. 1. The contract can also be found in ASR, *Notai segretari e cancellieri della R. Camera apostolica 1988*, fols 577v-590v.

sufficient resources to administer such a large contract on his own; in fact, as other documents show, the necessary financial means were actually furnished by the Genoese. Involved in this contract were the companies of Bartolomeo and Girolamo Sauli, of Tobia Pallavicini and Luca Giustiniani, of Cristoforo Sauli, as well as the Florentine company of the heirs of Girolamo Ubaldini; Francesco Iacobello from Foligno and Frangipane himself instead held only minor shares in the deal.[35] For the last two years (1551 and 1552) the Ubaldini company conveyed their 27.5% share to the Altoviti company, receiving in exchange 1,219.5 gold cameral ducats: of these, 388 went to the Olivieri company (the heirs of Benvenuto), shareholders, under the name of Ubaldini, with a 8.75% share.[36] Given the long-standing relationship between the Ubaldini and Olivieri families, it is quite probable that the Olivieri company was also involved from the first years of the contract.

The territories where the Apostolic Chamber had the power to farm taxes and where the relative offices were responsible were, both here and in the preceding case, described in great detail.[37] Just as it had done under the administration of the Olivieri company, the Apostolic Chamber continued to burden the local population with a large number of indirect taxes, and at times the addition of extraordinary taxes.

3. The Treasury of the Romagna

Like the Treasury of Perugia and Umbria, the Treasury of the Romagna was, from the 1510s, farmed out alternately to Florentine and Genoese bankers; again, like the Treasury of Perugia, more than an alternation it was in fact a collaboration, inasmuch as the official contract-holders conveyed shares to the others. However, the details of these collaborative efforts cannot always be traced and reconstructed because, as has already been noted, the documents of the Apostolic Chamber rarely kept trace of them. However, after the Genoese banker Giovanni Sauli (1513-14) came the Florentine Jacopo Salviati, a relative of Pope Leo X, until 1531.[38] In the 1530s it was Giovan Battista Galletti who held the post of treasurer, first with the Strozzi company, then with Francesco Tosignani, who eventually continued on his own.[39] Towards the

35 ASR, Camerale I, *Tesoreria provinciale di Umbria e Perugia*, buste 31-32; ASF, Galli Tassi 1847, fasc. 6.

36 ASF, Galli Tassi 1953, fol. 143.

37 '*Il lagho, il Chiusi tutto, il subsidio della ciptà e del contado compreso etiam rustichuli paghanti et ogni altro nome che soleva riscotere la ciptà avanti la rebellione, gabella grossa, gabella del vino, le cinque gabelle del contado, le gabelle de' quattropiedi, delle legne et paglia, cenciarie, mine, pegni, danni dati, ciabattini et di San Savino, pigioni delle botteghe, decime di compromessi della ciptà, li sussidi della provincia, tutte le gabelle et intrate di Fulignio, Spoleti et Todi et il terzo delle pene de' malefici della ciptà et contado di Perugia et provincia dell'Umbria con li honori et carichi soliti et consueti*' (ASF, Galli Tassi 1848, fasc. 2, fol. 1r).

38 ASR, Camerale I, *Tesoreria provinciale della Romagna*, buste 6-7.

39 ASR, Camerale I, *Tesoreria provinciale della Romagna*, buste 7-9; ASV, *Cam. Ap., Div. Cam. 112*, fol. 30r; ASF, Galli Tassi 1850, unnumbered folio referring to the shares of the Strozzi company.

end of the 1530s the company of the Genoese Luca Giustiniani and Tobia Pallavicini took over, in collaboration with, at least from 1541, the Florentine Antonio Ugolini.[40] It is possible for us to examine in much closer detail the subsequent administration, as the contract was held by the company of Benvenuto Olivieri, and is referred to in the Florentine documents.[41]

Olivieri had in fact already been acting as commissioner for the collection of the increase of the salt tax of Bologna and the Romagna since 1540 (for more detail see Chapter 7, pp. 150-153), and in 1542 he was involved in the collection of the *imposizione delle galere* (destined to the financing of the fleet), of the tithes and of the income from communes of the Romagna.

The Treasury of the Romagna was farmed out to Benvenuto Olivieri & Partners for seven years starting from 1 December 1545. At the stipulation of the contract the Olivieri company promised to loan to the Apostolic Chamber 25,000 *scudi d'oro in oro* to be repaid, without interest, over five years (one-fifth every year).[42] This sum was understood as '*pecuniis anticipationis appaltus*'.[43]

Given the vast sums of money they were obliged to lend, the farmers were always very careful to ensure their rights and to have sufficient guarantees that they would be repaid. Thus, Olivieri's predecessors, the Pallavicini and Giustiniani companies, for example, received from the incoming treasurer, by Chamber mandate, 10,000 *scudi d'oro in oro* '*pro redemptione pulcherrimi rubini preciosi*' on which they had foreclosed in lieu of the amount owed them by the Apostolic Chamber.[44]

As always happened, even if the names of only two or three merchant-bankers appeared in the contract, the numbers actually involved grew very quickly, with shares – some large, some small – being conveyed to other *mercatores*. The administration and the responsibility remained, however, in the hands of whoever had stipulated the contract with the Apostolic Chamber.

Thus, on 31 January 1546 Bastiano da Montauto & Partners signed an agreement with the Olivieri company to participate in the Treasury of the Romagna, with a 18.3% share, and undertook to contribute 4,583.3 *scudi* as their part of the loan of 25,000 *scudi*. The agreement provided that the Treasury continue to be administered by the Olivieri company, and that only in the case of the death of Benvenuto could the Montauto company intervene.[45] Another company that entered into the deal very early on was that of Girolamo Ubaldini, which, under the name of Benvenuto

40 ASR, Camerale I, *Tesoreria provinciale della Romagna*, buste 12-14.

41 To this period are relevant also ASR, Camerale I, *Tesoreria provinciale della Romagna*, buste 14-15.

42 ASF, Galli Tassi 1850, fol. 11; Galli Tassi 1921, fol. 39.

43 ASR, Camerale I, *Mandati Camerali 882*, fol. 98r. In another document it is defined as '*anticipatione della nostra condotta ... per tanti se ne servì detta Camera gratiosamente per rihavere ogni anno scudi cinquemila simili sopra li proventi di decta Thexoreria et contributione*' (Camerale I, *Tesoreria provinciale della Romagna*, busta 14, reg. 76, fols 8, 21).

44 ASR, Camerale I, *Mandati Camerali 882*, fol. 98r-v.

45 ASF, Galli Tassi 1850, fol. 11. Probably there was also the Altoviti company behind the Montauto company: Galli Tassi 1833, fol. 1 mentions the 18.3% share Montauto held for Altoviti.

Olivieri & Partners, purchased a 15% share.[46] Some months later, on 12 March 1546, the company of the Genoese bankers Tobia Pallavicini and Luca Giustiniani, who had already been treasurers of the Romagna in the period of the preceding contract, acquired a 36.7% share and agreed to pay 9,166.7 *scudi*.[47] On 5 July Giuliano Ardinghelli also entered into the deal, acquiring a 5% share in exchange for 1,250 *scudi*.[48] Complicating things even further, the Sauli company (Genoese) then bought a 7.5% share, under the name of Pallavicini and Giustiniani, which after three years they conveyed (in several instalments) to the Ubaldini (Florentines).[49] Thus, a few months after Benvenuto signed the contract with the Apostolic Chamber, the participants were the following:

Tobia Pallavicini and Luca Giustiniani & Partners	29.2%
Benvenuto Olivieri & Partners	25.0%
Bastiano da Montauto & Partners	18.3%
Girolamo Ubaldini & Partners	15.0%
Bartolomeo and Girolamo Sauli & Partners	7.5%
Giuliano Ardinghelli	5.0%

By 1548, however, the 36.7% share belonging to the Genoese (in the above list Pallavicini-Giustiniani and Sauli) was redistributed somewhat differently:

Tobia Pallavicini and Luca Giustiniani & Partners	21.7%
Cristoforo Sauli & Partners	7.5%
Heirs of Girolamo Ubaldini & Partners	3.9%
Bartolomeo and Girolamo Sauli & Partners	3.6%

Very soon afterwards, things changed yet again, when Bartolomeo and Girolamo Sauli transferred the remainder of their share to the Ubaldini company.

A few years later, in 1551 – therefore practically at the end of the contract – the participants in the 63.3% that can be defined as 'Florentine' (Olivieri, Montauto and Ardinghelli of the first list) were exactly the same, although Benvenuto Olivieri and Girolamo Ubaldini had been replaced by their heirs.[50]

All the agreements struck between the Olivieri company and the merchant-bankers who took shares in the Treasury followed the same lines as the agreement made with Montauto. The administration therefore continued to be controlled by

46 ASF, Galli Tassi 1953, fol. 143.

47 ASF, Galli Tassi 1850, fol. 13. The deed recording the agreement made with Pallavicini and Giustiniani, which witnesses, on 13 May 1546, the payment of the share, can also be found in Galli Tassi 1845, fasc. 3, fols 13v-14r and in Galli Tassi 1846, fasc. 1, fol. 14r-v.

48 ASF, Galli Tassi 1850, fol. 12; Galli Tassi 1955, fasc. 3, fol. 8.

49 ASR, Camerale I, *Tesoreria provinciale della Romagna*, busta 15, reg. 81, fol. 31. See ASF, Galli Tassi 1811, fol. 13v and Galli Tassi 1942, fol. 108 for a record of the Ubaldini's 7.5% share under the name of Pallavicini and Giustiniani; see also Galli Tassi 1951, fol. 156, which documents the presence of the Ubaldini company in both the Florentine and Genoese groups.

50 ASF, Galli Tassi 1850, fol. 15; Galli Tassi 1921, fol. 39. See also Galli Tassi 1811, fol. 10v.

the Olivieri company and the others could intervene only in the case of the death of Benvenuto.[51] None of the partners could set up individual business deals involving the Treasury, at the risk of being fined 1,000 *scudi*. If the Olivieri company had any private deal ('*alcuna incetta privata*'), it had to inform the others. The profits were calculated and distributed at the end of the year and the books were freely available for consultation to everyone. Eventual differences were to be resolved by consulting three other merchant-bankers, one chosen by each party and another to the agreement of both.[52]

The Olivieri company administered the Treasury of the Romagna for a total of three years and ten months from the stipulation of the contract in 1545; in other words until September 1549. During this period, as so frequently happened, there arose a dispute with the Apostolic Chamber, which demanded the payment of a number of debts it claimed it was owed. Unfortunately, no record of the outcome of this particular court case has survived.[53]

Several records of 1555, in other words three years after the expiry of the period of the contract, provide us with relatively reliable data on the profits earned from this particular farm.[54] However, because of the disputes mentioned above, it took some time to arrive at the final calculations. Moreover, some of the profits, probably fairly roughly calculated, were distributed during the period of the administration. Finally, some of the debts existing between the bankers were settled in separate deals. This was possible because of the close network that existed among the *mercatores* as well as between them and the Apostolic Chamber. However, a contemporary document speaks of the '*rata di lb. 16271.18.1*' [= approximately 4,043 *scudi d'oro in oro*]' as net profit from the Treasury of the Romagna.[55]

Other records provide us with even more significant data. For interests and profits calculated in the first three years, 3,630 *scudi d'oro in oro* were credited to Pallavicini and Giustiniani for their 29.2% share. A quick calculation thus gives us

---

51 According to ASF, Galli Tassi 1850, fol. 10, Bastiano da Montauto was administrator for part of the time; presumably from the end of 1549, that is after the death of Olivieri.

52 There were in fact at least two disputes between Olivieri, on the one hand, and Pallavicini and Giustiniani, on the other: the first was brought before Cornelio Malvasia and Roberto Ubaldini, 'common friends' and a merchant whose name is not known; the second before Silvestro Aldobrandini, Francesco Formento and Simone Guiducci (ASF, Galli Tassi 1850, fols 9-10).

53 ASF, Galli Tassi 1851, fol. 2. Galli Tassi 1850, fol. 18 shows a list of fines ('*contravenzion di Romagna*'). Among other things, Olivieri, in his capacity as treasurer, was accused of having failed to meet all his obligations: of not paying the 25,000 *scudi d'oro* (art. 2); not paying the subsidy and the loans for the '*fabbrica*' of the salt (art. 4); not paying all the expenses of the Treasury (art. 6); not paying the 800 *scudi d'oro* owed monthly to the Chamber (art. 9); including in the accounts services that should have been free (art. 10). The Olivieri heirs replied that Benvenuto had always acted correctly, complaining that they had always been (and still were) creditors of the Chamber (Galli Tassi 1938, fols 3-4).

54 ASR, Camerale I, *Tesoreria provinciale della Romagna*, busta 15, reg. 81, fols 1-41 ('*Conto degli eredi di Benvenuto Olivieri, Sebastiano di Montacuto, Tobia Pallavicini e Luca Giustiniani dal primo dicembre 1545 a l'ultimo dicembre* [actually November] *1552*').

55 ASR, Camerale I, *Tesoreria provinciale della Romagna*, busta 15, reg. 81, fol. 20.

for this period a total profit of 12,445 *scudi d'oro in oro*.[56] This result is confirmed by the records of the heirs of Girolamo Ubaldini & Partners, dated 1556: for the 15% share they held under the name of Olivieri in the seven years (until 30 November 1552), they made a profit of 3,148.3 *scudi d'oro in oro*; while for the 7.5% they held under the name of the Sauli company in the last four years, their share amounted to 634.7.[57] If these data are accepted as accurate, it can be calculated that the total profit for the participants came to 20,989 *scudi d'oro in oro* over seven years, 8,463.3 of which earned in the last four. This could have been due to poor results, or simply to the fact that the accounts of the more recent years might not yet have been closed. If the Olivieri company maintained, as it would seem, a 25% share for the entire duration of the contract, its profit and that of its heirs came to 5,247.2 *scudi d'oro in oro*. It should also be remembered that Benvenuto, in the name of his son Giulio, also held a 30% share in the Ubaldini company: this must have made him a further 1,135 *scudi*.

The following contract, again with a seven-year duration and ending therefore on 30 November 1559, was awarded to Bastiano da Montauto (and on his death his heirs, including Zanobi) and Francesco Iacobello of Foligno, who in previous years had already participated in the Treasury of Perugia and Umbria (pp. 132-136). Iacobello must have had close ties to the Genoese merchant-bankers, in that during the period of the old contract he acted as procurator of Pallavicini and Giustiniani (who, moreover, were probably also involved in the new contract), and during the period of the new contract he received a share from Bandinello Sauli, co-treasurer of the Romagna.[58]

4. The Treasury of Parma and Piacenza

Before taking over the administration of the Treasury of the Romagna, Benvenuto Olivieri's company had purchased a share in the Treasury of Parma and Piacenza. Despite the fact that chronologically this Treasury came first, it is discussed last for several reasons. First, the contract in this case was in the name of other bankers. Second, this Treasury was rather less important than that of the Romagna. And, finally, we have access to much less information, as very few documents referring to Olivieri's connection with it have survived.

From 1 October 1542 Tommaso Cavalcanti and Giovanni Giraldi & Partners of Rome farmed the Treasury and the increase of the salt tax of Parma and Piacenza for three years. The latter tax had already been in their hands for two years (in total five: 1 October 1540-30 September 1545). An initial loan of 18,750 *scudi d'oro in oro* was to be repaid in five years with the assignments coming from the Treasury and

56 ASR, Camerale I, *Tesoreria provinciale della Romagna*, busta 15, reg. 81, fol. 31; Galli Tassi 1952, fol. 184.

57 ASF, Galli Tassi 1953, fol. 143.

58 For this information see records in ASR, Camerale I, *Tesoreria provinciale della Romagna*, busta 15, reg. 81, fols 32, 33.

from the increase of the salt tax.[59] In exchange, the contract-holders agreed to make a monthly payment of 1,500 *scudi* to the depositary, for which they also received as collateral security various jewels.[60]

Benvenuto Olivieri's company also participated, purchasing a 30% share.[61] Under the name of the Olivieri company, Busini obtained a 10% share on behalf of Roberto Strozzi,[62] and the company of Pier Antonio and Alamanno Bandini purchased an analogous amount.[63] On 15 June 1542 Benvenuto's company received 750 *scudi d'oro in oro* as profits from the Treasury (a part of which went to Busini) and 100 *scudi* as the 5% commission on the increase of the salt tax in the province of Parma and Piacenza.[64]

5. Other Treasuries

Brief mention should also be made of the other Treasuries in which the *mercatores florentini romanam curiam sequentes* were involved: the provincial Treasury of Ascoli was administered first by Piero and Alessandro Del Bene (1526-31), then by Zanobi Biliotti (1531-35); during the pontificate of Paul III it was the turn of Sinibaldo Gaddi (1538-41), of Antonio Ugolini (1542), of Pietro Ugolini (1545-48) and of Bindo Altoviti (1548-50), the very wealthy Florentine banker who then became extremely influential in the provinces of the Marches and Ancona;[65] after 1559 the treasurer was Bartolomeo Bussotti, in collaboration with Piero Strozzi.[66] At Camerino we find again Altoviti (1539-41), followed, between 1545 and 1550, by Scipione Conti and Bastiano da Montauto.[67] The previous year, 1538, Altoviti had been treasurer of Fermo.[68] The province of the Marches was an unchallenged monopoly of the Florentines: it is not known who followed Luigi Gaddi (1515-23) in the role of treasurer, but it is certain that in those years and in the following ones the *Salara* was once again contracted out to the same Gaddi (1515-26) and then to Pietro

59 ASF, Galli Tassi 1865, unnumbered folio. Galli Tassi 1867, fasc. 7 seems to indicate that exactly the same conditions were in fact valid from 1538. According to Galli Tassi 1942, fol. 195r the duration of the contract of the Treasury was five years (until 30 September 1545), with a loan of 15,000 *scudi*.

60 For this clause see also ASR, Camerale I, *Mandati Camerali 874*, fol. 10v. In the same volume (fol. 95v) it is affirmed that the Cavalcanti and Giraldi, treasurers, could detract from the increase of the salt tax the 6,000 ducats that they had loaned plus the relative interests of 12%.

61 ASF, Galli Tassi 1865, fasc. 5.

62 Strozzi, who was owner of half of the social capital of Benvenuto Olivieri & Partners (see Chapter 2, p. 52), can be identified as the holder of Benedetto Busini's account marked '*a parte R.B.*' (ASF, Galli Tassi 1942, fol. 195r; Galli Tassi 2278, fol. 273). See also Chapter 9, p. 188.

63 ASF, Galli Tassi 1942, fol. 195r; Galli Tassi 1844, fol. 17; Galli Tassi 1946, fol. 22v.

64 ASF, Galli Tassi 2278, fol. 158.

65 ASR, Camerale I, *Tesoreria provinciale di Ascoli*, busta 6, regg. 22-25; busta 7, regg. 26-30, 32-35, 37.

66 Relative to these years are the registers ASF, *Strozzi Sacrati*, 528, 605, 606.

67 For all: ASR, Camerale I, *Tesoreria provinciale di Camerino*, busta 1.

68 ASR, Camerale I, *Tesoreria provinciale di Fermo*, busta 1.

Del Bene (1526-29).[69] In the following period the treasurers were Filippo Strozzi and Antonio Ugolini (1523-35),[70] Bindo Altoviti (1535-45), Pietro Ugolini and Giuliano Ardinghelli (1546-50). Altoviti kept the contract for the *Salara* for nearly two decades (1536-54) and was also commissioner for the collection of the Triennial Subsidy (1543-49).[71] In 1536 the treasurer of Norcia was Agostino Del Nero, while in 1543 this post was held by Francesco Porcella and in 1544 by Giovanni Degli Albizzi.[72] In the Treasury of Patrimonio, finally, throughout the 1530s and 1540s the Florentine banker Bartolomeo Pucci alternated with his fellow countryman Alessandro Del Bene and with the Genoese banker Sebastiano Sauli.[73] In other words, as emphasized in Chapter 1, even after the end of the Medici pontificates the Florentines continued to be very influential at the papal court.

69 ASR, Camerale I, *Tesoreria provinciale della Marca*, buste 22-24. BAV, *Vat. Lat. 7124*, fol. 157r; *Vat. Lat. 9960*, fols 65v-66v.

70 ASR, Camerale I, *Tesoreria provinciale della Marca*, busta 25. The contract naming Filippo Strozzi & Partners as treasurers from 1 January 1532 can be found in ASF, Galli Tassi 1977, fol. 73. The annual payment is given as 18,000 ducats *di moneta*. See Galli Tassi 1853 for more details on the participation also of Agostino Del Nero and of Lorenzo Gavotto of Savona (a draft of the contract can also be found in Galli Tassi 1843, fasc. 15). Relative to the years 1531-35 there also exist, again in the Archivio di Stato of Florence, four *filze* that, described in the inventory as '*lettere e calcoli riguardanti la Tesoreria di Romagna tenuta da Agostino Del Nero*', are instead relative to the Treasury of the Marches, of which Del Nero himself was vice-treasurer (*Torrigiani-Appendice*, filze 1-4). Although the contract was supposed to last until 1538, in 1535 the Treasury of the Marches was 'taken away' from Strozzi and given to Bindo Altoviti (Bullard, 'Bindo Altoviti', p. 35).

71 ASR, Camerale I, *Tesoreria provinciale della Marca*, buste 25-27; ASV, *Cam. Ap., Div. Cam. 127*, fols 106v-108r.

72 ASF, Diplomatico, *Dono Torrigiani-Appendice*, 7 September 1536; Galli Tassi 2278, fol. 327; ASV, *Cam. Ap., Div. Cam. 134*, fol. 124r.

73 ASR, Camerale I, *Tesoreria provinciale del Patrimonio*, buste 28-29. Alessandro Del Bene, nominated treasurer for seven years from 1 October 1542, sold ¾ of his share of the contract to Sauli (ASV, *Cam. Ap., Div. Cam. 127*, fols 42v-44r; *Cam. Ap., Div. Cam. 133*, fol. 18v). While the latter was treasurer, the Florentine, Roberto Ubaldini, was vice-treasurer (ASF, Galli Tassi 1980, *passim*). In Galli Tassi 1831, ins. 1, unnumbered folio, the contract regarding the *dogana dei pascoli* and Treasury of Patrimonio, farmed out for eight years from October 1549, at a price of 23,300 *scudi di moneta*; unfortunately, however, the name of the contract-holder is missing.

CHAPTER 7

Indirect and Direct Taxes

Towards the end of the Middle Ages taxation was mostly indirect, with direct taxation being applied prevalently in so-called extraordinary circumstances, although it should be pointed out that extraordinary circumstances were not in fact very rare.[1] The year 1543 was an important turning point. This was the year of the introduction of the first real direct State tax – the Triennial Subsidy. Like most other direct taxes, the subsidy was initially an extraordinary tax, but then, in practice, it became ordinary (see section 5). As Stumpo notes, however, if the distinction between direct and indirect taxes was clear at the central level, it was not so at all at the local level, where every commune could take an independent decision as to how taxes would be collected.[2] Direct taxation, which was applied only to owners of real estate, was generally calculated at the local level and was based on estimates that took into consideration the size and the agronomic conditions of the lands. There were, however, constant protests about both the estimates and the exemptions, as well as about the subsequent adjustments. These protests were directed not only towards the amount of money to be paid, but also towards the uncertainty as to how much this would actually be and towards the fact that there was unequal division between the taxpayers.[3]

As a result of the ever greater fiscal pressure exerted by the papacy, many taxes that were initially born as municipal taxes, in other words to cover the costs of the local administration, were then redirected to cope with the numerous needs of the Apostolic Chamber. Moreover, like the Subsidy, almost all began as extraordinary taxes, but were then prolonged so many times that they became ordinary.

However, rather than trying to outline a survey of the pontifical taxation of the second quarter of the sixteenth century, the following instead concentrates only on those aspects that directly involved the Florentine *mercatores*, and in particular the company of Benvenuto Olivieri. Moreover, although some general background will be provided in order to complete the picture, each individual problem will be looked at largely from the point of view of the *mercatores*, rather than that of the Papal State. The chapter begins with temporal finance, concentrating in particular on the

---

1 As is pointed out by C. Rotelli ('La finanza locale pontificia nel Cinquecento: il caso di Imola', *Studi Storici*, IX (1968): 111), all public works were considered extraordinary.

2 E. Stumpo, *Il capitale finanziario a Roma fra Cinque e Seicento. Contributo alla storia della fiscalità pontificia in età moderna (1570-1650)* (Milan 1985), pp. 90-91 and note 38. On the taxation in the sixteenth century and later see also E. Lodolini, 'Introduzione', in Archivio di Stato di Roma, *L'Archivio della S. Congregazione del Buon Governo (1592-1847). Inventario* (Rome, 1956), in particular pp. XLVIII-LXVI.

3 Rotelli, 'La finanza locale pontificia': 126.

indirect taxes: salt (section 1) and the customs or *gabelles* (sections 2-3); and then passes to the direct taxes, including a number of taxes (section 4) which were in part then replaced, in 1543, by the Triennial Subsidy (section 5); it concludes with the so-called spiritual finance, in particular with the tithes (section 6).

1. Salt taxes

The salt tax was an indirect tax with certain anomalies, since the consumption of this product was in a certain sense mandatory. Every commune, in fact, was assigned, after fairly rough calculations, fixed amounts that had to be purchased independently of the real necessities.[4] According to Rotelli, the rigidity of the system and the fact that Julius II's *Bolla d'oro* included a fixed annual tribute on salt, gradually transformed the salt monopoly into a real tax. Thus, when, in 1529 and in 1539, the State decreed an increase in the price of salt, the decision had the effect of a real general tax of a fixed amount.[5] The communes, in other words, had no choice but to purchase the amount assigned to them, and therefore had to pay the Apostolic Chamber a sum including the tax (the exact amount of which was estimated, at the moment of the subdivision between the various communes, according to the amount of salt).[6] Disputes often arose when the changing size of a commune was not matched by a change in the share of the salt assigned. In 1539 Paul III amended this traditional taxation, increasing the price of salt by 3 *quattrini* per pound, and extending the tax – which until that time had been limited to the communes of Patrimonio, Lazio, Sabina, Campagna and Marittima – to all the territories of the Papal State. It was this particular increase that led, as has already been mentioned (Chapter 6, p. 132 and note 11), to the rebellion of Perugia followed by the rebellion led by Ascanio Colonna. The repression of these uprisings cost the Papal State more money than that which was brought in by the tax. When, in 1543, the Triennial Subsidy replaced many of the numerous small taxes, the increase disappeared, although the original tax remained unaltered. The collection of the salt tax was always contracted out at the local level, and was often linked to the administration of the provincial Treasuries; it remained separate, however, from the farming of the *Salara* of Rome.

Not all the salt-mines were public property. Those of Ostia, for example, were divided into portions (55 to be exact), each belonging to a *porzionario* (or *salinaro*).

4 For more detail on the situation prior to the sixteenth century, see G. Tomassetti, 'Del sale e focatico del Comune di Roma nel Medioevo', *Atti della R. Deputazione di Storia Patria per le Marche*, s. IV, 1/2 (1924): 313-368, and M.L. Lombardo, *La Camera Urbis. Premesse per uno studio sull'organizzazione amministrativa della città di Roma durante il pontificato di Martino V* (Rome, 1970), esp. pp. 60 ff. For the early part of the sixteenth century, see instead M. Caravale, *La finanza pontificia nel Cinquecento: le province del Lazio* (Naples, 1974), pp. 26-41.

5 Rotelli, 'La finanza locale pontificia': 137-138.

6 A number of other interesting details can be found in ASF, Galli Tassi 1864, fol. 3, which contains the rules for the distribution and the payment of the salt of the commune of Castello, and Galli Tassi 1865, loose unnumbered folios which provide instructions on how the tax-farmers were to behave with the various authorities.

They were all, however, under the auspices of the Apostolic Chamber (on payment of an indemnity to the owners), which then contracted them out, with pluriannual contracts, to merchant-bankers.

The Salara of Rome

Unfortunately, as in the case of the customs, absolutely no Chamber documentation referring to the *Salara* of Rome in the sixteenth century has survived. The registers of the salt customs of Rome stop in 1500, to begin again only in 1621.[7] Some information about this period can, however, be gleaned from other sources.

The papal monopoly on the salt-mines of Rome dates back to the ninth century. It was then extended to the Romagna at the end of the thirteenth century and to the rest of the Papal State in the fourteenth.[8] From the fifteenth century the administration of the *Salara* of Rome was contracted out to private individuals. The proceeds initially went to the *Camera Urbis*.[9] By the beginning of the sixteenth century, however, all rights to – and revenue from – the *Salara* were claimed by the Apostolic Chamber, which handed over its administration to the highest bidder. There was an anomalous situation between 1519 and 1523, when Jacopo Salviati was in charge of all the papal *Salare*, which he then subcontracted out.[10]

In January 1531 the *Salara* of Rome was placed in the hands of the company of Bastiano da Montauto, one of the *mercatores florentini romanam curiam sequentes*. Tenders were called for, and in order to decide the winner the 'candle auction' (in which bidding time was measured by a burning candle and the winning bid was made before the candle burnt out) was used. The winner was not actually Montauto, but another Florentine, Zanobi Guidotti, *computista* of the Chamber, who had offered 18,500 ducats *di giuli 10* per ducat. The very same day, however, he transferred his rights to his fellow countryman.[11] After three years (in 1534), at the end of the contract, tenders were once again called for. The winner, this time without intermediaries, was the Genoese banker Sebastiano Sauli, who would pay 16,800 ducats per annum for the following five years.[12] It is interesting to note the overwhelming difference between these two figures and the 30,456 cameral ducats that had instead been paid in 1525.[13]

7 As already noted by Tomassetti, 'Del sale e focatico': 367.

8 P. Partner, *The Lands of St. Peter. The Papal State in the Middle Ages and the early Renaissance*, (Berkeley, 1972), p. 71.

9 Lombardo, *La Camera Urbis*, pp. 60 ff.

10 Caravale, *La finanza pontificia nel Cinquecento*, pp. 35-36.

11 Caravale, *La finanza pontificia nel Cinquecento*, pp. 62-63 (in particular, note 42). For the interminable list of the contributing communes mentioned in the contract see ibid., pp. 67-68 (note 63). The sum paid for the contract was 16,500 *scudi* according to ASF, Galli Tassi 1863, fasc. 15, fol. 1v.

12 Caravale, *La finanza pontificia nel Cinquecento*, p. 68. A different figure is given in ASF, Galli Tassi 1863, fasc. 15, fol. 1r: 18,700 *scudi di giuli 10 per scudo*.

13 M. Monaco, *La situazione della Reverenda Camera Apostolica nell'anno 1525. Ricerche d'archivio (Un contributo alla storia delle finanze pontificie)* (Rome, 1960), p. 79.

The next contract-holders were the companies of Benvenuto Olivieri, Luigi Gaddi and the Bolognese banker Jacopo Zambeccari, which were given the administration of the *Salara* for a period of three years (1 February 1539-31 January 1542). The *doganieri del sale*, that is the farmers of the *Salara*, agreed to pay 17,700 *scudi* per annum, to which was added a further 1,000 *scudi* (imposed by the Apostolic Chamber with a mandate of 26 June 1541), to cover the increase of the salt tax. In total, therefore, the contracting bankers paid out approximately 55,000 *scudi*.[14] Moreover, they had to pay their predecessors 15,000 *scudi di moneta*: this was a loan made to the Chamber which was added to every new contract and which the new administrators recouped on the monthly sales of salt.[15] They also had to make an annual payment of 13,340 *scudi di giuli 10 per scudo* to various colleges and offices, of which 12,340 for the *Salara* and 1,000 for the increase of the salt tax: 9,608 to the College of the presidents; 2,458 to the College of the knights of St Peter; 894 to the College of the portioneers of the port taxes (*porzionari di Ripa*); 380 to the College of the cubiculars and scutifers.[16]

Salt cost 34 *baiocchi* per *rubbio*.[17] In 1540 the production amounted to 44,038 *rubbi*, for which the contracting firms paid to the *salinari* almost 15,000 *scudi di moneta*, in three-monthly instalments.[18] In total the production of the three years

---

14 ASF, Galli Tassi 1864, fasc. 9, fol. 1; see also Galli Tassi 1949, fol. 138. To obtain the right to collect the increase, which would have given them a commission of 8%, the contract-holders also loaned 10,000 *scudi* at 12% (Galli Tassi 1825, fol. 3r).

15 ASF, Galli Tassi 1863, fasc. 12, fol. 5; see, for the subsequent contract, also Galli Tassi 1863, fasc. 14, fol. 11v. In both cases, at the changeover of administration, the incoming contract-holders also demanded a reimbursement (c. 150 *scudi* in the first case and c. 550 in the second) due to the devaluation of the *scudo* in the meanwhile. In 1542 it was Olivieri himself who loaned to Zambeccari 1,000 of the 5,000 *scudi* that the latter owed for his third of participation (Galli Tassi 2278, fol. 85). See also ASR, Camerale I, *Mandati Camerali 874*, fol. 71r. It should also be mentioned that in the first four months of the Olivieri-Zambeccari-Gaddi contract the *Salara* continued to be administered by Sauli (ASF, Galli Tassi 1863, fasc. 12, fol. 5); just as at the end of their contract Olivieri, Zambeccari and Gaddi did the same for their successors (see p. 149).

16 ASR, Camerale I, *Mandati Camerali 874*, fols 27v-28r; ASF, Galli Tassi 1864, fasc. 9, fol. 2. In the second year (1540) the sum came to 12,232 and in the third (1541) to 12,531. These sums were decided on at the end of the first year when the contract-holders, not having been paid the 1,200 *scudi* they were owed (and for which the Apostolic Chamber refused to take responsibility), did not want to pay the officials. The question was brought before the Chamber, where it was decided that the colleges would receive from the *Salara* only 12,235 *scudi* and would be compensated for the lost income from the *imposizione delle galere* and the income from communes (Galli Tassi 1863, fasc. 15, fols 1r-2r). See also Galli Tassi 1863, fasc. 4-5 (which are identical), fol. 1; and Galli Tassi 2278, fols 3, 57, 75, 226, where there is a slightly different distribution including, amongst the beneficiaries, also the College of the Archive.

17 In Rome the *rubbio*, when referring to salt, was equivalent to 164.6 litres: A. Martini, *Manuale di metrologia, ossia, Misure, pesi e monete in uso attualmente e anticamente presso tutti i populi* (Turin, 1883, reprinted Rome, 1976), p. 598.

18 ASF, Galli Tassi 2278, fols 286, 322; Galli Tassi 1863, fasc. 2, fol. 3.

came to 76,700 *rubbi* of salt, of which only 36,000 were sold; the remaining 40,700, as will be seen, were therefore transferred to the new contract-holders.[19]

The profits of the administration, once the expenses had been deducted, were equal to 3,522 *scudi*, which, when divided equally between the three participants, meant a sum pro capita of 1,174 *scudi*. An excellent result, especially if one also considers the collection of the *aumento* (increase), that is of the additional sum imposed on the salt tax, which reaped a profit for each of a further 1,253 *scudi* (total profit on the increase: 3,759 *scudi*).[20] However, unfortunately the contract-holders benefited little from the profits owing to them, as on 15 July 1542 they were subjected to a fairly substantial fine: 10,000 *scudi di moneta* because 'they had not sold the salt with the increased tax'.[21] In the end therefore, deducting, on the one hand, the fine, the bad debtors and other adjustments, and calculating, on the other, the profits, the commissions and other credits, the final result for the three *mercatores* was a loss of a total of approximately 2,800 *scudi*.[22]

Only Zambeccari participated in the successive three-year contract, with a share of one third, which he divided this time with other Florentines: Antonio Covoni & Partners, a company in which Olivieri was shareholder (see Chapter 2, pp. 59-60).[23] The passage from one administration to the next was obviously gradual, and a number of parcels of salt, as has been seen, remained in suspension between the new and the old contract-holders, although they were sorted out in the months which followed the handover. Among other things, for the first six months of the new administration the *Salara* continued to be administered by the old farmers, in exchange for which the Covoni company was credited with almost 6,800 *scudi di moneta*.[24] At the end of the first year of the new administration, the former contract-holders of 1539-41 (Olivieri and his partners) found themselves in the position of being owed by the new administrators a sum greater than 16,000 *scudi*, as a result of the following items: '*fabbricatura*' and transport to Ostia of 40,700 *rubbi* of salt (almost 14,000 *scudi*); transport from Ostia to Campidoglio, via Marmorata, of 23,800 *rubbi* (1,740 *scudi*); transport of a further 3,663 *rubbi*, consigned in various places in the vicinity of Rome.[25] It was agreed that the sum would be paid in the course of a year,

---

19 ASF, Galli Tassi 1863, fasc. 2, fol. 5. Every year the communes concerned received 6,476 *rubbi*, at the price of 42½ *baiocchi* per *rubbio* (fol. 1); there were, moreover, approximately 5,000 of '*extraordinario*'; plus approximately 450 for the Chamber.

20 ASF, Galli Tassi 1864, fasc. 11.

21 ASF, Galli Tassi 2278, fols 75, 322. In the same month, July 1542, Benvenuto commented bitterly that because of the fine 'a loss is more probable than a profit' (Galli Tassi 1825, fol. 3r).

22 ASF, Galli Tassi 1863, fasc. 9, fol. 6.

23 ASF, Galli Tassi 1863, fasc. 6, fols 7v-11r; Galli Tassi 2278, fol. 85. The first thing the new contract-holders had to do was to make a loan of 15,000 *scudi d'oro* (ASV, *Cam. Ap., Div. Cam. 131*, fols 145v-146r).

24 ASF, Galli Tassi 2278, fol. 195; Galli Tassi 1863, fasc. 6, fols 9v-10r.

25 ASF, Galli Tassi 1863, fasc. 6, fols 7v-8r: the cost of the transport from Ostia to Marmorata came to 4½ *baiocchi* per *rubbio*; the unloading cost 12 *giuli* per *barcata* (=360 *rubbi* approximately); transport from Marmorata to Campidoglio cost 2½ *baiocchi* per *rubbio*. Production plus transport to Ostia cost instead 34 1/5 *baiocchi* per *rubbio*: 32 *baiocchi* for the

between 1 August 1542 and 1 August 1543, and there is proof that in December 1542 the Covoni company paid 12,400 *scudi di moneta* to its predecessors for the salt consigned to them.[26]

As late as 1545, even though several years had passed since he had held the farm of the *Salara* of Rome, Olivieri participated in a number of transactions connected with the administration of the salt. On 19 April, for example, he made an agreement to sell 6,000 *rubbi* to the Duke of Castro; a month later he transferred the deal to the Romans, Carlo Paoloni & Partners, at that time contract-holders of the *Salara*. From this particular deal, on which he calculated a profit of 4,800 *scudi*, Olivieri would receive only the eighth part, but, at the same time would lose no money if the deal was unsuccessful.[27]

The price of the contract of 1 February 1551 was 18,000 ducats; the tender was won by the companies of the Florentine Pier Antonio Bandini and that of the heirs of Carlo Paoloni, who undertook to administer the *Salara* for seven years.[28]

The salt tax of the Romagna and Bologna and its increase

The communes of the Romagna extracted a predetermined quantity of salt every year from the salt mines of Cervia. This was then distributed throughout the territory, without any of it remaining unsold.

In 1539, as already mentioned, the Apostolic Chamber increased the price of salt by 3 *quattrini* per pound; considering that every sack of salt weighed 360 pounds, this meant an increase of 9 *lire* per sack.[29] The following year, on 31 March 1540, the collection of the increase of the salt tax of the Romagna and Bologna was taken over by Benvenuto Olivieri & Partners. The contract stated that Olivieri would be in charge of the administration for a period of five years, starting from 1 April. However, because of the imposition of the Triennial Subsidy, which replaced a series

---

salinari, ½ for transport to the warehouse of Ostia, ¾ for the expenses and commissions of guardians and ministers, 1/5 for the salary of the commissioners, ¾ for the rent of the warehouse of Ostia and for its guardian (Galli Tassi 1863, fasc. 12, fol. 21). It should be remembered that one *scudo di moneta* was composed of 10 *giuli* or of 100 *baiocchi*. These accounts presumably included the 21,000 *rubbi* purchased in 1539, but all the expenses of which would be paid by the new contractors (Galli Tassi 1864, fasc. 5, fol. 1r-v).

26 ASF, Galli Tassi 2278, fol. 195.

27 ASF, Galli Tassi 1865, fol. 10. For the agreements on the '*locatio salare urbe*' to Carlo Paoloni, for a sum of 17,850 ducats, see ASR, *Notai segretari e cancellieri della R. Camera apostolica 1988*, fols 307r-316v; some time later Cristoforo Sauli also entered into the deal (fol. 614r).

28 ASV, *Cam. Ap., Div. Cam. 157*, fols 186v-187v (contract of 29 May 1549).

29 For the quantity of salt attributed to each commune see ASF, Galli Tassi 1866: for example, Bologna was obliged to purchase 4,500 sacks, Imola 2,400, Rimini 2,100, Cesena and Ravenna 1,900, Faenza 1,800, Forlì 1,500 and so on. Interestingly the tax collector in the city and *contado* of Faenza was also paid an increase on the commission (12 *scudi d'oro* in addition to the 24 normally paid by the communes) because 'the business in that area was much more difficult than anywhere else in the province and therefore extra staff was necessary' (Galli Tassi 1866, fol. 63).

of taxes including the increase of the salt tax, the Chamber decided to suspend this contract exactly halfway through the period, after 30 months. In a protest sent to the '*magnifico messer Antonio*', one of Benvenuto's legal representatives demanded that *messer* Antonio take more of an interest in what was happening: Benvenuto had in fact loaned 12,000 *scudi*, which would be repaid without interest, in exchange for the right to collect the salt tax for five years. His profit would come from the 7% commission. Olivieri, in other words, assumed that he would earn 8,400 *scudi* as commission calculated on an estimated total of 120,000 *scudi*. In reality, on an actual collection of 50,000 *scudi*, he earned a commission of 3,500, or 4,900 less than he had calculated. And – he concludes – if 'he had thought he would receive only the revenue of 30 months, he would not have loaned the 12,000 *scudi* on which he earned no interest'.[30]

According to the initial contract, anyway, the *doganieri* of the salt, that is the contract-holders, were obliged to pay the Chamber 2,000 *scudi* a month, equivalent to the 24,000 *scudi* per annum it was estimated that would result from the sale of the salt. If at the end of the year the amount earned was greater than this, the extra money would become the property of the Chamber; if it was less, the contract-holders would have to make up the sum on the subsequent income. The *doganieri*, moreover, had to make an immediate loan to the Chamber of 12,000 *scudi* (the amount alluded to above), with an interest of 12% until the beginning of the tax collection, interest free afterwards. The commission – as mentioned – was 7%.[31] As early as July 1540, however, a number of amendments proved necessary, a clear reflection of both the difficulties faced by the Apostolic Chamber in respecting their side of the bargain, and, at the same time, the power they had to change the rules of the game at any time during the execution of the contract. Nevertheless, the deal remained lucrative for the *mercatores romanam curiam sequentes*, and they clearly wished to maintain the contract in order to recoup the money that the Apostolic Chamber continued to owe them. First it was decided that 2% of the 7% commission would be at the pope's disposal for three years; second, as the Chamber was not able to immediately repay the 12,000 *scudi* plus interest, it gave Olivieri 12 offices of knights of St Paul in pledge until repayment.[32]

As usual, the contract, even though it was in the name of Benvenuto Olivieri & Partners, also involved other *mercatores*. The loan of 12,000 *scudi* was in fact shared by: the heirs of Pandolfo Della Casa & Partners, who contributed 3,000 *scudi*; Tommaso Cavalcanti and Giovanni Giraldi & Partners, 2,000; Tobia Pallavicini & Partners, a further 2,000. Therefore the offices of knights of St Paul given in pledge

---

30 ASF, Galli Tassi 1864, fol. 1; a virtually identical document can be found in Galli Tassi 1844, fol. 9.

31 ASF, Galli Tassi 1865, fols 6, 7, 8 (these three documents are virtually identical). The contract speaks of 24,000 *scudi* for the first year and 30,000 for the following ones; from the above-mentioned complaint and from other sources it seems, however, that 24,000 *scudi* were calculated for all the years that the contract lasted.

32 ASF, Galli Tassi 1865, fol. 9. This information can also be found in Galli Tassi 1864, fasc. 13, where the Chamber is also debited with the interests for the three months between March and June which, calculated on the sum actually deposited of 11,428 *scudi*, amounted to 342 *scudi*.

were also handed out proportionately: 5 to Olivieri, 3 to Della Casa, 2 to Cavalcanti and Giraldi, 2 to Pallavicini.[33] Under the name of the Olivieri company (which held 41.6%) another two merchant-bankers participated, each with an 8.3% share: Jacopo Zambeccari and Luigi Gaddi, who had already been partners of Olivieri in the contract of the *Salara* of Rome.[34] Thus, the contributions to the loan were divided as follows:

Benvenuto Olivieri & Partners	25.0%
Heirs of Pandolfo Della Casa & Partners	25.0%
Tommaso Cavalcanti and Giovanni Giraldi & Partners	16.7%
Tobia Pallavicini & Partners	16.7%
Jacopo Zambeccari & Partners	8.3%
Luigi Gaddi & Partners	8.3%

The situation is slightly different, however, when the commission of 7% is taken into account, as at this point the then treasurer of the Romagna, Antonio Ugolini, is included with a share of 2/7 (=28.6%).[35] The shares of the others must therefore be calculated on the remaining 5/7:

Antonio Ugolini	28.6%
Benvenuto Olivieri & Partners	17.9%
Heirs of Pandolfo Della Casa & Partners	17.9%
Tommaso Cavalcanti and Giovanni Giraldi & Partners	11.9%
Tobia Pallavicini & Partners	11.9%
Jacopo Zambeccari & Partners	5.9%
Luigi Gaddi & Partners	5.9%

In actual fact, of the first 2,100 *scudi d'oro in oro* that were distributed of the 2,661.75 total (that is 7% of the 38,025 that were collected in three years) 625 went to Olivieri, 600 to Ugolini, 375 to the heirs of Della Casa, 250 to Cavalcanti-Giraldi and to Pallavicini.[36]

Bernardo Machiavelli, commissioner for the tax collection, was entitled to 2% of the sums collected.[37] On the 38,025 *scudi d'oro in oro* that were collected in the three years, therefore, he obtained a commission of 760.5 *scudi*.[38]

33 ASF, Galli Tassi 2278, fol. 98. Until November 1541, 'for the interest on the 5 knighthoods of St Paul which we have in pledge', Olivieri received 781.5 *scudi di moneta* (fols 54, 151).

34 ASF, Galli Tassi 1942, fol. 195v. All the details of the contract and the shares of participation can also be found in Galli Tassi 1825, fol. 2r.

35 In fact: 'the commission is 7%; on the first three years 2% has to be given to Ugolini' (ASF, Galli Tassi 1942, fol. 196v).

36 Commissions matured on 8 November 1542 (ASF, Galli Tassi 1864, fasc. 13; Galli Tassi 2278, fol. 157).

37 As confirmed in ASF, Galli Tassi 1942, fol. 196v, which spoke optimistically (from Olivieri's point of view) of 2% at the most.

38 ASF, Galli Tassi 2278, fol. 314.

On 27 July 1542, of the 83,735 *lire di bolognini* (=approximately 21,750 *scudi d'oro*) collected, Benvenuto Olivieri and his partners were entitled to 5,813 (=1,505).[39] In the following period, until March 1543, of the 62,662 *lire* (=16,275 *scudi*) collected, 4,386 (=1,139) went to Olivieri and his partners as commission. On 15 May 1545, presumably for arrears for the period 1540-43, of the 57,038 *lire* (=14,800 *scudi* approximately) a share of 3,993 *lire* (=1,037) was attributed to the contract-holders. On the same date, Bernardo Machiavelli, commissioner for the increase of the salt tax on behalf of Olivieri, credited to Benvenuto Olivieri & Partners 19,000 *lire di bolognini* (=approxiamately 4,935 *scudi*) for their commission on approximately 69,300 *scudi*, which would be collected over five years if the contract regarding the increase of the salt tax of the Romagna and Bologna continued.[40]

The initial requests of the representatives of Olivieri therefore had a positive outcome: instead of being calculated on the increase of the salt tax, the 7% commission was calculated on the Triennial Subsidy of the Romagna and Bologna. By this time the new tax had become an essential source of income, and, initially intended to be provisory, was then repeatedly prolonged, until it became a true ordinary tax. (This is treated in more detail in section 5 of this chapter.)

The salt tax of the Marches, Umbria, and Parma-Piacenza

In passing it is worth mentioning that between 1530 and 1531 the companies of Ciriaco Mattei, Filippo Strozzi and Bindo Altoviti (of which Olivieri was partner), which at the time were already managing the customs of Rome (see Chapter 5, p. 115), managed the collection of the increase of the salt tax in the Marches, Umbria and the duchy of Spoleto.[41] Bindo Altoviti was subsequently administrator of the *Salara* of the Marches at the end of the 1530s and beginning of the 1540s.[42] Sometimes the administration of the local *Salara* and/or the collection of the increase of the salt tax were included in the contract of the Treasury, thus becoming part of the responsibility of the treasurers. Such was the case, for example, of Olivieri and his partners in Umbria and Perugia and of the Cavalcanti and Giraldi in Parma and Piacenza.[43]

2. The *gabella dello Studio*

One of the indirect sources of income was a rather particular tax, the so-called *gabella dello Studio*. This was a duty applied to the wine sold by retail in Rome, which served to finance the activity of the University of Rome.

---

39 ASF, Galli Tassi 1866, fols 66-67. Galli Tassi 1864, fol. 15 differs slightly, calculating on a collection of nearly 81,000 *lire di bolognini* a commission of 5,663.

40 ASR, Camerale I, *Tesoreria di Romagna*, busta 14, reg. 70, fol. 25; reg. 71, fol. 43.

41 ASF, Galli Tassi 1865, fasc. 1.

42 ASR, Camerale I, *Tesoreria provinciale della Marca*, buste 25-27. See also Chapter 6, p. 143.

43 See Chapter 6, pp. 133-134, 141-142 and the sources quoted there.

The University, or *Studium*, of the City of Rome was founded by Boniface VIII by a papal bull of 20 April 1303. In 1431, it was reorganized by Eugene IV, immediately after his ascension to the papal throne. As part of this reorganization he ordered that the University be financed by the increase of a *gabella*, or duty, on imported foreign wine (previously its financing was rather more haphazard, deriving from various sources, including, for example, the customs of Ripa). Originally this duty amounted to 6 *denari* per pound of wine; Eugene IV ordered this to be increased by 3½ *soldi* per pound and that it be destined '*pro salario doctorum per eos ad legendum in dicto Studio conductorum, et omnium expensarum in Studio hujusmodi occorrentium*'. At the same time it was expressly forbidden that it be destined for other uses. The *gabella*, therefore, was collected on foreign wine sold by retail. Within 24 hours of purchase innkeepers and tavern-keepers were obliged to declare the quality and quantity of the wine, so that the tax could be calculated. Given its new destination, this *gabella vini forensis ad minutum* was from then on known as the *gabella Studii*.[44]

Initially the duty was paid directly to the *Camera del popolo romano* – it was, in other words, a communal tax – and it was administered by the magistrates of the city. By the end of the fifteenth century, however, the control had fallen into the hands of the Apostolic Chamber. Like most of the Apostolic Chamber's sources of revenue, the collection of this duty was contracted out to merchant-bankers resident in Rome. The price, which was proclaimed publicly, amounted, at the end of the fifteenth century, to 14,000 Roman florins, which were increased by 2,000 ducats in 1500, the Jubilee year.[45] For the whole of the fifteenth century the *gabella* was an excellent source of income and therefore was a much sought after contract among the bankers. As an aside, it should also be mentioned that, despite the veto proclaimed in 1431, the proceeds of the duty were in part destined to other uses (for example, the construction of bridges, buildings or roads).[46]

In the three years from 1504 to 1506 the *gabella* was contracted out to the Sienese banker Jacopo de' Bertini for 4,000 gold cameral ducats, and in the following three years (1507-09) to his fellow citizen, Stefano Ghinucci (of whom Bertini

---

44 E. Lo Sardo, *Le gabelle e le dogane dei Papi in età moderna: inventario della serie Dogane della Miscellanea camerale per materie* (Rome, 1994), p. 161. For the history of this *gabella* in relation to the University in the fifteenth and sixteenth centuries, see, as well as the bibliography cited in the notes which follow, also the interesting articles by R. Avesani ('Appunti per la storia dello "Studium Urbis" nel Quattrocento') and P. Pavan ('Il Comune romano e lo "Studium Urbis" tra XV e XVI secolo') in *Roma e lo Studium Urbis. Spazio urbano e cultura dal Quattro al Seicento*, Atti del Convegno, Rome 7-10 June 1989 (Rome, 1992), pp. 69-87, 88-100.

45 D.S. Chambers, 'Studium Urbis and *gabella studii*: the University of Rome in the fifteenth century', in C.H. Clough (ed.), *Cultural aspects of the Italian Renaissance. Essays in honour of Paul Oskar Kristeller* (Manchester, 1976), p. 77.

46 Chambers notes that in 1497, against an income of 13,050 florins, the expenses were 7,901: this difference was immediately appropriated by the Apostolic Chamber, contributing, together with other factors, to the disappointing results of the *Studium*, which remained 'more Roman (which, paradoxically, meant more provincial) than a *Studio generale* should have been' ('Studium Urbis and *gabella studii*', pp. 77, 86-87).

was '*socius et institor*'). After this the Florentine dominion, which was already becoming clear in the field of papal finances, was confirmed by the assignment of the contract, for three and a half years (1510-13) at 7,850 gold cameral ducats, to Antonio Segni and Guidetto Guidetti;[47] they were succeeded by Bonifacio Donati. When the city magistrates, thanks to Leo X, regained control of the administration of the *gabella dello Studio*, they tried but failed to find sufficiently wealthy Roman merchant-bankers, and thus in December 1515 had little choice but to entrust the administration for four years to another Florentine, Giovanni Ardinghelli, for 6,260 gold cameral ducats. According to Polverini Fosi, the pope wished to demonstrate the University's total dependence on Florentine money and to tie the hands of the Campidoglio, which, deprived of every decisional power, was thus each time forced to make a deal with the Curia and its financiers.[48] Leo X's spendthrift politics, which included very generous treatment of the lecturers of the University, however, meant that the revenue from the *gabella* no longer sufficed.[49] Moreover, against the will of the city magistrates, who invited him to be somewhat more prudent, the pontiff always took good care of the merchant-bankers who had contracts with the Chamber, guaranteeing, among other things, reduction of their debts. After Ardinghelli came the Florentine Bernardo da Verrazzano and the Roman Giuliano Maddaleni Capodiferro. In April 1524 it was Strozzi and his partners who obtained the contract. In December 1525, however, after various arguments and accusations, it was conveyed to another Florentine: Luigi Gaddi, one of the most influential merchant-bankers in the period of the Medici pontificates.[50]

With the Sack of 1527 the University was closed down and Clement VII redirected the proceeds of the *gabella* on the wine towards the increase of the assignments of the *conservatori* and of the other officials of the *popolo romano*, and towards the maintenance of the city walls and other public buildings of the city until the *Studio* was reopened in the first years of the pontificate of Paul III. By 1539 the University was once again functioning well.[51]

During the pontificates of the two Medici popes, therefore, the Florentine bankers maintained a virtual monopoly over the *gabella dello Studio*. This was not, however, due to the favours that Leo X and Clement VII bestowed lavishly on their fellow countrymen, but rather to a very real dependence. This was demonstrated, for example, when, during the first Medici pontificate, in an attempt to tender out the *gabella* to Roman merchants, the *conservatori* were unable to obtain offers

---

47 The case of Antonio Segni is rather unusual: he reached the peak of his success at the beginning of the sixteenth century, then fell into disgrace with the election of Leo X, because of the support given to Cardinal Soderini (I. Polverini Fosi, 'I mercanti fiorentini, il Campidoglio e il papa: il gioco delle parti', in *Roma e lo Studium Urbis*, p. 177). The latter controversial individual is the subject of a study by K.J.P. Lowe, *Church and Politics in Renaissance Italy. The Life and Career of Cardinal Francesco Soderini, 1453-1524* (Cambridge, 1993).

48 Polverini Fosi, 'I mercanti fiorentini, il Campidoglio e il papa', pp. 177, 183.

49 F.M. Renazzi points out that '*col favore e per munificienza di Leon X giungono le lettere in Roma al più alto grado di coltivamento e di gloria*' (*Storia dell'Università degli Studi di Roma* (4 vols, Rome, 1803-06, reprinted Bologna, 1971), II, pp. 1-30).

50 Polverini Fosi, 'I mercanti fiorentini, il Campidoglio e il papa', pp. 182-184.

51 Renazzi, *Storia dell'Università*, II, pp. 91, 97.

greater than 1,500 ducats, compared with the 7,000 that the Florentines were able to guarantee.[52] Not surprisingly, therefore, even though there was a non-Medici pope on the throne the situation remained much the same.

After the company of Mario de' Bellis, depositary of the '*gabelle gymnasij alme urbis*' in 1539,[53] it was Bernardo Corbinelli who won the contract from the senate of the *popolo romano*, for five years starting from 1 January 1540 (therefore, until 31 December 1544), in exchange for a total sum of 12,000 *scudi di moneta*.[54] Benvenuto Olivieri & Partners of Rome acquired a 25% share. On 31 December 1542 (but presumably this was the situation from the beginning) there were four participants, each with a share of 25%: Bernardo Corbinelli, Carlo Paoloni, Filippo Carducci & Partners (in which the Olivieri held 53.3%) and Benvenuto Olivieri & Partners.[55] On 1 January 1543 the Olivieri company then transferred a 5% share to Antonio Covoni & Partners of Rome, which contributed 120 *scudi* per annum, obtaining a profit of 84.3 *scudi*, equal to 35.1% of the capital paid in.[56] From this it can be deduced that in the same period (1 January 1543-31 December 1544) the Olivieri company made a profit of 337.2 *scudi*.

In the first two years, each of the four participants had made a profit of 800 *scudi*.[57] For the third year, 1542, the Olivieri company were guaranteed a profit of 250 *scudi* (it should be recalled that at this time they held a 25% share because the Covoni company had not yet entered the deal).[58] In the five years that they participated in the administration, Benvenuto Olivieri & Partners earned a profit of 1,387.3 *scudi*, after an outlay of 2,760 *scudi*, which naturally was paid back to them in the course of the operations. Analysing the overall profits, a falling trend can be noted, from 1,600 *scudi* on average in the first two years, to 1,000 in the third year, to 843 in the fourth and fifth years.

3. Other indirect taxes

The three customs of Rome have already been dealt with in considerable detail in Chapter 5, because of their importance for both the contracting bankers and for the Chamber, and thus need not be dealt with again here. This leaves a few similar

52 Polverini Fosi, 'I mercanti fiorentini, il Campidoglio e il papa', p. 181.

53 ASR, Camerale I, *Mandati Camerali 872*, fol. 32r-v. On this occasion de' Bellis was asked to pay 75 ducats to the medical doctor, Giustiniano Finetto of Montelupo (probably for part of his salary as lecteur).

54 ASF, Galli Tassi 1832, fol. 1; Galli Tassi 1942, fol. 195r.

55 ASF, Galli Tassi 1942, fol. 195r.

56 The Covoni company specified that their share was on behalf of the Capponi of Florence, who then indicated that the orders of Francesco del Nero be followed; Del Nero in his turn said that the wishes of his brother Agostino be followed, and thus it was to this last that the Olivieri company would have had to pay the profits (ASF, Galli Tassi 1832, fol. 2). See also Galli Tassi 2278, fol. 339.

57 ASF, Galli Tassi 1941, fol. 443r.

58 ASF, Galli Tassi 2278, fol. 35, account of '*Filippo Carducci e c. depositari della dogana dello Studio*'.

means of taxation – again often contracted out to private individuals – which are described below.

Generally linked to the Treasury of the Patrimonio, at least from 1480, was the *dogana dei pascoli* on the area around Rome (that is, the duty on the right of common, or grazing rights). The papacy held the monopoly on this duty, which was administered for many years by the Genoese banker Sauli, at times joined by the Florentines Bartolomeo Pucci, Alessandro Del Bene and Roberto Ubaldini.[59]

In 1544 Donato Acciaiuoli wrote to Benvenuto Olivieri: 'in exchange for the administration of the customs on animals [*dogana del bestiame*], I would like you to open a bank with a capital of 5,000 to 6,000 *scudi*'; this, according to Acciaiuoli, would result in annual earnings of the amount of 5,400 *scudi*, deriving from the 15% imposed on '*ciascheduno condotiere*'.[60] Unfortunately this is not referred to in any other source, and thus the outcome remains unknown to us, but, nevertheless, it is worthwhile noting Acciaiuoli's letter as it provides a glimpse of another aspect of Olivieri's various activities.

Little information has survived, either, with regard to the *dogana dei cavalli* (or customs on horses). All that is known is that in September 1545 it was in the hands of Carducci, and under his name Benvenuto Olivieri. The latter then handed over his profits to Mariotto Della Palla.[61]

In 1548 those merchants who had loaned 100,000 *scudi* to the pontiff had the right to the 25,000 *scudi* (which then became 35,000) of revenue from the *gabella della farina* (tax on flour) (see Chapter 3, pp. 90-93). Between 1544 and 1546 the Florentines, Antonio and Bernardo Corbinelli, had had an important role in the administration of this tax.[62]

The *gabella dei contratti* (tax on contracts) was also in Florentine hands, at least from the end of the 1530s. It is not known with any certainty if and with what share the company of Benvenuto Olivieri (or of Filippo Strozzi before him) participated in the business deal, but it is certain that in the six years of the contract, which ran from 1 January 1538 to 31 December 1543, Tommaso Cavalcanti and Giovanni Giraldi & Partners held a 25% share in the *gabella* and the related '*pene e quarti*'. The Apostolic Chamber received an initial loan of 15,000 *scudi d'oro in oro* (16,500 *di moneta*) and, it can be assumed, an annual *rente*, although there is no record of this. In the six-year period Cavalcanti and Giraldi made a profit of nearly 3,000 *scudi*.[63]

59 Caravale, *La finanza pontificia nel Cinquecento*, pp. 41-46, 60-62, 79-81. See also Chapter 6, note 73.

60 ASF, Galli Tassi 1824, fol. 17.

61 ASF, Galli Tassi 1806, ins. 2 and here, Appendix, doc. 3, p. 222.

62 ASV, *Cam. Ap., Div. Cam. 139*, fols 60v, 90r, 158v-159r, 180r; *Cam. Ap., Div. Cam. 142*, fol. 15v.

63 ASF, Galli Tassi 1832, fasc. 15, fols 1-4. The profits derived from the 8% commissions on the first 10,000 ducats collected and of 10% on the rest; and then of 25% on the '*pene*' (for the latter, the rest was subdivided thus: 25% to the questors, 25% to the lawyers, notaries and mandataries, 25% to the commissioner).

Rodolfo Dotti, appointed by the Chamber to collect this *gabella*, received in return one-fifth of all the sums collected, after deducting the expenses.[64]

4. Direct taxes

In a study of this kind, which centres on the activity of a single merchant-banker, it is not always easy to accurately identify all the various sources of income of the Papal State. As in the previous cases, a banker – or more frequently a consortium of bankers – loaned large sums of money which would be repaid from the future revenues of the Chamber. If, however, the contract in question was not very large, then the repayment might well come from other sources: for example, the *imposizione delle galere* (destined to the financing of the fleet and instituted in 1533), the income from communes (*entrate delle comunità*) and the *vigesima* (a twentieth part) on the assets possessed by the Jews.[65] All of these were direct taxes, ordinary or extraordinary, the collection of which was contracted out to the *mercatores* who were owed money by the Chamber. These taxes as a source of income for the *mercatores* can be passed over here, as they were described in Chapter 3, section 3, dedicated to the loans. They were discussed in the earlier chapter rather than here as there were often various items of income involved in any single loan operation, and it was the final amount rather than the individual items that was the most significant aspect from the point of view of this study on Benvenuto Olivieri.

5. The Triennial Subsidy

The Triennial Subsidy was introduced in 1543 as a way of replacing the increase of the salt tax and the other extraordinary taxes (including '*le maggiori intrade delle Comunità, il Sussidio delle Galere, e de' Censi*') with a single tax.[66] The Subsidy was applied to all the communes and was a real 'State tax', in the sense that it affected all the territories of the Papal State.[67] It also diminished the difference between lands which were *mediate subiecte* and those which were *immediate subiecte*, given that they were all subject to this taxation. According to Gardi, the Triennial Subsidy, which no longer admitted any exemptions for non-ecclesiasts, but affected all

64 ASF, Galli Tassi 1832, fol. 10-11. See ASV, *Cam. Ap., Div. Cam. 153*, fols 183r-184r for the statutes of the *gabella dei contratti*.

65 It was Adrian VI (1522-23) who imposed on the Jewish population the payment of the '*vigesimam partem omnium et singulorum bonorum, jurium, actionum, fructuum, redituum et proventuum ac pecuniarum quarumcumque et usuraria pravitatis ad eos spectantium*' (Monaco, *La situazione della Reverenda Camera Apostolica*, p. 51). For more detail on this tax and on the papal fiscal policies with regard to the Jews, see K.R. Stow, *Taxation, Community and the State. The Jews and the Fiscal Foundations of the Early Modern Papal State* (Stuttgart, 1982), esp. pp. 1-36.

66 ASR, Camerale II, *Gabelle*, busta 1, fasc. 10, fol. 370r (p. 89 of the printed booklet).

67 Caravale, *La finanza pontificia nel Cinquecento*, p. 82.

taxpayers, can be considered the model tax of the modern Papal State.[68] However, its application differed from commune to commune as its exact definition was decided on by the local authority. While each commune had to pay very precise shares (which were sometimes amended following the recurrent protests), it could freely choose how to apply this new tax. For example, it could choose to collect a part of the total by way of various duties: in Imola the authorities placed taxes on grain and forage, as well as on woods, vineyards, pastures, etc.[69] The Triennial Subsidy, while failing, in practice, to lessen to any real extent the privileges of the clergy, did at least destroy once and for all those of the nobles (who until then had even extended the exemptions to their peasants).[70]

Although the protests and subsequent negotiations quickly brought the amount below the 300,000 *scudi* initially calculated, the instrument revealed itself immediately to be efficient and versatile both from the financial and the political point of view, and was thus immediately renewed.[71] Particularly clear are the words of the encyclical of 13 June 1545, with which Pope Paul III decided to prolong the Triennial Subsidy for a further three years. This encyclical explains that the Subsidy substituted the increase of the salt tax, income from communes, the *imposizione delle galere* and the *censi*, with the double aim of reducing the tax burden on the communes and of having liquid assets available as quickly as possible. However, increasing needs for the 'defence of the Catholic Faith' and the 'war against the infidels' meant that the alternative was then to either reintroduce the abolished taxes, or to prolong the Triennial Subsidy. The choice fell on 'the path that will create less damage and annoyance to the subjects', or, in other words, the renewal of the Subsidy.[72]

This was not, however, the only time that the Triennial Subsidy was prolonged, as it was clearly considered by the Chamber to be an efficient and simple way of extracting taxes from the population. In 1548 it was prolonged for a further three years, while the third extension was proclaimed by Julius III in a papal bull of 16 March 1551. The last extension, again for three years, was proclaimed by Marcellus II in a bull of 18 April 1555.[73] At this point the Triennial Subsidy became ordinary and perpetual rather than extraordinary and temporary. Over time, however, the collection of this tax evidently became less efficient, as by around 1560 it rendered only 165,000 *scudi*, against the 300,000 calculated at the beginning.[74] Stumpo has demonstrated that the continual negotiations between the communes and the Chamber almost immediately prevented the Subsidy from exceeding 200,000 *scudi*.

68 A. Gardi, 'La fiscalità pontificia tra medioevo ed età moderna', *Società e Storia*, 33 (1986): 537.

69 Rotelli, 'La finanza locale pontificia': 128-129.

70 Rotelli, 'La finanza locale pontificia': 121-122.

71 Gardi, 'La fiscalità pontificia': 538.

72 ASR, Camerale II, *Gabelle*, busta 1, fasc. 10, fol. 370r-v (pp. 89-90 of the printed booklet).

73 ASR, Camerale II, *Gabelle*, busta 1, fasc. 10, pp. 106 ff.

74 According to a statement made by the Venetian ambassador, Mocenigo: E. Albèri, *Relazioni degli ambasciatori veneti al senato (Relazioni della corte di Roma nel secolo XVI)* (Florence 1846), series II, vol. 4, p. 27.

He suggests, however, that the real error was that of replacing the gold coin (initially used to calculate the amount of the Subsidy) with silver coin, which was subject to a progressive devaluation.[75] Nevertheless, the Subsidy constituted a model which, at least until the end of the century, the pontiffs often copied when they imposed new taxes.

Every area or province had its own depositary or commissioner for the collection of the taxes: in the case of the Romagna, the first three-year period (1543-46) was administered by the Genoese bankers, Pallavicini and Giustiniani.[76] Benvenuto Olivieri, who then became treasurer from December 1545 together with these two bankers, was commissioner for the collection of the Triennial Subsidy from 1546 to 1549, for 30,000 *scudi* in Bologna and 40,000 in the Romagna.[77] The appointment to this role was not necessarily linked to the contract of the Treasury; nevertheless, it was often the treasurer himself, or a person close to him, who covered both offices. Altoviti, who had firm control of the province of the Marches, naturally dealt with the collection of the Subsidy in that province.[78]

In 1549, as was described in great detail in Chapter 3, p. 92, a large consortium of bankers acquired the right to 106,000 *scudi* from the Triennial Subsidy as a partial repayment of a loan of 128,000 *scudi d'oro in oro*.[79] The Olivieri company, whose share of the loan came to 19,000, therefore had the right, proportionally, to 15,734 *scudi*.

6. Tithes

The other important area of income for the papacy is frequently referred to as the area of 'spiritual finance', in other words, the area that included the tithes and the taxes on the clergy in general. These were extraordinary taxes, dictated by urgent necessities of defence and of protection of the Catholic faith, which from the end of the thirteenth century were applied to the earnings of almost all the ecclesiastical institutions of Christendom (a number of institutions were guaranteed exemptions). Between that time and the fifteenth century approximately 20 tithes, some annual and others pluriennial, were imposed in Italy.[80] In general, from the second half of the fifteenth century there was a reduction of the spiritual income and by the sixteenth century the tithes were limited to the clergy of only the Italian States: the main aim remained the same, but could be broadened to include the maintenance of the papal fleet, as a means of protecting and ensuring the security of the State of the Church.

---

75 Stumpo, *Il capitale finanziario a Roma*, pp. 103-104.

76 ASF, Galli Tassi 1850, loose folio; ASR, Camerale I, *Tesoreria di Romagna*, busta 14, reg. 74.

77 ASR, Camerale I, *Mandati Camerali 888*, fol. 104r; ASV, *Cam. Ap., Div. Cam. 141*, fol. 25r-v. Even earlier, in 1544, however, the company of Olivieri had loaned 10,000 *scudi d'oro*, receiving in exchange the right to collect the Subsidy of Bologna (ASR, *Notai segretari e cancellieri della R. Camera apostolica 1988*, fol. 265r-v; see also Chapter 3, p. 89).

78 ASR, Camerale I, *Mandati Camerali 874*, fol. 59r.

79 ASF, Galli Tassi 1828, fasc. 4. The sum of 106,000 *scudi* was divided among the provinces as follows: Marches 30,000, Bologna 25,000, Ravenna 20,000, Umbria and Perugia 20,000, Patrimonio and Civitavecchia 6,000, Campagna and Marittima 5,000.

80 Stumpo, *Il capitale finanziario a Roma*, p. 184.

The collection of the tithes and their transfer to Rome were traditionally delegated to the most influential merchant-bankers, the only ones originally able to reach, thanks to their close-knit and well-organized networks, the most remote markets of Europe (see also Chapter 1, pp. 6-7). By Benvenuto Olivieri's time the problems of distance and the technical difficulties that had previously made the merchant-bankers the necessary interlocutors for the collection of this tax no longer existed. Nevertheless, the Apostolic Chamber continued to entrust the *mercatores* with this task, as often these taxes were used as a means of repaying their debts. In practice, the bankers acquired rights on the collection of the tithes in certain areas until the original loan plus the interest (12% per annum) had been repaid in full, and in general they were also entitled to a commission of 5% for the service of tax collection.

The commissioner appointed to collect the taxes from the communes of the Papal State was in general linked to the treasurer of the province, even if he was not necessarily one of his partners or employees. For example, when Benvenuto Olivieri was treasurer of Umbria and Perugia (1541-46)[81] and of the Romagna (1545-49),[82] the accounts for the collection of the tithes all passed through his hands.

These cases are only briefly mentioned here, as they have already been dealt with in the section dedicated to the loans made to the Apostolic Chamber, Chapter 3, section 3. This seemed to be the logical choice, because, as has just been pointed out, the income deriving from the tithes (and also from the *imposizione dei mezzi frutti* which had to be paid by the clergy) often did not remain for long in the coffers of the Apostolic Chamber, but rather was used to repay the loans that the latter had received. Moreover, these sums of money were more often than not repaid using proceeds deriving from various sources, including sources of a temporal nature (see p. 158). An exception has been made for two cases, however, both relative to territories outside the Papal State. The first is mentioned briefly here because it concerns a circumstance of which little is known but the results, and the second because it concerns a particularly interesting situation.

In 1539-42 the company of Benvenuto Olivieri took a share of a third in a contract worth 20,000 *scudi* stipulated by the Pallavicini-Giustiniani company for the collection of the tithes in the Kingdom of Naples. The bankers had the right to a premium of 2,000 *scudi* and a commission of 10%. Of the 6,667 *scudi* of the Olivieri company, however, two shares of 2,000 *scudi* each were transferred to Cavalcanti-Giraldi and to Bandini.[83] In the following years it was Michele and Alessandro Olivieri of Naples who occupied themselves materially with the collection of the tithes of the Kingdom of Naples.[84]

81 Information on Umbria and the duchy of Spoleto in 1543 can be found in ASF, Galli Tassi 1872-1873.

82 In 1546, of the tithes collected in the Romagna for the war of Germany, 5% was the commission of the commissioner Andrea Zanini, while the remaining 8,047 *lire* were attributed to Benvenuto Olivieri as treasurer, on behalf of the Apostolic Chamber (ASF, Galli Tassi 1874).

83 ASF, Galli Tassi 1825, fol. 7r; Galli Tassi 2278, fol. 150.

84 ASV, *Cam. Ap., Div. Cam. 142*, fol. 49.

In 1546-47 the pontiff imposed a tithe to pay for the war of Germany. For the share reserved for the Duchy of Florence he made very precise agreements with Cosimo I de' Medici, which regarded very closely also Benvenuto Olivieri & Partners. The latter in fact promised to pay 50,000 *scudi d'oro in oro*, of which 20,000 immediately to Bartolomeo Gualterotti & Partners '*della magona del ferro*' and 30,000 in three instalments to Cosimo. Moreover, Olivieri undertook to pay Tobia Pallavicini, then depositary general of the Chamber, 24,300 *scudi*, again relative to the assignment on the tithes (Olivieri and Gualterotti were guarantors for the duke). The duke undertook to repay the entire 74,300 *scudi* in four years, adding an interest of 12% per annum. Furthermore, taking into account that normally the Olivieri would have employed their money in trade and exchange, therefore enjoying higher profits, as compensation they were exempted from paying any of the taxes, and were also paid a commission of 5% on the collection. Furthermore, they were nominated commissioners and collectors of the tithes, *mezzi frutti*, *quarti di frutti* and arrears, and their appointment could not be revoked until both the loan and the interests had been repaid in full. The Olivieri delegated the actual collection in the duchy of Florence to Matteo Delle Macchie, promising him an annual recompense of 300 ducats.[85]

It can be assumed that the operation described below was part of the 24,300 *scudi* loaned directly to the Chamber, via its depositary. On 14 August 1546 Benvenuto Olivieri's company loaned the Chamber two diamonds to the value of 7,000 *scudi d'oro in oro* and promised a further 11,000 *scudi*, making a total of 18,000 *scudi*, which would be repaid after a year from the tithes of the State of Florence. One of the diamonds (which was worth 3,200 *scudi*) belonged to Bartolomeo Gualterotti, who also promised to give Olivieri half, every time he made a payment on the mandate of the Chamber towards the 11,000 *scudi*.[86] Clearly, he too, apart from being the guarantor of Cosimo I, contributed directly to the deal. One strange point is that the sum was divided into three lots of 4,000, 4,000 and 2,000 *scudi*, the last of which were defined '*pro residuo*'.[87] It is possible, therefore, that the real agreement was for Benvenuto and Bartolomeo to loan only 10,000 *scudi*, but that they would then be given an extra 1,000 on repayment.

7. The overall picture

At this point we can begin to see the overall picture of the relationship between the Apostolic Chamber and Benvenuto Olivieri and his partners. Table 13 provides a visual summary of the participation of the Olivieri company and those connected with it (see Chapter 2, pp. 56-61) in the administration of the various pluriennial contracts stipulated with the Chamber. What is very clear, even at first glance, is the heterogeneity of the business deals with the Chamber in which Benvenuto's company participated. Moreover, while it is probable that the contracts shown in this table were the most important and substantial of the company's business

85 ASF, Galli Tassi 1867, fasc. 8, fols 1r-3r.

86 ASF, Galli Tassi 1843, fasc. 3; see also Galli Tassi 1867, fasc. 3.

87 ASF, Galli Tassi 1831, fols 10-12.

deals, it should also be remembered that they represented only a part of its activity. Benvenuto Olivieri & Partners were also involved in tax-farming resulting from loans, as well as investments in shares of public debt and in venal offices. Therefore, the picture drawn in Table 13 is partial, but, remembering what has been said in the previous chapters, it nevertheless renders the idea of the role of the *mercatores romanam curiam sequentes*.

The depositary was the most important papal banker, whose job it was to make clearly defined payments on behalf of the Apostolic Chamber. In exchange for this he was assigned fonts of revenue, the sources and amounts of which were indicated very precisely by contract (even if in practice this precision became somewhat blurred). This role had therefore to be covered by a bank that was considered solid and capable of furnishing indisputable guarantees. Clearly Benvenuto Olivieri & Partners possessed these characteristics, because they were appointed depositary for approximately three years (with a short interruption), between 1540 and 1543, and again for a further two years, between 1545 and 1546. Unlike the administration of the large contracts (which will be examined shortly), the administration of the Depositary seems to have always been the prerogative of a single company.

An affair in which Benvenuto was involved throughout the 1540s was that of the customs of Rome, administered first of all by the Strozzi company and then by that of Olivieri. In the second case particularly, the wealth of documentation that has survived makes it possible to examine closely the details of their administration. From 1543 the customs were contracted out to two Florentine companies: that of Benvenuto Olivieri and that of Bastiano da Montauto. The contract stipulated with the Apostolic Chamber shows that the two companies each had a 50% share. As is shown in Table 13, however, the former almost immediately dropped its share to between 1.5 and 4.4%. This is due to the fact that from the very beginning other companies and individuals purchased shares, and by approximately halfway through the duration of the contract the number of participants had risen to fifteen. Included among them were Antonio Covoni & Partners, with an initial share of 10%, which was then withdrawn (in the last years the company was replaced by Antonio Covoni as an individual). Among the participants were also the Ubaldini, who, holding shares under the names of both Olivieri and Montauto, maintained a constant 5.5% of the total. The case of the customs is a perfect example showing how in reality the company of Benvenuto did not have the financial means to manage such large contracts on its own, but rather obtained from others most of the money necessary, using its resources to lead groups of investors. As the balance-sheet of 1543 shows (see Table 14, p. 186), the money flows were transparent. The Olivieri company was owed considerable amounts of money by the Apostolic Chamber, in return for its services. At the same time, however, the Olivieri company owed equally large sums to other merchant-bankers who had acquired shares in the farms under Olivieri's name.

Table 13 – Shares in the tax-farms of the Apostolic Chamber belonging to the Olivieri company and other companies in which he had an interest

YEAR	DEPOSITARY	CUSTOMS OF ROME	TREASURY OF PERUGIA	TREASURY OF THE ROMAGNA
1538		Strozzi 21.3%		
1539		Strozzi 21.3% (?)	from May Olivieri 50.0% (?)	
1540	from July Olivieri 100%	Strozzi 21.3% (?)	Olivieri 50.0% (?)	
1541	Olivieri 100%	Strozzi 21.3% (?)	Olivieri 25.0%	
1542	Olivieri 100%	Strozzi 21.3% (?)	Olivieri 25.0%	
1543	from March Olivieri 100%	Olivieri 12.5% later 2.5% Covoni 10.0% Ubaldini 5.5%	Olivieri 20.0% Covoni 5.0%	
1544		Olivieri 2.5% Covoni 10.0% Ubaldini 5.5%	Olivieri 20.0% Covoni 5.0%	
1545	Olivieri 100%	Olivieri 2.5% Covoni 10.0% Ubaldini 5.5%	Olivieri 20.0% Covoni 5.0%	from December Olivieri 100.0%
1546	Olivieri 100%	Olivieri 2.5% Covoni 10.0% Ubaldini 5.5%	Olivieri 8.7% Ubaldini 18.8%	Olivieri 25.0% Ubaldini 15.0%
1547		Olivieri 1.5% later 4.4% Ubaldini 5.5%	Olivieri 8.7% Ubaldini 18.8%	Olivieri 25.0% Ubaldini 15.0%
1548		Olivieri 4.4% Ubaldini 5.5%	Olivieri 8.7% Ubaldini 18.8%	Olivieri 25.0% Ubaldini 15.0%
1549		Olivieri 4.4% Ubaldini 5.5%	Olivieri 8.7% Ubaldini 18.8%	Olivieri 25.0% Ubaldini 22.5%
1550			Olivieri heirs 8.7% Ubaldini 18.8%	Olivieri heirs 25.0% Ubaldini 22.5%

Treasury of Parma and Piacenza	*Salara* of Rome	Increase of the salt tax of the Romagna	*Gabella dello Studio*
	Olivieri 33.3%		
	Olivieri 33.3%	from April Olivieri 25%	Olivieri 25% Carducci 25%
	Olivieri 33.3%	Olivieri 25%	Olivieri 25% Carducci 25%
from October Olivieri 10%	Covoni 33.3%	Olivieri 25%	Olivieri 25% Carducci 25%
Olivieri 10%	Covoni 33.3%		Olivieri 20% Covoni 5% Carducci 25%
Olivieri 10%	Covoni 33.3%		Olivieri 20% Covoni 5% Carducci 25%
Olivieri 10%			

The treasurer of one of the provinces of the Papal State was another office of prestige. Apart from the Marches, over which Bindo Altoviti & Partners had a virtual monopoly, the Treasury of Perugia and the Treasury of the Romagna also represented sources of substantial earnings. Benvenuto Olivieri & Partners were directly involved with these last two treasuries (being in both cases among the contract-holders), but never at the same time. From the end of the 1530s until 1545 they were involved with the Treasury of Perugia; from the end of 1545 until 1549-50 they instead covered the role of treasurers of the Romagna. The Treasuries required less investment in financial terms than did the customs, and thus the contract could be divided among a smaller number of people. At Perugia, for example, the Olivieri company initially possessed perhaps half of the shares, and only after eighteen months did they drop their share to 25%, and then to 20%, having conveyed 5% to Antonio Covoni & Partners. When, in December 1545, the Olivieri company began their administration of the Treasury of the Romagna, the Ubaldini company took over 27.5% of the Treasury of Perugia. Under the name of the latter, however, Benvenuto Olivieri & Partners maintained a share of 8.7%, but this time without any direct involvement in the administration. As far as the Treasury of the Romagna is concerned, the Olivieri company maintained a constant participation of 25%; the Ubaldini, on the other hand, in the fourth year increased their share from an initial 15% to 22.5%. Moreover, between 1540 and 1543 Benvenuto Olivieri & Partners also had other business interests in the Romagna, where they collected the increase of the salt tax.

Besides the large contracts, another important source of profit for the bankers was the loan operations. In these cases the Apostolic Chamber very rarely made the repayment in cash, but more often through the bestowal of the right to collect determined fiscal revenues: from the *imposizione delle galere* to the tithes, from the *vigesima* of the Jews to the Triennial Subsidy, the Chamber alienated its own future revenue to the bankers. Furthermore, as the following chapter will show, there were other services that, while not directly regarding the papal tax system, were nevertheless connected to the papal finances. One example is the alum: in this case the Olivieri company was not involved in the production itself (an operation which would have placed it in direct contact with the Apostolic Chamber), but only in the distribution, for which it made very detailed agreements with the contract-holders who dealt with the production, the Grimaldi company of Genoa. Another such service was the Mint. In the period 1540-45 the Olivieri company held a 25% share in a separate company created specifically for the administration of the Mint. These services will be looked at in the next chapter.

CHAPTER 8

Other Activities

This chapter examines a series of contracts that, while still linked to the Apostolic Chamber, differ from those of the preceding chapters because they are not connected to the papal taxation system.

1. The alum mines at Tolfa

In May 1462 Giovanni di Castro (godson of Pope Pius II and at the time commissioner general of the province of Patrimonio) discovered that alum could be mined near Civitavecchia, on the Tolfa mountains. This was an unexpected stroke of fortune for the Papal State, as it found itself the possessor of a notable source of wealth, and – perhaps even more importantly – the discovery of alum placed it in a position to liberate itself once and for all from its detested dependency on the Turks. Until that time, in fact, alum had been discovered in Italy in useful quantities only in the vicinity of Naples. The amount found there was not, however, sufficient to meet demands and therefore alum had to be imported from Spain, or, even worse from the papal point of view, from the Ottoman Empire (the most famous mines were those of Focea, which had been owned by the Genoese until 1455). Moreover, in order to pay the 300,000 ducats that were on average necessary every year to purchase the product from the Levant,[1] Christendom found itself obliged to include arms as part of the deal, thus in practice financing, both directly and indirectly, the Turkish military campaigns against itself.

Alum was used in particular for the tanning of skins and as a mordant for the dyeing of woollen cloth. It was also a common ingredient in the manufacture of glass, as well as in pharmacopoeia, where it was used as an astringent and haemostat. What rendered it particularly precious was the fact that there were virtually no acceptable substitutes. Thus, when, more or less by chance, large deposits of alum ore were discovered within its territory, the Papal State attempted to acquire the monopoly and to exploit the commerce not only for financial reasons, but also as a way of gaining ground in the struggle against the infidels. Many years later, in 1543, reference was still made to the 'great delight and joy and celebration of all of Christendom' when alum, 'by divine revelation and human ingenuity', had been discovered on the Tolfa mountains.[2]

1 P. Pecchiai, *Roma nel Cinquecento*, Storia di Roma, vol. XIII (Bologna, 1948), p. 276.

2 ASF, Galli Tassi 1830, fol. 15.

Pope Pius II (1458-64), therefore, immediately proclaimed his right to the land where the alum had been discovered, pledging the future revenue of the mines directly to the crusade against the Turks. His successor Paul II (1464-71) went even further, expressly forbidding all Christian countries to import Turkish alum. To make their claim to the alum mines valid, however, the papacy had to pay the Frangipane family, lords of Tolfa, 17,000 *scudi d'oro* and 300 florins.[3]

The first contracts regarding the exploitation of the mines, stipulated with Castro and other financiers in partnership with him, stated that the Apostolic Chamber would purchase a minimum of 30,000 cantars[4] of alum per annum, which it would then sell. The results cannot, however, have been very encouraging, given that in 1466 the Medici, the new contractors, signed a contract greatly modified with respect to the preceding ones. The new agreement was certainly more satisfactory for the Apostolic Chamber because it stated that the commercialization of the product was no longer to be dealt with by the Chamber, but instead by the private contracting party. The Medici family held the monopoly over the alum mines until 1476, when they came into conflict with Pope Sixtus IV, who consequently decided to award the contract to another company currently enjoying papal favour: the Pazzi company.[5]

The financial return of the alum mines towards the end of the century can be estimated at around 40,000 ducats annually.[6] The custom of contracting the mines out, however, meant that the Papal State earned less than this, as the bankers obviously sought to increase their part of the profit. Initially, in the first decades after the discovery of the mines, all the revenue was poured into the war against the Turks. Later, however, the money made from the alum was used for other purposes: in particular, for the repayment of loans or for the gratuities of certain important individuals (above all the clerks of the Chamber and the apostolic secretaries).[7]

It was not easy for the popes to impose a monopoly on the alum of the Tolfa. First, the quantity produced had to be maintained at a level that did not saturate the market, in order to prevent an excessive lowering of the prices. Second, the papal imposition that this monopoly be respected was not always accepted by the European sovereigns; rather, they tended to reserve the right to import alum from all over Christendom, as

3 O. Montenovesi, 'Agostino Chigi banchiere e appaltatore dell'allume di Tolfa', *Archivio della Società Romana di Storia Patria*, 60 (1937): 110.

4 In the 1440s, the cantar was equivalent to 150-156 *libbre*, or pounds (see here, p. 170, art. 4 of the contract of 1541). Since in Rome a *libbra* was equal to 339 grams (A. Martini, *Manuale di metrologia, ossia, Misure, pesi e monete in uso attualmente e anticamente presso tutti i populi* (Turin, 1883, reprinted Rome, 1976), p. 598), it can be deduced that a cantar weighed between 50.85 and 52.88 kg.

5 R. De Roover, *The Rise and Decline of the Medici Bank (1397-1494)* (New York, 1966), pp. 153-154, 164; pp. 152-164 of the volume discuss the monopoly of the alum administered by the Medici.

6 Pecchiai, *Roma nel Cinquecento*, p. 276.

7 This is the tendency, existing at least from the second quarter of the sixteenth century, that we have already seen in preceding chapters in relation to many of the contracts. With regard to the alum, for example, in 1548 a group of Florentine and Genoese bankers, with the loan of 128,000 *scudi d'oro in oro*, acquired the right to, among other things, 16,363 *scudi* from the alum mines of the Tolfa (cf. Chapter 3, p. 92). See here also note 14.

well as, on occasion, from the Levant. One of the countries where the pontiffs had the most difficulty establishing a monopoly was France, which in contravention of Paul II's interdict with regard to Turkish alum – renewed by Julius II in 1506 – imported large quantities of alum from Spain and also from North Africa.[8]

The normal process followed by the Chamber in farming out the mines was that a contract was written up placing the administration of the Tolfa mines in the hands of a banker, or more often a consortium of bankers. The bankers would pay a fixed sum to the Apostolic Chamber, in exchange for which they would oversee the mining of determined quantities of alum and then manage its commerce in all the countries of Christendom. In December 1500 the '*appaltum alluminum Sanctae Cruciatae et Camerae Apostolicae*' was assigned for 12 years (the administration was to begin in the following May) to the companies of the Sienese bankers Mariano Chigi and the heirs of Ambrogio Spannocchi, who subsequently also took over the contract of the Agnano mines (near Naples).[9] After Chigi and Spannocchi it was the turn of Andrea Bellanti & Partners, in partnership with Mariano Chigi's son, Agostino (who held a 20% share in the operation). In return, Bellanti and Chigi made a loan to Pope Leo X (who was in great need of money, having sustained enormous expenses for his coronation ceremony) of 75,000 ducats *di carlini*, which they were entitled to recoup over the following ten years directly from the proceeds deriving from the alum mines.[10] In 1520 the administration of the mines was once again placed in the hands of Agostino Chigi and the Spannocchi company; they were then followed by the Gaddi, Florentine bankers.[11]

1 August 1531 saw the beginning of a period of administration shared equally between the companies of the Genoese banker Ansaldo Grimaldi and the Sienese banker Girolamo Venturi, who contracted to pay an annual 15,000 ducats *di carlini* and to produce 20,000 cantars of alum.[12] Venturi, however, finding himself unable to meet his financial obligations, borrowed money from various merchant-bankers, promising in return a consignment of alum. Giulio and Lorenzo Strozzi & Partners, together with the heirs of Pandolfo Della Casa & Partners, stood surety for Venturi, who therefore had little choice in the matter of how to dispose of the alum: for example, 3,250 cantars had to be consigned to the Strozzi company and 2,000 to the Della Casa company by 1 March 1537.[13] In 1541, when the books were balanced, the heirs of Girolamo Venturi (who died in 1537) found themselves owing Benvenuto

---

8 J. Delumeau, *L'alun de Rome XVe-XIXe siècle* (Paris, 1962), pp. 48-51.

9 Montenovesi, 'Agostino Chigi': 111-112. The contract was divided thus: 60% to Mariano Chigi & Partners (the partners were Mariano himself with 40.62%, his son Agostino 'the Magnificent' with an equivalent share, and Francesco Tomasi with 18.76%) and 40% to the heirs of Ambrogio Spannocchi & Partners. Agostino Chigi's involvement in these and the following years is also dealt with by *Il Magnifico Agostino Chigi* (Rome, 1970), pp. 301-323.

10 Montenovesi, 'Agostino Chigi': 109, 113. According to Delumeau, the contract cost 15,000 ducats annually (*L'alun de Rome*, 98, tab. I).

11 Montenovesi, 'Agostino Chigi': 113; P. Pecchiai, *Roma nel Cinquecento*, p. 276.

12 Delumeau, *L'alun de Rome*, p. 99, tab. I.

13 ASF, Galli Tassi 1830, fol. 9, fasc. 11. The act in which the Strozzi company, represented by Benvenuto Olivieri, and the Della Casa company, with Luigi Rucellai, guaranteed for the Venturi company is dated 1536 (fasc. 10).

Olivieri & Partners of Rome almost 16,500 *scudi di giuli 10 per scudo*. This large sum of money was a result of the surety that first the Strozzi company and then the Olivieri company, who took over from them, had guaranteed for the payments that Venturi had to effect on behalf of the Apostolic Chamber, and in particular for the sums to be paid to the colleges of the knights of St Peter, of the Archive and of the clerks of the Chamber.[14]

On 1 August 1541 the Tolfa alum mines were under the administration of the Genoese merchant-bankers Ansaldo Grimaldi & Partners. The contract between them and the Chamber, which stipulates a period of 12 years, is dated 1538, at which time Grimaldi, apart from already being the contract-holder, was also depositary general of the Apostolic Chamber (Girolamo Sauli, who acted as his procurator, was vice-depositary).[15] Grimaldi had the right to nominate his heirs or successors. The contract laid down that in 12 years the contract-holder could produce 360,000 cantars of alum (therefore, an annual production of 30,000 cantars) at 150 pounds per cantar '*a peso grosso*', that is, 156 '*del sottile*' (art. 4). Moreover, they could produce a further 1,500 cantars per annum for their own use, paying a fixed price to the clerks of the Chamber (art. 5); the contract-holder was entitled to 1.5% on the alum produced (art. 7); in exchange for the contract he had to pay an annual 28,333.3 ducats *di carlini 10* per ducat (art. 46) as well as an initial sum of 40,000 ducats, which, however, would be repaid to him in annual shares of 3,333.3 ducats, thus reducing the annual sum to be paid to 25,000 (art. 47); Pope Paul III, however, reserved the right to nominate at his own discretion a person to whom the Grimaldi would have to transfer ⅓ of the contract (art. 59).[16]

In the mid-sixteenth century, therefore, the Genoese had a firm monopoly over the Tolfa alum mines, which lasted until 1578: the Sauli were in charge from 1553 to 1565, and the Pallavicini from 1566 to 1578.[17] Only in the last quarter of the century did Florentine names reappear: Ridolfi, Altoviti and Guicciardini, often in

---

14 ASF, Galli Tassi 1830, fol. 8. For the payments that the Strozzi company made on behalf of the Venturi company to the clerks of the Chamber (2,000 ducats a year) and to the knights of St Peter (7,920) see numerous looseleaf folios in Galli Tassi 1830; and the accounts, albeit very confused, relative to 1537-38 in Galli Tassi 1953, fols 147-155. In Delumeau, *L'alun de Rome*, p. 158 there is a list of the institutes that had assignment on the alum for the period 1553-65.

15 The death of Venturi (partner in the contract of the preceding period) might also have had some influence on the date of the renewal.

16 ASF, Galli Tassi 1830, fasc. 7: this very detailed contract consists of 59 articles occupying 31 pages (the most significant are summarized here). In ASV, *Cam. Ap., Div. Cam. 112*, fol. 35r-v there is a list of the jewels given as pledge in 1538, in exchange for the advance loan of 40,000 ducats: among these stand out '*unam Punctam Adamantinam, vulgariter dictam la Puncta Bella, qual sol star nel fermaglio del piviale di N.S., et fo comprata da pp. Julio II*' (fol. 35v). The share of ⅓ was initially assigned to Orazio Farnese who, however, after a year, was replaced by Luca Giustiniani (*Cam. Ap., Div. Cam. 131*, fols 32v-33r).

17 Delumeau, *L'alun de Rome*, pp. 99-100, tab. I, which shows also that between 1565 and 1566 the Apostolic Chamber had decided not to farm the alum mines out. For the contract with Bandinello Sauli, again for the sum of 28,333.3 ducats *di carlini* per annum, see ASV, *Cam. Ap., Div. Cam. 157*, fols 185v-186v.

partnership with the Olgiatto family, natives of Como.[18] On the production side, the quantity of which was precisely laid down in very detailed contracts, there was scant room for other merchant-bankers. Certain aspects of production, such as the quantity of alum and the percentage of the price of the product that could be retained, were totally in the hands of the contract-holders.

On the distribution side, however, the contract-holders necessarily had to avail themselves of the collaboration of other merchant-bankers. Delumeau, using the accounts kept by the Grimaldi company during their second contract, has demonstrated that in the period 1541-53, 392,661 cantars of alum were exported (therefore, something more than the 360,000 laid down in the contract). Of the 370,824 that can be traced, the Grimaldi personally handled only 21.4%, with a greater percentage passing through the hands of Martin Ayala, a Spanish merchant from Burgos (27.4%).[19] The same records show that Benvenuto Olivieri exported 8,285.139 cantars of alum to Marseilles and Aigues-Mortes between 1541 and 1544, as well as 2,000 cantars to Florence (2.8%).[20] The data available in the Fondo Galli Tassi not only confirm this, but also add more detail, providing us with a much more complex picture of investment, partnership and profit sharing.

Concerning export to Florence there is very little information: only that, in February 1548, 1,000 cantars of alum were sent to the *provveditori* of the Arte della Lana.[21]

There is, however, much more information regarding export to France, an important market outlet. The heirs of Ansaldo Grimaldi, who were administering the Tolfa mines at the time, gave Benvenuto Olivieri, for the 12 years between 1 March 1540 and 1 March 1552, the right to export alum to the following ports: Rouen, 4,000 cantars per annum; Brittany, La Rochelle and 'Potto', 3,500; 'Provence' (this appellation refers to anywhere in the French Midi), 3,000.[22] Almost all the alum destined for France was transported to either the Atlantic ports or the Mediterranean ports of 'Provence' (Marseilles and Aigues-Mortes).

18 Delumeau, *L'alun de Rome*, p. 100, tab. I: to be exact, the contracts were held by Olgiatto and Ridolfi (1578-90), Olgiatto, Ridolfi and Altoviti (1590-1602), Guicciardini and Ridolfi (1602-14).

19 Delumeau, *L'alun de Rome*, pp. 209-211, tab. XVI: among others, a significant contribution was made by the Florentines, Del Bene and Sertini (11.2%), who dealt with exports to France, and the Genoese, Giustiniani (10.5%).

20 Delumeau, *L'alun de Rome*, p. 210, tab. XVI. In those years 5,000 cantars were also sent to Florence in the name of Giovan Battista Puccini, and, in 1550-51, approximately 1,600 cantars were sent in the name of the heirs of Girolamo Ubaldini, with whom Olivieri had been connected (ibid., pp. 210-211, tab. XVI).

21 ASF, Galli Tassi 1830, fol. 4. This is the document that shows the cost of insurance against all the risks for the voyage between Civitavecchia and Pisa: a large number of *mercatores* guaranteed for a certain sum, receiving as a premium 5% of the sum itself, until an insured value of 2,000 *scudi d'oro* was reached.

22 ASF, Galli Tassi 1829, fol. 10.

The ports of La Rochelle, Brittany, Rouen, Dieppe

The ports situated beyond the Strait of Gibraltar, and in particular Rouen, were the favoured destination for Italian alum sold in France: according to Delumeau, between 1531 and 1553, 77.9% of a quantity exceeding 169,000 cantars.[23]

Olivieri together with various partners were among those who obtained the right to export 7,500 cantars per annum to the Atlantic ports of the north of France. In the first year of their contract (1541-42) Benvenuto Olivieri's company sent four ships with 7,566 cantars of alum to La Rochelle, Dieppe and Rouen, to their agents and associates Giovan Francesco Bini & Partners of Lyons. For the ⅜ (=37.5%) that it held, the Olivieri company spent in cost and insurance 7,102.57 gold cameral ducats. When it arrived in France, the alum must have been sold for 23,616 ducats, given that the Olivieri company obtained net receipts of 8,856 ducats and a consequent profit of 1,753.43 (the total profit must therefore have been of 4,675.81 ducats).[24] It was certainly a good business deal, given that in 12 months the profit for the *mercatores* reached 24.7% of the investment made, that is more than double the rate of interest normally applied to loans. The data available, moreover, allow us to estimate at 2.50 ducats per cantar the cost of the purchase (that by contract came to 2.25 ducats per cantar), the transport and the insurance, and at 3.12 the money received from the sale.

While during the first year the export of alum must have been prevalently in Florentine hands (it is known, for example, that besides Olivieri, also the Bini company's Lyons branch held a significant share), from the following year (1542-43) it was administered directly in Rouen by Castro and Malvenda, Spanish merchant-bankers from Burgos. In 1542 Castro and Malvenda possessed a share of ¾, while the share of the Olivieri and Bini companies had fallen considerably, to only ⅛ each.[25] In these 12 months, nevertheless, on their share of the 10,258 cantars sold (1,282.25),[26] the Olivieri company made a profit of 1,038.09 ducats, against net receipts of 3,922.65 and a cost that therefore must have been of 2,884.56.[27] These calculations do not, however, take into consideration the cost of insurance and of transport, as they were made on 2.25 ducats per cantar, or, in other words, the simple price of purchase paid by the contractors for the alum, according to the contract. The proceeds of the sale amounted this time to 3.06 ducats per cantar and were therefore less than those of the preceding year.

---

23 Delumeau, *L'alun de Rome*, pp. 244-245, tab. XXI.

24 ASF, Galli Tassi 2278, fols 133, 153.

25 ASF, Galli Tassi 1942, fol. 195v; Galli Tassi 2278, fol. 133. The important role played by the merchants of Burgos in the export of the alum of Tolfa has already been mentioned: see p. 171.

26 Also in this case the alum was transported on four ships: one belonging to Mini of Leovilla, one to Gerard Marvel, one to Piero Balnar and the last from Dieppe (ASF, Galli Tassi 2278, fol. 205).

27 ASF, Galli Tassi 2278, fol. 133: in this case the cost is not clearly indicated, as it is added to that of the other shares relative to the successive years, of which there are no financial records. The transport by ship must, however, have cost 0.20 *scudi* (=0.19 ducats) per cantar (fol. 205).

The ports of Provence

Compared with Atlantic France, Mediterranean France was a secondary destination for the commerce of alum. Between 1531 and 1553, for example, compared to the 131,754 cantars that were shipped to the ports of the French Atlantic, only 37,468 were unloaded in those of the Mediterranean (a ratio of 3.5 to 1).[28]

Nevertheless, Benvenuto Olivieri & Partners were involved here as well. In 1540 the Grimaldi company sold them the right to export every year, for 12 years, 3,000 cantars of alum, in exchange for 2.25 ducats per cantar in three annual instalments.[29] As in the first phase of commerce with the ports of the Atlantic, it was Giovan Francesco Bini & Partners of Lyons who administered *in situ* the business transactions regarding the arrival of the product. Giovan Francesco Bini purchased a 31.3% share, half of which he then conveyed to Piero, his brother. Moreover, although the amount of his share is unknown to us, it is certain that, under the name of the Bini company, Luigi di Gino Capponi also took part in the deal. The investment was then extended to other partners, as can be seen in the following list:[30]

Benvenuto Olivieri & Partners	31.3%
Luca Giustiniani	25.0%
Giovan Francesco Bini & Partners	15.6%
Piero Bini	15.6%
Raimondo Vidal of Avignon	12.5%

In the agreement that provided for the transfer of ¼ of the contract to the Genoese merchant-banker Luca Giustiniani, it was also stipulated that Olivieri would – if the necessity arose over the following four years – loan him up to 5,000 *scudi* per annum, which would be repaid with an 8% interest. In practice, therefore, Benvenuto made it possible for Giustiniani not to pay the price of the alum, by agreeing to do it himself in exchange for an interest of 8% per annum.[31]

For the Olivieri, the expenses relative to the 6,325 cantars produced in the first and second (and part of the third) year amounted to 5,295.4 gold cameral ducats, that is in all to 16,945.3 (=2.68 ducats per cantar). For the operations of the first two years, Olivieri's company, probably imagining a retail price of around 3.15 ducats per cantar, had calculated that they would make a profit close to 1,000 ducats, equivalent to approximately 18.9% of the initial investment.[32] In this period the costs of the loading, transport and insurance were in fact particularly high, equal to approximately 0.43 ducats per cantar, although in the following years they returned to more normal levels.

In July 1542 Benvenuto Olivieri & Partners hired the ship S. Maria Maggiore, property of the Florentine Francesco Gucci and with Giovanni Corso as patron, to

28 Delumeau, *L'alun de Rome*, pp. 244-245, tab. XXI.

29 Thus the sum reached 6,750 ducats per annum (ASF, Galli Tassi 2278, fol. 132).

30 ASF, Galli Tassi 1732, fol. 3; Galli Tassi 1830, fol. 13; Galli Tassi 1942, fol. 194v.

31 ASF, Galli Tassi 1829, fol. 10. See also Galli Tassi 2278, fol. 76.

32 ASF, Galli Tassi 2278, fol. 134.

transport at least 3,000 cantars of alum from Civitavecchia to Aigues-Mortes. The alum, once it reached its destination, would be consigned to Raimondo Vidal, who was a partner of the Olivieri company in this business venture. The cost of transport amounted to 1 *scudo d'oro in oro* for every 8½ cantars (the transport of 3,000 cantars must therefore have cost approximately 353 *scudi d'oro in oro*, that is 345 gold cameral ducats). Between August and the following September the alum was loaded onto the ship and insured, all for a sum of approximately 430 ducats (=440 *scudi*). In total, therefore, the cost of insuring and transporting around 3,000 cantars amounted to 775 ducats (=793 *scudi*). If this sum is added to the 6,750 ducats necessary for the purchase of the alum, the total is 7,525 ducats, or, in other words, a sum of approximately 2.5 ducats per cantar.[33]

At the end of the four years, in 1544, it was calculated that on the 10,595 cantars of alum shipped and partly sold the 'certain' profit amounted to ⅔ of a *scudo* (=0.65 ducats) per cantar. This meant 7,063.3 *scudi* (=6,902.8 ducats), to which had to be added the profits on the 1,405 cantars remaining that, calculated in proportion, would bring the total to 8,000 *scudi* (=7,818.2 ducats).[34] The final profits, therefore, were equal to 28.96% of the initial investment; not an exceptional result, but considerably more than that estimated at the end of the second year.

As has been mentioned numerous times, the business ventures of the various merchant-bankers looked at in this book were closely intertwined with each other and with the tax-farms of the Apostolic Chamber. The way in which Olivieri repaid Giustiniani a part of the capital stock and part of the profits from this venture is a perfect example of this. Olivieri transferred 4,803 *scudi* to the Genoese merchant-banker as a share on the 10,000 he had by assignment on the Triennial Subsidy of Bologna during the period 1543-44. It should, moreover, be noted that the commissioners of this Subsidy were Giustiniani and his partner Tobia Pallavicini.[35]

At times the alum was sold to third parties before being transported to its final destination. A very detailed description of such a transaction has survived in the Fondo Galli Tassi. On 10 March 1542 Olivieri and his partners sold 250 cantars of alum while the product was still in Civitavecchia to a merchant from Marseilles, Giovanni Vernet, provided that the latter shipped it to Marseilles under the same conditions agreed by Olivieri with Grimaldi. In reality the price agreed on for the transaction was quite high, 2.93 gold cameral ducats (=3 *scudi d'oro in oro*) per cantar; Vernet thus paid 731.72 ducats (=750 *scudi*). Not all of this sum, however, ended up in the pockets of Olivieri and his partners: 7.32 ducats (=1%) went to the brokers; 1.85 (=0.25%) went to the consulate of the Florentine nation; 14.63 (=5%) was the commission pertaining to the Olivieri company. The remaining 707.52 ducats were instead shared amongst the participants in the usual proportions, meaning that Benvenuto Olivieri & Partners received 221.23 ducats net.[36] Therefore, calculating that the price of purchase of the alum was 2.25 ducats per cantar, Olivieri's outlay, for his share, must have been 175.78 ducats: consequently his profit must have

33 ASF, Galli Tassi 1833, unnumbered folio; Galli Tassi 2278, fol. 81.

34 ASF, Galli Tassi 1830, fol. 12.

35 ASF, Galli Tassi 1830, fol. 12.

36 ASF, Galli Tassi 2278, fols 111, 134, 143.

amounted to 45.45 ducats (=25.9% of the investment), plus the above-mentioned commission of 14.63 ducats.

An analogous operation took place a year later: this time it was Agostino di Giovanni Corso who purchased 150 cantars of alum at Civitavecchia. The note regarding the destination of this alum is interesting, as it indicates 'Provence or the land of the Moors and nowhere else' – clear proof that the papal interdiction had lost, if it had ever really possessed, a great part of its power.[37] What is particularly surprising, however, is that Corso paid only 1.95 ducats (=2 *scudi*) per cantar of alum, considerably less than the price paid by the Olivieri company and associates when they bought the alum from the Grimaldi contract-holders (2.25 ducats). It might be hypothesized, however, that this very low price hid a recompense for operations connected to the transport of alum, since Agostino was the son of the above-mentioned Giovanni Corso of Civitavecchia, patron of a ship used by Olivieri for commerce with Provence.

Atlantic Spain

The flow of traffic towards Atlantic Spain (Seville and Cadiz) was fairly limited. Delumeau has calculated that this area, in the period 1531-53, imported little more than 30,000 cantars of alum from the Tolfa (4.9% of the total).[38] At the end of 1544 the Grimaldi company sold 2,500 cantars of alum to a group of merchants from Burgos (the heirs of Girolamo de Castro; Giovanni de Castro; the heirs of another Giovanni de Castro; Francesco, Luigi, Diego, Alfonso Malvenda and their procurator Martin Ayala). This alum, which was destined for the ports of Cadiz and Seville, was sold for the sum of 5,000 *scudi d'oro*, to be paid after a year. However, in June 1545, well before the date scheduled for the payment, the debt was cleared by the companies of Pier Antonio and Alamanno Bandini (for ¾) and of Benvenuto Olivieri (for ¼).[39]

At the beginning of the twentieth century Zippel argued that there had been a rapid decline in the commerce of alum from the sixteenth century onwards; Delumeau, on the contrary, in his volume dedicated to the alum of Rome, argues that it was exactly halfway through the Cinquecento that production of alum reached its peak, and that

37 ASF, Galli Tassi 2278, fol. 143. At least two Florentines (Tommaso Sertini and Albizzo Del Bene, who have already been mentioned as being among the most active exporters, note 19) were, when operating in France, given authorization by the king to trade in Roman alum with the 'infidels'; this news, when it reached Rome, caused the pontiff great distress (Galli Tassi 1830, fasc. 15-20).

38 Delumeau, *L'alun de Rome*, pp. 214-215, tab. XVII. Delumeau's calculations include the ports of Ceuta and Lisbon.

39 ASF, Galli Tassi 1830, fol. 6. The Bandini company must, however, have been agents of the group of Burgos (see Galli Tassi 2278, fols 133, 134); in fact, Galli Tassi 1830, fol. 14 (document undated) probably refers to this same operation, as it speaks of 2,577 cantars of alum, ¼ of which belonging to Olivieri and ¾ to the Spaniards Malvenda, Salinas and Ayala. With regard to this last family, mention has already been made of Martin (p. 171), an important exporter of alum, in particular towards Flanders and London, but also towards the French ports of the Atlantic and, albeit in lesser measure, towards the Atlantic ports of southern Spain.

only towards 1650 did it go into decline.[40] It was also precisely between the years 1540 and 1550 that Benvenuto Olivieri was at his zenith. While his company played only a supporting role in the commerce of alum, the fact that it played a role at all is definitely a significant sign of how the *mercatores romanam curiam sequentes* sought to become involved in all the economic-financial sectors connected, directly or indirectly, to the Apostolic Chamber. Olivieri owed part of his success in the business venture of the alum to the fact that he was able to exploit the various connections that he possessed in Italy and abroad. Naturally, being a Florentine, he had contacts in Florence, which he had continued to nurture; moreover, since he carried out his business activities in Rome, he was in continuous contact with the other merchants connected to the Curia, both Florentines and Genoese. Finally, Olivieri and his partners profited from their connections with Florentines who were active in the extremely important financial market of Lyons, and who were thus the fulcrum for the operations that involved France.

2. The importation of grain

Clearly the provision of foodstuffs was of primary importance to all States, and the Papal State was no exception. The failure to ensure the provision of adequate quantities of cereal had – as is easy to imagine – serious consequences from the point of view of public order. It was, therefore, essential for the State to do its best to ensure constant reserves at reasonably low prices. Like other cities, Rome had its own office of the *Annona* which was responsible for all operations regarding the provision of food. While in the past the city authorities had dealt with it, in the sixteenth century the papal bureaucracy took control. As in other areas of its jurisdiction, however, the papacy handed over the right to import cereals to merchants, thus leaving this delicate field open to the risk of notable abuses.[41] While this question is clearly of some considerable importance, it is, unfortunately, beyond the scope of this book to treat it in any great detail. However, as Benvenuto Olivieri and his company were

40 Delumeau, *L'alun de Rome*; G. Zippel, 'L'allume di Tolfa e il suo commercio', *Archivio della Società Romana di Storia Patria*, 30 (1907): 5-51, 389-462 (431 for the above statement).

41 Dedicated in particular to the fourteenth century is the volume by L. Palermo, *Mercati del grano a Roma tra Medioevo e Rinascimento*, vol. I: *Il mercato distrettuale del grano in età comunale* (Rome, 1990); more recently, the author has returned to the same theme in *Sviluppo economico e società preindustriali. Cicli, strutture e congiunture in Europa dal medioevo alla prima età moderna* (Rome, 1997), pp. 283-349. The fifteenth-century organization and the transformation of the *Annona* from a Roman communal office to State structure are again analysed by L. Palermo in 'L'approvvigionamento granario della capitale. Strategie economiche e carriere curiali a Roma alla metà del Quattrocento', in S. Gensini (ed.), *Roma capitale (1447-1527)*, Atti del IV Convegno di studio del Centro studi sulla civiltà del tardo Medioevo, San Miniato (Pisa) 27-31 October 1992 (Pisa, 1994), pp. 145-205. For problems regarding specifically the sixteenth century, see: L. Falchi-M.G. Pastura Ruggiero-D. Sinisi, 'L'Annona di Roma nel sec. XVI', in *Gli archivi per la storia dell'alimentazione*, Atti del convegno, Potenza-Matera 5-8 September 1988 (Rome, 1996), pp. 568-589; M.G. Pastura Ruggiero, 'Lo Stato e la "res frumentaria" a Roma nella prima metà del Cinquecento', *Dimensioni e problemi della ricerca storica*, 2 (1990): 17-70.

also involved – albeit only marginally – in the importation of grain to Rome, it will be briefly looked at inasmuch as it touched on his activities.

In the immediate area of Rome grain was obtained from the provinces of Patrimonio and Campagna. Beyond Rome, but still within the borders of the Papal State, cereal was also often procured from the Ancona area in the Marches, and more rarely from Umbria and the Romagna.[42] Transport by land was quite expensive for bulky merchandise of low value for weight, and grain was therefore more often transported by sea. If there were no impediments of a political or political-financial nature, it was therefore more convenient and economical (given that the trip to Civitavecchia was shorter) to have the cereal brought from Sicily, the so-called 'grain store of the Mediterranean'.[43] In the sixteenth century all the popes relied on Sicilian grain, often using Italian merchants resident in Rome to administer the purchase and transport of large quantities.[44] Beyond the Italian peninsula, 'Provence' (this refers, as was also true when speaking of alum, to anywhere in the French Midi) was a relatively important source of grain; conversely, at times the Roman countryside was also a source of grain for France. In years of particular crisis, however, it became necessary to import grain from the Levant, or, in other words, from the greatly detested Turkish enemy; with Spain, on the contrary, there was little or no commerce.[45]

The company of Filippo Strozzi (in which, it should be remembered, Benvenuto Olivieri was a partner) took a very active part in importing grain from the south. In the years 1532-33, for example, either on its own or in association with the Bernisone family, natives of Savona, the Strozzi company stipulated agreements with the Apostolic Chamber for the importation of grain from Sicily and, to a lesser extent, from Calabria.[46] The crisis that occurred during the years 1533-34, as a result of a shortage of grain, has already been mentioned in Chapter 1 (pp. 15-16). Problems of food provisioning had pushed Clement VII to make arrangements for importing Sicilian grain, and he placed the actual task of doing so in the hands of Filippo Strozzi. The marriage between Catherine de' Medici (niece of the pope) and Henry of Orleans, however, angered Charles V to such an extent that he revoked the previous agreement. Strozzi therefore had to fall back on French grain, but the delays in its arrival led to the first unrests among the populace of Rome, with a number of violent protests directed against agents of the Florentine banker. The need to procure grain from ever further away (Flanders), the loss of several merchant-ships together with the loads they were transporting and the damages suffered by the loads of others pushed Strozzi's agents to sell the small quantity of grain which had arrived (there were no reserves from the previous year) at a price double that which had been agreed on. Shortly thereafter Clement VII died, at which point the masses gave vent to

---

42 J. Delumeau, *Vie économique et sociale de Rome dans la seconde moitié du XVIe siècle* (2 vols, Paris, 1957-59), II, pp. 626-633.

43 F. Braudel, *The Mediterranean and the Mediterranean World in the Age of Philip II* (2 vols, London, 1972), I, pp. 602-604.

44 See Delumeau, *Vie économique et sociale*, II, pp. 634-639 (in particular, pp. 634-635 for the first half of the century).

45 Delumeau, *Vie économique et sociale*, II, pp. 640-642, 646-649.

46 ASF, Galli Tassi 1875, fasc. 5, 6, 7, 8, 9.

their anger, with Filippo Strozzi as their favourite target: his warehouses were sacked, his bank and its agents seriously threatened. The city council, having decided to make a public example of Strozzi, fined him to the tune of 700,000 *scudi*; Paul III, however, first reduced the sanction to 17,500 *scudi*, and then decided to suspend it, and, despite the overwhelming disapproval of most members of the council, maintained his own deposit with the Florentine bank.[47]

Certainly, compared to information we have about the Strozzi company, there is far less documentation directly regarding the company of Benvenuto Olivieri. However, even if the sources available seem to indicate that among the Florentines operating in the Eternal City the most active in the commerce of grain were the Cavalcanti-Giraldi and Montauto companies, Benvenuto Olivieri & Partners had some part in the import of grain to Rome.[48] To make the following discussion clearer, it should be pointed out that *salma* and *rubbio* were dry measures: in Sicily the *salma* was equivalent to 275.09 litres (=222.81 kg); the *rubbio* was more variable, and in various parts of the peninsula went from 280 to 314 litres, while in Rome it was equivalent to 294.46 (=238.5 kg).[49]

In 1539 a contract to import grain was stipulated by the companies of Alessandro Deti and Bastiano da Montauto, and afterwards a share of 1/5 divided in half was conveyed to the companies of Cavalcanti-Giraldi and Olivieri in exchange for 1,100 *scudi di moneta* to each of the first two companies.[50]

Again in 1539 the *Congregazione* (supervisory committee headed by cardinals) of the Annona purchased grain for 25,000 *scudi* from Tommaso Cavalcanti and Benvenuto Olivieri.[51] In 1541 the same two men, plus the partner of the former, Giovanni Giraldi, furnished 3,000 *salme* of Sicilian grain as part of 10,000 *salme* (which the two companies divided in half) stipulated in a contract of 1540.[52] They continued, until April 1543, to furnish grain in quantities that met or even exceeded those laid down in the contract: in the period 1540-43, for example, Paul III received 12,353 *salme* of grain at 5 *scudi* per *salma*. Presumably, then, they imported other quantities independently.[53]

47 For further details, see M.M. Bullard, *Grain Supply and Urban Unrest in Renaissance Rome: the Crisis of 1533-34*, in P.A. Ramsey (ed.), *Rome in the Renaissance. The City and the Myth* (Binghamton N.Y., 1982), pp. 279-292; the information which follows is also taken from this work.

48 There are numerous references to their participation in ASF, Galli Tassi 1875; Galli Tassi 1876. For the Montauto, see also Delumeau, *Vie économique et sociale*, II, pp. 634-635.

49 Martini, *Manuale di metrologia*, pp. 439 (for the *salma*), 597 (for the *rubbio*).

50 ASF, Galli Tassi 2074, fols 7-8.

51 Pastura Ruggiero, 'Lo Stato e la "res frumentaria"', p. 51: having available only 12,000 *scudi*, the pope asked the *Congregazione* to procure the remaining 13,000 as a loan from the officials of the Curia.

52 Pastura Ruggiero, 'Lo Stato e la "res frumentaria"', p. 54 (note 85). The transport by sea to Civitavecchia for these first 3,000 *salme* cost 1,269 *scudi* (ASF, Galli Tassi 1876, fol. 4).

53 ASF, Galli Tassi 1876, fols 9, 23, 27.

In 1541 Benvenuto Olivieri paid 13,290 *scudi di moneta* to the Cavalcanti and Giraldi company for 2,658 *rubbi* of grain, which served for the bread for the troops fighting the war against Ascanio Colonna.[54]

In 1544-45 the Olivieri company bought 1,000 *salme* of wheat under the name of Montauto, who, together with the Ubaldini company, had promised to supply 10,000 *salme* to the Apostolic Chamber.[55]

In July 1545, the Cavalcanti-Giraldi and Olivieri companies were again given the task of importing Sicilian grain, each investing 2,300 *scudi* [56] and obtaining as a guarantee the collection of the Triennial Subsidy.[57] It was this, in fact, that mostly interested the merchants that supplied the grain: not so much the business deal in itself, often not particularly profitable (although there was the occasional exception, as will be seen shortly), but the revenue that they could earn from the various offices, from the shares of the *Monte* and more generally from the proceeds of the various taxes of Rome or of the provinces of the Papal State, that the Apostolic Chamber was forced to hand over as guarantee. Again in 1545, Benvenuto Olivieri, who at that time was treasurer of Perugia, must in some way have been involved in the commerce of the grain in that area, whether imported to Perugia or transferred from there to Rome.[58]

In August 1548 the companies of the Florentine banker Montauto (for ⅔) and of Bernardini and Spada from Lucca (for ⅓) made a deal with the Apostolic Chamber for the importation of 10,000 *salme* of grain from Sicily.[59] Benvenuto Olivieri & Partners paid 3,750 ducats for a 25% share of what their co-nationals had (therefore they eventually owned 1/6 =16.67%). The share of the Montauto company was then divided further between the Cavalcanti-Giraldi and Rucellai companies, ¼ each. In the end, the deal was divided thus:

Martino Bernardini and Vincenzo Spada & Partners (Lucchese)	33.33%
Bastiano da Montauto & Partners	16.67%
Benvenuto Olivieri & Partners	16.67%
Tommaso Cavalcanti and Giovanni Giraldi & Partners	16.67%
Luigi Rucellai & Partners	16.67%

54 ASF, Galli Tassi 1875, fol. 4.

55 ASF, Galli Tassi 2074, fol. 5.

56 ASF, Galli Tassi 1951, fol. 72; ASR, *Notai segretari e cancellieri della R. Camera apostolica 1988*, fols 561r-567r: Girolamo Ubaldini was also then named as a participant (fol. 567r); ASV, *Cam. Ap., Div. Cam. 142*, fols 45v-46v.

57 Pastura Ruggiero, 'Lo Stato e la "res frumentaria"', p. 54 (note 85); connected to this operation Olivieri obtained the right to import tax-free a further 2,000 *rubbi*, on top of the supply to the Chamber. There are also other references to relatively small quantities of grain that Benvenuto Olivieri & Partners traded independently from the Apostolic Chamber (ASF, Galli Tassi 1876, fol. 23; Galli Tassi 1951, fols 80, 83, 84).

58 ASF, Galli Tassi 1875, fol. 1; ASR, *Notai segretari e cancellieri della R. Camera apostolica 1988*, fols 567v-570v.

59 ASF, Galli Tassi 1952, fols 45, 49. Delumeau, *Vie économique et sociale*, II, pp. 634-635, claims that of the 9,910 *salme* that actually left Sicily only 9,218 reached the port of Ripa: in fact, in the voyages from the island 690 *salme* of grain were lost in shipwrecks (Galli Tassi 1875, fol. 10).

From a total investment of 22,500 ducats the bankers made an overall profit of 5,108 (22.7% of the sum initially paid in), of which 851 went to Benvenuto Olivieri & Partners.[60]

3. The Mint of Rome

The Mint of Rome has already been mentioned in Chapter 1 (pp. 13-14) as an example of the favouritism shown by every pontiff towards his own fellow countrymen: in 1515, for instance, Leo X had removed its administration from the German Fuggers, to give it to the Florentines. His Fleming successor, Adrian VI, who had been guardian of Charles V, once again broke the contract in order to hand it over to a certain Saver, agent of the Fuggers, who by that time had become the bankers of the Spanish sovereign. With Clement VII, however, the Mint once again changed hands and was contracted out to the 'consuls and councillors of our Florentine nation'.[61] In 1540, therefore, under Paul III, the Mint continued under Florentine management. From September of that year Tommaso Cavalcanti and Giovanni Giraldi & Partners took over the contract, choosing their fellow countryman Lorenzo di Raffaello Pintelli as manager and partner. Cavalcanti and Giraldi paid the sum of 2,000 *scudi d'oro in oro* (declaring themselves ready to pay out a further 2,000 in case of necessity) to establish the company that would manage the Mint. The company, like the contract itself, was to be of five-year duration, renewable if the administration was reconfirmed, and was to be given the name of Lorenzo Pintelli & Partners. The initial division of the profits would be 60% to the Cavalcanti and Giraldi company and 40% to Pintelli, to whom the former would also make available 1,000 *scudi* for the expenses of the company (rents, household furnishings, etc.) and a further 380 per annum for the upkeep of his own personal household.[62]

A few days later, on 30 September, the Cavalcanti and Giraldi company transferred half of its share to Benvenuto Olivieri & Partners, who paid 1,500 *scudi d'oro in oro* as their half of the social capital (since to the initial 2,000 *scudi* had been added the 1,000 for the expenses of the company). In their turn the Olivieri company transferred a 5% share to Giovan Battista Bettini, who in exchange paid them 250 *scudi*.[63] To sum up, therefore, considering that Pintelli earned his part through his activity in the administration of the Mint and not from having deposited a part of the social capital, the profits would be shared as follows:[64]

---

60 ASF, Galli Tassi 1952, fol. 49.

61 For all this information see A. Schulte, *Die Fugger in Rom 1495-1523* (2 vols, Leipzig, 1904), I, pp. 205, 209, 219 and II, pp. 122, 146.

62 ASF, Galli Tassi 1824, fols 1-2.

63 ASF, Galli Tassi 1824, fols 1-2; Galli Tassi 2278, fols 94, 99. A record of all the contracts and agreements mentioned so far in this section can be found in Galli Tassi 1824, fol. 14. Giovan Battista Bettini, incidentally, was brother of the same Bartolomeo who was at that time collaborating with the Cavalcanti and Giraldi company and who later would become administrator of the estate of Benvenuto Olivieri.

64 This is confirmed by ASF, Galli Tassi 1942, fol. 194v, which, however, gives the beginning of the contract as 1 July 1540.

Lorenzo Pintelli	40%
Tommaso Cavalcanti and Giovanni Giraldi & Partners	30%
Benvenuto Olivieri & Partners	25%
Giovan Battista Bettini	5%

After the stipulated five years the contract was not renewed, but was taken over by three other bankers: Giovan Battista and Lorenzo Degli Albizzi, and Vincenzo de Castello.[65]

Only after lengthy disputes with the Roman Senate did the papal authority, under the papacy of Eugene IV (1431-47), succeed in obtaining control of the Mint. For some time it had been the custom to contract it out to private individuals. The *zecchiere* (farmer of the Mint) was obliged by the Apostolic Chamber to mint a fixed quantity of coin, in gold, silver and copper, under the close supervision of the chamberlain and, above all, of the treasurer general. Among the rights of the *zecchiere*, on the other hand, were a fixed annual remuneration (albeit not particularly high – on average 500-1,000 *scudi* per annum), and above all the possibility to mint, as well as the quantity fixed by the Chamber, also all the coin that he wanted, using metals provided by himself or other private individuals.[66] Olivieri, Roberto Strozzi and others, for example, took various objects of silver to the Mint in order to have them turned into coin.[67] The *zecchiere* was obliged to mint coin brought to him by private individuals, but could keep for himself 0.5% of the gold and 1% of the silver. Moreover, he could, on authorization of the president of the Mint, export all the coins he minted in addition to the quantity requested by the Apostolic Chamber, using also, free of charge, the papal galleys for the transport.[68] It was this last right that allowed the *zecchiere* to earn the money that made it profitable for him to take the office. Some risk existed, however, when oscillations of the value of the metals were not followed by changes in the value of the coins: when this happened it was no longer a good financial move for private individuals to take metals to be coined at the Mint.[69]

To sum up, this chapter has shown how Benvenuto Olivieri's company readily became involved not only in sectors that were formally connected to the fiscal apparatus of the Chamber, but also in what might be referred to as peripheral sectors that nevertheless could still be considered as part of the overall set of services offered to the Apostolic Chamber. The variety of activities included in the working relationship between the *mercatores* and the papal financial body therefore confirm the existence of a very tight-knit collaboration between one and the other. By this time

---

65 L. Londei, in M.G. Pastura Ruggiero, *La Reverenda Camera Apostolica e i suoi archivi (secoli XV-XVIII)* (Rome, 1984), p. 153. In a list of merchants of 1546 L. Degli Albizzi & Partners were described as '*zechieri*' (ASF, Galli Tassi 1868, fasc. 1, fol. 4v; transcribed in the Appendix, doc. 1).

66 Londei, in Pastura Ruggiero, *La Reverenda Camera Apostolica*, pp. 149, 160-161; S. Balbi De Caro-L. Londei, *Moneta pontificia da Innocenzo XI a Gregorio XVI* (Rome, 1984), pp. 8-10, 18-20.

67 ASF, Galli Tassi 2278, fols 59, 152.

68 Londei, in Pastura Ruggiero, *La Reverenda Camera Apostolica*, p. 160.

69 Balbi De Caro-Londei, *Moneta pontificia*, pp. 20-22.

– the mid-sixteenth century – the *mercatores* had become inextricably intertwined with the finances of the Papal State. The Papal State was so deeply in debt to these bankers that it had to continue taking out new loans in order to pay the old ones. The Apostolic Chamber was no longer able to survive without the Florentine and Genoese merchant-bankers. The merchant-bankers, similarly, were inextricably involved with the Chamber: on the one hand, they profited financially and socially from this collaboration, but, on the other, they had no choice but to continue to supply money and services, because their loans were almost never paid back in full, but more often than not deferred with assignments on other sources of income.

CHAPTER 9

The Business Turnover

Clearly, the main focus – and most original aspect – of this book is Benvenuto Olivieri's activity as a papal banker. However, while this was his main role and an undercurrent in all his transactions, and even though all the sums of money that passed through his hands on other markets, prevalently foreign, served in the final analysis to finance the loans that he made to the Chamber, not all his banking activity was directly connected to the Apostolic Chamber. Since there was no overt relationship between the two, however, this chapter takes a more general look at the business turnover of Olivieri's company, and examines its relations also with companies or individuals not connected to the papal finances. The historiography provides numerous examples of merchants who used Italian or foreign marketplaces to transfer sums of money or to conceal loans. However, as has been repeated several times, there are no other cases like that of Benvenuto Olivieri, and no other collection like the Fondo Galli Tassi has come to light which allows us to analyse in such detail the relations between private bankers and the Apostolic Chamber.

This chapter examines the flow of money – at times quite substantial amounts – between Rome and other Italian and foreign cities, in particular Lyons. Between this French city and Rome there was a notable business turnover: while Lyons was the established centre of financial transactions at the European level, by this time Rome too had acquired an important position and by the beginning of the sixteenth century it was considered an important marketplace for bills of exchange.[1] A hundred years later, at the beginning of the seventeenth century, 20% of the business deals negotiated at the fairs of Piacenza originated in Rome.[2] The ability of the bankers to play with the exchange rates allowed them to loan money through the fairs, and thus make a profit. Naturally each transaction necessitated two bills of exchange: one that transferred the money to Lyons and the other that from Lyons transferred the money back to a beneficiary in Rome. These operations, moreover, allowed the bankers to avoid running foul of the anti-usury laws, because the eventual profit was not a fixed sum as a percentage on the money, but rather a recompense for the risk, which varied from day to day. The interest rate was by this time an accepted part of financial dealings (and was attached to all the loans conceded to the Apostolic Chamber), but it was always specified that it was due to *lucri cessantis*.

---

1 M.T. Boyer-Xambeu-G. Deleplace-L. Gillard, *Monnaie privée et pouvoir des princes* (Paris, 1986), p. 164. For an exhaustive study of Lyons, principal European financial marketplace in the sixteenth century and home to four fairs, one book is sufficient: the classic R. Gascon, *Grand commerce et vie urbaine au XVI*[e] *siècle. Lyon et ses marchands (environs de 1520-environs de 1580)* (2 vols, Paris, 1971).

2 J.G. Da Silva, *Banque et crédit en Italie au XVII*[e] *siècle* (2 vols, Paris, 1969), p. 119.

The Roman bankers (including those discussed in this book) therefore often used Lyons, even when they were transferring money privately between each other. Thus, even though the overwhelming majority of the operations carried out by Benvenuto Olivieri & Partners regarded the business affairs of the Apostolic Chamber, the name of Lyons – and also of other foreign financial markets – frequently appears in the accounts of the company.[3]

1. The balance sheet of 1543

In the central chapters of this book all of the contracts that the Olivieri company was party to were analysed individually. In this section instead an attempt will be made to photograph a single moment in the life of this company, looking at all the activities in which Benvenuto Olivieri & Partners were involved at that point in time. The best way to do this would, of course, be to have an original and complete balance sheet in our possession, but unfortunately no such document exists in the Fondo Galli Tassi.[4] Nevertheless, useful information can be gleaned from the '*libro azzurro di debitori e creditori di Benvenuto Olivieri e compagni di Roma, segnato A secondo*' (ASF, Galli Tassi 2278), which holds the records of the company from 1 January 1542 to 31 January 1544 inclusive. This volume is the second of three; it follows, in other words, and somewhat obviously, the '*libro azzurro A primo*' and precedes the '*libro azzurro A terzo*', neither of which, unfortunately, seem to have survived to the present day.[5]

The only way, therefore, of obtaining a balance sheet able to give us a picture of the overall business turnover of the Olivieri company of Rome was to choose a date and calculate the balance of all the accounts active on that day. There was actually

3 Concerning the Italian bankers and, in particular, the Florentine bankers in Lyons, see M. Cassandro, *Le fiere di Lione e gli uomini d'affari italiani nel Cinquecento* (Florence, 1979); R. Gascon, 'Les Italiens dans la renaissance économique lyonnaise au XVIe siècle', *Revue des études italiennes* (1958): 167-181; E. Picot, *Les Italiens en France au XVIe siècle* (Bordeaux, 1918, reprinted with an introduction by N. Ordine, Rome, 1995), esp. pp. 75-124.

4 There are fragments of a balance sheet of the '*libro azurro primo segnato A*' of 18 November 1542 (ASF, Galli Tassi 1946, fols 18r-24r), which indicate the presence of 55 accounts of creditors and 85 of debtors; amongst the first stand out profits for 16,698 gold cameral ducats (fol. 20v). It was not considered suitable, however, as apart from being incomplete no supporting sources were found. Nor, moreover, was it possible to use the '*spoglio del libro azzurro segnato A secondo e terzo*' (Galli Tassi 1920) because this contains records spanning too long a period of time (and in reality there is only one relative to the *libro secondo*): it seems to be an annotated list of accounts that had not yet been settled between the heirs of Benvenuto Olivieri and the account-holders, in the years up until 1570.

5 It is important to keep this fact in mind, because in the volume used here there are accounts which refer to either the first or third of the volumes. And, unfortunately, in neither case can they be considered a balance sheet, because in both the transactions took place not on a single day, but during the three years. It seems therefore clear that – presumably in order to save paper (the writing is very small and close together in almost all the volume) – the accountant of the Olivieri company kept more than one book at a time, recording the accounts in the successive one once he ran out of space.

little choice – the only possible date was 13 February 1543. The following day, in fact, the accounts started to be carried forward to the *libro A terzo* and, presumably, these accounts became active in the *libro terzo* on the same day. Luckily, 1542-43 was in any case one of the peak years in business terms for Benvenuto Olivieri & Partners. At that time, to name only the more important business deals in which it was involved, the company was under contract to administer the three customs of Rome, the Treasury of Perugia and Umbria and the *Salara* of Rome, as well as being, for most of the period, depositary general.

Having chosen the date, all the accounts were then examined and the balance of those open at the time was calculated. The result is a balance sheet composed of 312 accounts (153 in credit and 159 in debit), which provides a complete overview of the activity of a *mercator romanam curiam sequens*. The full version can be found in the Appendix, Doc. 7, but a summary in table form is also provided in this chapter. This summary will be taken as a starting point for the discussion that follows, although, naturally, occasional reference will be made to the accounts of the complete balance sheet in the course of the analysis. It should be noted that in constructing Table 14 some of the sums included were, for reasons of greater clarity, processed, with the result that the numbers do not always correspond exactly to those given in the complete version.

It is immediately noticeable that there is a slight difference (equivalent to 0.96%) between the total of the *Avere* side (credit) and that of the *Dare* side (debit). This discrepancy, however, is so slight that can be considered insignificant and may be a result of either errors made by the original accountant or of an oversight on my part. Moreover, as has been noted also by De Roover commenting on a similar mistake in the balance sheet of the Roman company of the Medici of 1427, 'in any case, the reason why the books did not quite balance was human failure – *errare humanum est* – rather than ignorance of accounting principles'.[6]

We should not be misled by the high percentages of the sections called 'Correspondents, holders of current accounts and miscellaneous credits/debts': these are truly miscellaneous. Not necessarily, in other words, do the accounts there included belong to the sphere of private transactions, that is separate transactions unconnected to the Apostolic Chamber. In these sections, as well as the highlighted subcategories, accounts are registered to single individuals and colleges, functionaries, tax-farmers and partners of the company, as well as tax-collecting services and even merchandise. Moreover, even those Italian or foreign companies included in a separate section might nevertheless be linked to the Chamber contracts – but not always, and not necessarily (not even those with headquarters in Rome). Tellingly, the balance sheet demonstrates what a vast amount of money was owed to the Olivieri company by the Apostolic Chamber. It should be noted, however, that these loans had not been made by Benvenuto Olivieri & Partners alone. Rather, they (independently from the Chamber) had made private agreements with many other merchant-bankers, who provided a good part of these sums directly or through foreign financial marketplaces.

6 R. De Roover, *The Rise and Decline of the Medici Bank (1397-1494)* (New York, 1966), p. 99.

Table 14 – Balance sheet of Benvenuto Olivieri & Partners, 13 February 1543 (values in gold cameral ducats and percentages): the figures are rounded to the nearest ducat. In the section called 'Correspondents, holders of current accounts and miscellaneous credits/debts' single accounts with balances over 3,000 ducats are listed except for those that have already been included in the various categories (for example, companies and so on).

ASSETS		ducats	%
Apostolic Chamber		117,509	38.39
Olivieri & Partners depositaries, acc. a parte		14,634	4.78
Olivieri & Partners treasurers of Perugia		3,805	1.25
Correspondents, holders of current accounts and miscellaneous credits		124,650	40.72
Companies in Rome, 11.30%	34,594		
Clergy, 5.78%	17,691		
Companies abroad, 4.55%	13,935		
Companies in Italy (outside Rome), 2.03%	6,218		
Raffaello Gherardini of Milan, 1.91%	5,856		
Salinari, 1.66%	5,079		
Alum, 1.62%	4,964		
Andrea Malvenda of Rouen, 1.46%	4,450		
Benedetto Busini, acc. a parte R.B., 1.20%	3,684		
Farmers of the *Salara* of Rome, 1.09%	3,331		
Others, 8.12%	24,848		
Interest, premiums and advances on accounts of third parties		7,619	2.49
Cash		33,837	11.06
Total credits		302,054	98.69
Losses on fair of 1541		4,021	1.31
TOTAL		306,075	100.00
Discrepancy		2,977	0.96

Source: author's elaboration from ASF, Galli Tassi 2278

LIABILITIES		**ducats**	**%**
Olivieri & Partners depositaries, current acc.		9,753	3.16
Correspondents, holders of current accounts and miscellaneous debts		253,279	81.95
Companies in Rome, 23.15%	71,532		
Companies abroad, 15.21%	47,007		
B. Machiavelli for salt of the Romagna, 8.99%	27,768		
N. Capponi, his acc., 7.90%	24,421		
College of *Monte della Fede*, 6.08%	18,803		
Companies in Italy (outside Rome), 3.63%	11,220		
Clergy, 2.50%	7,740		
B. Olivieri, his current acc., 2.24%	6,922		
Luigi Gaddi, 1.08%	3,347		
Francesco Bartoli, broker of exchanges, 1.05%	3,236		
Others, 10.12%	31,283		
Other Olivieri companies in Italy		3,058	0.99
Register of charges and fees to be paid		1,424	0.46
Libro Azzurro A primo		11,575	3.75
Prior companies		6,401	2.07
Total debts		285,490	92.38
Social capital		20,000	6.47
Various profits		3,562	1.15
TOTAL		309,052	100.00

When the company began its activity, as has been seen (Chapter 2, p. 52), on 1 September 1539, it had a social capital (*corpo*) of 24,000 gold cameral ducats. In Table 14 this is given as 20,000 ducats. This discrepancy can be easily explained: the actual contributions were 17,000 ducats from Benvenuto Olivieri, 2,000 from Benedetto Busini and 1,000 from Simone Guiducci, while the remaining 4,000 were a promised contribution plus the capitalization of the service of Busini and Guiducci (*stima della persona*). Roberto di Filippo Strozzi's name does not appear on the list of partners, but it is known that he contributed 12,000 ducats hidden behind the name of Benvenuto Olivieri. Roberto's wish for discretion is mirrored in the ledger, where there is no account registered to him directly (although there is mention of Filippo Strozzi's heir – no name is specified). Nevertheless, it can be safely assumed that he was the holder of the substantial account '*Benvenuto Ulivieri per conto a parte R*'.[7] With almost equal certainty the even more substantial account '*Benedetto Busini per conto a parte R.B.*' can also be attributed to Strozzi.

Some space should now be given to a discussion of profits and losses. The situation on 13 February was one of loss. Against the 3,562.19 ducats of profit on various operations, 4,020.87 ducats were lost at the Fair of All Saints of 1541. The final balance, therefore, was a loss of 458.68 ducats.[8]

This was an unusually unfortunate moment for the Olivieri company. Just over a month later, in fact, on 17 March 1543, the loss of the account registered to the Fair of All Saints of 1541, which had in the meantime increased, was virtually cancelled out, thanks to 4,037.11 ducats 'made good by the depositary for exchange operations'.[9] Furthermore, on the same day (on which, it should be remembered, the contract for the Depositary ended: cf. Chapter 3, pp. 72, 76) the considerable sum of 14,175.96 ducats was also credited to the profit and loss account by the depositary.[10] Overall, the company was successful – on 31 January 1544, for example, its accountant credited the profit and loss account of the *libro terzo* with a sum of approximately 21,400 ducats. It is to do justice to an activity that certainly, in these years, was relatively profitable, that the profit and loss account is provided in its entirety in the Appendix (Doc. 8) and in a summarized form in Table 15. It should, moreover, be considered that on 7 September 1543 there had already been a first distribution of profits, equal to 1,600 ducats, between Olivieri, Busini and Guiducci.[11] Therefore, as can be seen

7 In ASF, Galli Tassi 1920, fol. 24 this account is referred to in the following terms: 'these sums belong to Roberto di Filippo Strozzi, partner in this company for 10 *soldi per lira* [=50%] behind the name of Benvenuto'.

8 ASF, Galli Tassi 2278, fols 11, 137, 150, 151, 158. The last four accounts are relative to four distinct operations. The account at fol. 11, on the contrary, is the profit and loss account, which provided the final balance of the profits or the losses made on the various business deals as they occurred, and also of the other four accounts, once they were balanced.

9 ASF, Galli Tassi 2278, fol. 137.

10 ASF, Galli Tassi 2278, fol. 11.

11 ASF, Galli Tassi 2278, fol. 362. On the same 7 September, 210 ducats were paid out in salary to the employees. As has already been discussed (Chapter 2, pp. 52-53), they were Giovan Francesco Ridolfi, Francesco Del Riccio and Guglielmo Dei; in addition, working on the administrative side, and recompensed exclusively from the division of the profits, were Simone Guiducci, half of whose participation in the social capital was capitalization of his

in the table below, the net profit obtained in the 25 months was of approximately 23,000 ducats, equal to an annual average of 11,040.

Table 15 – Profit and loss account of Benvenuto Olivieri & Partners, 2 January 1542-31 January 1544. Values in gold cameral ducats rounded to the nearest ducat

PROFITS	**ducats**	**%**	**ducats**	**%**
Operations with the Apostolic Chamber			20,510	70.93
Depositary General	14,176	49.02		
Salt of Rome and the Romagna	3,024	10.46		
Treasuries (Romagna and Parma-Piacenza)	1,668	5.77		
Vigesima+subsidy of the Jews	822	2.84		
Others	820	2.84		
Various commissions			2,965	10.26
Distribution of alum			2,047	7.08
Covoni company			1,100	3.80
Various profits			2,294	7.93
Total profit			**28,916**	**100.00**
LOSSES	**ducats**	**%**	**ducats**	**%**
Italian merchant-bankers			2,213	37.41
Neri Capponi	636	10.75		
Olivieri & Partners of Naples	616	10.41		
Others	961	16.25		
Operations with the Apostolic Chamber			1,685	28.48
Salt of Rome and the Romagna	1,285	21.72		
Venal offices and *Monti*	400	6.76		
Employees, expenses for the bank, alms			831	14.05
Exchanges			379	6.41
Dispatch of letters			231	3.91
Various losses			576	9.74
Total loss			**5,915**	**100.00**
Net profit			**23,001**	
Annual average			11,040	

Source: ASF, Galli Tassi 2278, fols 11, 311, 362

If therefore the profits and losses are examined in their entirety, the sectors of greatest profit can be identified. Between 16 January 1542 and 31 January 1544 the entries of the *Avere* side added up to a total of 28,916 gold cameral ducats, almost half of which, as has been seen, came from the Depositary. Approximately 4,000 ducats

service, and Benedetto Busini, who worked at a 'higher' level, on occasion even representing the company.

(from which 1,000 have to be subtracted because, as specified in the entry on the *Dare* side, 'they were credited by mistake') came from commissions, that is the 2-3% that the bank retained on some financial transactions. The third entry in order of value, 1,404.90 ducats, was the profit from the increase of the salt tax of Rome and the Romagna. A further sum of 1,009 ducats is recorded as the profit from the *Salara* of Rome, but because of a disagreement with the financial administration it was not collected, and is therefore also recorded in the loss column. Slightly larger (1,100.18 ducats) was the share of profits belonging to the Olivieri company that had been distributed by Antonio Covoni & Partners. A further two substantial entries (1,038.09 and 1,000 ducats) were the profit calculated on the first two years the company was involved in the commerce of alum, respectively with Atlantic France and with Provence. Most of the lesser profits came again from operations connected to the Apostolic Chamber: 702.45 as interest on a loan connected with the Treasury of the Romagna; 609.76 as commission on the increase of the salt tax in the same region; two entries of 431.66 and 390.25 were the profits from the *vigesima* and the subsidy of the Jews respectively; a further 365.82, 214.64 and 146.14 ducats were the result of operations connected to the Treasury of Parma and Piacenza; the third year of the administration of the *gabella dello Studio*, finally, resulted in a profit of 243.92 ducats. In other words, with few exceptions, the sources of profit were linked directly or indirectly (for example the commerce of alum) to the papal finances.

The sum of the entries on the *Dare* side came instead to 8,515 ducats: 1,000 of them, as mentioned above, were necessary to 'cancel' an entry on the *Avere* side and 1,600 were the profits already distributed. The most substantial single sum is the 1,009 ducats of missed profits on the *Salara* of Rome, which was referred to above. Almost 600 ducats, on the other hand, were recorded as a loss in the account held in Naples by the Olivieri company. The other entries, all of which, with one exception, were less than 300 ducats, included numerous small sums given to charitable causes, as well as sums used for various reasons, from general company expenses (rent of the premises, books, etc.) to exchange operations.

After this minor detour to examine the profit and loss account, the balance sheet can now be analysed. On 13 February 1543 the debts still remaining in the account registered to the *libro azzurro primo* exceeded 10,000 ducats. As was mentioned at the beginning of this section, even when the *libro secondo* was well under way, entries continued to be recorded in the *libro primo*. Two accounts can be taken as an example: a current account containing a sum of 6,084.71 ducats, and another 'relative to divers debtors and creditors', with a balance of 5,490.76 ducats.[12] It should be noted that at the end of the book the balance of the first was included in the second, destined then to be debited to the *libro terzo* with a sum exceeding 6,300 ducats (a relatively high sum, but nevertheless reduced compared to the 11,575.47 to which amounted the total of the two accounts on 13 February 1543).[13]

Benvenuto Olivieri & Partners's debts with the prior companies – Giulio and Lorenzo Strozzi & Partners and Filippo Strozzi & Partners – were recorded as coming to slightly more than 2% of the total loss. Obviously the debt with the first

12 ASF, Galli Tassi 2278, fols 88, 266.

13 ASF, Galli Tassi 2278, fols 332, 383.

was greater (4,615.21 ducats against 1,785.88), given that chronologically it was the more recent. Both debts, however, were paid relatively quickly and in September and December 1543 respectively were transformed into credit (albeit a very small sum), and as such were then carried forward to the following book.[14]

Before analysing the accounts relative to the diverse operations in which Benvenuto Olivieri & Partners were involved, a brief glance will be given at the cash account, which included all those sums of money that materially entered or exited the coffers of the company. According to the records, this money was handled by Simone Guiducci and Guglielmo Dei.[15] On 13 February 1543 the coffers held 33,837.45 ducats, 24,781.67 of which 'in the hands of' Guiducci and 9,055.78 in those of Dei. In total, the sum held in cash came to 11.06% of the assets.[16]

A fundamental part of the activity of the Olivieri company was, as has been amply documented in the central part of this volume, that of the papal finances; or, more accurately, the company's relations with the Apostolic Chamber, which was in charge of the handling of these finances. In the relevant section of Table 14 five separate accounts have therefore been placed together. These accounts are registered to, first, 'various deals' – the *imposizione delle galere*, the tithes, the income from communes (*entrate delle comunità*) and a loan of 55,000 *scudi* (73,170.76 ducats); second, the increase of the salt tax of the Romagna (32,408.92 ducats); third, the customs of Rome (5,853.70 ducats); fourth, the *imposizione dei mezzi frutti* on the monasteries (4,682.93 ducats); and, lastly, the *vigesima* of the Jews (2,276.41 ducats).[17] These five accounts constitute almost 40% of all the credit items of the balance sheet. The first and largest account, which draws together a number of separate yet related operations, has already been dealt with in some detail in Chapter 3, where it was pointed out that, in repayment for the two loans of 20,000 and 55,000 *scudi*, the Olivieri company and their partners were given the right to the collection of taxes of various types, both temporal and spiritual (pp. 86-87). This confirms once again that the *mercatores* loaned enormous sums to the Apostolic Chamber; of the more than 73,000 ducats of the first account, moreover, almost 62,000 were registered in a single day, 7 September 1542.

Another very large credit, recorded on 13 February 1543, was the 32,408.92 ducats claimed by the Olivieri company from the administration of the salt tax of the Romagna. It should not, however, be forgotten that, as often occurred, a good part of this sum went to other merchant-bankers who were acting under the name of the

14 ASF, Galli Tassi 2278, fols 128, 276, 360.

15 ASF, Galli Tassi 2278, fols 8, 36, 54, 76, 83, 104, 108, 122, 141, 142, 144, 147, 156, 161, 175, 178, 183, 190, 193, 216, 219, 225 (for Guiducci), 227, 233, 247, 252, 254, 264, 267, 275, 298, 300 (for Dei). Roughly, Guiducci managed the cashbox until 7 October 1542 and Dei from 9 October 1542 to 22 September 1543; however, for a certain period of time the two accounts overlapped.

16 It is difficult to establish if this was a high or low percentage, given that there are no specific studies on this matter. Two examples, relative to a Corsi company of 1582 and a Strozzi company of 1484, can be found, however, in R.A. Goldthwaite, 'Banking in Florence at the End of the Sixteenth Century', *The Journal of European Economic History*, 27 (1998): 530, 532.

17 ASF, Galli Tassi 2278, fols 97, 100, 101, 197.

Florentine company (cf. Chapter 7, pp. 151-152). The 5,853.70 ducats relative to the customs, corresponding to 6,000 *scudi d'oro in oro*, were the half of the 12,000 *scudi* that the Olivieri and Montauto companies, farmers of the three customs, had to loan to the Apostolic Chamber as a first instalment of the loan of 52,000 *scudi* promised in exchange for the contract (for more details on this sum, see Chapter 5, pp. 117-118). Furthermore, the Apostolic Chamber owed almost 4,700 ducats to the Olivieri company as repayment of a loan that had been made at the end of 1541 by a consortium of Florentine and Genoese bankers (amongst whom then further shares were transferred: see Chapter 3, p. 85), in exchange for the collection of the '*mezzi frutti*'. The last credit entry, equal to 2,276.41 ducats, came from a loan which guaranteed rights on the collection of the *vigesima* of the Jews, transferred by the Olivieri company to the Genoese Pallavicini-Giustiniani company (again, see Chapter 3, p. 88).

In the same book, separate accounts were also kept in the name of Benvenuto Olivieri & Partners as holders of specific posts, in particular as depositaries general and as treasurers of Perugia. The reason for this was that they wished to keep the sums and accounts relevant to these posts separate from those of the normal activity of the company. On 13 February 1543, for example, three accounts connected to the Depositary were open: two current accounts and a *conto a parte*. The two current accounts present contrasting balances, one positive for 17,368.89 ducats, the other (the 'new one') negative for 27,121.73.[18] The third account was opened specifically for and only to register the capital (*corpo*) of the Depositary and was closed on 17 March 1543 at the end of Olivieri's period of management (cf. Chapter 3, pp. 72, 76). In the balance sheet this contributed 14,634.13 ducats (equal to 15,000 *scudi di giuli 10 per scudo*) to the profits, equal to 4.78% of the total. However, as already mentioned, the movements of sums of money between the accounts of the company and those of the depositaries or treasurers did not in reality affect the liquid assets or the profits of the company, but only provided evidence of and information about the constant borrowing and lending of money between the company and the various posts it covered, formally distinct, but in practice coinciding.[19]

The situation was similar with regard to the two accounts in the name of Benvenuto Olivieri & Partners in their role as treasurers of Perugia, one relative to 1542, the other to 1543. Both show a positive balance, meaning that the treasurers were in debt to the company, because it was the latter, obviously, which advanced the sums that by contract the treasurers themselves had to pay to the Apostolic Chamber. In the total amount of 3,805.21 ducats, the account relative to the year 1543 (138.64 ducats) obviously has little weight, having been opened only a month and a half previously.[20]

---

18 ASF, Galli Tassi 2278, fols 201, 260.

19 In the case just mentioned, the 15,000 *scudi* were first placed at the Chamber's disposal in the account of the depositaries '*per conto a parte*' (ASF, Galli Tassi 2278, fol. 7); then, at the end of the administration of the Depositary, this sum was credited to the same account and debited to the current account of the depositaries (fols 7, 290); this last account would be balanced against those of the company. On the *conti a parte*, see below.

20 ASF, Galli Tassi 2278, fols 203, 266.

In Table 14 there is another large section called 'Correspondents, holders of current accounts and miscellaneous credits/debts', which gathers together most of the accounts both in credit (134 out of 153 = 87.6%) and in debit (132 out of 159 = 83%). The percentages are less well balanced, however, when the accounts are analysed in terms of value: the sum of the credits amounts to 124,650 ducats (equal to an average of 930.22 per account), that is to 40.72% of the total assets; that of the debts, on the other hand, reaches the considerable figure of 253,279 ducats (in other words 1,918.78 for each account), and the share of 81.95% of the total debt. This imbalance was necessary to compensate for the difference of 126,195 ducats between the credit and the debit in operations connected with the Apostolic Chamber (including those of the Depositary and the Treasury). All of the nucleus of this study, as well as the brief considerations made at the beginning of this section, have highlighted the figure of Benvenuto Olivieri & Partners as coordinators of the papal contracts; not that this role was of their exclusive competence, but it has been seen how often they were the ones who officially signed the original contracts before parts of them were conveyed to other Florentine – or Genoese – bankers.

In general, if the balance of an account is relatively small this does not necessarily indicate an operation of minor importance, but might instead indicate the tail-end of an important business venture. For this reason, small sums have not been automatically ignored, but where indicative of something more important they have instead been highlighted.

As to assets, 43.92% of the money recorded in the 'Correspondents, holders of current accounts and miscellaneous credits' section is held in accounts which can be divided into three categories: accounts in the names of companies with headquarters in Rome (27.75% of the figure of this section and 11.30% of the total credit); accounts of companies with headquarters in other Italian cities (4.99% of the sum of this section and 2.03% of the total credit); and, thirdly, accounts of companies with headquarters in foreign cities (11.18% of the sum of this section and 4.55% of the total credit). Interestingly, 86.85% of the money in this last category (which will be discussed in more detail later in this chapter) came from companies with headquarters in Lyons. Another category that stands out is that of accounts in the name of individuals belonging to the clergy, to whom the Olivieri company obviously believed that it made good business sense to open a line of credit (14.19% of the sum of this section and 5.78% of the total assets).

On the debit side the accounts registered to the companies make up 51.23% of the total of the sums of the section 'Correspondents, holders of current accounts and miscellaneous debts'. Among these, the category that contains the most substantial sum of money (28.24% of the section and 23.15% of the total debit) is yet again that which holds the accounts belonging to companies operating in Rome. The category of foreign companies instead contains 18.56% of the sums of the section, or 15.21% of the total debit. This time the companies have a more varied origin: Lyons 31.98% of the total of the category, Valladolid (thanks above all to the Strozzi company) 31%, Antwerp 13.85%, Burgos 12.10% and Besançon 10.65%.

Before analysing these items in more detail, however, several preliminary observations should be made on the types of accounts that were set up. Above all, those *mercatores* with whom the Olivieri company had more frequent dealings often held simultaneously more than one kind of account: *conti correnti* (current accounts), *conti a parte* (separate accounts) and *conti de' tempi* (time accounts), followed alternatively by the attributes *nostro* (ours) and *loro* (theirs).

Of the *conti correnti* little needs to be said, given that their function was analogous to that of today. The *conti a parte* were opened for two possible reasons: either for particular operations or for individuals who wished to remain anonymous. In the first case, to the name of the holder of the account was added the indication '*a parte*' (separate) and the type of operation concerned, for example alum, increase of the salt tax of the Romagna, *imposizione delle galere*; or even the social capital of the company. In the second case, the name of the holder plus '*a parte*' was followed by a letter or letters, generally the initials of the name of the person who wished for reasons of his own to remain anonymous, and thus remained hidden behind the name of the account-holder.

The *conto de' tempi* instead indicated long-term operations. The different terms of payment were also indicated by the recurrent note, '*per quando riscossi saranno*' (when they will be collected). Normally, therefore, if Banker X entered into a business deal under the name of the Olivieri company, he became a creditor of the Olivieri company for the sum with which he participated, in a *conto loro de' tempi*. Naturally, as the sums were collected, Olivieri credited them to X, diminishing his debt to the latter. In most cases this type of account will therefore be found on the debit side of the balance sheet. In contrast, when Benvenuto Olivieri & Partners acted under the name of X, then it was they who became creditors (X must give) in a *conto nostro de' tempi*, the balance of which was normally written on the credit side of the balance sheet. The two terms *a parte* and *de' tempi* could also be combined.

This miscellaneous section of the balance sheet obviously also includes accounts relative to operations linked to the Apostolic Chamber, which are registered either to individuals or to the operations themselves. Doc. 7 in the Appendix shows the accounts of this section, both on the *Dare* and the *Avere* sides, in decreasing order of value. By far the most substantial is the account of Bernardo Machiavelli, commissioner for the increase of the salt tax of the Romagna: the 27,768.19 already collected by him (which therefore appear on the debit side) would then be transferred to Rome to the Olivieri company through bills of exchange drawn by the Cattani company of Bologna.[21] Machiavelli, who was frequently involved in tax-farming in Bologna and in the Romagna, also held another account, relative to the *imposizione delle galere* and recorded on the debit side of the balance sheet for a sum of 1,932.05 ducats.[22] For somewhat different reasons it would seem that Tobia Pallavicini held 1,858.53 ducats in a *suo conto de' tempi*: this sum corresponded to 2,000 *scudi di moneta*, that is a sixth

21 ASF, Galli Tassi 2278, fols 96, 211. Closely linked to these operations are also another two accounts: one belonging to Bernardo Machiavelli, which records his commissions for tax-collection services, with a balance of 2,094.33 ducats (fol. 31); the other belonging to Antonio Ugolini, this too for a commission, equal to 585.37 ducats (fol. 93). For the involvement of these two men in the operations relative to the increase of the salt tax of the Romagna, see Chapter 7, pp. 150-153.

22 ASF, Galli Tassi 2278, fol. 213.

of the 12,000 that the Olivieri company had paid to obtain the contract of the increase of the salt tax of the Romagna, in which Pallavicini subsequently participated.[23]

Further, on the *Avere* side there are accounts containing fairly substantial figures registered directly to the operations that involved the Olivieri company in its role as tax-farmer on behalf of the Apostolic Chamber: the *vigesima* of the Jews of the Romagna and Bologna (1,611.73 ducats), the tithes of the Romagna (1,278.08) and the tithes of Perugia (931.47).[24]

Similar to the accounts registered to tax-collection operations are those opened for the various colleges, which, as was discussed in Chapter 4, gathered together those who had the right to collect revenues either because they were holders of offices or because they were holders of bonds of the public debt. The latter is the case of one of the largest accounts on the *Dare* side of the balance sheet: 18,802.70 ducats. This was the amount owed by Benvenuto Olivieri & Partners to the College of the *Monte della Fede*, for which they were depositaries (they were responsible for the payment of the annuities).[25] Evidently, therefore, they kept account of the sums for which the College had an assignment on the customs of Rome, but they also used this account to pay out to the holders of the bonds of the *Monte* (or, in other words, the members of the College) their bimonthly income. Other items were registered by Olivieri and his partners because, in their role of farmers of the customs, of the *Salara* of Rome or of the Treasury of Perugia, they were obliged by contract to pay to the following colleges or, rather, to the depositaries of these, the assignments to which these had the right: the College of the portioneers of the port taxes (*porzionari di Ripa*), the College of the cubiculars and scutifers, the College of the presidents, the College of the apostolic secretaries, the College of the knights of St Peter, the College of the clerks of the Chamber and the College of the Archive.[26]

On the credit side of the balance sheet are the accounts registered to '*più salinari*' and to the '*doganieri della Salara di Roma*', containing 5,078.58 and 3,330.97 ducats respectively. In the first account were initially recorded all the payments in cash made to the functionaries who were involved in the distribution of the salt; only subsequently were these partially balanced out by sums 'made good' by the salt tax-farmers ('*doganieri della Salara*').[27] The second account, which registers the tax collections on the salt distributed, presents as debt the sums paid to the *salinari*, the assignments to various colleges and, above all, the sum of 8,869.27 ducats that the account-holders

23 ASF, Galli Tassi 2278, fol. 98.

24 ASF, Galli Tassi 2278, fols 195, 220, 281. Also in the balance sheet, but with much lower amounts, are the tithes of Campagna (fol. 249) and of Patrimonio (fol. 277). Linked to the tithes are the accounts of the commissioners: Bernardo Machiavelli (fol. 241), Luca Tommasini (fol. 265), Guido Machiavelli (fol. 271), Giovan Battista Bonsi (fol. 271). Virtually all these sums can be found in the *Avere* side, since they were the collections from the various areas; eventually they were 'made good' to the Apostolic Chamber, thus contributing to a reduction in the latter's debt to the Olivieri company (fol. 317).

25 ASF, Galli Tassi 2278, fol. 259.

26 ASF, Galli Tassi 2278, fols 3, 4, 57, 153, 226, 239.

27 ASF, Galli Tassi 2278, fols 44, 286.

'are obliged to give … according to the agreement made with the pope, because they did not sell the extraordinary amount of salt with the increased tax'.[28]

The accounts in the name of members of the clergy can be considered a special case. Most of the credit the clergy owed to the Olivieri company derived from payments carried out on their mandate. In other words, the bankers opened a special line of credit, believing that in this way they could curry favour with the higher echelons of the papal hierarchy, and be remembered when, for example, it was decided to whom contracts would be awarded. In the case of Giovanni Poggio, nuncio to Spain, whose account registers a balance of 6,245.38 ducats, it was necessary to resort to the mediation of the Strozzi company of Valladolid.[29] Cardinal Trivulzio is recorded as owing in excess of 6,300 ducats to the Olivieri company, while Cardinal Antonio Pucci owed less than 1,500 (still a substantial sum).[30] None of the other cardinals, bishops or abbots was overdrawn for more than 1,000 ducats.[31] The sums that instead are found in the debit side refer to entries 'made good' to the Olivieri company by other banks: it was the latter, in other words, who had loaned money to the ecclesiastics, in the hope of enjoying the favours mentioned above. Among the prelates Giovanni Poggio, in the double role of nuncio to Spain and of general treasurer, stands out again, with a sum of 5,074.94 ducats.[32] The balances of the others were instead of a decidedly lesser amount, with two Florentine cardinals, Antonio Pucci and Giovanni Salviati, in the lead.[33]

Moving on to the other accounts, the first which should be mentioned are those in the name of the partners: the current account of the *maggiore* (senior partner) Benvenuto Olivieri, for example, shows that the company owed him the substantial amount of 6,922.45 ducats:[34] Benvenuto, in other words, had made an investment '*fuori dal corpo*' (above and beyond his share in the social capital).[35] Benedetto Busini, another partner in the company, had decidedly less in his current account: 394.27 ducats.[36]

Among the personal accounts of other individuals, one that stands out in particular is that of Neri Capponi of Venice, containing 24,421.36 ducats. This enormous sum was the result of a large number of movements of money, among which should be noted, on the dates 16 December 1542 and 20 January 1543, two entries of

28 ASF, Galli Tassi 2278, fol. 75; cf also Chapter 7, p. 149.

29 ASF, Galli Tassi 2278, fol. 277.

30 ASF, Galli Tassi 2278, fols 89, 192, 204, 205. For more information on this prelate, who was of some importance for Benvenuto Olivieri and his family, see Chapter 2, note 92.

31 Girolamo Capodiferro Recanati, apostolic nuncio to France was among them: the Bini company of Lyons acted as intermediary (ASF, Galli Tassi 2278, fol. 281).

32 ASF, Galli Tassi 2278, fol. 182.

33 ASF, Galli Tassi 2278, fols 132, 140, 281.

34 ASF, Galli Tassi 2278, fol. 257.

35 Among the sums listed here two in particular should be noted, of 5,000 ducats each, paid by Benedetto Busini on 16 December 1542 and 20 January 1543, on behalf of the account *a parte R.B.*: or, in other words, on behalf of Roberto Strozzi, who acted hidden behind the name of Benvenuto (ASF, Galli Tassi 2278, fol. 257). For the '*sopraccorpo*', and more precisely for the investments '*fuori dal corpo*', see De Roover, *The Rise and Decline*, pp. 100-101.

36 ASF, Galli Tassi 2278, fol. 212.

20,000 ducats each 'made good' to Benedetto Busini's *conto a parte R.B.*[37] This last account, as has been mentioned, was in reality the property of Roberto Strozzi, who had made a large contribution to the social capital of the company but preferred to remain hidden. The relationship between Neri Capponi and Filippo Strozzi (and, after the latter's death, his heirs) is well documented: the two were partners in the Strozzi company of Lyons, and Neri, together with Benvenuto Olivieri, was among the executors of Filippo's will.[38] The hypothesis can therefore be made with a fair degree of certainty, that these extremely substantial deposits constituted investments '*fuori dal corpo*' made anonymously by the Strozzi family in the Olivieri company (which was the successor, in Rome, of those belonging to Filippo and later Giulio and Lorenzo).

As well as the above accounts, there are various others in the name of single individuals, amongst which will be mentioned here only those containing amounts exceeding 1,000 ducats. On the credit side, it should be noted that the 5,855.91 ducats in the account of Raffaello Gherardini of Milan all came from a single bill of exchange delivered for him to the Bini company of Lyons at the 1542 Fair of All Saints.[39] Signorino Signorini held an account for bills of exchange paid by him in partnership with Rinaldo and Giovan Battista Strozzi & Partners of Valladolid, which on 13 February 1543 showed a balance of 2,731.19 ducats;[40] the 1,727.40 ducats of the heirs of Girolamo and Fabio Venturi were also the result of exchange operations.[41] Among the others, it is worth mentioning the accounts of Lorenzo di Piero Ridolfi, brother of the cardinal (1,227.12 ducats), of the above-mentioned heir of Filippo Strozzi (1,169.04), of Antonio di Leonardo from Bergamo (1,150.38) and of Jacopo Zambeccari (1,055.61).[42]

On the debit side are the accounts of the following individuals: Luigi Gaddi (3,346.55 ducats), Francesco Bartoli, broker of the exchanges (3,235.63), Diego Fernandez Neto, Portuguese (2,759.59), Ciriaco Mattei, Roman (2,350.35) and again Lorenzo Ridolfi, for a *conto nostro a parte* belonging to Paolo Riccardi (1,311.71).[43]

Among the companies with headquarters in Rome there were naturally a large number of Florentine partnerships and a somewhat smaller number of Genoese. As to assets, the total balance comes to 34,593.72 ducats, of which only 5,664.82 (16.38%) come from the Genoese, more precisely from Luca Giustiniani & Partners. As to liabilities (debts owed by the Olivieri company), the sum comes instead to 71,532.16, of which 24,385.91 (34.09%) in accounts of Genoese companies: 12,195.13 of Luca

37 ASF, Galli Tassi 2278, fol. 234. Again, on 4 April (for which reason it is not included in the balance sheet), it would seem that a further 20,000 ducats must have been transferred: half to the heir of Filippo Strozzi, the other again to Benedetto Busini '*a parte R.B.*'.

38 See Chapter 2, note 62.

39 ASF, Galli Tassi 2278, fol. 255.

40 ASF, Galli Tassi 2278, fol. 177.

41 ASF, Galli Tassi 2278, fol. 124.

42 ASF, Galli Tassi 2278, fols 40, 85, 93, 107.

43 ASF, Galli Tassi 2278, fols 48, 84, 102, 237, 299. The account of Ciriaco Mattei had been opened for the tax-farm of the customs (Chapter 5, p. 120); Paolo Riccardi had purchased instead a share of an office of secretary.

Giustiniani and Cristoforo Sauli, 8,827.53 again of Luca Giustiniani, 3,363.25 of Girolamo Grimaldi. The value of the sums registered to Florentines, therefore, on the credit side reaches 83.62% of the total of the money relative to firms active in Rome; on the debit side this percentage drops to 65.91%. This underlines yet again the privileged relationships that existed with other individuals and companies from within one's own nation, for which reason the *mercatores* preferred whenever possible to collaborate with their own co-nationals. It also shows, however, that there was a need too of the additional help of others, in particular the influential Genoese bankers. Moreover, the fact that the total on the debit side was greater than that on the credit side clearly indicates that Benvenuto Olivieri & Partners were in debt to the Genoese bankers, rather than the contrary.

Among the Genoese, Olivieri would seem to have had a special relationship with Luca Giustiniani, while among the Florentine companies his closest relationship was without a doubt with Antonio Covoni & Partners. As mentioned (Chapter 2, p. 59), Benvenuto Olivieri & Partners were a shareholder in their company. In fact, virtually the entire amount of the positive balance of the Covoni company's account (8,292.70 ducats) corresponds to the 8,500 *scudi d'oro in oro* the Olivieri partnership had contributed to the social capital of the former; 3,784.90 ducats instead belong to a *conto nostro de' tempi*, with many cross-entries in the current account, in a 'game' of giros, rather than real transactions.[44] On the other side, there is a very substantial balance in 'our current account for money drawn and delivered', equal to 14,306.65 ducats: a notable overdraft made by the Olivieri company, which evidently, thanks to its share in Antonio Covoni & Partners, had access to large amounts of credit which it could use for its own exchange transactions.[45] Again on the debit side should be noted the 4,878.05 ducats of the *conto loro de' tempi*, relative to operations with the Apostolic Chamber such as the *imposizioni dei mezzi frutti* and *delle galere*, and the 4,084.67 of the current account referred to above.[46]

Another of the associated companies that should be mentioned is that of Girolamo Ubaldini (cf. Chapter 2, p. 57). With reference to this company there is a positive balance of 2,926.82 ducats in the *conto nostro de' tempi*, a result of various operations with the Apostolic Chamber: the *imposizione delle galere*, the income from communes and the tithes of Patrimonio.[47] There were however much greater sums on the debit side, further proof that the Olivieri company was usually first contract-holder and then conveyor of shares of the contracts stipulated with the Chamber: 5,853.67 ducats in the *conto loro de' tempi* and 4,148.82 ducats in the *conto loro corrente*.[48]

---

44 ASF, Galli Tassi 2278, fol. 199.

45 ASF, Galli Tassi 2278, fol. 269.

46 ASF, Galli Tassi 2278, fols 196, 274.

47 ASF, Galli Tassi 2278, fol. 200.

48 ASF, Galli Tassi 2278, fols 180, 198. With regard to the operations with the Apostolic Chamber, the apparent anomaly of the contemporaneous presence of two accounts, one with credit balance, the other debit, can be explained in the following way: Benvenuto Olivieri & Partners were the contract-holders, they then conveyed a share to Girolamo Ubaldini & Partners and later came into possession of a half of the same. In fact the first figure, corresponding to 3,000 *scudi d'oro*, is half of the second, in other words the 6,000 *scudi* that

Another special case is that of Filippo Carducci & Partners. As has been mentioned (Chapter 2, pp. 60-61), Benedetto Busini was a partner in this company as a representative of Benvenuto Olivieri & Partners. In the balance sheet of February 1543 there is a *conto loro corrente* with a deficit balance equal to 552.41 ducats.[49] In the same document Filippo Carducci & Partners also appear as depositaries of the *gabella dello Studio* (see Chapter 7, p. 156). Clearly, in this case the balance is in credit for the Olivieri company, which had taken a share under the name of the Carducci company, signatory of the contract with the Apostolic Chamber.[50]

Among the other Florentines, the company with which the Olivieri company had the closest ties was that of Tommaso Cavalcanti and Giovanni Giraldi. There are three relevant credit items in the balance sheet: a *conto loro corrente* (2,391.59 ducats); a *conto nostro de' tempi* regarding operations relative to the Treasury of the Romagna and to the Mint (784.36 ducats); a current account held by the Cavalcanti and Giraldi company in their role as *zecchieri* of the Mint of Rome (249 ducats).[51] Much greater are the two sums on the debit side, resulting from contracts with the Apostolic Chamber of which the Olivieri company was the main signatory: these sums are recorded in two *conti loro de' tempi*, one relative to the customs of Rome (6,431.47 ducats) and the other to the increase of the salt tax of the Romagna (1,858.53 ducats).[52]

Another family with which the Olivieri company had frequent business dealings was the Montauto family, as has been seen in preceding chapters: the 1543 balance sheet shows a *conto nostro de' tempi* regarding operations on the salt tax of Rome and the Romagna, in the name of Salvestro da Montauto & Partners, in credit for 1,951.17 ducats.[53] Another important Florentine company was that of the heirs of Pandolfo Della Casa: on the credit side they had a balance of 2,374.74 ducats in an account regarding the customs of Rome, while on the debit side, in a *conto de' tempi*, they had 1,951.23 ducats, deriving from operations linked to the increase of the salt tax of the Romagna.[54]

The recently begun contract to administer the customs saw the involvement of the company of Alessandro and Giovan Battista Del Bene. At the beginning of the contract this company (under the name of the Benvenuto Olivieri & Partners) owned a share of 7.5%, which gradually diminished in time: the balance on 13 February 1543 was among the liabilities, for an amount of 3,170.75 ducats.[55]

Among the accounts of other Florentine companies, all with a positive balance for Benvenuto Olivieri & Partners, besides that with 1,739.95 ducats of Vanni and Girolamo Signorini & Partners, should perhaps be mentioned only the *conto a parte de' tempi* of Lorenzo Pintelli & Partners, a firm created for the administration of the

---

the Olivieri company had initially conveyed to the Ubaldini company. For the business deal concerned, part of a larger transaction of 55,000 *scudi*, see Chapter 3, p. 87.

49 ASF, Galli Tassi 2278, fol. 103.

50 ASF, Galli Tassi 2278, fol. 35: the figure in the balance sheet is 2,317.51 ducats.

51 ASF, Galli Tassi 2278, fols 94, 152, 250.

52 ASF, Galli Tassi 2278, fols 98, 102.

53 ASF, Galli Tassi 2278, fol. 99.

54 ASF, Galli Tassi 2278, fols 98, 278.

55 ASF, Galli Tassi 2278, fol. 103.

contract of the Mint, in which the Olivieri company held a 25% share (see Chapter 8, pp. 180-181).[56]

Of the Genoese, Olivieri and his partners preferred – as mentioned – to work with Luca Giustiniani. With the company that he had created in Rome together with Cristoforo Sauli, Giustiniani found himself, on 13 February 1543, in the position of creditor for 12,195.13 ducats, following operations relative to the *imposizione delle galere*, to the income from communes and to the tithes.[57] There was also the considerable number of nine accounts still open on that date in the name of Luca Giustiniani & Partners, some with a positive balance, others with a negative balance. This is not surprising given that, as shown in preceding chapters, their company is often named when Benvenuto Olivieri was involved in large operations with the Apostolic Chamber. Among the accounts listed on the credit side of the balance sheet, the largest is the *conto de' tempi* for Giustiniani's share of the alum of Provence, which has a balance of 4,527.17 ducats; besides this was a *conto a parte*, again opened for operations relative to the alum, with a balance of 897.58 ducats.[58] Of lesser importance, but nevertheless worth noting, are the *conto loro corrente* and the *conto a parte* for the *imposizione delle galere* and the tithes of the Romagna.[59]

Turning to the accounts listed on the debit side of the balance sheet, the first to be noted is a *conto loro de' tempi* of Luca Giustiniani & Partners, containing registrations of sums relative to the customs and to the *vigesima* of the Jews, for a total of 2,601.64 ducats.[60] There are also another three accounts, all with figures close to 2,000 ducats, that include transactions regarding the commerce of alum, or more precisely: a *conto loro de' tempi a parte* for the alum of Provence, a generic account 'for alum' and a *conto a parte* belonging to the heirs of Girolamo and Fabio Venturi.[61] The last (in terms of size) is another *conto a parte*, containing operations linked to the income from communes of the Romagna, the balance of which amounts to 414.63 ducats.[62]

Returning briefly to the alum, 3,363.35 ducats were also recorded among the liabilities in an account belonging to Girolamo Grimaldi & Partners, heirs of the company that for more than ten years held the contract of the Tolfa alum mines.[63]

Without a doubt Olivieri also maintained relations with other merchant-banking firms scattered throughout the peninsula, although these played a more marginal role.

---

56 ASF, Galli Tassi 2278, fols 59, 251. The balance of Pintelli's account amounted to 248.60 ducats.

57 ASF, Galli Tassi 2278, fol. 198. This figure was equivalent to the 12,500 *scudi d'oro* with which the Genoese company entered into the above-mentioned deal of 55,000 *scudi* (Chapter 3, p. 87).

58 ASF, Galli Tassi 2278, fols 76, 135. These operations are discussed in depth in Chapter 8, pp. 173-174.

59 ASF, Galli Tassi 2278, fols 149, 238: the first amounted to 411.37 ducats, the second to 98.70.

60 ASF, Galli Tassi 2278, fol. 102.

61 The sums are respectively: 2,022.35 ducats (ASF, Galli Tassi 2278, fol. 208), 1,926.51 ducats (fol. 73) and 1,862.40 ducats (fol. 238).

62 ASF, Galli Tassi 2278, fol. 238.

63 ASF, Galli Tassi 2278, fol. 132.

As has been seen, in their business dealings with the Apostolic Chamber linked to the territories of the Papal State, Bologna and the Romagna were of primary importance for the interests of Benvenuto's company. Their main point of reference, *in situ*, were the heirs of Carlo Cattani & Partners, who were holders of a number of accounts. At least four of their accounts showed a positive balance: a *conto loro corrente* (for the sum of 1,940.55 ducats) and three *conti nostri a parte* – one relative to the tithes (724.62 ducats), one regarding the *imposizione delle galere* (197.40 ducats) and the last concerning the increase of the salt tax of the Romagna (197.40 ducats).[64] It can be seen in these three last cases that the Olivieri company found it more useful to keep completely separate accounts with the Cattani company in Bologna, each one referring to a single operation regarding tax-farming at the local level.

The case of the Cattani company's largest account with a negative balance is quite different: 4,292.66 ducats mostly resulting from the participation of 5,000 *scudi d'oro* (=4,878 ducats) that the Cattani company had taken under the name of Benvenuto Olivieri & Partners, who had underwritten a loan of 20,000 *scudi* with the Apostolic Chamber.[65] The last account is the *nostro corrente* that the Olivieri company had opened with the Cattani company in order to cover the advance loans necessary to deal with expenses it had to meet in the Bologna-Romagna area.[66]

Only a small number of other business deals have left a trace. One, for example, was a *conto loro* in the name of the Florentine company of Jacopantonio Busini (father of Benedetto, loyal partner of Benvenuto Olivieri), with a positive balance for the Olivieri company equal to 1,345.13 ducats.[67] There was also a *conto nostro de' tempi* of Damiano Pallavicini & Partners of Genoa, for operations linked to the import of grain from Sicily. Although the credit for the Olivieri company, on 13 February 1543, stood at only 591.50 ducats, this was the remainder of a much larger operation.[68] Lorenzo and Alessandro Strozzi & Partners of Venice must also be remembered, even though no large sums are connected with their name; but the fact that they are mentioned was nevertheless one of the many signs of how important this family was for Olivieri.[69] Given that Neri Capponi (also based in Venice) transferred large sums to the Roman company of the Olivieri family, it is probably not a coincidence that Olivieri was in debt for the sum of 3,062.42 ducats to a Florentine firm of the Capponi family (Piero and Luigi Capponi & Partners) in the *conto nostro corrente*[70] and that there was also a *conto loro corrente* belonging

64 ASF, Galli Tassi 2278, fols 213, 244, 262.

65 ASF, Galli Tassi 2278, fol. 200; see also Chapter 3, p. 86.

66 ASF, Galli Tassi 2278, fol. 246: the balance of the account is 2,515.27 ducats.

67 ASF, Galli Tassi 2278, fol. 50.

68 ASF, Galli Tassi 2278, fol. 94. Of smaller importance were on the other hand the operations with Lorenzo Guicciardini & Partners of Ferrara, the heir of Baldassarre Machiavelli & Partners again of Ferrara, Jacopo Giacomini & Partners of Ancona (fols. 34, 60, 194).

69 See ASF, Galli Tassi 2278, fols 240, 253 for the two accounts *nostri* with a credit balance, and fols 13, 284 for the accounts *loro corrente* and *nostro* with a debit balance. The relations with other Strozzi, those of Valladolid, will be discussed shortly.

70 ASF, Galli Tassi 2278, fol. 268. At fols 32, 263 the accounts *nostro corrente* and *loro corrente* with a very small credit balance.

to Giuliano and Piero Capponi & Partners of Pisa with a negative balance of 641.31 ducats.[71]

Separate mention must be made of the relations with the other companies of the Olivieri family to which the Roman company was in debt on 13 February 1543 to the tune of 3,058.05 ducats. In particular, Benvenuto had frequent business dealings with Michele and Alessandro Olivieri & Partners of Naples and with Michele and Giovanni Olivieri & Partners of Florence.[72] With the first company in particular the business transactions were extremely frequent and the accounts open on this date relatively numerous. Besides a *conto nostro corrente* (with a negative balance of 1,173.40 ducats) and two *conti loro correnti* (negative, respectively, for 390.89 and 56.92 ducats),[73] there are also two *conti a parte*, for operations that clients of the Olivieri company of Rome intended to undertake in the Naples area: one, the *conto a parte O*, can be traced to Ottavio Farnese; for the other, the *conto a parte D.F.*, it has not been possible to trace the real account-holder.[74] With regard to the balance of the first, which comes to only 247.75 ducats, it should be underlined that this comes from an exchange operation of 25,000 *scudi d'oro in oro* paid in Naples on the mandate of the pope, with Michele and Alessandro Olivieri acting on behalf of Benvenuto, 'for the purchase of the Principality of Altamura, in favour of Ottavio Farnese and of his consort, Margherita d'Austria'.[75]

Also as far as the Florentine company is concerned, both the *conto nostro corrente* and the *conto loro corrente* have a debit balance. The sum of the former is much greater (1,103.94 ducats) – a further indication that Benvenuto Olivieri continued to maintain relations with Florence from his headquarters in Rome and that he made use of his relatives' company to carry out payments in that city.[76]

Of the *mercatores* working in foreign cities, those with the closest and most constant ties with the Olivieri company of Rome were Giovan Francesco Bini & Partners of Lyons. Besides being agents for exchange transactions in the most important financial market of Europe, they were also partners of the Olivieri company in the distribution of the alum on French soil (see Chapter 8, pp. 172-175). In 1542-43 this operation was at its peak and the balance sheet shows various accounts concerning it. In particular, there are among the assets: the *conto nostro de' tempi a parte L* for alum of Provence belonging to Luca Giustiniani, the Genoese who had entered into the business deal purchasing a quota under the name of Olivieri (balance of the account: 2,022.35 ducats); the *conto loro de' tempi* for alum (879.95 ducats); the *conto nostro a parte* for the alum of Rouen, Dieppe and La Rochelle (505.85 ducats).[77] Among the debts is the *conto loro de' tempi* for the sale of the

71 ASF, Galli Tassi 2278, fol. 21.

72 A very small debt was owed to Paolo Olivieri and Giandonato Barbadori & Partners of L'Aquila, who were in credit, in the '*conto loro corrente*', for only 6.33 ducats (ASF, Galli Tassi 2278, fol. 28). For information regarding the Olivieri companies in Italy, see Chapter 2, pp. 30-34.

73 ASF, Galli Tassi 2278, fols 256, 270, 285.

74 ASF, Galli Tassi 2278, fols 150, 174.

75 ASF, Galli Tassi 2278, fol. 150.

76 ASF, Galli Tassi 2278, fols 217, 272.

77 ASF, Galli Tassi 2278, fols 77, 153, 207.

alum to Rouen, Brittany and La Rochelle (3,922.65 ducats); and the *conto nostro de' tempi* for the sale of the alum to Provence (385.42 ducats).[78] Further proof of the exceptionally close relationship between the two companies is the existence of a *conto loro corrente nuovo*, in which sums were registered regularly, independently of the exchange transactions carried out at the fairs.[79] Also related to the commerce of alum are the two accounts belonging to Castro and Malvenda of Burgos, partners of the Olivieri company for the distribution of alum both in Atlantic France and, to a lesser extent, in Spain: the *conto nostro a parte de' tempi* has a positive balance of 1,024.42 ducats; the *nostro de' tempi*, on the other hand, has a negative balance of 5,689.49.[80] Another *conto nostro de' tempi*, with a large positive balance (4,450.13 ducats), is in the name of Andrea Malvenda of Rouen alone; this account records sums of money 'they owe us when they will receive it'.[81]

The other transactions carried out with foreign companies tended more often to have a negative balance. The balance sheet of 13 February 1543 shows the situation of the accounts with the Tuscan companies which Benvenuto Olivieri & Partners dealt with in France. For the sake of clarity the accounts will be examined fair by fair. First, there was the above-mentioned loss of 4,020.87 ducats for the Fair of All Saints 1541. From the Epiphany Fair of 1542 there remained a negative balance of 1,593.75 ducats in a *conto nostro* of Giovan Battista and Vincenzo Pinelli Adorni and Francesco de' Franchi & Partners of Besançon.[82] For the following Easter Fair the only significant sum still to be settled was that of 1,729 ducats, listed among the assets in a *conto nostro* of Antonio and Ludovico Buonvisi & Partners of Lyons.[83] With regard to the August Fair of 1542, on the credit side there are four *conti a parte D* (unfortunately belonging to an unknown individual), respectively in the name of the Sertini company, Bartolomeo Panciatichi, Simone Panciatichi and the Buonvisi company (for a total of 1,589.52 ducats);[84] and on the debit side two, respectively a current account of Simone Panciatichi & Partners and a *conto a parte R.B.* (Roberto Strozzi) of the Sertini company.[85] For the Fair of All Saints 1542 there are two *conti nostri correnti*: one belonging to the Bini company, with a positive balance of 3,300 ducats, and one to Damiano Pallavicini and Paolo Doria & Partners of Besançon, with a negative balance of 3,410.81 ducats.[86] The 1543 Epiphany Fair (the last fair before the balance sheet of 13 February) left a negative balance of 6,489.31 ducats in the *conto nostro* of Giovan Francesco Bini & Partners, one of 1,134 in the *conto*

78 ASF, Galli Tassi 2278, fols 206, 207.

79 ASF, Galli Tassi 2278, fol. 255: the account has a debit balance of 1,176.76 ducats.

80 ASF, Galli Tassi 2278, fols 134, 177.

81 ASF, Galli Tassi 2278, fol. 205. On the debit side various items are 'made good' by the Bini company to the Olivieri company 'for their half'.

82 ASF, Galli Tassi 2278, fol. 23.

83 ASF, Galli Tassi 2278, fol. 91.

84 ASF, Galli Tassi 2278, fols 155, 184.

85 ASF, Galli Tassi 2278, fols 155, 192: the balances come to 120.24 and 481.25 ducats respectively.

86 ASF, Galli Tassi 2278, fols 228, 278. There are also accounts of the Sertini, Panciatichi and Rinieri companies of Lyons with very small balances (fols 228, 231, 232).

nostro of Andrea Rinieri & Partners and one of 1,087 in the *conto nostro corrente* of Bartolomeo Panciatichi & Partners.[87]

Foreign, however, did not mean only Lyons, Besançon or operations connected to the commerce of alum. The company of Giovan Carlo Affaitati of Cremona, for example, had its headquarters in Antwerp; a *conto nostro corrente* of this company can be found on the debit side of the balance sheet for the large sum of 6,219.37 ducats.[88] Rinaldo and Giovan Battista Strozzi & Partners of Valladolid were of considerable importance to the Olivieri company, as they were the latter's correspondents in Spain for operations in the main fairs in that area. Against the 400 ducats listed on the credit side for a *conto nostro a parte G*, we find on the debit side the following extremely substantial entries: 5,378.47 ducats in the *conto nostro* for the Fair of October 1542; 5,123.07 ducats in the *nostro corrente* for the Fair of Villalòn; 3,621.29 ducats in a *conto loro corrente nuovo*.[89]

It is not clear if the operations made with foreign companies consisted in speculations on the exchange rates (on their own behalf and on behalf of third parties) or in money loaned or borrowed: probably both things were true, but the brevity of the records does not allow us to establish to what degree. Certainly we know that at least a part of the money that passed through Lyons came from Rome and to Rome was destined to return, to be included in the enormous business turnover of the papal contracts.

A separate section has been created for 'Interest, premiums and advances on accounts of third parties'. The item which stands out here is that of the 'premiums on coins and gold', which came to 4,239.74 ducats. This account obviously has entries on both the *Dare* and the *Avere* sides, but the balance profited greatly from the 4,432.36 ducats 'made good' to the depositary general. On 17 March (the final date of the contract of the Depositary, see Chapter 3, p. 76) 10,385.49 ducats would be credited to the same account.[90] This account served the bankers to credit and debit the differences deriving from the exchange rate between gold coins and silver coins. Since silver devalued continuously compared to gold, it was necessary, when loan operations involving silver coins were carried out over a long period of time, to calculate the fluctuating difference in value between the two metals during this time.[91] The existence of entries such as this is not at all surprising, given that, as has been seen, the operations with the Apostolic Chamber included large advances on the part of the *mercatores*. What is however curious is the simultaneous presence among the assets of both the commissions and the expenses related to the collection of the increase of the salt tax of the Romagna. Naturally the first account is positive (balance: 2,048.86 ducats): on the *Avere* side can be found the tax-collection money owed to the company, from which were then subtracted, on the *Dare* side, the

87 ASF, Galli Tassi 2278, fols 245, 253, 278.

88 ASF, Galli Tassi 2278, fol. 224; Giovan Battista and Lorenzo Guicciardini & Partners were also to be found in the same city (fols 22, 25).

89 ASF, Galli Tassi 2278, fols 177, 209, 249, 258. There is, again on the debit side, also a *conto nostro* relative to another important Castillian fair: that of Rioseco (fol. 136).

90 ASF, Galli Tassi 2278, fol. 86.

91 For more details on money issues, see the Note on Moneys, p. xiii.

amounts owed to the other bankers who participated in the contract under the name of Olivieri. The presence of the expenses can instead be explained by the fact that these had in reality been sustained on behalf of third parties (for example, Bernardo Machiavelli) and appeared therefore as a credit for the Olivieri company.

The last two accounts that should be mentioned among the assets are registered as, first, 'household expenses' and, second, 'household furnishings (*masserizie*)', with respective balances of 2,162.65 and 1,058.61 ducats.[92] These were sums owed to the Olivieri company by the family of Benvenuto for having sustained, on behalf of the latter, substantial costs.

This detailed analysis of the balance sheet confirms what has already been shown by the previous chapters: Benvenuto Olivieri & Partners dealt mainly with the Apostolic Chamber, and all the other business operations were instrumental for these dealings. The company directed its largest investments towards the papal finances, juggling a great variety of business deals in order to do so, and, thanks to the collaboration of other bankers, were able to concede very substantial loans and advances to the Chamber. The reason for this was, of course, that of all his business ventures, Benvenuto's greatest profits came from his dealings with the Chamber.

There are very few studies of Florentine banking companies between the fifteenth and sixteenth centuries, and the Olivieri documents are a unique source for information about bankers and the papacy in the Rome of these years.[93] In a recent article, Richard A. Goldthwaite compared the 1582 balance sheet of Simone and the heir of Giovanni Corsi & Partners of Florence with those of some fifteenth-century companies, thus demonstrating that the total value of the 'assets under management' (that is the sum of the balances of the accounts open at the moment of the balance sheet) of the former was much greater compared to those of the others.[94] If we compare the 178,374 *scudi d'oro* of the Corsi company with the more than 300,000 of the Olivieri company, we can see how the latter had a notably superior volume of business transactions; and if the inflation of 40 years were taken into consideration, the difference would be even greater.

Business dealings with the papal court had always offered notable opportunities for investment, as can be seen also from the fact that in one single year, 1427, the balance sheet of the Roman company of Giovanni di Bicci de' Medici had a turnover of 25% greater than that of his Florentine company.[95] It is necessary, however, to be extremely cautious when evaluating these figures. As has been seen in the course of this research, the Olivieri company managed an enormous number of investments,

---

92 ASF, Galli Tassi 2278, fols 7, 180. The household expenses were all paid in cash, as is demonstrated by the fact that the cross-entry was always in the cash account. The household furnishings were included on the credit side, their value based initially on the price of purchase; their value gradually depreciated and accordingly appropriate sums were inserted on the debit side.

93 See also in this regard, Goldthwaite, 'Banking in Florence': 472-473.

94 Goldthwaite, 'Banking in Florence': 492 (tab. 5). The author points out that in the 1580s the Corsi company 'was large but presumably not among the largest' (475).

95 See again Goldthwaite, 'Banking in Florence': 492 (tab. 5) for a comparison in a single monetary unit; and De Roover, *The Rise and Decline*, pp. 206-207, 226-227 for the complete balance sheets.

but also conveyed substantial shares to other companies. Consequently, only a relatively small part of the large sum recorded in the balance sheet came directly from the coffers of Benvenuto Olivieri & Partners.

Conclusion

This book centres around the life and work of Benvenuto Olivieri, an influential Florentine merchant-banker in Rome in the first half of the sixteenth century. Olivieri moved to the Eternal City during what might be referred to as 'boom years' for the Florentines in Rome, that is during the 20-year reign of the Medici popes. Interestingly, however, he actually reached the peak of his success during the papacy of Paul III Farnese (1534-49), by which time the Florentines, although still holding important posts, were no longer in the position of absolute dominion that they had had in the preceding years.

Olivieri spent virtually all of his professional life in the service of the Apostolic Chamber, the body that managed the pontifical finances. The discovery of a substantial collection of *filze* and volumes held in the Archivio di Stato of Florence – the Fondo Galli Tassi – has made it possible to study in some depth the various facets that characterized the financial aspects of the relations between the Chamber and the papal bankers in the sixteenth century. This documentation, in fact, mostly consists of accounts of Benvenuto Olivieri's company relative to business operations connected to the papal finances. The discovery of these documents can be considered extremely fortunate, particularly as no other analogous examples of collections of private manuscripts have come to light. It is for this reason that the studies carried out to date have all been based essentially on Chamber documents and thus necessarily biased towards the point of view of the Apostolic Chamber.

On one hand, the lack of specific works dedicated to the subject might be seen as a disadvantage; on the other, however, it might also be seen as an advantage in that it makes this research even more interesting, as it is the first to look at the medieval papal finances from the point of view of the private banker. Until today, for example, we only had a very vague idea of exactly how the *mercatores* administered the contracts farmed out to them by the Chamber. What has been made very clear by the documents in the Fondo Galli Tassi is that there was a complex network of shareholders involved in every contract: while only two or three merchant-bankers were the actual signatories of the contract, many more (in some cases even a dozen) either already owned or acquired shares during the period of its validity. There was, in other words, a dense network of relations linking the bankers with each other and to the various sources of income of the papacy; a dense network which – it should be underlined – was not static but in continual movement. It has also become clear that the bankers' link with the Chamber was at this time indissoluble, as the latter, with its constant need for ever more money, never found itself in the position of being able to extinguish its debts. All it was able to do was convey the rights to collect on future revenue.

When Benvenuto Olivieri began his career as a banker he appears to have been a man of modest means. There was no strong tradition of banking in his family, even though other Olivieri of his generation (brothers or cousins) also became involved in merchant-banking, participating in companies active on the various Italian and foreign marketplaces. The young Benvenuto moved to Rome from Florence, where he attached himself to one of the most powerful *mercatores* of the period, Bindo Altoviti. He worked with Altoviti for a long time – 15 years – first as an employee and then as a junior partner. Olivieri must have made the most of this experience, ready to soak up all the advice that was offered to him, as by the beginning of the 1530s he was held in such high esteem that he found himself being fought over by the principal Florentine banking houses operating in Rome. On one hand, there was Altoviti, who had no wish to lose his protégé; on the other, Filippo Strozzi who, at the time was very closely connected to Pope Clement VII, did all in his power to attract the young banker to work with him. Benvenuto chose Strozzi, who set up a new company in Rome, the administration of which was entrusted to Olivieri, together with Francesco Del Nero. To have taken such a step, Filippo Strozzi clearly must have had enormous faith in Benvenuto Olivieri's capacities, proof of the high esteem in which he was held, esteem that must have been the result of the work he had done in the course of the years passed in the company of the Florentine merchant-bankers linked to the Curia. Moreover, when, after the death of Clement VII, Filippo, increasingly caught up in political activity, found himself in great difficulty, he handed over the administration of his Roman companies to Olivieri. There are a number of clear indications that the relationship between Benvenuto and Filippo must have gone beyond the realms of a simple working one: between the two a sincere friendship must have developed, which Strozzi did not omit to underline in his testament, in which he entrusted to Olivieri the guardianship of his children ('*non recusi pigliare in morte la persona del secondo padre*'). Even after the death of Filippo, Benvenuto continued to retain extremely close ties with his friend's family. In 1539, for example, Olivieri headed a company in which, well hidden behind his name, Roberto di Filippo Strozzi invested a substantial sum of money.

At least until the end of 1545 Roberto Strozzi was an important investor behind the name of Benvenuto. A careful study of the accounts in the ledger reveals that he contributed a number of very substantial sums, most of which were sent from Lyons, or from Venice, by Neri Capponi. That it was Capponi who transferred most of these large sums of money was no coincidence, as he had been a faithful companion to Filippo Strozzi in the firm of Lyons. This is an interesting point, since as well as Capponi others of those with whom Olivieri did business most frequently had previously been agents or associates of Strozzi. The Bini family, for example, had been partners of the Strozzi family in Lyons from the 1520s on, and in the 1540s were the primary contact of Benvenuto Olivieri & Partners in that city, where they were involved both in the distribution of alum in the territory of France, and in carrying out exchange operations at the fairs. Or the Covoni family: in 1530 Migliore was partner of Filippo in the firm of Rome; in the 1540s Antonio transferred shares of the company that carried his name to Benvenuto Olivieri and to his company.

To sum up, it is clear that being a satellite in Strozzi's orbit carried with it both advantages and disadvantages: while certain roads were facilitated, at the same time Benvenuto found himself having to move with great caution and ability to conquer positions that might, for political motives – Strozzi's opposition to the Medicean regime in Florence – have been barred to him. The marriage of Benvenuto Olivieri to Isabella Ridolfi can be seen as a seal of the relationship between the two men: the marriage deed sanctioning the union was stipulated by Maria di Filippo Strozzi, and the fact that she herself was married to a Ridolfi would seem to suggest that she had a direct interest in such a union between Benvenuto and a Ridolfi. However, it should be pointed out that, even though, as is probable, this was a matrimony entered into for reasons of family politics, Olivieri never failed to manifest sincere affection towards his young wife.

In general, therefore, it can be noted that the personal relationships that existed or developed among the various merchant-bankers were of great significance for their business relationships. These relationships could be of kinship: such is the case of Giovan Francesco Ridolfi, brother of Benvenuto's wife and his employee in the Roman companies; of Simone Guiducci, partner of Olivieri and husband of his niece; or of Girolamo Ubaldini, brother-in-law of Benvenuto (he too was married to one of the Ridolfi sisters), with whom he began working in 1542. Or the connections could be limited to the business context; however, in this case there always developed preferential relations. Remaining in the Roman context, one of Olivieri's favourite business partners was Antonio Covoni, who, as a member – as has just been mentioned – of a family with interests very closely linked to those of the Strozzi family, had then maintained the same sort of relationship with the Olivieri company.

By the 1540s, Benvenuto, thanks to both his personal and business capacities, had become the representative of the Strozzi family in Rome, keeping, however, a lower profile than that of Filippo and his heirs. With the passing of time he achieved fame and prestige in his own right, but it is unlikely that he ever freed himself completely from this tie. This doubtless gave him advantages, as has been seen, but also disadvantages: for example, it drew upon him the anger and the thirst for revenge of an individual such as Francesco Del Nero, who had been partner and friend of Strozzi long before Benvenuto came on the scene. Del Nero's anger, which had already manifested itself during Benvenuto's lifetime, reached its peak in the years following his death, when he persecuted Olivieri's heirs, even to the extent of taking it on himself to attack them over tax discrepancies between Benvenuto and the Chamber ('*in luogo del fisco a saldare i conti che Benvenuto haveon con la Camera*'). Del Nero's thirst for revenge is perhaps one of the main reasons none of Benvenuto's sons followed in their father's footsteps. Another reason was certainly the fact that Giulio, the eldest, had just turned seven when his father died and therefore too much time would have passed before he was capable of administering autonomously the business affairs that he had inherited. The documents, which refer to problems with Benvenuto's inheritance as late as the 1570s, do not however shed any light on the type of activity carried out by the sons of Benvenuto, who therefore would appear to be the only member of the family to have achieved a certain fame in Rome. Another contributing factor is probably that Benvenuto had enjoyed the last burst of glory of the Florentines at the papal court, whereas by the time his heirs came of age it was the Genoese who were flourishing in Rome.

Olivieri, moreover, did not even manage to place any of his relations in the higher echelons of the papal bureaucracy: probably the fact that he was the first in his family to work in Rome, and without personal financial means behind him, did not facilitate a task that in any case was certainly not an easy one. At the peak of his career Benvenuto only held several minor offices, which, moreover, appear to have been more a good speculative investment than a first step towards a career in the ecclesiastical hierarchy. Nevertheless, he (and, it must be added, the money that he was capable of furnishing, fundamental in such relationships) was held in high esteem by the upper echelons of the papal bureaucracy, as can be seen also by a letter in which the general treasurer urged the commissioner of Perugia to treat Olivcri with respect, because 'he is the depositary and servant of His Holiness, and treasurer, not simple administrator ... His Holiness does not wish those words to be used again against m. Benvenuto ... because this would upset His Holiness.'[1]

In order to succeed in penetrating the network of relations of the Apostolic Chamber two things were necessary: first, money, and, second, links with influential members of the Curia who acted as patrons to the bankers. Whoever did not have the fortune to possess a member of the family in the highest echelons of the ecclesiastic hierarchy usually relied as second best on his co-nationals. Benvenuto Olivieri, coming from a relatively modest family, had therefore to seek the patronage of Florentine prelates. (He did, as mentioned, have the support of the influential Strozzi family, but this – because of the political interests of the latter – was a two-edged sword.) He succeeded in finding a patron in Antonio Pucci, cardinal of the Santi Quattro Coronati, and then in his successor, Roberto Pucci. His relationship with Cardinal Antonio appears to have been an important one for Benvenuto, as is underlined by the fact that Antonio Pucci was named one of the godfathers of Giulio, firstborn son and chosen heir of Benvenuto.

The Florentines had an excellent comprehension of the intricacies of the papal finances, a comprehension developed in the course of the previous centuries, during which they had had absolute control of the administration of the numerous services required by the papacy. These services included the collection of Peter's pence, which came to Rome from all corners of Christianity thanks to the network of agents that only the large Florentine banking houses were capable of organizing; the commerce of luxury goods, imported in order to satisfy the demands of the pope, the cardinals and the members of their courts; and, closest in time to the years dealt with in this volume, the farming (*appalto*) of a large part of the tax collections that the Apostolic Chamber continued to impose in ever greater numbers. The definitive seal on the Florentines' power in this period was the 20 years of the Medici pontificates (1513-22, 1523-34): in these decades the Florentines wielded an influence that they would never again experience.

1 'M. Baccio [Ghini, commissioner of Perugia], M. Benvenuto [Olivieri] si è lamentato con il N.S. che subbito che sete arrivato in Perugia havete fatto pigliare tutti li libri e scritture della Thesoreria e levati li ministri nella salara e Thesoreria con usar parole molto impertinenti contra l'honore suo, senza considerare che lui è Depositario e servitore di Sua Santità e conduttore della Thesoreria e non amministratore. Et perché N.S. non vuole che s'usino simili termini contra esso m. Benvenuto e ci ha commesso, ve lo scriviamo caldamente: per questa vi diciamo che vi governiate di modo nelle vostre commissione che non venghino più simili querele, perché dispiacerebbe a Sua Santità. E state sano. Da Roma, addì v di decembre 1542. B. Helvinus Thesaurarius' (ASF, Galli Tassi 1847, fol. 8).

It has, however, emerged from the research into the following period – the pontificate of Paul III Farnese – that the weakening in the Florentines' authority and prestige was not immediately perceptible, despite the fierce Genoese competition. Even between the end of the 1530s and the 1540s, in fact, there was a solid presence of Florentine banks capable of administering papal financial affairs.

A very interesting aspect highlighted by this study is that of the considerable importance of networking. In every tax-farming operation or in every loan, the signatories (one, two or at the most three) stipulated private agreements with a smaller or greater number of other bankers, some of whom acquired quite considerable shares. It could, therefore, be said that there existed a parallel market thanks to which there was a reliable source ready to supply the enormous sums required by the papal coffers and that single banking houses could not, on their own, guarantee.

These agreements were independent of the contracts with the Apostolic Chamber, which dealt exclusively with the few signatories. It is precisely for this reason that the discovery of the Fondo Galli Tassi is of such importance, as it provides us with the point of view of an individual banker. Until now the papal documentation had been the principal, if not the only, source for the study of Chamber contracts in the first half of the sixteenth century. This has necessarily resulted in a partial understanding of these operations, since they made visible only the presence of a few contract-holders, ignoring the consortia of bankers involved behind the scenes. But, as has emerged in this volume, the official signatories did not necessarily maintain large shares in the contract they were responsible for. Private banking documents are the only source of information on this 'secondary market', thanks to which the most important business deals could be shared out amongst many merchant-bankers. The tardiness with which the Chamber repaid the money loaned placed the *mercatores* in a constant position of being creditors and therefore did not allow them the continuous investment of large sums. A further point that can be noted, and that until now had not emerged with such clarity, is the close collaboration that seems to have existed between the Florentines and the Genoese: almost every farm in this period included exponents of both the first and the second nation.

Personal relations are an important part of business networking. In the Fondo Galli Tassi the same names constantly recur over the years in conjunction with Benvenuto Olivieri. Among the Genoese he must have had a preferential relationship with the company of Luca Giustiniani, with or without the latter's partner, Tobia Pallavicini. Among the Florentines he obviously had more than one close relationship. In the Carducci, Covoni and Ubaldini companies, for example, Olivieri (alone or with his own company) was a shareholder. He also had important relationships with the two Montauto companies (that of Bastiano and that of Salvestro), as well as with Tommaso Cavalcanti and Giovanni Giraldi & Partners. Other Florentine names also recur frequently, a further demonstration that, although the colony no longer had individual companies of the ilk of Strozzi, it still possessed a strong contingent of enterprising firms. Surprisingly there seems to have been little contact with Bindo Altoviti & Partners, whose name only appears in the largest deals stipulated between consortia of bankers of various nations and the pontiff. There would seem to be two possible reasons for this. On one hand, one might suspect a 'cooling off' of the relations between Bindo and Benvenuto after the events of 1531, when, despite the opposition of the former, Olivieri detached himself from him to link himself up with the Strozzi company; on the other, in the 1540s Bindo Altoviti & Partners had virtual total financial control over the Marches, the richest province of the Papal State, and the company therefore probably concentrated most of its resources in this province, to administer the Treasury, the salt tax and its increase, the Triennial Subsidy and almost all the other taxes which were collected locally.

It is not easy to estimate how much Benvenuto Olivieri managed to earn in his 30 years in Rome. What is certain is that he arrived in the city of the popes with a fairly small amount of capital: there is no indication that the inheritance from his father Paolo was particularly substantial, and moreover it must have been shared among many brothers. However, even if money was initially scarce, he must have inherited from his family a certain mercantile-banking spirit, as he was not the only member to enter into business: several of his brothers and cousins worked in important Italian and foreign marketplaces. Benvenuto, therefore, arrived in Rome presumably with a small amount of money, but armed above all with goodwill. After his professional experience with Bindo Altoviti, certainly profitable and gratifying, by the beginning of the 1530s he had the means to invest 4,000 gold cameral ducats in the company of Filippo Strozzi. As soon as he began working for Strozzi, until the death of Clement VII (September 1534), Olivieri found himself involved in huge business deals, Strozzi being the favourite banker of the pope. In the five years that followed Benvenuto must have been a very able administrator and representative of the companies owned by Filippo first and by his sons afterwards. This was a very delicate moment, in which the opposition to the Strozzi family came both from Florence and from Rome; even if it should be pointed out that in the latter city it was the population that considered damaging the presence of this family, more than the Apostolic Chamber and the ecclesiastic hierarchy, which presumably were in no financial position to abruptly cut off all contact from such important bankers.

In the 1540s Benvenuto Olivieri was at the height of his powers, with many years of business experience behind him. His companies participated in most of the principal business deals with the Apostolic Chamber. Over a decade Benvenuto Olivieri & Partners administered various important entities, such as the Treasury of Umbria and Perugia and that of the Romagna, the customs and the *Salara* of Rome, the increase of the salt tax of Rome and the Romagna (see Table 13, pp. 164-165). His company also purchased shares in other farms, when the Apostolic Chamber needed loans of some substance. Finally, for a total of approximately five years (not consecutive) they administered the Depositary, the concession of which was certainly an acknowledgment of solidity and trustworthiness on the part of the higher echelons of the Chamber hierarchy. As well as in the area of papal finances, the Olivieri company also acted in sectors indirectly connected to the Apostolic Chamber, such as the commerce of the alum or of grain. All of this activity was embedded in a complicated network of relationships that, as has been seen, was subject to constant change and involved a large number of merchant-bankers in multiple simultaneous investments.

Benvenuto Olivieri & Partners of Rome, on the other hand, took little or no part in mercantile activity. Such activity was instead the province of Filippo Carducci, among whose partners we find the Olivieri company, but no relevant accounting books have survived the passage of time. The fact that Benvenuto's company focused exclusively on banking activities is not surprising, considering the amount of work being a *mercator* of the Curia generated.

As mentioned, it is not easy to estimate how much wealth was acquired by Olivieri in his years of activity in Rome: the document which seems to be the most reliable is a brief signed memorandum, dated 3 September 1545 (four years before his death). According to this in that moment the assets of Benvenuto came to approximately 40,000 *scudi d'oro*. His efforts thus must have left his heirs comfortably off, even if not particularly rich. This was, however, no small achievement, as he was a 'self-made man'. He could not rely on family wealth that would have allowed him to immediately begin his career near the top of the ladder. He had instead to begin at the bottom rung and slowly work his way up, increasing his wealth as he went. His business acumen allowed him to understand and penetrate the mechanisms governing the papal finances. Aided presumably also by the position of depositary that he covered for approximately five years, he was very quick to notice and take advantage of occasions for profit, and he created for himself a certain role as coordinator of farms for the Apostolic Chamber. Clearly, he was in no position to be able to enter into any of these transactions on his own, and, despite being in his name, they were in reality financed by consortia of Florentine and Genoese bankers.

The fact that he came from a modest background is another reason that Benvenuto Olivieri is a particularly interesting man to study. He was not one of those great bankers who have become part of history because their wealth allowed them to become major players, both economically and politically. He was instead a fairly ordinary Florentine who decided to try his luck in Rome and, thanks to his successful networking and collaboration with other businessmen, succeeded – despite the fact that he was working during the reign of Paul III Farnese, when the fortune of the Florentine nation of Rome was beginning its gradual decline – in achieving a more than respectable position. He was, in other words, one of many, and as such an exemplary case.

Appendix

Doc. 1: List of Florentine 'merchants', 1546

(ASF, Galli Tassi 1868, fasc. 1, fols 4r-5r)
List of merchants who participated in financing the church of S. Giovanni dei Fiorentini and their contributions (expressed in *scudi*).

[fol. 4r] yhs 1546 Nota di mercatanti potrebono contribuire alla spesa della fabrica di S. Jo. Baptista della nation fiorentina:

Mag^{co} m. Bindo Altoviti	300
Mag^{ci} rede di Pandolfo Della Casa e comp.	300
Mag^{ci} Strozzi	300
Mag^{ci} Cavalcanti et Giraldi e comp.	300
Mag^{ci} Bastiano da Montauto e comp.	300
Mag^{ci} rede di Alexandro Deti	300
Mag^{ci} Pier Antonio et Alamanno Bandini	200
Mag^{ci} Benvenuto Olivieri e comp.	200
Mag^{ci} Girolamo Ubaldini e comp.	200
Mag^{ci} Bernardo Acciaioli et Francesco Scarlatti e comp.	100
Mag^{ci} Alamanno Alamanni e comp.	100
Mag^{ci} Raphaello Griseldi e comp.	100
Mag^{ci} Agostino Del Nero e comp.	100
Mag^{ci} Pier Antonio Guasconi e comp.	100
Mag^{co} Donato Buonsignori e comp.	50
Mag^{co} Antonio Ubertini e comp.	50
Mag^{co} Zanobi Masini e comp.	50
Mag^{co} Bartolomeo Ruspoli e comp.	50
Mag^{co} Francesco Buonafé e comp.	50
Mag^{co} Girolamo da Ceuli	50
[fol. 4v] D. Alamanno et Vincenzo Romoli	50
D. Francesco Gu[cc]i	25
D. Alexandro Be[tti]ni	25
D. Alexandro Bartoli	25
D. Calvano Calvanesi	25
D. Raphael Benozzi	25
D. Vincenzo Luperelli	25
D. Antonio Pintassi e comp.	25
D. Simone da Firenzola	25
D. Bernardo Corbinelli	25
D. rede di Bartolomeo Angelini	25

D. Bernardo Alberighi	25
D. Signorino Signorini	25
D. rede di Francesco Della Fonte	25
D. Matheo da Cataniano	25
D. Giannotto Giannotti	25
D. L. delli Albizi zechieri e comp.	25
D. Phylippo Carducci	25
D. Manno dalla Mole	15
D. Octavian del Tignoso	15
D. Nicolò Campoli	15
D. Lotto Lotti	10
D. Antonio Fratini e comp.	10
D. F. Gucci banderaio	25
[fol. 5r] D. Simone Serragli	10
D. Nicolò Pancatichi	10
D. Piero Mannucci e comp.	10
D. Giramonte G.	10
D. Girolamo Fineschi	10
D. F. Gamberaia	10
D. [capitano] Clemente da Pisa	10
D. Jo. Ceperello [e Bart. suo fratello]	10
D. D. Girllandaio	10
D. Jo. Della Fonte	10
D. rede di Francesco d'Antonio Seragli	10
D. Francesco Bartholi	10
D. L. Boccacci	10
D. L. Del Caccia	10
D. L. Rondolini	10
D. Vectorio dalla Mole	10
D. P. de Corella	10
D. B. Scapella	10
TOTAL	3945

Doc. 2: Benvenuto Olivieri's will, 1544

(ASF, Galli Tassi 1810, ins. 2)
First draft of Benvenuto Olivieri's will, written five years prior to his death.

[fol. 1r] Perché delle cose di questo mondo nessuna è più certa che la morte, et venendo improvisa a chi ha mogle et figloli piccoli, non trovandosi memoria come si habia a procedere nelle cose loro, i figloli et le loro substantie restono qualche volta in potere et cura di chi non ha quello amore che haverebbono quelle persone a chi el più li lassassi, racomando come la experientia delle cose paxate ne admaestra. Et però, conoscendo Io Benvenuto di Paulo Ulivieri fiorentino, et per privilegio etiam ciptadino romano, quanti danni potrebbono succedere a' miei figloli et alle cose mia, se io da questa vita mancassi senza havere facto memoria delle cose mie, mi sono resoluto per questo scripto lasciare a' miei posteri quello che voglio et desidero si facci dopo la mia morte, quale prima prego l'Omnipotente Idio et Salvatore Nostro Ihesu Christo che permetta che la venga quando sia più salute della ‹...› mia et Suo sanctissimo servitio al quale la‹...›ndo in fini ‹...› pregandolo per la sua infinita pietà et misericordia si degni giudichi luogo di salvatione amen.

[fol. 1v] In prima succedendo la morte a Roma, el mio corpo sia mandato alla ecclesiastica sepultura con funerali convenienti, non excedendo li statuti romani nella spesa. Et che si faccino dire le messe et altri officii soliti per morti. El luoco sia quando paia alli infrascripti executori in la chiesa di S.to Gio. Baptista della nation fiorentina. Seguendo a Firenze sia in S.ta Maria Novella in qualche luogo dove si facci uno sepulcro o lapide o altrimenti come parrà alli exequtori conveniente.

Et perché in Roma sono morti tre miei fratelli, Raphaello, Francesco et Lorenzo, voglio si facci una memoria di loro in la detta chiesa di S. Jo. Baptista, con spesa in tutto al più di scudi cento d'oro, della quale habino cura il governatore et consigliori che per li tempi saranno della Compagnia della Pietà della nation fiorentina.

Et perché sia pregato per l'anime loro et mia, lascio alla dicta Compagnia scudi cinquanta d'oro con charicho che debino ogni anno fare dire in la chiesa da' preti uno anniversario et nella Compagnia uno officio per XXX anni et quel più tempo che loro paressi[1]. [fol. 2r] Item lascio alla Compagnia della Misericordia scudi XXV d'oro, con charico che ogni anno faccino dire uno anniversario per l'anima mia, tanti anni quanti a loro parrà conveniente.

Item prego i miei heredi et chi harà cura de loro sino sieno in età legittima che ogn'anno in Roma standoci, se non in Firenze, faccino qualche limosine come ho fatto sempre io in vita alli poveri et monasterii di frati et monache et spedaly et altri, secondo parrà loro conveniente per l'anima mia et perché Dio presti loro gratia di, nella gratia Sua, aumentare nelle virtù et beni della fortuna. Et questo rimetto alla lor discretione. Bene ricordo lor che quanto più facian più si troveran contenti. Et

1 The following paragraph has been crossed out, but is reproduced here because it provides some interesting information: 'Item lascio alla Compagnia detta una mia casa posta a Ripa a compagnia per 1/4 con li Fossi, quale al presente paga di censo alle monache di S.ta Cecilia duc. 15 di carlini et alla ‹...› di Ripa duc. 5 di carlini ogni 6 mesi et s'appigiona scudi 60 l'anno che me ne tocha 45.'

racomando loro le povere vergine che s'ingegnino substentarle non tanto quelle de' monasterii che tucte l'altre cognoschino che meritino.

Alla mia carissima consorte Isabella di Pagnozzo Ridolphi lascio che habia la sua dote et più in tutto sino a scudi dumila d'oro in oro et l'usufrutto di altri mille et altro, sechondo aparisce per uno scripto di mia mano che ha apresso di lei, quale voglio siano i miei heredi obligati servando. Et a lei raccomando i miei figloli et figlole nati di lei secondo in detto scripto li ho detto.

[fol. 2v] Alle mia figlole Ginevra et Maria legittime et naturale nate di detta Isabella, perché sendo nate a Roma potrebbono volere usare li statuti et godere privilegio di romane, declaro che non voglo che habino della mia heredità se non la dota conveniente sino a scudi ijMD d'oro in oro per ciascuna il più, et il manco scudi ijM d'oro in oro. Et da 2M a 2500 stia in arbitrio delli infrascripti exequtori quali, considerato le qualità della mia heredità, la gravino o sgravino di detti scudi 500 per ciascuna. Et a quella habino a stare quiete, né si possino maritare senza lor licentia et consenso, et faciendolo non possino dimandare più di scudi 1000 per ciascuna. Et se monache si facessino habino convenienti doni in modo parrà alli miei exequtori.

Prego li miei heredi et exequtori che voglino quanto prima comodamente si potrà por mano su tanti danari, che depositandoli o impiegandoli in qualche luogo che sia c‹...›to possino honestamente augmentare, in modo che ‹...› sappino dove sarà la loro dote. Et se si troverà che ne habino parte come spero si acresca quello fussi necessario per la somma predetta sino a scudi 2500, come è detto.

In tutti li altri liei beni mobili et inmobili presenti et futuri lascio mio herede universale [fol. 3r] Julio mio figlolo legittimo et naturale nato della detta mia mogle Isabella.

Se Dio ci concederà altri figloli, sendo femine habino scudi ijM d'oro in oro di dote; sendo maschi participino per rata parte con Julio secondo la quantità saranno.

Al quale Julio, et li altri se ne haveremo, comando che sia obediente a sua matre et alli altri su[oi] superiori et sino ad anni venti finiti non voglio che della heredità possa né possino disporre in modo alcuno, se non in quel modo che possono disporre e popilli et in pupillare etate constituti.[2]

Quali figloli, figlole et mogle voglo che si mandino a Firenze e quivi si nutrischino et allevino li maschi sino a tempo conveniente et le femine sino si maritino.

[fol. 3v] Lascio et voglo che dopo la morte mia tutte le mia ragioni et compagnie si finischino. Et allo stralcio d'epse, volendo piglare la cura, stia dua anni Benedetto di Jacopo Antonio Busini, quale sempre me è stato affectionatissimo. Et lo prego così perseveri co miei figloli et aiuti stralciare et finire et ridurre al netto ogni cosa più presto potrà. Et perché lo possi fare più amorevolmente, voglo che habia in detti dua anni delli miei heredi per suo premio scudi 20 il mese mentre starà a detto stralcio. Et non volendo o [po]tendo tal cura, lo [pre]go non manchi di consiglare, come informato ch'egl'è delle cose mia, a chi miglore tal cura quale si dia a qualche persona simile, con quel salario che parrà alli executori.

2 Same as note 1: 'Prego che vogla studiare et diligentemente ingegnarsi d'imparare in modo che crescendo diventi virtuoso et tale che facci honore a me et a tutta la casa et posterità nostra et se sarà solo non si curi di sequitare l'arte mercantile perché è pericolosissima.'

Finite che saranno e ritratti d'epse de' primi danari, dopo accomodati quelli e le dote delle mie figlole predette, si comperi per sino a scudi 2000 d'officii in persona di Julio mio figlolo, e frutti de' quali serviran per li suoi bisogni cotidiani, de' quali frutti possi disporre a suo modo; et se già ne havesse simil somma o parte, comperisi quel mancassi, et mentre che sarà piccolo che non spenderà quel avanzerà si riprenda in officii o altra cosa simile a sua disposition. [fol. 4r] Di poi di quello di mano in mano si verrà al netto si comperi, non sendo comprati alla mia morte oltre a quelli mi trovo al presente, beni stabili in quel di Firenze per scudi quattromila incircha, coè 2000 in una casa in Firenze et ijM altri in una possessione o più che sia utile e non pomposa; et il desiderio mio sarebbe si comprasse in quel di Prato o luogo simile, come sa mia moglie.

Del restante vorrei che si comprasse in Roma o suo territorio tanti beni stabili di case o casali con più beneficio de' miei heredi che si puotrà. Et parendo a miei executori comperare sino a iijM altri scudi d'officii a Julio, lo faccino.

La memoria delle cose mie si troverà su uno libro di ricordanze che ho comincato a questo effetto; et quando non fusse quivi, per e mia conti a libri della mia compagnia con li Strozzi et della mia ragione si troverrà tutto, perché non ho curato [fol. 4v] tenere altro libro proprio continuato, ma sempre tutto girato per el banco dove si harà di tutto lume.

La cura et tutela de' miei figloli, volendola la Isabella mia mogle et loro matre, non si rimaritando et stando dove loro, se li dia et sia sua fino a che figloli maschi habino xx anni. Et l'entrate delle possessioni et masseritie che ho et che si comprerranno in Firenze, come è detto, ne habia la cura lei. Et facciale servire al loro vitto et uso et non sia tenuta di quelle a rendere conto nessuno a nessuno. Et caso che si rimaritassi, che per essere ancor hoggi molto giovane, li figloli et mia fratelli l'habino per excusata. In tal caso la cura resti a Michele, mio fratello maggiore honorando, et mancando lui ad Alexandro, pure mio magior fratello, con le facultà che la Isabella.

Se per caso Julio mio figlolo mancassi senza ha[ver] figloli, succedino a lui li miei fratelli Michele et Alexandro sendo vivi; se non et non sendo vivi detti miei fratelli, succedino li loro figloli, se ne haveran, per equal parte: la metà quelli di Michele et la 1/2 quelli di Alexandro.

[fol. 5r] Exequtori di questo mio testamento et ultima voluntà siano Michele et Alexandro, miei fratelli maggiori honorandi, chi di loro vorrà et l'uno succeda a l'altro, et m. Bartolomeo Bettini et m. Gio. Baptista Accaiuoli, miei compari et affectionatissimi, quali voglo che uno de' miei fratelli predecti con decti m. Bartolomeo et m. Jo. Baptista o al manco con uno di loro d'acordo possino fare et exequire quanto in questo si contiene, et habino quella auctorità soglono havere simili exequtori. Et mancando nessuno de' dicti Bartolomeo o Jo. Baptista, succeda in luoco del primo[3] Benedetto Busini, in luoco del secondo m. Girolamo Ubaldini mio carissimo cognato; et mancando tutti e due e fratelli, succeda a loro 2[4] Benedetto o Girolamo, in modo che se è possibile restino sempre tre, et dua d'acordo posseno fare come è detto. Quali tucti prego, i fratelli per l'obligo et per l'affiction fraterna,

3 In superscript the name of 'Pagnozzo Ridolphi' has been added; he is Benvenuto Olivieri's father-in-law.

4 'Pagnozzo' in superscript.

et alli altri per l'affiction che me hanno sempre portata, che voglino allegramente piglare questo peso per amore di Dio et mia, et procedere verso i miei figloli come se loro fussino. Et nel maritare della [fol. 5v] Ginevra, per essere figloccia di m. Bartolomeo, non si facci senza suo consenso; et della Maria, per esser figloccia di m. Jo. Baptista, non si facci senza suo consenso, sendo vivi. Che Dio a tucti presti lunga vita.

Raccomando principalmente la mia consorte et li mia figloli alli Reverendissimi et Illustrissimi Cardinali monsignor Antonio Pucci et monsignor Guido Ascanio, Cardinale Santa Fiora Camerario et a Ascanio Cardinale di Rimini et monsignor Hieronimo Ricenas episcopo maurianeto[5] et alli magnifici signori tucti miei compari et patroni, quali prego che voglino in tucte le occurentie et bisogni aiutare li miei figloli come hanno fatto me. Et precipue il Reverendissimo et Illustrissimo Santi Quattro, quale confesso in le mie adversità non havere havuto el più affectionato protettore et defensore et col quale prego li miei exequtori et heredi sempre si consiglino in le loro actioni. Al quale et alli altri volentieri harei lassato il peso d'exequtori, ma per non li fastidire più che si voglino non lo ho facto, dico bene che se alcuno di lor vorrà intervenire come exequtore, voglio che habia quelle medesime auctorità che li altri exequtori predicti et con li 2/3 di quelli si possi far tutto.

Facto a dì 6 di ottobre 1544. Ita est Benvenuto Olivieri proprio.

5 The following sentence has been crossed out: 'tutti miei compari et patroni et alli magnifici signori Piero et Ruberto di Phylippo Strozzi'.

Doc. 3: Benvenuto Olivieri's property and holdings (*substantie*), 1545

(ASF, Galli Tassi 1806, ins. 2, unnumbered folio)
Self-executed list of property and holdings, of 3 September 1545, detailing his current economic situation (buildings, investments, activities).

Substantie di me Benvenuto Ulivieri. Questo dì iij di septembre 1545

Una casa posta a Ripa di Roma comprata a 24 di gennaro 1540 a nativitate a libro di Roma de' mia del banco azuro, c. 15. E paga di censo sc. 27.18, affitasy sc. 36, costo	sc.	180
Le possessione et casamenti del Chiasso comprati dall'erede di m. Leonardo Tornabuoni addì 28 di luglio 1541. Costò sc. 3600 et la gabella sc. 279	sc.	3879
La mia casa di Roma comprata da Albertaccio del Bene e fratelli sc. 1883 et di più li sc. 650 in circha di migloramenti: pagala di banchi duc. 125 di carlini di censo. Restasene a pagare sc. 941.10 a Natale 1546; affittasi al banco, sc. 200 d'oro. Della compra è rogato Lodovico Roydetti. Bisogna la retification de' fratelli d'Alberto. Quando si pagerà sc. 941½	sc.	2500
Le possessione patrimoniale a Firenze in Valdisieve et Mugello per circa sc. 1000. Apare in le divise	sc.	1000
A libro azuro segnato A tertio di Benvenuto Ulivieri e compagni sono creditore di duc. 9847.15.8 di Camera che ‹…› pagono x per cento. Vaglono	sc.	10094
Item ho havere la mia rata delli utili fattisi et che restano ancora a dividersi. Sono creditore di duc. 35528.3.3 di camera vecchi. Tochamene s. v d. x per lira. Non ci sono li utili della Thexoreria di Perusa che saran da sc. v mila. Ragiono	sc.	10000
Antonio Covoni proprio mi debbe duc. 224.1.8 per resto del corpo. Item sc. 1250 che ha cedula di Luigi del Riccio. Item m'à assegnato duc. 831.10.1 a riscontro della Camera per conto del prestito delle doane per d. vii per lira assegnatone sotto nome delli Olivieri. In tutto	sc.	2332
Item mi debe Antonio Covoni proprio el sexto delli utili facti in dicta compagnia d'Antonio Covoni e Co. che sono creditori avanzi duc. 6173.18.3. Non v'è l'utile del partito di Perusa. Ragiononsi 6000 netti et presti	sc.	1000

Girolamo Ubaldini proprio mi debbe per lo partito datomi a 31 d'agosto 1545 duc. 3723.18.4. Item li utili di dua anni della ragion, che saran da 800: holli dati a Iulio mio figlolo che li ha messi in la ragion nova in somma duc. VI mila, che il restante s'à a porre di questo Natale	sc.	4500
Dohana de cavalli sotto nome de' Carduci: quelli utili vi si fanno li ho donati sin hora a Mariotto della Palla et così, vivendo lui, farò sino al fine della condotta	sc.	181
[Sub-total	sc.	35666]
Quello si cavasse de' debiti che restano della ragion con li Strozzi a libro bianco K 3°, che li avanzi sono creditori di duc. 7480. Me ne tocha el sexto [1247], son mal debitori		
Quello più si cavasse delli debiti della ragion con li Strozzi de libro verde segnato B, che li avanzi sono creditori di duc. 3926.18.4. Buon debitore, me ne tocha s. v d. x per lira [1145]		
Uno officio di Cavaliere di S. Paulo: costòmi sc. 1000, vale 850. Vaca per obitum		
L'officio d'abreviatore che ho in persona mia non vaca per obitum: è della ragion de libro azurro 3° che ne ha 2/3 Niccolò della Riccia		
Miei fratelli et parenti mi sono debitori circa sc. ij mila che non ‹…›do da lor a rendermeli più ‹…› lassarli lor et li lasso in dono		
Della ragion delli Altoviti havuta compagnia con lor sotto nome di Baptista Puccini, resto creditore buono. Somma come apare al mio libro rosso A proprio, tenuto mentre stetti con loro. Credo vi sia maturo per me da ‹…› sc. se il Pucino li havesse fare d'avere la rata et stiasene a quello dirà m. Bindo		
E bilanci delle mie ragioni sono tutti nello mio scriptoio mio di Roma		
A libro gallo de' mia di Roma il conto è circa pary: non v'è sc. 100		
[Estimated grand total	sc.	40000]

Doc. 4: Partnership agreement among B. Olivieri, B. Busini and S. Guiducci, the participation of R. Strozzi, and dissolution, 1539-43

(ASF, Galli Tassi 1826, fols 3v-5v)
Three documents are shown here: the initial agreement among Benvenuto Olivieri, Benedetto Busini and Simone Guiducci (18 July 1539); the participation of Roberto Strozzi hidden behind Olivieri's name (18 August 1539); the dissolution of the company (17 March 1543).

Partnership agreement among benvenuto Olivieri, Benedetto Busini and Simone Guiducci (18 july 1539)

[fol. 3v] yhs. Al nome di Dio

Sia noto et manifesto a qualunche leggerà o leggere udirà la presente scritta come col nome di Dio Benvenuto di Paolo Ulivieri, Benedetto di Iacopantonio Businі et Simone di Mariotto Guiducci, cittadini et mercanti fiorentini, sono convenuti infra di loro di far compagnia per Roma o dove la corte romana si trasferissi, con le conditione et patti che appresso si narreranno:

Son d'accordo che dettsa compagnia dica in Benvenuto Ulivieri e compagni et usi il segno qui in margine adnotato et duri anni tre, principiando a dì primo di luglio prexente 39.

Son dacordo che il corpo di detta raggione sia di duc. xxiiij mila d'oro di Camera, de' quali Benvenuto Ulivieri sia tenuto di mettere duc. xviiij mila, cioè duc. xvij mila in contanti et duc. dua milia ad ogni suo beneplacito; Benedetto Bussini duc. tremila d'oro di Camera, cioè duc. ij mila contanti et duc. mille nella stima della sua persona; Simone Guiducci duc. duamila, cioè duc. mille contanti et duc. mille nella stima della sua persona. El quale corpo debba per ciascuno de' detti compagni esser messo fra dua mesi dal dì che comincia la detta compagnia et chi manchassi habbia a rifar la compagnia a raggione di xv per cento a capo d'anno.[1]

Sono d'accordo che il governo et l'administratione di detta compagnia[2] sia di tutti li compagni che in sul luogo alla giornata fussino, ma Benvenuto non sia obligato starvi più né altrimenti che a llui bene venga; solo Benedetto et Simone non possino partirsi dalla cura et governo d'essa et sieno tenuti continuamente col corpo et animo exercitarsi a benefitio di detta et ogni anno mettere in saldo et mandare bilancio a Benvenuto, essendo assente, distincto, particolare et chiaro, acciò che esso possi apertamente vedere in che stato la raggione si trovi.

Sono d'accordo che non si possi per alcun di detti compagni trarre cosa alcuna[3] de' corpi et utili di detta raggione, se non alla fine d'essa, né possa anchora servire amici di denari, robbe o promesse, se non per [fol. 4r] apparente benefitio di detta raggione. Et chi trahessi o altrimenti gravassi per alchuno modo retto o inderetto

1 In the margin: 'corpo duc. xxiiij mila / Benvenuto … duc. 19000 / Benedetto … duc. 3000 / Simone … duc. 2000 / duc. 24000'.

2 In the margin: 'governo'.

3 In the margin: 'non si possa trarre né servir amici'.

la detta raggione sia tenuto rimborsarla et conservarla a raggione di xv per cento a capo d'anno. Solo alli detti Benedetto et Simone si concede trarre ogni anno per lor bisogni et giornalmente duc. sessanta d'oro per ciascuno; de' quali ne habbino a ir debitori in lor conto et alla fine di detta raggione ragguagliarne gli altri compagni.

Sono d'accordo che chi al governo si trovarà possa exercitare detto corpo in mercantie, cambii, speditione, appalti di lumiere, dohane, depositeria et che altro a proposito indicassi;ma nessuno senza espressa licentia de l'altro possi negotiare in Roma o dove la corte romana si trasferisse sotto suo nome o d'altri per la sua proprietà; et negotiando, ogni utile facessi s'intenda applicato alla compagnia, sendovi danno sia suo. Possa bene Benvenuto Ulivieri fuori di detta Roma et corte far tutto quello che bene li viene, ma solo Benedetto et Simone né quivi né altrove negotiare o far negotio possino.

Sono d'accordo che occorendo altri giovani per servitio di detta raggione, li habbia a prendere Benvenuto Ulivieri con quel salario parerà conveniente.

Sono d'accordo che alla fine di detta compagnia Benedetto et Simone sieno obligati stare allo stralcio d'essa al manco sei mesi a spese di detta[4] raggione senzo altro salario; et mancando per qualsivoglia cagione, possi detto Benvenuto prendere uno in loco di quello che mancassi, a spese del mancante per detto tempo allo stralcio. Et la prima cosa si habbino a pagare tutti li creditori del più vivo vi sarà, et quando le sustantie della raggione, per non essere ancora leste, non bastassino, ciascuno de' detti compagni sia tenuto provedere quello bisognassi per la sua rata secondo la tratta in contanti; et non lo facendo, sia lecito a Benvenuto, per la preservatione del nome et honor suo, pigliarli a cambio et ricambio tante volte quante occoressi, overo in deposito a quelli prezzi et per quelli tempi et luochi che a llui parrà, a conto di detta raggione, quella somma occoressino; et inoltre vendere robbe et substantie della raggione a contanti et stagliare dette a quelli prezzi troverà per satisfare alli creditori di detta raggione; et quelli pagassi habbino a trarre li corpi secondo le messe in contanti, mercantie o debitori, secondo saranno. Et di poi partire gli utili in questo modo, cioè: a Benvenuto Ulivieri,[5] per li suoi duc. xviiij mila di Camera, cioè duc. 17 mila in contanti et duc. ij mila che debbe mettere ad arbitrio suo, s. 15 d. 10 per lira; a Benedetto Bussini [fol. 4v], per li sua 3 mila duc. d'oro, cioè duc. ij mila contanti et duc. mille per la stima della sua persona, s. ij d. 6 per lira; a Simone Guiducci per li sua duc. ij mila, cioè duc. mille contanti et duc. mille per la stima della sua persona, s. i d. 8 per lira. Et così s'habbia a dividere infra di loro la perdita quando vi fussi, che Dio ne guardi. Et delli utili che Dio ne concederà, sono d'accordo che se n'habbia a dare per l'amor de Dio a' poveri bisognosi cinque per cento, ma ciascuno de' sopradetti compagni habbia a distribuire la parte sua secondo la tratta di detti utili.

Sono d'accordo che mancando nessuno di detti compagni per morte, di che Dio ne guardi, la compagnia s'intenda finita come se l'ultimo giorno fosse venuto.

Item che alla fine di detta compagnia le scritture restinoa Benvenuto Ulivieri, con obligo di farle commune alli altri compagni et lassarne prendere copia a loro piacere.

---

4 'stralcio' repeated in the margin.

5 In the margin: 'discussione degli utili'.

Item che avanzando danari a Benvenuto, li possa cambiare o inpiegare in cedole o altre mercantia o partiti sotto nome et a' libri di detta raggione et non altrimenti; et facendolo observisi el capitolo quinto, possa bene il detto Benvenuto intervenire nelle industrie et magone di Lunghezza per la sua proprietà senza alcuno preiuditio.

Et tutte le sopradette cose in capitoli xi contenute promettono li detti compagni l'uno a l'altro inviolabilmente observare sotto pena, oltre alle predette, di duc. trecento d'oro di Camera da pagarsi per chi contrafacessi a qualsivoglia parte delle sopradette conventioni alli observanti; et tante volte s'intenda essere incorso in detta pena, quante volte contrafacessi sottomettendosi ciascuno d'essi a tutte le corte, iuditii et fori temporali et spirituali dove raggione si tenessi et particularmente alla Mercantia di Firenze, et obligando ciaschuno sé et suoi heredi e beni presenti et futuri in quelli miglior modi che di raggione far si può, et renuntiando ad ogni privilegio, legge o statuto che qual si voglia di loro far potessi.

Et quando difficultà o dubbio alcuno nascessi infra li detti compagni, o per non essere bene dichiarato qualche cosa delle soprascritte, o per qualche caso non venuto in consideratione nel formar la presente scripta, intendono et vogliono tutto sia da ogni iudice equamente a puro et buono inteletto, secondo lo stile de' reali mercanti interpretato, supplito et deciso. Et in fede della verità si sottoscriveranno qui a piè di lor propria mano.

Io Benvenuto Ulivieri sono contento, prometto et m'obligo a quanto [fol. 5r] in questa scritta si contiene et per fede ho fatto questa soscrittione di mia propria mano questo dì xviij de luglio 1539 in Roma, laus Deo.

Io Benedetto Bussini sono contento, prometto et m'obligo a quanto in questa scritta si contiene et per fede ho fatto questa soscrittione di mia propria mano questo dì 18 de luglio 1539.

Io Simone Guiducci sono contento, prometto et m'obligo a quanto in questa scritta si contiene et per fede ho fatta questa soscrittione di mia propria mano questo dì 18 di luglio 1539 in Roma.

Participation of Roberto Strozzi (18 August 1539)

Dichiarasi per la presente il dì soprascritto è copia de verbo ad verbum della[6] originale scritta di compagnia fatta fra il soprascritto Benvenuto Ulivieri, Benedetto Bussini et Simone Guiducci, quale è appresso d'esso Benvenuto, et come in la participatione del detto Benvenuto et sotto nome suo il Magnifico m. Roberto Strozzi proprio debbe mettere duc. dodicimila d'oro in oro di Camera et participare sotto nome d'esso Benvenuto per s. dieci per lira[7] di tutti gli utili et danni che seguisseno in detta compagnia; de' quali duc. dodicimilia per el corpo et li utili che si faranno in epsa compagnia, che Dio li accrescha, el detto Benvenuto promette rendere fedele et reale conto al detto m. Ruberto, et pagargnene come, nel modo et quando li riscoterà lui, et fargliene cessione di quello accadessi liberamente et senza nessuna eccettione. Et il

6 In the margin: 'deciaratione della participatione di Ruberto Strozzi in la compagnia per duc. xij mila'.

7 The situation is summarized in the margin: 'Strozzi … duc. 10 / Benvenuto … duc. 5.10 / Simone … duc. 1.8 / Benedetto … duc. 2.6 / duc. 20'.

detto m. Ruberto s'obliga et promette, per detta rata sua di s. 10 per lira, conservare il detto Benvenuto quando danno vi fussi, di che Dio guardi, nel modo et come è obligato lui alli detti sua compagni Benedetto et Simone, liberamente et senza alcuna exceptione, promettendo et obligandosi in tutto et per tutto l'uno a l'altro et l'altro a l'uno observare in la soprascritta horiginale scritta si contiene inviolabilmente, come se in detta originale scritta di detto m. Ruberto espressamente fussi per detta rata fatto mentione sotto le pene et sumessione predette, qual vogliono qui tutte s'abbino per repetite. Et per fede et cautela di ciaschuno s'è fatto la presente dichiaratione che sarà sottoscritta di dette parte.

Io Benvenuto Ulivieri proprio dichiaro, prometto et obligomi a quanto in questa scritta si contiene et in fede ho fatto questa soscrittione di mia propria mano a dì 18 d'agosto 1539 in Roma.

Dissolution of the company (17 March 1543)

[fol. 5v] Consule et Consiglieri della nation fiorentin di Roma
Ad instanti et requisitione di Benvenuto Ulivieri e compagni di Roma,[8] universalmente a tutti et singuli mercanti et negotianti in Roma et in la corte romana et spetialmente a quelli di nostra natione, per virtù della presente si fa intendere come la raggione la quale per il passato fino a questo giorno ha canto sotto et in nome di Benvenuto Ulivieri e compagni di Roma è secondo che si asserisce finita et disdetta fra loro di comune consenso et non intendano segua più avanti, né che alcuno de loro negotii o faccia facende sotto nome della detta raggione. Et negotiando in detto nome ciascuno oblighi sé proprio et no la detta raggione, né li compagni di quella, del che dicano essersene protestati infra di loro et di nuovo si protestano contra li negotianti, acciò che ne habbino piena notitia. Et se pure il prefato Benvenuto Ulivieri da hoggi per l'avenire negotiassi, come si crede negotiare, sotto il medesimo nome di Benvenuto e compagni di Roma, dichiarano et danno notitia a tutti che non vogliono s'intenda né s'intendon della raggione et compagnia finita at disdetta come di sopra, né de' medesmi compagni et sotto detto nome. Et acciò che alcuno delli detti mercanti et negotianti non possa excusarsi et allegare ignoranza, gli si fa questa generale intimatione con expresso et repetito protestatione come di sopra in ogni miglior modo et che di raggione et stile mercantile si può et debba fare.

Intimat. die xvij Martii 1542 [=1543]

8 In the margin: 'disdetta della compagnia'.

Doc. 5: Depositary contract, 1545

(ASF, Galli Tassi 1851, fasc. 10, fols 1r-4v)
Trascription of the contract farming out the administration of the Depositary to Benvenuto Olivieri & Partners for the years 1545 and 1546

+ M.D.XLVI Contracto del Partito per conto de' pagamenti ordinarii della Depositeria per la Camera apostolica per dua anni 1545 . 1546
X Januarii 1545
[fol. 1r] IN NOMINE DOMINI AMEN

Presentis publici Instrumenti seriem visuris, lecturis pariter et audituris evidenterpateat et sit notum quod anno a nativitate D.N. Jesu Christi Millesimo Quingentesimo Quadragesimo Quinto Indictione Tertia Die vero Sabbati Decima mensis Januarii, Pontificatus Sanctissimi in Christo Patris et Domini Nostri D. Pauli divina providentia PP tertii anno undecimo. In mea publici et Camere apostolice notarii testiumque infrascriptorum ad hec specialiter voatorum et rogatorum presentia personaliter congregati et cohadunati existentes Reverendissimus et Illustrissimus Dominus ac Reverendi in Christo patres et domini Guido Ascanius Sfortia Sancti Eustachii Diaconus Cardinalis de Sancta Flora nuncupatus Sanctissimi D.N. prefati et Sancte romane ecclesie Camerarius ac Bernardinus Helvinus electus anglonensis prefati D.N. PP Thesaurarius generalis Julius Gonzaga ex comitibus Novellarie ac Petrus Lippomanus episcopus veronensis Camere apostolice Clerici assistente etiam R.D. Julio de Grandis dicte Camere presidente, Cameram apostolicam representantes et facientes ac illius negocia more camerali pertractantes habito ut asserverunt inter eos super infrascripto partito faciendo tractatur colloquio etiam cum Sua Santitate ac ex ipsius mente et voluntate ipsorumque matura deliberatione nomine prefati Domini Nostri ac sedis et Camere apostolice auctoritate ipsorum officii agentes ex una et Magnificus vir D. Benvenutus Oliverius civis et mercator florentinus romanam curiam sequens partibus ex altera non vi, dolo, melu aut aliqua sinistra machinatione circumventi sed eorum sponte et ex certa scientia omnibus melioribus modo via iure causa et forma quibus melius et efficacius ac de iure validius fieri posset seu deberet ad infrascriptam interesse conventiones et mutuas promissiones dictis respective nominibus per antea ut dixerunt firmatas, discussas et consideratas devenerunt et deveniunt infrascripti tenoris vz.

Per servitio di N.S. è stato ragionato non tenere più Depositaria ma dare assignamenti a tutti li pagamenti della Camera come si è cominciato a fare, perché a Sua Excellentia è dato assignamento per il suo quartiere et per le galere sopra la contributione del novo subsidio [fol. 1v] in Romagna et nel Patrimonio, al Maestro di Casa nella Marca et al Quartiero de' Cavalli se desegna ne l'Umbria o altri luochi et perché alli pagamenti che si fanno in Roma per la guardia di Sua Santità per monsignor Governatore, monsignor Castellano, Bargello, Cappella, Populo Romano et altri provisionati non si può dare comodamente l'assegnamento per ciascuno, si è pensato di dare un assegnamento fermo che basti per fare il pagamento ogni mese di questi ordinarii quali se calculano cinque mila settecento scudi in circa il mese et che uno habbi cura di rescotere detto assegnamento et pagare et renderne conto. Per questo, essendo recercato il mag.co m. Benvenuto Olivieri mercante fiorentino di corte, lui proptamente secundo il suo solito ha acceptato questo peso per fare servitio a Sua Beatitudine con li capituli et pacti infrascripti da osservarsi inviolabilmente vz.

In primis la Camera apostolica concede ogn'anno per dui anni cominciati a kalende di gennaro presente mese al soprascritto m. Benvenuto e compagni, per assegnamento della pacha de' detti ordinarii annotati qui sotto, le infrascripte entrate, le quale non possano divertirsi né assignarsi per altro in modo alcuno et, non li essendo pagati a l'infrascritti tempi, la Camera ve li habbi a provedere subito de contanti vz.

Censi de Napoli, Ferrara, Urbino, Pesaro, Sinigaglia et tutti gli altri che se pagano alla festa di San Pietro del mese de Giugno, che sogliono ascendere alla somma de scudi dicessette millia et a questo effecto sia depositario. Sc. 17000	17000
Quarto de' fructi delle congregationi de fratrarie che ascendano alla somma de sc. vintiunmila d'oro in oro da pagarsi ne li termini delle obligationi fatti presso li atti di me Michelangelo notaro. Scuti	21000
Vigesime delli hebrei del Stato Ecclesiastico computati quelli de Avignone et conta venaysino da pagarsi per tutto il primo d'Agosto. Scuti octo mila	8000
Una decima de tutto il Stato Ecclesiastico con il quarto de' frutti de' beneficii regulari extra congregationes da ritenerse dal primo de giugno a tutto decembre per ciascuno de' detti doi anni. Scuti otto mila	8000
[fol. 2r] Maleficii di Roma tutti et non fruttando scudi quattro mila d'oro per tutto l'anno 1545 et altretanti per l'anno 1546 se li habbi a dare altro assegnamento vivo per detta somma de scudi quattro mila overo quello che mancharà	4000
Item sopra la contributione del terzo anno di Parma et Piacenza scudi sei mila d'oro in oro da pagarsi ne' primi otto mesi, cioè per tutto 1545 et riscuotersi pro rata con l'altri assignamenti vi sono o seranno	6000

Et ad effetto delle receptioni soprascritte solamente sia depositario.

Che tanti faranno insieme la somma de	64000

Il detto m. Benvenuto per detti ordinarii promette pagare insino a la somma de cinque millia settecento scudi in circa ogni mese alle persone che saranno annotate in la lista infrascritta et non ad altri per mandati però dal reverendissimo Camerlengo et Thesoriere generale secundo il solito da spedirsi giornalmente per doi anni proximi incominciando, anzi anticipando dal principio di gennaro presente con il soprascritto assegnamento il quale non possa esserli tolto, divertito né impedito in tutto o in parte in modo alcuno, ma se intenda esser applicato a detto m. Benvenuto per assegnamento de' detti ordinarii per detti doi anni firmissimamente; et levandosi o applicandosi ad altri o mancando d'essere pagati a' detti tempi cessi subito l'obligo del sborso per rata, anzi in tal caso sia in facultà d'esso m. Benvenuto non seguitare più avanti et la Camera sia obligata restituirli subito quello havessi forsi sopra pagato et non pagandolo corra l'interesso a dodici per cento a capo et ragion de anno.

Et perché ogni faticha desidera premio la Camera dà et concede al detto m. Benvenuto licentia di potere retenere a detti pagamenti la retentione solita secundo hanno retenuto li mag.[ci] m. Thobia Pallavicino et m. Luca Justiniano depositarii, la quale serva per l'occupatione de' danari che terrà sborsati de' soi detto m Benvenuto in questa impresa et per le fatiche et spese sue et de' ministri che se adopraranno in questa cosa.

Item sono d'accordo che detto m. Benvenuto debbia accordare li notarii di Camera delle loro retentioni de mandati et similmente monsignore Reverendissimo Camerlengo et il Signore Thesoriere et li Signori Chierici di Camera et altri [fol. 2v] camerali delli loro regali a conto suo.

Item sono d'accordo che si debbino pagare li assignamenti fatti a' signori secretarii participanti, Archivisti, Cubicularii e Scudieri sopra la Depositaria a conto della Camera insino a la somma de scudi seicento cinque l'anno.

Item la Camera debbia deputare commissarii et riscuotere la decima, quarto de' fructi et vigesima a nominatione di m. Benvenuto con li soliti emolumenti et provisione.

Item la Camera debbia fare expedire et concedere brevi patente et altre scritture necessarie et opportune per riscuotere li soprascritti assegnamenti con ogni prestezza, facilità et favore et ordinare alle congregationi et hebrei che debbano obligarsi pagare al detto m. Benvenuto a nome della Camera per detti dui anni.

Compositione del quarto de' frutti per l'anno 1545

	gold cameral ducats	*scudi d'oro in oro*
Cassinensi	6000	6540
Olivetani	3000	3270
Scopettini	909	1000
Lateranensi	3000	3270
Camaldulensi	1000	1090
Certusini	4000	4360
Vall'Umbrosa	550	600
San Giorgio in Alga	250	272
Celestini	200	218
Cistello di Lombardia	150	163
Silvestrini de Fabriano	25	27
Cruciferi	100	109
San Girolamo		100
Cistello di Toscana		100
	19284	[21119]

Compositione della vigesima delli hebrei

	scudi di moneta	*scudi d'oro in oro*
Marcha		2500
Romagna	950	863
Avignone		200
Conta Venayssino		800
Bologna		2000
[fol. 3r] Roma		327
Campagna et Marittima		
Benevento		
Patrimonio et Orvieto		
Umbria		1310
		[8000]

Censi di San Pietro

	gold cameral ducats	*scudi d'oro in oro*
Napoli et Sicilia	7000	7175
Ferrara	7000	7175
Urbino	1340	1460
Pesaro e Mondaino	850	926
Altri censi piccoli in circa	274	274
	[16464]	[17010]

Apresso sarà la nota di quello ha a pagare m. Benvenuto Oliverio a conto del soprascritto partito

	mensuatim	annuatim
Guardia	1328.14	15944. 8
Signor Jo. Battista Savello	250	3000
Mancie	150	1800
Castellano e Bombardieri di Sancto Angelo	431. 3.10	8174
Fonditor dell'Artellarie	18. 6. 8	220
Cappella di nostro Signore	353. 7. 8	4240.12
Bibliothecario	4	48
Cappellani della libraria	6	72
Instauratori de' libri greci	8	96
Castellano de Hostia	36	432
Zecca et altri ministri	40	480
Signor Alexandro Colunna	100	1200
Capitaneo Alexandro da Terani	50	600
Cap° Nicolò da Piombino	25	300

Offitiale de le nove cathene	4	48
Cancellaria del R.mo Farnese	24	288
Governatore di Roma	173. 3	2077.16
Bargiello di Roma	320	3840
[fol. 3v] Thesauriero	60	720
Presidente	48	576
Abbreviatore de Curia	11	132
Advocato fiscale	8. 6. 8	100
Advocato de' poveri	8. 6. 8	100
Procuratore fiscale	8. 6. 8	100
Visitatore de carcere	4	48
Substituto fiscale	3	36
Commissario della Camera	20	240
Compotista della Camera	11.10	138
Mensario di notaro di Camera	6	72
Sollicitatore della Camera	3.10	42
Dui scrittori secreti	8	96
Portonaro di Porta Borgia	4	48
Racamatore	6	72
Banderaro	6	72
Pellicciaro	4	48
Medico fisico	45.17	550. 4
Alexandro riparo	10	120
Gaio gioiellerio	10	120
Zoppo scopatore	3	36
Savoia giardinero	3	36
Jaco Melenchino	10	120
Soprastante di Fonte di Sancto Pietro	3	36
Julio Americi	12	144
Custode del Palco Santa Maria Maiore	2	24
Signor Fabritio Varano	20	240
Gieronimo Grosso collaterale	15	180
Cap° Jo. Francesco Monte Mellino	25	300
Cardinale di Loreno	12.10	150
Pigione di Torre di Nona	2. 2	25. 4
Castellano di Terracina	60	720
[fol. 4r] Augumento del Castello Civita Vecchia	12	144
Spitiale palatino	6	72
Augustino hermolao	25	300
Signor Astorre Baglione	40	480
Gabbani et Tappi di Castello	12.15	153
Pascasio	4	48
Vittorio Clementino	8	96

Camerlengo del populo romano	205	2460
Conservatori di Roma	107	1284
Caporioni	56. 7.11	676.15
Senatore	180	2160
Confalone	31	372
Diversi altri offitiali	294	3528
Archivio	29	348
Cubicularii et scudieri	12	144
Secretarii apostolici participanti	8. 8. 4	101
Reverendissimo Farnese	110	1320
Nuntio di Francia	363	4356
Bini de Lione	55	660
Cera per la Candellora	62.10	750
Pallii di mezo agosto	22	264
Vestire de' palafreneri	100	1200
Scabelli	8. 6. 8	100
		[69318.19]

Item ch'el detto m. Benvenuto sia obligato render conto de ttre in tre mesi secundo il solito et delle somme soprascritte così de l'introito come de l'exito si debba attendere alla verità di quel che con effetto si riscuote et paga non obstante il specificato di sopra et di totto rendere bon conto.

Item promettono il suddetto m. Benvenuto far confirmare il presente contratto da Nostro Signore per suo motu proprio ad ogni requisitione sua in forma valida:

Que omnia et singula capitula et conventiones suprascritta promiserunt [fol. 4v] dicte partes altera alteri mutuo et vicissim perpetuo et inviolabiliter attendere et observare et contra non facere, dicere vel venire per se ipsos vel alios quovis quesito colore de iure vel de facto in iudicio vel extra alias ad omnia damna, expensas et interesse per alteram ipsarum partium premissa servantem per partem inobservantes patientes, substinentes et incurrentes, reficienda, restituenda et resarcienda teneri partes ipse voluerunt super quibus quidem damnis et interesse illorumque quantitate stare et credere voluerunt solo et simplici verbo damnum passi absque alia probatione iudicis, taxatione vel curie decreto. Pro quibus quidem omnibus et singulis sic ut premittitur tenendis, attendendis, complendis et inviolabiliter observandis, Prefati Reverendissimus et Reverendi Domini Camerarius, Thesaurarius et Camerales dictis nominibus omnia et singula dicte Camere bona mobilia et stabilia presentia et futura etiam iocalia preciosa quecunque dictus vero Benvenutus se ipsum suosque heredes ac bona sua et eorundem quecunque mobilia et immobilia, presentia et futura, ubicunque existentia sub penis et in pleniori et ampliori forma Camere apostolice cum renunciationibus, submissionibus procuratorum constitutione et aliis clausolis in ampliori forma Camere apponi solitis et consuetis, quandocunque latissime extendentes hypothecarunt et obligarunt iuraveruntque ad Sancta Dei Evangelia apponentes manus eorum dextras ad pectus more cardinalis et prelatorum ac tactis respective scripturis sacrosanctis. De et super quibus omnibus et singulis partes ipse rogarunt Notarium infrascriptum ut unum vel plura publicum seu publica conficerem Instrumentum seu instrumenta. Actum Rome in Palatio apostolico in stantiis residentie Prefati Reverendissimi et illustrissimi D. Cardinalis Camerarii in eius cubili sub anno, Indictione, Die, mense et Pontificatu quibus supra. Presentibus ibidem Magnificis viris D. Bartholomeo Bettino et Jo. Baptiste Perino civibus et mercatoribus florentinis romanam curiam sequentibus testibus ad premissa vocatis specialiter atque rogatis. Fine

Et ego Michelangelus Thomasinus de Ripatransone Clericus firmans dictae Camerae Apostolicae Notarius quia praemissis rogatus interfui, presens instrumentum subscripsi et publicavi, signoque meo tabellionatus consueto munivi requisitus in fidem et testimonium veritatis.

Doc. 6: Contract for the Treasury of Perugia and Umbria farmed out to Benvenuto Olivieri & Partners, 1541

(ASR, Camerale I, *Tesoreria provinciale di Umbria e Perugia*, busta 30, reg. 129, fols 1quattuor r-10r)
Transcription of the contract, in Latin, in which the Treasury of Perugia and Umbria is farmed out to Benvenuto Olivieri & Partners on 10 June 1541 for five years.

[fol. 1quattuor r] In nomine Domini amen. Per hoc presens publicum instrumentum cunctis sit notum quod anno a nativitate Domini Millesimo quingentesimo quatragesimo primo in dictione decima qu‹...› die vero decima mensis Junii pontificatus Sanctissimi in Christo Patris et Domini Nostri domini Pauli divina providentia PP tertii anno septimo. In mea Camera apostolica notarii testimonium infrascriptorum ad hoc spetialiter vocatorum et rogatorum presentia coram reverendis presentibus dominis Joanne Poggio prothonotario et secretario apostolico S.D.N. PP thesaurario, Johanne Gaddo decano, Balthassarre de Piscia, Johanne de la Casa, Hieronimo Sauli archiepiscopo barensis, Andrea Cornelio electo brixiensis et ‹...› Gonzaga ex comitibus Nuvellarie camere apostolice clericis presidentibus. In edibus monasterii Sancte Marie de Pace in camera apostolica ad iura reddendum et negocia camere apostolice utilt peragendum de mane ut moris est congregatis et coadunatis assistens eis, reverende presente domino Johanne Baptista Cicacurie causarum camere apostolice generali auditor, ac eximiis J.V. doctoribus d. Antonio Gabrielis advocato et Benedicto de' Valentibus procuratore fiscalis comparvitet se presentavit Magnificus vir dominus Benvenutus de Oliveriis civis et mercator florentinus romanam curiam sequens et ad presens eiusdem camere depositarius generalis qui tam suo quam sociorum suorum nominibus, eisdem R.P.D. thesaurario et clericis presidentis quoddam mandatuam in forma motus proprii manu [fol. 1quattuor v] S.D.N. PPe signatum exibuit et putavit tenoris sequentis vz.

Paulus ppa tertius motu proprio etc. Nuper post concessionem de Thesaureria civitatis Perusie et provincia Umbries nostrae dilecto filio Francisco Bencio civi florentino ad certum tempus non dum elapsum et sub certis pactis, conditionibus et conventionibus tunc expressis per certas nostras in forma brevis seu motus proprii litteras instrumento desuper in Camera apostolica fortsan celebrato factam cupientes paci et tranquillitati ac securitati dicte civitatis Perusie ac civium et incolarum eiusdem providere unam arcem seu fortallitium per quam seu quod civitas predicta ab hostium insidiis defendi posset et seditiosi si qui essent compesci valerent in ipsa civitate construi mandavimus et per alias nostras in forma brevis litteras certa assignamenta cum quibus fabrice arcis prefate subvenire voluimus fecimus pro ut in singulis litteris predictis latius continetur cum aut intentionis nostre sit ut Arx predicta quantocitius posset ad sui perfectionem perveniat et assignamenta predicta de presenti non suppetant alicuique Camere apostolice facultates aliis suis et urgentissimis necessitatibus non sufficiant et propterea constituerimus dictam Thesaureriam cum anticipatione infrascripte pecuniarum summme cum qua fabrice dicte arcis subvenire possit de novo locare accedente tamen ad hoc espresso dicti Francisci consensu, exactam diligentiam fieri fecimus pro honeris locationis de novo facienda nec inveniremus qui meliores nostras et [fol. 2r] et Camere apostolice condictiones fecerit quos dilectos filios Benvenutum de Oliveriis et socios modernos depositarios nostros, qui Thesaurariam predictam ad nostram requisitionem anticipata infrascripta pecuniarum summa conducere parati sunt. Igitur intentionem nostram hominis omnino exequi volens motu proprio et ex certa nostra scientia ac de apostolice potestatis plenitudine concessionem dicto Francisco de dicta Thexauraria ut prefertur factam, suo ad hoc ut prefertur expresso accedento consensu harum ferie revocantes, prefatum Benvenutum et soci civitatis Perusie et provincie Umbrie predictarum Thesaurarios, ad quinquennium proxime future pontificatus nostri anno septimo incohante cum omnibus et singulis privilegiis indultis, facultatibus, membris, honoribus et oneribus ac emolumentis solitis et consuetis facimus, constituimus et deputamus eisquam Thesauraria prefatam liberam inmunem et desbrigatam a prefato Francisco Bencio, ac omnia et singula eius membra infrascripta vz: lacum Trasimenum seu Perusinium nuncuptum, salariam cum augmento pretii salis nuper per nos impositi, gabellam magnam et vini quinque gabellas comitatus; nec non gabellas quadrupedum, lignorum et palearum, conciarie eminarum, pignorum, damnorum, datorum et Sancti Sabini pensiones apotecarum et decimas compromissorum [fol. 2v] civitatis prefate, focularia eiusdem civitatis alias exigi solita que per vos exigi et per illos qui antea illa persolvi consueverant ad que Cameram apostolicam reintegamus persolvi volumus et mandamus, nec non subsidium civitatis: totum Clusium, Montem Malbum, omnia subsidia provincie comprehensa in concessione facta prefato Francisco Bencio de dicta Thesauraria omnes gabelas et introitus civitats Fulginei, Spoleti, Tuderti et Assisii, augmentum precii salis civitatis Castelli, Montonis, Citerne et castri Plebis. Maleficia penas bannitorum et condennatorum et bonorum confiscationes Perusie et provincie predictarum infra dictum quinquennium occurentes et signanter omnia et singula membra suprascripta pro precio et nomini precii florenorum quinquaginta octo milium octingentorum nonaginta octo solidorum viginti monete perusine camere cum omnibus et singulis privilegiis, facultatibus, indultis, fructibus, redditibus, proventibus, emolumentis ac honoribus et oneribus predictis ac facultate thesarariam prefatam per substitutum exercerdum locamus, concedimus et assignamus per presentes. Ex quibus quidam florenis quinquaginta octo milibus octingentis et nonaginta octo solidis viginti dictos, Benvenutum et socios teneri et obligatos esse volumus ad solvendum annuatim omnia salaria, expenses et provisiones ac officialium in dictam thesauraria participantium assignationes in una cedula manu dilectorum filiorum Guidonis Aschanii Sfortie, Sancte Marie in Cosmedin diaconi [fol. 3r] cardinalis nostri et S.R.E. camerarii, nec non Hieronimi Ricenatis, generalis Thesuararii subscribenda et in libris dicte Camere registranda que constituunt summam florenorum vigintiquinque milium centum viginti solidorum quatraginta residuo vero dictorum florenorum quinquaginta octa milium ottingentum nonaginta octa solidorum viginti pro intero precio prefato ademptis et defalcatis dictis florenis vigintiquinque milibus centum viginti solidis quatraginta facit summam florenorum triginta trium milium septingentorum septuaginta septem solidorum viginti constituentes scuta decem et novem milia de julis decem pro quolibet scuto dicti conductores tenerent ad solvendum illi ultra illis cui ultra quibus per nos aut Cameram nostram apostolicam ordinatum fuerit singulis annis in tribus solitionibus hoc est de quatrimestre in quatrimestre et in cuius licet quatrimestris fine a die adepte pacifice possessionis computantis in civitate Perusie in monetis in dicta civitate currentis et exigentis, ac teneantur et solvere omnes exitus ordinarios Camere prefatarum civitatum Fulginei, Spoleti, Tuderti et Assisii, et si contingat per nos aut Sedem et Cameram apostolicam aliquam gratiam, concessionem et seu reintegrationem officiorum et aliarum rerum et bonorum aut aliarum restaurarum non tamen occasione maleficiorum fieri dicte Camere nostre apostolice et in diminutionem dicti precii seu census cedat [fol. 3v] si autem dicti conductores minus solverint de exitu in dicta cedula notando et exprimendo cedat ad commodum dicte Camere nostre apostolice, declarantes in locatione, concessione et assegnatione hominis non comprehendi confiscationis bonorum rebellium vigore ultime rebellionis per perusinos facte, nec eorum compositiones quas pro nobis et dicta Camera per presentes reservam volumus et que ex eo que ex maleficiis ut supra dictis conductoribus assegnatis ultra summam trium millium ducatorum et de focularibus civitatis ultra summam quinque milium florenorum per dictos conductores exigi contingat, deu tertie partes dicte Camere nostre apostolice spectent et pertineant alia vero tertia parte conductoribus. Et eidem ultra dictam summam scutorum decem et novem milium solvere teneant si vero ex dictis focularibus minus dictorum quinque milium florenorum absque tamen culpa dictorum conductorum aut ministrorum eorundem exactum fuerit cedat danno dicte Camere et illud mius eidem Camere ex precio suprascripto solvere teneantur. Volumus autem dictos conductores teneri ad solvendum prefato Francisco Bencio duas tertias partes florenorum octo milium pro quibus fuit locato lacus pro anno incepto kalendas Maii proximi e preterit et finientis ultima aprilis proxime futuri, de quibus idem Franciscus tenentur reddere computum et idem observandum teneri volumus [fol. 4r] dictorum conductorum successores in dicta Thesauraria dictis conductoribus ultimo anno presentis locationis ut fabrice dicte Arcis subvenire valeamus. Dicti conductores teneantur anticipata solutione non expectantis terminis dictarum solutionum scuta tria milia auri de julis decem pro scuto quolibet in subsidium dicte fabrice exbursati ex pecuniis introituum predictorum in fra terminum unius anni in fine cuiuslibet quatrimestris tertiam partem volumus insuper ac motum scientia et potestatis plenitudine similibus declaramus aliquas compositiones remissiones aut absolutiones per legatos, vicelegatos, gubernatores, locotenentes aut alios officiales in causis maleficiorum et penarum tam Perusie quam provincie predictarum et rerum dicte ultime rebellionis fieri non posse absque dictorum Thesaurariorum aut eorum ministrorum presentia et spetiali consensu in scriptis faciendo et alter facte nullius sint roboris videlicet momenti. Dantes et concedentes eisdem conductoribus plenam et liberam facultatem omnia et singula membra dicte Thesaurerie et gabellas predictas locandi et dislocandi aut per se ipsos retinendi et ministrandi ac officiales lacus deputandi, deputatos et per nos dummodo ex causa onerosa deputati non sint amovendi, decernendi nihils nullas irritas et inanes quascumque locationes [fol. 4v] de dictis membris aut gabellis et rebus supra eis concessis et locatis aut eorum aliqua altra que per ipsos conductores facta etiam si per nos aut Cameram apostolicam fieri contingeret et si (quod absit) inductis civitate et provincia aut aliquo loco dicte provincie bella, pestis aut aliud iustum impedimentum occurerent, Camerarius, presidentes et clerici Camere predicte infra duos menses a die requisitionis perductos conductores in Camera facte indicare habeant danna passa que diminui et retineri debeant ex fictu dicte Thesaurerie et si in fine locationis huiusmodi dicti conductores in aliquo creditores Camere remanerent ex qua vis causa aut prenderent nullo modo possint a dicta Thesauraria et membris predictis amoveri nisi prius liquidato eorum credito in dicta Camera et eis effectualiter et integraliter satisfacto et huiusmodi locationem durare voluimus donec credita liquidata et ipsi cum effectu satisfacti fuerint et teneantur ipsi conductores per duos menses ante finem huiusmodi locationis ad dandum computa in dicta Camera de eo in quo se creditores esse pretenderent et insuper indemnitati dicti Francisci Bencii ut parest succurrere volentes decernimus dictos conductores teneri ad satisfacendum prefato Francisco quicquid dictus Franciscus occasione officii Thesauraria pro annis [fol. 5r] prefatis creditor existit, facta prius in Camera apostolica liquidatione de dicto suo credito omnino satisfacere teneantur et id quod propterea dicti conductores solverint ad comptum dicte Camere ponant, et de precio prefato absque alio mandato retineant et retinere possint et valeant mandantes prefatis camerario, Thesaurario, presidentibus clericis dicte Camere quantas partes in eadem Camera a‹…›ttant, et in libris eiusdem Camere registrari desuperque instrumentum publicum, litteras patentes et alias scripturas tam publicas quam privatas pro ut requisiti fuerint confici et celebrari ac tradi mandent et faciant ac pecunias per dictos conductores presentium vigore retentas in eorum comptis admittant, dictosque tres mille ducatos in subventione dicte fabrice solvendos per ordinarium introitum et ex dicte Camere describi faciant, communitatibus vero universitatibus et aliis particularibus personis tam civitatis Perusie quam aliarum civitatum, terrarum et locorum dicte provincie eisdem conductoribus pareant et obediant, nec non legatis, vice legatis, gubernatoribus, locatenentibus ceterisque officialibus civitatis et provincie predictarum nunc et pro tempore existente, et aliis ad quos quomoltus spectat vel dum quorum et quando pro parte dictorum conductorum requisiti fuerit [fol. 5v] eisdem eorumque ministris faveant et assistant contradictores quoslibet per censuras ecclesiasticas et alias pecuniarias penas de quibus eis videbitur aliaque remedia opportuna auctoritate apostolica apparenter postposita compescendo invocato et si opus fuerit ausilio bracchiis secularis, non obstantibus premissis ac constitutionibus et ordinationibus apostolicis, nec non legibus imperialibus et in locationibus similibus ultra alienationem rerum fiscalium certam exquisitam formam servantes requirentes et decretum irritans continentes quibus illorum omnium tenores presentibus pro sufficiente expressis habentes harum serie spetialiter et expresse derogamus, ceterisque contrariis quibuscunque volumus autem presentium solam signaturam sufficere in iudicio et ex‹…› incontrarium edita non obstante et que antequam Thesaurariam huiusmodi exercere incipiant de illud fideliter exercendo et de reddendo legale computum in Camera se obligent et iurare teneantur. Placet et ita motu proprio concedimus et mandamus A Illudque recipi et admitti at super illo sibi dictisque sociis suis instrumentum iuxta illius formam confici debita cum instantia postulavit quiquidem R.P.D. Thesaurarius et clerici presidentes dictum mandatum seu motum proprium ea qua decuit reverentia receperunt et admiserunt illiusque viso [fol. 6r] et me notario alta voce illud legente percepto tenore mandatis apostolicis, ut parest, morem gerentes et inherentes ac ipsius mandati seu motus proprii tenorem insequentes eorum sponte, certa scientia et spontanea voluntate non vidolo fraude aut aliter circumventi omnique meliori modo quo de iure potuerunt prefati S.D.N. PP et Camere apostolice nomine concessione supra et infrascripte Thesaurarie Perusie et Umbrie et illius membrorum soprascripto domino Francisco Bencio ut in dicto preinserto motu proprio fit manu eiusdem Francisci ad hoc accedente consensu primo et ante omnia revocantes locaverunt, concesserunt et assegnarunt prefato magnifico domino Benvenuto de Oliveriis et sociis, domino Benvenuto presenti et pro se et dictis sociis absentibus suisque et illorum heredibus et successoribus quibuscumque una mecum notario publico infrascripto stipulanti et recipienti ac conducenti dictam Thesaurariam civitatis Perusie et provincie Umbrie liberam, inmunem et disbrigatam a prefato domino Francisco Bencio ac omnia et singula eius membra infrascripta vz. lacum Trasimenum sive Perusinum nuncupatum salariam cum augmento precii salis nuper per S.D.N. PP impositi, gabellam magnam, et vini quinque gabellas comitatus, nec non gabellas quadrupedum, lignorum et palearum, conciarie eminarum, pignorum, dannorum, datorum et Sancti Sabini pensiones apotecarum et decimas compromissorum civitatis prefate [fol. 6v] focularia eiusdem civitatis alias exigi solita nec non subsidium provincie comprehensa in concessione facta prefato domino Francisco Bencio de dicta Tesauraria, omnes gabellas et introitus civitatis Fulginei, Spoleti, Tuderti et Assisii augmenti precii salis civitatis Castelli, Montonis, Citerne et Castri Plebis, maleficia penas bannitorum et condennatorum et bonorum confiscationes Perusie et provincie predictarum. Infra desigantum quinquennium occurrens, ad tempus et pro tempore quinquem annorum proxime futurorum kalende januarii proxime preteriti pontificatus prefati S.D.N. PP anno septimo inhoatorum et ut sequitur finiens cum omnibus et singulis privilegiis indultis facultatibus membris honoribus et oneribus ac emolmentis solitis et consuetis pro precio et nomine precii florenorum quinquaginta octo milium octingentorum nonaginta octo et solidorum viginti monete perusine camere anno quolibet, convenientes prefati R.di D. Camerales ex una et D. Benvenutus dictis respective nominibus ex alia partibus pacto expresso solenni stipulatione hinc inde interveniente firmato quod dicti D. Benvenutus et socii ex dictis florenis quinquaginta octo milibus octingentis nonaginta octo solidis viginti teneantur et obligati sint annuatim solvere omnia salaria, expensas et provisiones ac officialium in dicta Thesauraria participantium assignationes in una cedula manibus R.mi D. Guidonis Ascanii Sfortie Sancti Eustachii Diaconi Cardinalis de Sancta [fol. 7r] Flora S.R.E. Camerarii ac R.di D. Hieronimi Ricenatis de Capite Ferreo S.D.N. PP generalis Thesaurarii subscripta et in Camera apostolica registrata ac inferius de verbo ad verbum inserta que constituunt summam florenorum viginti quinque milium centum et viginti ac solidorum quatraginta similium residuum vero dictorum florenorum quinquaginta octo milium octingentorum nonaginta octo et solidorum viginti pro integro precio prefato quod demptis dictibus florenis viginquinque milibus centum viginti et solidis quatraginta facit summam florenorum triginta trium milium septingentorum septuaginta septem et solidorum viginti constituens scuta decem et novem mille de juliis decem pro quolibet scuto. Prefatus D. Benvenutus dictis nominibus solvere et pagare promisit illi ultra illis cui ultra quibus per prefatum S.D.N. aut Cameram apostolicam ordinatus fuerit singulis igitur in tribus solutionibus hoc est de quatrimestre in quatrimestre et in cuiuslicet quatrimestris fine a die adepte pacifice possessionis computans in civitate Perusie predicta currens et exigens convenientes et prefati quibus sopra nominibus contrahentes pacto expresso mutua stipulatione firmato quod dicti Benvenutus et socii conductores teneant solvere dictos exitus ordinarios Camere prefatarum civitatorum Fulginei, Spoleti, Tuderti et Assisii et si contingat pr prefato S.D.N. PP aut sedem et Cameram apostolicam aliquam gratiam, concessionem seu [fol. 7v] reintegrationem officiorum et aliarum rerum et bonorum aut aliquem restaurum non tantum occasione maleficiorum fieri danno dicte Camere apostolice et in diminutionem dicti precii seu census cedat. Si aut dicti conductores minus solverint de exitu in dicta cedula notante et experimente cedat ad comodum dicte Camere cum declarationibus decretis, pactis, condictionibus, capitulis et clausulis in dicto preinserto mandato seu motu proprio contentis, expressis, specificatis et annotatis, que hic pro denuo specificatis ac repetitis dicte partes contrahentes habere voluerunt ac alie in omnibus et per omnia iuxta dicti mandati seu motus proprii formam, continentiam et tenorem. Que omnia et singula premissa ac supra et infrascripta et on presenti instrumento contenta prefati contrahentes vz: Reverendus Dominus Thesararius et Clerici presidentes ex una et Dominus Benvenutus ex alia partibus quibus supra nominibus tenere, attendere, complere firmiterque et inviolabiter observare in nulloque contrafacere, dicere vel venire aliqua ragone vel causa promiserunt sub expressa hypoteca et obligatione omnium et singulorum prefate Camere spiritualium et temporalium ac ipsius Domini Benvenuti et sociorum respective bonorum mobilium et inmobilium presentium et futurorum quoruncumque reflectioneque et integra restitutione omnium et singulorum dannorum sumptuum interesse et expensarum per ipsas partes aut alteram ipsarum in iudicio vel extra quovismodo patiendorum et substinendorum super quibus quidem damnis sumptibus, interesse et expensis credere et stare voluerunt soli et [fol. 8r] simplici verbo illius ipsarum partium damna sumptus expensa et interesse huiusmodi patientes et substinentis absque testium productione iudicis taxatione vel quavis alia probatione. Pro quibus omnibus et singulis sic habendis, tenendis et observandis prefati R.D. Thesaurarius et clerici presidentes quibus supra nominibus prefate Camere apostolice bona omnia mobilia et inmobilia, spiritualia et temporalia, presentia et futura, iura, res et actiones dicti vero Dominus Benvenutus et quibus supra homnibus se ipsum suosque socios predictos ac suos heredes et successores suaque et dictorum heredum et successorum ac sociorum bona mobilia et inmobilia presentia et futura, iura, res et actiones quecumque iuxta supra inserti mandati seu motus proprii formam et tenorem respective vicissim obligarunt in ampliori forma Camere apostolice cum renunciatio [om]nibus submissionibus, suppositionibus constitutione procuratorum et aliis clausulis et cautelis solitis et consuetis obligarunt et hipotecarunt et sic prefati Reverendus Dominus Thesaurarius et clerici presidentes positis eorum manibus ad pectora more prelatorum dictus vero Dominus Benvenutus factis scripturis sacrosantis ad Sancta Dei evangelia respective iuraverunt rogantes me notarium infrascriptum ut depremissis omnibus publicum confecerem instrumentum acta fuerunt hec Rome in plena Camera apostolica in edibus dicti monasterii de Pace, presentibus ibidem Dominis Alexandro Repario Causidico Senensi Jacobo Paganello, Camere apostolice vice computista et Petro Gomez, S.D.N. PP cursore, [fol. 8v] testibus ad premissa vocatis et rogatis Λ generali F damno σ dictis annis approbo. M.

Tenor vero cedule suprascripte sequitur et est talis vz. esito della Thesauraria di Perugia quale il M.co m. Benvenuto Ulivieri Thesoriero è obligato di pagare ogn'anno durante il tempo della sua Thesauraria e tutto quello pagasse meno cede ad utile della R.da Camera apostolica.

[At fols 8v-10r there is a list, here summarized, where the figures of the second column are expressed in florins *perugini* and the figures of the third column are their equivalent in *scudi di moneta*.]

	florins of Perugia	*scudi di moneta*
Al R.mo legato per provisione	1600	900
Officiali di Roma vz portioni, cavalieri, cubicularii et scudieri	7111.10	4000
Collegio dell'Archivio	355.50	200
R.di Sig.ri Chierici di Camera per li regali di Natale	115.50	65
Detti per la rocca di Cesis	327.10	184
R.di Sig.ri secretarii apostolici per le tasse alienate et stinte	1246.36	701.10
Lettori dello Studio per provisione ordinaria	2666.60	1500
Detti per la provisione straordinaria et salario delli advocati fiscali	553.18	311.17½
Bargiello della provincia	4266.60	2400
Guardia del R.mo legato	1450.60	816
Spese del Thesaurario	711.10	400
Carta, cera et tinta per le cancellerie	60	33.75
Cappellani di certe capelle per offerte	82	46.12
Salario di dua rocche vz. Castiglione e la Fratta	600	337.50
Censo della casa dove abita il Thesaurario	27.70	15.62
Certe elemosine a luoghi pii	158.70	88.31½
Cinque cavallari et quattro mandatari per salario ordinario	397.30	223.50
Bargiello del Laco	300	168.75
Procuratore fiscale	106.60	60
Palii et lance per dua festività	110.60	62.25
Octo balii	106.60	60
Spazzatori della piazza	8	4.50
Soprastante della fonte per reparatione e mantenimento	246.60	138.75
Tre panni bigi si danno a' poveri d'Iddio	48.10	27.06¼
Cera per la purificatione	90	50.62½
Fabrica del dormitorio di Santo Francesco	88.80	50
Spedale della Misericordia	17.70	10
Spese per mandare atorno lettere e messi	300	178.75
Notario della Camera apostolica	68.74	38.71¼
Frati di S. Domenico per reparation del convento	150	84.37½
Monasterio delle Vergini per elemosina	4.40	2.50
Monasterio di Monte Luce per elemosina	31.64	17.83¾
Isola Maggiore per l'esentione	116.88	65.80
Repertorio de' banniti	13.30	7.50
Potestà di Monte Castello	64	36
Frati di S. Francesco observanti per sale	4.40	2.50

La cera solita per li lumi a' luoghi pii ma non a' cittadini	580	326.25
Cinque maestri di scquola	400	225
Cinque trombetti	533.30	300
TOTAL	25120.40	13239.75

G. As. Cardinalis Camerarius
Hier. Thesaurarius

Et ego Michelangelus Thomasinus de Ripatransone clericus firmans dicte Camere apostolice notarius quia premissis rogatus interfui, presens instrumentum mano propria subscripsi et publicavi, signoque meo Thabellionatus consueto munivi requisitus in fidem et testimonium veritatis.

Doc. 7: Balance sheet of Benvenuto Olivieri & Partners, 13 February 1543 (author's elaboration from ASF, Galli Tassi 2278)

ASSETS

APOSTOLIC CHAMBER		
Various contracts [*imposizione delle galere*, tithes, income from communes, loan of sc. 55000]	73170.76	
Increase of the salt tax of the Romagna	32408.92	
Customs	5853.70	
Imposizione dei mezzi frutti levied on the monasteries	4682.93	
Vigesima of the Jews	2276.41	
		118392.72
BENVENUTO OLIVIERI & PARTNERS, DEPOSITARIES		
Current acc.	17368.89	
Acc. *a parte* [social capital]	14634.13	
		32003.02
BENVENUTO OLIVIERI & PARTNERS, TREASURERS OF PERUGIA		
Current acc. [year 1542]	3666.57	
Current acc. [year 1543]	138.64	
		3805.21
COMPANIES IN ROME		
Covoni Antonio & Partners		
our acc. *a parte*	8292.70	
our acc. *de' tempi*	3784.90	
Giustiniani Luca & Partners		
acc. *de' tempi* for his share of the alum sold to Provence	4527.17	
acc. *a parte* for alum	897.58	
their current acc.	411.37	
acc. *a parte* for *imposizione delle galere* and tithes of the Romagna	98.70	
Ubaldini Girolamo & Partners, our acc. *de' tempi*	2926.82	
Cavalcanti Tommaso and Giraldi Giovanni & Partners		
their current acc.	2391.59	
our acc. *de' tempi*	784.36	
farmers of the Mint of Rome, current acc.	249.00	
Della Casa heir of Pandolfo & Partners for the customs of Rome	2374.74	
Carducci Filippo & Partners, depositaries of the *gabella dello Studio*	2317.51	
Montauto Salvestro & Partners, our acc. *de' tempi*	1951.17	
Signorini Vanni and Girolamo & Partners	1739.95	
Ubellotti Giovan Battista & Partners		
for dispatches	732.67	

for a protest returned from Lyons	631.00	
Pintelli Lorenzo & Partners, our acc. *a parte de' tempi*	248.60	
Bartoli Leonardo and Alessandro & Partners	201.60	
Del Benino Niccolò & Partners, their current acc.	32.29	
		34593.72
COMPANIES IN ITALY (OUTSIDE ROME)		
Cattani heir of Carlo & Partners of Bologna		
their current acc.	1940.55	
our acc. *a parte* for the tithes	724.62	
our acc. *a parte* G for the *imposizione delle galere*	197.40	
our acc. *a parte* S [increase of the salt tax of the Romagna]	113.83	
Busini Jacopantonio & Partners of Florence, their acc.	1345.13	
Capponi Piero and Luigi & Partners of Florence		
our current acc.	53.04	
their current acc.	10.26	
Strozzi Lorenzo and Alessandro & Partners of Venice		
our current acc.	766.53	
our old current acc.	131.02	
Pallavicini Damiano & Partners of Genoa, our acc. *de' tempi*	591.50	
Guicciardini Lorenzo & Partners of Ferrara, their current acc.	337.51	
Giacomini Jacopo & Partners of Ancona, our acc.	6.11	
		6217.50
COMPANIES ABROAD		
Bini Giovan Francesco & Partners of Lyons		
our current acc. for the past All Saints' fair	3300.00	
our acc. *de' tempi a parte* L for alum sold to Provence [Luca Giustiniani]	2022.35	
their acc. *de' tempi*	879.95	
our acc. *a parte* for alum sold to Rouen, Dieppe and La Rochelle	505.85	
Rinieri Andrea & Partners of Lyons, our acc. *a parte*	1924.08	
Buonvisi Antonio and Ludovico & Partners of Lyons		
our acc. for the next Easter fair [1542]	1729.00	
our acc. *a parte* D for the August fair [1542]	312.94	
Sertini Tommaso & Partners of Lyons		
our acc. *a parte* D for the August fair [1542]	481.25	
our current acc. for the next Epiphany fair [1543]	28.25	
our acc. for the next All Saints' fair [1542]	5.53	
Panciatichi Bartolomeo & Partners of Lyons		
our acc. *a parte* D for the August fair [1542]	412.40	
our acc. for the next All Saints' fair [1542]	51.09	
Panciatichi Simone & Partners of Lyons, our acc. *a parte* D for the August fair [1542]	382.93	
Salviati Averardo and Piero & Partners of Lyons, our acc. for the August fair [1542]	67.17	

Del Bene Riccardo & Partners of Paris, our acc.	33.43	
Pallavicini Damiano and Doria Paolo & Partners of Besançon, our acc. for the Easter fair [1542]	7.00	
Castro heir of Girolamo, Perez di Malvenda Francesco, Diego, Alfonso & Partners of Burgos, our acc. *a parte de' tempi*	1024.42	
Strozzi Rinaldo and Giovan Battista & Partners of Valladolid, our acc. *a parte* G	400.00	
Briz Girolamo & Partners of Valladolid, through the Strozzi of Valladolid	367.58	
		13935.22
CLERGY		
Poggio rev. m. Giovanni nuncio to Spain, acc. *a parte* through Luigi de Torres, Giovanni da Montepulciano, Niccolò Casulano and two others	6245.38	
Trivulzio rev. m. Agostino, cardinal		
new acc.	3449.60	
acc. *a parte* through the heir of Filippo Strozzi	2926.85	
Pucci rev. m. Antonio, cardinal Santi Quattro		
his current acc.	1451.89	
through Alessandro Deti & Partners	39.10	
Dandino rev. m. Girolamo, apostolic scriptor and protonotary	913.44	
Capodiferro Recanati rev. Girolamo, apostolic nuncio to France, through G.F. Bini & Partners of Lyons	759.28	
Cervino rev. m. Marcello, cardinal S. Croce	464.64	
Spinola, heir of the late rev.mo Antonio, cardinal and chamberlain		
new acc.	391.79	
[old acc.]	250.10	
Pucci rev. m. Roberto, cardinal	213.96	
Farnese rev. m. Alessandro, cardinal	138.06	
Cornaro rev. m. Andrea, bishop of Brescia and clerk of the Chamber	130.06	
Carducci rev. Atto, abbot of S. Presedia, and his successors	121.95	
Ardinghelli rev. m. Niccolò, bishop of Fossombrone and datary	97.56	
de' Cavalieri rev. m. Pier Vincenzo, through Sebastiano Gualterio	97.55	
		17691.21
OTHER CORRESPONDENTS, HOLDERS OF CURRENT ACCOUNTS AND MISCELLANEOUS CREDITS		
Gherardini Raffaello of Milan	5855.91	
Salinari	5078.58	
Alum on our account	4964.29	
Malvenda Andrea of Rouen, our acc. *de' tempi*	4450.13	
Businі Benedetto, his acc. *a parte* R.B. [Roberto Strozzi]	3684.23	
Farmers of the *Salara* of Rome, current acc.	3330.97	

Signorini Signorino, for letters paid together with the Strozzi of Valladolid	2731.19	
Expenses for the household	2162.65	
Busini Benedetto at the papal court, when he went to Perugia	2059.10	
Venturi heir of Girolamo and Fabio	1727.40	
Ridolfi Lorenzo di Piero	1227.12	
Strozzi heir of the late mag. m. Filippo	1169.04	
Antonio di Leonardo from Bergamo	1150.38	
Household furnishings	1058.61	
Zambeccari Jacopo, his current acc.	1055.61	
Capponi Neri of Venice, his acc.	720.64	
Tofia Giovanni, deputy of the notary of the chancery	635.38	
Stabbia/Anguillara ill. s.or Flaminio, current acc.	606.31	
College of the *Porzione*	580.97	
Jewels on our account	531.71	
Guiducci Simone di Mariotto, his current acc.	462.93	
Buontempi Federigo of Perugia	439.92	
Torres Luigi de', apostolic secretary	433.50	
Paganelli Jacopo	431.82	
Vidal Raimondo of Avignon, his acc. *de' tempi a parte*	420.47	
Zacherella Giulio from Norcia	417.54	
Tasca Noferi, through ill. s.re Flaminio d'Anguillara	413.67	
San Giovanni galleon, one half of which belongs to us	390.25	
Olivieri Benvenuto our senior partner (*maggiore*), his acc. *a parte* M	384.15	
Congregazione and monks of Vallombrosa	336.58	
Gentili Alessandro and brothers in Rome	317.07	
Della Palla Mariotto	299.65	
College of cubiculars and scutifers	261.72	
Corbinelli Bernardo, his current acc.	235.65	
Dei Guglielmo, our employee	233.74	
Tommasini Luca, formerly commissioner for the tithes of Urbino	227.69	
Dinello Antonello of Naples	212.70	
Tommasini Michelangelo, notary of the Chamber, through m. Evangelista de' Cesis	185.75	
College of the knights of St Peter	172.19	
Del Conte Jacopo, painter	107.32	
Brokerage fees	101.89	
Buonagurio Bernardino, collector of the College of the Archive	100.83	
Epifanio Piero, our petitioner	89.83	
Porcella Francesco, treasurer of Norcia	88.76	
Gavotto Lorenzo of Savona, his current acc.	72.20	
Serafino Galeazzo	66.30	
Farnese Orazio ill. s.or	61.77	
De Anguillara Maddalena Strozza	48.80	
Capodiffero Recanati Girolamo, datary	44.22	

Ridolfi Giovan Francesco	43.42	
Bettini Bartolomeo	39.03	
Expenses for letters	34.96	
Ubaldini Girolamo, his personal acc.	27.27	
Giannino, master furrier	24.40	
College of the Archive	22.45	
Consulate of 'our nation'	21.10	
Crescentii heir of Girolamo, Bolognese	20.02	
Casulano Niccolò	19.87	
Mozzi Luigi de' at the imperial court	19.67	
Coscolla Piero of Naples, his acc.	16.03	
Monte della Fede, our acc. in the name of B. Busini	14.00	
Soap belonging to the Olivieri of Naples	13.75	
Mellini Antonio	12.68	
Benci Francesco, his personal acc.	11.72	
Cechi Domenico, tailor in Venice	11.62	
Cai Bastiano	9.77	
Del Riccio Francesco di Giulio, our employee	5.87	
Porto Paolo	4.43	
		52214.16
INTEREST, PREMIUMS AND ADVANCES ON ACCOUNTS OF THIRD PARTIES		
Premiums on coins and gold	4239.74	
Commissions on the collection of the increase of the salt tax of the Romagna	2048.86	
Interest on various offices	534.03	
Expenses relative to the 40000-*scudi* loan	363.08	
Interest on offices belonging to Jacopo Zambeccari	304.84	
Expenses relative to the collection of the increase of the salt tax of the Romagna	116.08	
Expenses relative to the lawsuit against Girolamo Spannocchi	12.39	
		7619.02
CASH		
Cashbox in the hands of Simone Guiducci	24781.67	
Cashbox in the hands of Guglielmo Dei	9055.78	
		33837.45
LOSSES		
Losses incurred by the All Saints' fair 1541	4020.87	
		4020.87
TOTAL		**324330.10**
Discrepancy		2976.50

LIABILITIES

APOSTOLIC CHAMBER		
Imposizione delle galere	727.82	
Income from communes	156.10	
		883.92
BENVENUTO OLIVIERI & PARTNERS, DEPOSITARIES		
New current acc.	27121.73	
		27121.73
COMPANIES IN ROME		
Covoni Antonio & Partners		
our current acc. for money drawn and delivered	14306.65	
their acc. *de' tempi* [*imposizione mezzi frutti* and *galere*]	4878.05	
current acc.	4084.67	
Giustiniani Luca and Sauli Cristoforo & Partners of Rome, their acc. *de' tempi*	12195.13	
Cavalcanti Tommaso and Giraldi Giovanni & Partners		
their acc. *de' tempi* [customs]	6341.47	
their acc. *de' tempi* [increase of the salt tax of the Romagna]	1858.53	
Ubaldini Girolamo & Partners		
their acc. *de' tempi* [*imposizione delle galere*, income from communes and tithes of Patrimonio]	5853.67	
their current acc.	4148.82	
Grimaldi Girolamo & Partners, farmers of the Tolfa alum mines	3363.25	
Del Bene Alessandro and Giovan Battista & Partners of Rome, their acc. *de' tempi* [customs]	3170.75	
Giustiniani Luca & Partners		
their acc. *de' tempi* [customs and *vigesima* of the Jews]	2601.64	
their acc. *de' tempi a parte* [alum of Provence]	2022.35	
for alum	1926.51	
acc. *a parte* belonging to the heir of Girolamo and Fabio Venturi	1862.40	
acc. *a parte* for the income from communes of the Romagna	414.63	
Della Casa heir of Pandolfo & Partners of Rome, their acc. *de' tempi* for the 12.000 *scudi* repaid via the increase of the salt tax of the Romagna	1951.23	
Carducci Filippo di Bartolomeo & Partners, their current acc.	552.41	
		71532.16
COMPANIES IN ITALY (OUTSIDE ROME)		
Cattani heir of Carlo & Partners of Bologna		
their acc. *de' tempi* for the 20.000-*scudi* loan repaid via the *imposizione delle galere*	4292.66	
our new current acc.	2515.27	
Capponi Piero and Luigi & Partners of Florence, our current acc.	3062.42	
Busini Jacopantonio & Partners of Florence, their acc. *a parte* I	5.64	

Capponi Giuliano and Piero & Partners of Pisa, their current acc.	641.31	
Strozzi Lorenzo and Alessandro & Partners of Venice		
our current acc.	611.81	
their current acc.	39.78	
Machiavelli heir of Baldassarre & Partners of Ferrara, their current acc.	50.83	
		11219.72
COMPANIES ABROAD		
Bini Giovan Francesco & Partners of Lyons		
our acc. for the next Epiphany fair [1543]	6489.31	
their acc. *de' tempi* for money received from the sale of alum to Rouen, Brittany and La Rochelle	3922.65	
their new current acc.	1176.76	
our acc. *de' tempi* for alum sold to Provence	385.42	
our acc. *a parte* for alum	0.35	
our acc. *a parte* under the name of the Cattani of Bologna	0.25	
Panciatichi Bartolomeo & Partners of Lyons		
our current acc. for the next Epiphany fair [1543]	1087.00	
their current acc.	3.06	
Panciatichi Simone & Partners of Lyons		
our current acc. for the current August fair [1542]	120.24	
their current acc.	5.03	
Rinieri Andrea & Partners of Lyons		
our acc. for the next Epiphany fair [1543]	1134.00	
our acc. for the next All Saints' fair [1542]	19.76	
Sertini Tommaso & Partners of Lyons		
our acc. *a parte* R.B. for the current August fair [1542]	481.25	
our current acc. for the current Easter fair [1542]	12.50	
their acc. *a parte* R	2.10	
Buonvisi Antonio and Ludovico & Partners of Lyons, our acc. for the next Epiphany fair [1543]	193.17	
Pallavicini Damiano and Doria Paolo & Partners of Besançon, our current acc. for the next All Saints' fair [1542]	3410.81	
Pinelli Adorni Giovan Battista and Vincenzo, de' Franchi Francesco & Partners of Besançon, our acc. for the next Epiphany fair [1542]	1593.75	
Affaitati Giovan Carlo & Partners of Antwerp, our current acc.	6219.37	
Guicciardini Giovan Battista and Lorenzo & Partners of Antwerp		
our current acc.	264.45	
their current acc.	24.67	
Castro heir of Girolamo, Malvenda Francesco, Luigi, Diego, Alfonso & Partners of Burgos, our acc. *de' tempi* [alum of Rouen, Brittany, La Rochelle]	5689.49	
Strozzi Rinaldo and Giovan Battista & Partners of Valladolid		
our acc. for the next October fair [1542]	5378.47	
our current acc. for the next fair at Villalòn	5123.07	

their new current acc.	3621.29	
our acc. for the next fair at Rioseco	9.13	
Lotti Antonio and Francesco & Partners at the imperial court, through the Strozzi of Valladolid	441.27	
Capponi Piero and Luigi and Neretti Mariotto & Partners of London, their acc. *a parte* G.M.	198.59	
		47007.21
CLERGY		
Poggio rev. m. Giovanni, general treasurer and nuncio to Spain	5074.94	
Pucci heir rev. m. Antonio, cardinal Santi Quattro		
current acc.	705.33	
acc. *a parte*	30.90	
Salviati rev. Giovanni, cardinal	603.50	
Gonzaga rev. m. Giulio, clerk of the Chamber and earl of Novellara	581.34	
Faverello rev. m. Tommaso, cubicular and scutifer	302.15	
Cornaro rev. Francesco, cardinal	225.89	
Mignanelli Fabio, bishop of Lucera	163.99	
De Santes Benedetto, bishop of Alessandria.	33.66	
Cornelio rev. mons. Francesco, cardinal	17.63	
Coria, bishop of, through the Strozzi of Valladolid	1.05	
		7740.38
OTHER CORRESPONDENTS, HOLDERS OF CURRENT ACCOUNTS AND MISCELLANEOUS DEBTS		
Machiavelli Bernardo, commissioner for the increase of the salt tax of the Romagna	27768.17	
Capponi Neri of Venice, his acc.	24421.36	
College of the *Monte della Fede*, its Depositary	18802.70	
Olivieri Benvenuto, our senior partner (*maggiore*), his personal current acc.	6922.45	
Gaddi Luigi	3346.55	
Bartoli Francesco, broker of the exchanges	3235.63	
Fernandes Neto Diego, Portuguese	2759.59	
Mattei Ciriaco, Roman, his acc. *de' tempi*	2350.35	
Machiavelli Bernardo, commissioner of the increase of the salt tax of the Romagna, acc. *a parte* for his commission	2094.33	
Machiavelli Bernardo, commissioner of the *imposizione delle galere*	1932.05	
Pallavicini Tobia, his acc. *de' tempi*	1858.53	
Vigesima of the Jews of the Romagna and Bologna	1611.73	
Ridolfi Lorenzo, our acc. *a parte* [Paolo Riccardi]	1311.71	
Tithes of the Romagna	1278.08	
Busini Benedetto, acc. *a parte* R.B. for his acc. *de' tempi* for the Treasury of Parma and Piacenza	1097.54	

Bonsi Giovan Battista vice-treasurer of Parma and Piacenza, acc. *a parte*	1068.87	
Fregapane Mario, Roman	975.63	
Offices of knights of St Paul in pledge	975.63	
Tithes of Perugia	931.47	
Zambeccari Jacopo, his acc. *di compagnia*	844.87	
Starnocchio Ippolita and Marzia, daughters of master Leonardo	780.50	
Mattei Ciriaco, Roman	751.23	
Farnese s.or Rinuccio	703.38	
Pallavicini Tobia, for the tithes on the Jews [sic]	620.87	
Ugolini Antonio, his commission	585.37	
Olivieri Benvenuto, our senior partner (*maggiore*)	576.28	
Deti Ludovico, cashier of the custom of Terra	505.53	
Scarlattini Antonio from Perugia	488.33	
Bonsi Giovan Battista, commissioner of the tithes of Parma and Piacenza	487.81	
Busini Benedetto, his current acc.	394.27	
Randoli Alberto, for the *Salara* of Perugia	337.04	
Galletti rev. m. Giovan Battista, formerly treasurer the Romagna	315.57	
Mellini Antonio at the French court, his acc. *de' tempi*	315.50	
Greco Giorgio, *trombone di Castello*	292.95	
Alum on our account	285.35	
Tithes of Campagna	274.42	
Olivieri Benvenuto, for the mills of Ravenna	273.20	
Strozzi Giovanni di Zaccaria, our employee at the Depositary	261.62	
Bettini Giovan Battista, his acc. *de' tempi*	243.91	
College of the presidents	191.49	
College of the apostolic secretaries	175.10	
Machiavelli Guido, commissioner of the tithes of Bologna	168.53	
Vidal Raimondo of Avignon, his current acc.	164.33	
Spinelli Niccolò	163.39	
Bonfio Achille (formerly commissioner of the income from communes and *guastatori* of Patrimonio)	133.03	
Servants of the household	119.67	
Cortesi Jacopo rev. m., for interest on a knight of St Peter	94.90	
College of the clerks of the Chamber	90.92	
Starnocchio Leonardo, tailor in Rome	86.50	
Dispatches	84.70	
Panteo Giovan Antonio of Verona, his current acc.	48.78	
Frescobaldi Giovan Battista of Toulouse, his current acc.	39.04	
Machiavelli Bernardo	29.28	
Tommasini Luca, commissioner of the tithes of the 'Stato nuovo'	24.83	
Alicorno Traiano	19.30	
Tithes of Patrimonio	16.97	
da Castiglione Giovan Battista, through Alamanno Alamanni & Partners	9.78	

Machiavelli Guido, commissioner of the tithes of Bologna	8.87	
Farnese Ottavio ill. s.or, his current acc.	6.87	
Isar Arrigo heir of Gabriello of Zaragoza, through the Buonvisi of Lyons	6.37	
Vidal Raimondo of Avignon, his current acc.	5.24	
di Santo Stefano Agostino of Zaragoza, through Antonio and Ludovico Buonvisi of Lyons	3.48	
Tantucci Francesco of Siena, his current acc.	3.17	
Mellini Antonio, through Simone Panciatichi & Partners of Lyons	2.27	
Nuti Francesco of Naples, his acc.	1.80	
Simoni Niccolò of Paris, through Giovan Francesco Bini & Partners of Lyons	0.88	
Adimari Corso of Florence, through Michele and Giovanni Olivieri & Partners of Florence	0.72	
Mancini Andrea, postmaster of Lyons	0.18	
		115780.76
OTHER OLIVIERI COMPANIES IN ITALY		
Olivieri Michele and Alessandro & Partners of Naples		
our current acc.	1173.40	
their current acc.	390.89	
acc. *a parte* O [Ottavio Farnese]	247.75	
their current acc.	56.92	
our acc. *a parte* D.F.	30.96	
Olivieri Michele and Giovanni & Partners of Florence		
our current acc.	1103.94	
their current acc.	47.86	
Olivieri Paolo and Barbadori Giandonato & Partners of L'Aquila, their current acc.	6.33	
		3058.05
REGISTER OF CHARGES AND FEES TO BE PAID		
Our commissions	687.27	
Interests on 12 offices of knight of St Paul relative to the increase of the salt tax of the Romagna	475.82	
Interests on *Monte* bonds due to various individuals	213.24	
Expenses for alum	30.19	
Interest on an office of portioneer belonging to us and to the Cavalcanti-Giraldi	17.40	
		1423.92
LIBRO AZZURRO A PRIMO		
Olivieri Benvenuto & Partners, our *Libro azzurro A 1°*, current acc.	6084.71	
Balance ('*Per conto di più debitori et creditori*') of *Libro azzurro A 1°*	5490.76	
		11575.47

PRIOR COMPANIES		
Strozzi Giulio and Lorenzo & Partners *della ragione del libro verde B*	4615.21	
Strozzi Filippo & Partners *del libro bianco R 3°*, their current acc.	1785.88	
		6401.09
SOCIAL CAPITAL		
Olivieri Benvenuto our senior partner (*maggiore*), his acc. *a parte*	17000.00	
Busini Benedetto di Jacopantonio, his acc. *a parte*	2000.00	
Guiducci Simone di Mariotto, his acc. *a parte*	1000.00	
		20000.00
VARIOUS PROFITS		
Profits and losses on our account	2615.35	
Profits on our account, acc. *a parte* for the increase of the [salt] tax of the Romagna	762.53	
Profits, acc. *a parte* for the Treasury of Parma and Piacenza	97.56	
Profits, acc. *a parte* for the tithes of Naples	86.75	
		3562.19
TOTAL		**327306.58**

Doc. 8: Profit and loss account of Benvenuto Olivieri & Partners, 1542-44

(ASF, Galli Tassi 2278, fols 11, 311, 362)
This is the profit and loss account of the Olivieri company, taken from the ledger (*Debitori e creditori*), 2 January 1542-31 January 1544 (the figures are in gold cameral ducats).

dare **side**

[fol. 11] yhs M.D.xlj

Avanzi et disavanzi di nostro chonto deon dare addì ij di gennaio grossi dieci dati alla Compagnia di Hiesù, portò m. Pietro Cadosio per limosina. Cassa havere in questo a carte 8 -.10. -

E addì iij di gennaio scudi tre d'oro in oro pagati a Giovanni delle Machie come disse il nostro Benedetto, che sono per uno errore che si fecie più fa in certi danari che si pagano al signore Giovan Jacopo. Cassa in questo a 8 2.19. -

E addì 7 detto scudi dicianove s. iiij pagati a Petrone portatore per rubbia di grano et portatura d'esso dato per noi a x reghole come per la nota in filza. Cassa in questo a 8 18.15. -

E addì detto scudi cento d'oro in oro pagati a Salvestro da Montauto e co., posto Zanobi da Montauto contanti. Et sono per pigione della chasa et bancho che abbiamo dalli Strozzi per sei mesi. Cassa a 8 97.11. 3

E addì 7 di febraro scudi ventinove s. iij di juli x per scudo pagati a Giovanni Strozzi capssiere del dipoxitario per la metà di scudi 58.6 che dette per le mancie solite al capodanno proximo paxato. Cassa in questo a 54 28. 9. -

E addì xj detto s. 5 dati per limosina come disse il nostro maggiore. Cassa a 76 -. 5. -

E addì 3 di marzo scudi quatro d'oro pagati a uno amicho per scudi 1600 hauto da lui a ¼ per cento a contare per suo conto a 83 3.18. 6

E addì 29 d'aprile scudi dua d'oro pagati a maestro Jacopo per marzo et aprile presente. Cassa in questo a 141 1.19. 6

E addì 6 di maggio scudi venti di moneta fansi buoni alli Ulivieri di Firenze per noi per tanti pagati scudi 12 a Michele Ulivieri et scudi 8 a Jacopo Antonio Busini per dare limosine. Havere in questo a 92 19.10. 6

E addì detto scudi venticinque s. iij d'oro inn oro fannosi buoni a detti per tanti che si perde in uno conto a parte o per noi. Havere in questo a 92 24.11. -
E addì 22 di maggio scudi sei pagati a Giovanni Pandolphini proquratore del consolato per elemosine a frati della Minerva per fare capitolo, pagato contanti. Cassa in questo a 144 5.17. 6

E addì 9 di giugnio scudi quatro d'oro pagati al consolato di nostra natione per la festa di Santo Giovanni proximo, a 147 3.18. 6

E addì 15 detto ducati dugentocinquantauno s. iiij d. j d'oro di camera pagati a Francesco Bartoli per li emolumenti della c[edo]la di ducati 3300 che così siamo stati d'achordo. Cassa in questo a 156 251.14. 6

E addì 28 detto scudi dieci d'oro inn oro dati per Dio, come disse il nostro maggiore, al Monasterio delle Vergine. Pagato il signore Luigi de Torres contanti. Cassa a 161 9.15. 6

E addì 30 detto scudi dua d'oro pagati a maestro Jacopo Mini per maggio et giugnio s[econ]do il solito. Cassa a 161 1.19. 3

E addì 13 di luglio scudi cento d'oro inn oro pagati alle rede di m. Phylippo Strozzi et per lor a Salvestro da Montauto e co., pagato Zanobi lor cassiere et sono per la pigione cominciata a Santo Giovanni paxato della casa di bancho, a 178 97.11. 3

E addì 2 d'aghosto s. xij pagati per la festa di Santa Maria mezzo aghosto. Cassa a 183 -.12. -

E addì xj detto s. x pagati al caporione di Ponte per la candela d'aghosto. Cassa a 183 -.10. -

E addì 28 di luglio scudi dieci pagati al signore Luigi de Torres per conto dei poveri. Cassa in questo a 183 9.15. 6

E addì 21 d'aghosto s. iiij dati a dua frati per Dio. Cassa a 190 -. 4. -

E addì 5 di settembre scudi dua d'oro pagati a maestro Jacopo Mini per la sua solita provisione per luglio et aghosto, a 216 1.19. 3

E addì 12 detto ducati dicianove s. xiiij d'oro di camera fannosi buoni a Giovanni Martino de' Blevi per utile della sua metà di ducati 500 del cambio, per sua prima, fatto a comune et rimesso per sua lettera fino adì primo di marzo. Havere al quaderno di cassa a c. 216 19.14. -

E addì detto ducati viij.xiij.ij d'oro di camera fannosi buoni alli Ulivieri di Napoli per nostro conto a parte G attenente a Girolamo Ubaldini e co. et sono per li utili di danari che dovevono rimettere più più per lor che non facemo. Havere in questo a 174 8.13. 2

E addì 30 d'ottobre scudi dua d'oro pagati a maestro Jacopo Mini per la sua provisione di settembre et ottobre. Cassa in questo a 247 1.19. -

E addì 6 di novembre scudi dua d'oro pagati a m. Alexandro Deti per dare alla Compagnia del Corpus Domine per limosina, a 247 1.19. 6

E addì 15 detto scudi quatro d'oro inn oro pagati per limosina al Monasterio di Santa Caterina delle Zitele, pagato Giovanni de Cabreri, a 252 3.18. 3

E addì 18 detto ducati xv.xviiij d'oro di camera si perdano al conto de' Salviati d'Anversa per nostro conto a 75 15.19. -

E addì 23 di dicembre scudi sette s. v.viij d'oro inn oro per scudi 8 di moneta pagati al maestro della posta di Napoli per havere fatto spacciare una staffetta a Napoli. Cassa in questo a 264 7. 2. 2

E addì 30 detto scudi dua d'oro pagati a maestro Jacopo Mini per la sua pagha di novembre et dicembre paxato. Cassa in questo a 267 1.19. -

E addì 2 di giennaio s. xviij d'oro di camera pagati a Vincenzo Cozzone per havere cavalcato la mula. Cassa in questo a 267 -.18. -

E addì detto ducati xLj.xij.ij d'oro di camera fansi buoni al signore Giovanni Baptista Savello per cambi di danari tenuti di suo, a 87 41.12. 2

E addì 19 detto juli xiiij pagati a Domenico Prochaccio per porto di scudi 1400 da Firenze a qui, a 275 1. 5. 6

Et in dì 13 detto ducati cxxvj.xviij.ij di camera fannosi buoni a Neri Capponi di Vinetia a tre per cento di ducati 4292.11.8 che habbiamo tenuto di suo a Lione; habbiamo a restituire a 20 di questo. Havere in questo 234 126.18. 2

E addì 27 di giannaio s. 10 pagati al Riccio Prochaccio per porto di scudi 500 da Firenze a qui, c. 298 -.10. -

E addì 10 di febraro juli 24 pagati a Domenico Prochaccio per porto di scudi 2400 da Firenze, c. 300 2. 2. 8

E addì 17 detto scudi uno d'oro inn oro dati per Dio di comune del nostro maggiore a certi frati, c. 310 -.19. 6

E devon dare addì 17 di marzo scudi trecentoquattordici s. v di moneta fannosi buoni al signore Luigi de Torres: et sono scudi 222 per li frutti di scudi 6000 di credito di Monte per 4 paghe finite a l'ultimo di febraro 1542 a nativitate che si comperò il secretariato et ducati 92 s. 5 per li frutti di ducati 1500 per 5 paghe finite a l'ultimo di dicembre proximo paxato. Valgono d'oro inn oro scudi 285.14. Havere a 293 278.15. -

Et in dì primo di marzo scudi dua d'oro inn oro pagati a maestro Jacopo per giennaio et febraro. Cassa in questo 315 1.19. -

E addì 17 detto ducati v.xvij.viiij d'oro di camera che tanti perde uno conto di Lorenzo Antinori e co. di Milano per noi. In questo 28 5.17. 6

E addì xvij di marzo ducati dugentoseptantacinque s. x di camera fannosi buoni Antonio Covoni e co. per quello hanno patito per lo sborso de' sali facto avanti il tempo et altri conti simili di danari prestatoci d'acordo sino addì ij del presente. Posto havere in questo a carta 274 275.10. -

E addì xvij di marzo scudi novanta d'oro in oro pagati a uno amico B per storno d'uno cambio a libro vecchio, a 349 87.16. -

E addì 24 detto scudo uno di moneta donato per Dio a Bernardino luchese per maritare sua figliola, c. 349 -.19. 6

Et per resto di questo conto tirato avanti. In questo 310 [=311] 17299.14.10

[fol. 311] yhs M.D.xliij

Avanzi di fronte deono dare addì iiij d'aprile scudi decy s. xviij.iij d'oro in oro per scudi 12 di juli pagati a Francesco Lisca per li cubicularii et scudi 22 per el mese di novembre paxato per la depositeria, a 350 10.13. 3

E addì detto ducati dua di camera nuovi pagati a Bartolomeo Capponi per la scriptura de' libri della depositeria, a carte 350 2. 2. 8

E addì iiij d'aprile scudi cento d'oro in oro pagati a rede di Philippo Strozzi e co. et per lor a Salvestro Montauto e compagni per la pigione di casa del semestre che finirà per tutto gugno proximo al 64, a c. 350 97.11. 3

E addì v d'aprile ducati cinquecento otto s. xv d'oro di camera vechi fannosi buoni a Neri Capponi di Vinetia per li cambi di ducati 24421.7.2 tenuti di suo la fiera d'apparitione d'acordo. Avere 283 508.15. -

E addì detto scudi ventiquattro d'oro in oro fannosi buoni a Cavalcanti e Giraldi per li cambii di scudi 1821 sborsatoci avanti che li risquotessino da Luca Iustiniani e co. Havere a 94 23. 6. 9

E addì 10 detto scudi dodici di juli x per scudo pagati a Mattio maestro delle poste di Firenze per porto delle lettere del Procaccio per tutto uno anno. Portò Michelagnolo suo garzone contanti, a 350 10.13. 2

E addì detto scudi cinquantauno s. viij d'oro inn oro sono per mancie date a più persone per le feste di Natale come per la lista copiata al memoriale a 14. Cassa in questo a 350 50. 3. -

E addì xj d'aprile ducati venti s. xiij d'oro di camera vechi pagati a Giovanni Martino de' Blevis per la metà delli utili di fiorini 640 d'Aragonia rimessi a metà in Spagna in fiera d'ottobre. Pagato contanti cassa in questo a 350 20.13. -

E addì 12 detto ducati dugentoventisette s. vij.viij d'oro di camara si perdono al conto delli Affetati. Per noi in questo a 224 227. 7. 8

E addì 17 detto ducati LXXXj.iiij.v si perdono al conto de' Capponi di Firenze. Per noi in questo a 322 81. 4. 5

E addì detto ducati LXX.v.viiij si perdono al conto delli Strozzi di Vinetia. Per noy in questo a 139 70. 5. 9

E addì detto ducati cxxxj.-.iiij si perdono al conto delli Strozzi di Vinetia. Per noi in questo a 253 131. -. 4

E addì detto scudi milletrentaquatro s. iiij.iiij di moneta fannosi buoni a' Doghanieri della Salara di Roma et sono per rincontro d'altanti fattoci buoni a buon conto delli utili si speravano in detta salara per la nostra terza parte, che per havere di poi hauto a pagare alla Santità D.N.S. scudi X^{M} non vi sono stati. Posto detti dohanieri havere in questo a 322 1009. -. -

E addì 23 detto scudi dieci d'oro inn oro pagati a madonna Isabella per valuta di uno roccetto lavorato fatto venire da Firenze per donare al Rev.mo Triultio Thexoriere generale. Cassa in questo a 353 9.15. 6

E addì 12 di maggio juli xij si persono in su scudi 12 di moneta mandata il Machiavello a 353 -.19.10

E addì detto juli 5 pagati per rogo d'uno contratto di scudi 600 di Monte stato resignato a m. Benvenuto, a c. 353 -. 9. -

E addì detto scudi nove s. xv d'oro inn oro fannosi buoni alli Ulivieri di Napoli per noi per costo d'una staphetta spacciataci con la quietanza delli scudi XXV^{M} et per costo della quietanza. Havere a 256 9.10. 3

E addì detto ducati Dcvij.x.xj d'oro di camera si perdono al conto delli Ulivieri di Napoli per noi. In questo a 256 598. -. 8

E addì detto ducati vij.-.j simili si perdono al conto de' Palavisino et Dori di Bisanzone. In questo a 123 7. -. 1

E addì 28 detto scudi venticinque d'oro inn oro fannosi buoni a Simon Guiducci per tanti n'eron debitori al quaderno di cassa che serviron quando andò a Napoli. Inposte per conto di XXV^{M} scudi, a 356 24. 8. -

E addì detto ducati LXXij.x.vj d'oro di camera si perdono al conto de' Salviati di Lione per noi in agosto paxato. In questo a 188 72.10. 6

E addì 5 di luglio ducati -.j.v si mettono a conto de' Covoni per pareggiarlo. In questo a 339 -. 1. 5

E addì sino xxvj di febraio scudi quaranta d'oro in oro si fanno buoni a Nicolò Spinelli per denari ttenuti di suo 49 39. -. 6

E in dì 26 di gugnio juli 8 ½ pagati per limosina alla sorella di Lorenzo Ferrara, a c. 357 -.16. -

E in dì 30 detto scudi dua d'oro inn oro pagati a maestro Jacopino per suo salario di 2 mesi finiti questo dì, a c. 357 1.14. -

E addì viij di luglio ducati ottantaquattro d'oro di camera fannosi buoni a Ghulielmo Dei nostro giovane, et sono ducati 24 per salario di mesi vj finiti a l'ultimo di gugno 1542 et ducati 60 per suo salario d'uno anno finito all'ultimo di gugno 1543. Posto havere in questo a c. 87 84. -. -

E addì detto scudi quaranta d'oro in oro fannosi buoni a Cavalcanti e Giraldi per li cambii di scudi ijM anticipatoci ij mesi che s'avevon havere da Santi iiij [Antonio Pucci] et per lui d'Alexandro Deti, quale li paga a' detti Deti et poi si li fa buoni, a 89 39. -. 6

E addì detto ducati ottantasepte s. i d. xj d'oro di camera per sicurtà et altre spese procedute al conto di Girolamo a Genova a coomune con Palavisini che per erore nel saldare al libro vecchio non s'aconcan per nostra rata, c. 94 87. 1.11

E addì 14 detto scudi venti d'oro inn oro pagati per Francesco Boni in più volte che se li donano per servitii di dua anni stato nel banco et n'era debitore al quaderno di cassa dove se ne fa creditore. Cassa in questo a 364 19.10. 6

E per resto di questo conto tirato avanti in questo a 362 20198. 6. 4

[fol. 362] yhs M.D.XLiij

Avanzi di fronte deono dare addì viij d'agosto scudi ventiquattro d'oro in oro fannosi buoni a m. Decio Alberico da Cesena per la provision di dua anni che finiranno a l'ultimo de presente per esser procurator del banco. Posto havere a c. 355 23. 8. 6

E addì detto scudi xxxij di juli fannosi buoni a Bartolomeo Sguerrini libraro a buon conto de' libri datoci per questa ragione et per la depositeria. Posto havere in questo 348 28. 8. 6

E addì detto ducati cinque s. vj di camera in conto a fructi de Monte di Fede. In questo a c. 284 5. 6. -

E addì detto scudi centodicassette s. xiij.iiij d'oro in oro per li fructi d'una compagnia di scudi 400 per 6 mesi finiti a 19 di marzo et ‹...› et scudi 91 ⅔ per li fructi di scudi 1000 d'una compagnia di x mesi finita a xviij di questo sotto nome di Lorenzo Ridolphi a xj per cento. Avere a 237 114.16. -

E in dì 6 detto ducati trentatre s. v.viiij d'oro di camera fannosi buoni a' Bini di Lione per danari tratti loro la valuta da' Covoni a 59 ¾ voleva dire a ducati 62 3/5 per marco. Havere a 340 33. 5. 9

E addì 8 detto scudi cinquantatre s. x.x di juli x per scudo fannosi buoni a' Dohanieri della Salara per valuta di rubbia 27 di sale datoci per casa a scudi 2 il rubio ch'eron andati creditori a libro vechio in più somma, a 322 52. 4.10

E addì 20 detto ducati centocinquantatre s. xvij.vij d'oro di camera si perdono al conto delle senserie per quello che s'è cambiato per nostro conto da luglio 1539 a tutto marzo 1542. Havere in questo a 299 153.17. 7

E in dì 29 di marzo scudi nove di moneta picoli a' Clerici di Camera per resto di lor regali della Depositeria per Natale paxato che si paga moneta et hanno voluto oro. Posto il Dipoxitario havere a 292 8. -. -

E addì 7 di settembre scudi - s. vj fansi buoni alli Ulivieri a parte R per porto d'uno gruppo da Firenze, a 372 -. 6. -

E addì detto ducati centottanta d'oro di camera vechi fannosi buoni a Giovan Francesco Ridolphi nostro giovane alle scripture per suo salario di mesi xviij finiti a l'ultimo di gugno paxato, c. 185 180. -. -

E addì detto ducati milledugentosexantsei s. xiij.iiii d'oro di camera vechi fannosi buoni al nostro magiore Benvenuto Ulivieri per la sua rata di ducati 1600 divisi a buon conto, c. 342 1266.13. 4

E addì detto ducati dugento d'oro di camera vechi fannosi buoni a Benedetto Busini per la sua rata di ducati 1600 divisi a buon conto questo dì. Posto li debba havere in questo a c. 352 200. -. -

E addì detto ducati centotrentatre s. vj.viij d'oro di camera vechi fannosi buoni a Simone di Mariotto Guiducci per la sua rata di ducati 1600 divisi a buon conto questo dì. Posto havere a 14 133. 6. 8

E addì detto ducati trenta di camera fannosi buoni a Giulio di Francesco del Riccio per suo salario di mesi xv finiti a l'ultimo di gugnio paxato. Posto havere in questo a 240 30. -. -

E addì 25 detto ducati trentatre d'oro di camera fannosi buoni a Antonio Scarlattini per ricambio di scudi 500 tenuti di suo per il tempo ch'è finito a l'ultimo d'ottobre proximo. Posto avere a 265 33. -. -

E addì detto scudi cinquanta d'oro in oro fannosi buoni a Benvenuto Ulivieri per el prezzo d'una sua mula fornita di velluto e copertina donata più fa al S. Thexoriere, a c. 372 48.15. 9

E ducati cinquantuno s. v d'oro di camera fansi buoni a Leonardo Starnochio per utili de' sua denari scudi 800 ch'è creditore Hippolita et Marzia sue figliuole per tutto agosto 1542. Havere a 51 51. 5. -

E addì xxvj dixembre scudi cento d'oro in oro si fan buoni al detto per mercie delle denari di dette sue figliuole a x per cento dal primo di settembre 1542 fino al primo di gennaio proximo futuro 1543 ab incarnatione. Havere a 51 97.11. 3

E ducati venticinque d'oro di camera si fanno buoni alli Strozzi di Valladulit che non ce gli fecion buoni che se nono messi lor in conto per provision del pagato a' cortigiani. Havere in questo a c. 378 25. -. -

Et ducati dugentoquaranta s. xvj anzi scudi septanta d'oro in oro si fan buoni a Benedetto Busini spesi in andar a Vinezia in poste et tornar con un S.re l'anno 1541 di febraio ab incarnatione. Havere in questo a c. 381 68. 6. -

E addì 31 di gennaio scudi venti di moneta fannosi buoni a' Carducci per più robe havute da lor per fare impannature et altro per il banco. Posto havere in questo 363 17.14.10

E deon dar addì xxxj di gennaio anzi fino a 14 di settembre scudi uno s. xvj di moneta pagati a Ruberto da Pavia per lli frutti di ducati 100 di credito di Monte che comperò da noi, per lle paghe di novembre et dicembre, genaio et febraio. Cassa in questo 382 1.12. 3

E in dì xviij di magio 1543 ducati - s. viiij d'oro per limosina alli Scapumini, a c. 353 -. 9. -

E in dì 14 di settembre ducati tre s. ii.ii di camera picoli per tre consensi di portione vendute più fa, a c. 382 3. 2. 2

Et ducati mille di camera che per errore sono fatti troppo creditori in la partita di ducati 3964.10.4 per le provisioni che volea dire ducati 2964.10.4. Posto havere in questo a c. 368 1000. -. -

E in dì xiiij di settembre ducati ventitre s. xii.iiii d'oro di camera pagati a Ghulielmo Dei per tanti spesine in fogli, limosine et altre spese minute del banco da settembre 1540 a settembre 1542. Posto capsa in questo a c. 382 23.12. 4

E addì 31 di gennaio ducati dugentonove s. x.iiij di camera per porti di letere di varii luoghi et il ‹…›amo di Firenze per 4 anni. In questo 95 209.10. 4

E ducati xxj^{M}ccccj s. iiij.v di camera si fa creditore il nostro libro 0/3. In questo a c. 383 21401. 4. 5

AVERE side

[fol. 11] yhs M.D.XLj

Avanzi et disavanzi di nostro chonto di nostro chonto di fronte deon havere addì xvj di gennaio scudi venti di juli x per scudo rechò Simone Ghuiducci contanti da uno amicho segnato B. Cassa dare in questo a 36 19.10. 6

E addì xviiij detto scudi tre d'oro rechò Simone Guiducci. Cassa dare in questo a 36 2.18. 9

E addì 3 di febraro scudi otto di moneta hauti da m. Aschanio Danepi contanti. Cassa in questo a 53 7.16. 3

E addì 18 d'aprile ducati sessanta s. v d'oro di camera vechi levati da uno conto di speditione. In questo a 115 60. 5. -

E addì detto s. x facci buoni Pietro Coscholla per uno prot°. Dare in questo a 105 -.10. -

E addì 8 di giugnio scudi trecento d'oro inn oro facci buoni il Rev.mo cardinale Triultio et sono per li cambii patiti per tutto giugnio presente. Dare in questo a 123 292.13. 9

E addì 6 di luglio scudi centoventi d'oro inn oro rechò Benedetto Busini contanti, disse per certo cambio fatto con Baldassar Olgiatto. Posto cassa, dare in questo a 175 117. 1. 6

E addì x detto scudi milletrentaquatro s. iiij.iiij di moneta hauti dalli dohanieri del sale et per lor da Lorenzo Altoviti per il nostro ⅓ di scudi 3102.13.2 siminli, contanti. Cassa a 175 1009. -. -

E addì 26 detto scudi tre d'oro hauti da m. Sebastiano Gualterio contanti, a 183 2.18. 9

E addì 3 d'aghosto scudi novanta d'oro inn oro rechò Benedetto Busini contanti disse hauti dall'Olgiatto, a 183 87.16. 3

E addì 12 di settembre ducati lij.xviiij.viiij d'oro di camera si avanzano al conto per noi di fiera di Villalone. In questo a 23 52.19. 9

E addì detto ducati dieci d'oro di camera per uno cambio fatto con Diegho di Salzedo. Dare li Strozzi per noi in ottobre, in questo a 209 10. -. -

E addì detto ducati xxxiiij.xvj.vij d'oro di camera facci buoni il signore Ottavio Farnese. In questo a 60 34.16. 7

E addì 15 detto ducati uno s. viij d'oro di camera hauti da' Beni. Cassa in questo a 216 1. 8. -

E addì 16 detto scudi centoventi d'oro inn oro rechò il nostro magiore da uno amicho. Cassa in questo a 219 117. 1. 6

E addì 8 di novembre scudi novanta d'oro inn oro rechò Benedetto Busini da uno amicho a parte B, a 247 87.16. 3

E addì 14 detto scudi dodici s. ij di moneta rechò il nostro magiore. Cassa in questo a 252 10.14. 6

E addì 18 detto scudi ventisei s. xiij.iiij d'oro inn oro fannoci buoni li Bini di Lione per ricambio di lb. iij^{M} trattisi depositati per la fiera d'aghosto a 2 per cento. Dare in questo a 121 26. -. -

E addì detto ducati cvij.vj d'oro di camera che si avanzano al conto di Francesco Corsini di Valladolid per noi, a 59 107. 6. -

E addì 18 detto ducati xxxviij.viiij d'oro di camera ci fa buoni Lorenzo Ghomez episcopo di Sarni. Dare a 89 38. 2. -

E addì xvj di gennaio scudi trecentoseptantacinque d'oro in oro per lla mia rata delli avanzi di Parma e Piacenza, a 178 365.16. 6

E addì detto scudi dugentoventi s. ij di moneta ci fanno buoni li Cavalcanti e Giraldi per ducati 13500. Frutti pagati in Piacenza a comune con loro per metà, dare a 250 214.12. 9

E addì detto scudi secentoventicinque d'oro in oro per la nostra rata a buon conto di scudi 2100 divisi alli 8 di novembre per conto delle provisione dello augmento del sale di Romagna. Dare in questo a 157 609.15. 2

E addì 31 detto scudi centocinquantanove s. j.x d'oro in oro per scudi 175 di moneta per il salario della dipositeria del Monte della Fede dal primo di novembre 1541 fino a tutto dicembre 1542, a 298 155. 3.10

E addì 17 di marzo scudi quattordicimila cinquecentotrenta s. vij.j di juli x per scudo fattoci buoni il dipositario D.N.S. che tanti restava loro creditore avanzi. Dare in questo a 292 14175.19. 3

E addì detto scudi centoquarantanove s. xvij.vj che tanta avanza il conto del V. Thexoriere di Parma et Piacenza, a 164 146. 2. 9

E addì detto scudi centonovantasei s. viiij.ij ci fa buoni il Collegio del Monte della Fede per il Monte in persona di Benedetto Busini per tutto aprile paxato et Benvenuto Ulivieri per tutto dicembre. Dare frutti di Monte a 284 191.14. 2

E addì detto scudi quattrocentoquarantadua s. viiij d'oro in oro in conto alla Camera per la vigesima delli hebrei, a 100 431.13. 2

E addì detto scudi quattrocento d'oro in oro a buono conto de l'utile del partitto del subsidio delli hebrei, a 291 390. 5. -

E in dì 28 di febraro s. x d'oro hauti da uno amico segnato L.G. Cassa in questo a 315 -.10. -

[fol. 311] yhs M.D.xLiij

Avanzi di nostro conto per conto corrente debbono havere per resto di simil conto per tirarlo avanti posto li debbino dare a quello in questo a carte 11 17299.14.10

E addì iiij d'aprile scudi centoseptantuno s. ij d. ij d'oro in oro per li frutti di 7 mesi finiti a 31 di marzo dell'entrata di scudi 293 ⅓ l'anno che habiam sopra la Thexoreria di Romagnia sotto nome d'Antonio Covoni e co. Posto dare al per noi de' tempi in questo a 199 166.18. 9

E addì detto scudi septecentoventi d'oro in oro fannoci buoni Cavalcanti et Giraldi e co. di Roma per nostro conto de' tempi et sono per tanti riscossine da Luca Iustiniano e co. Thexorieri di Romagnia per li interessi di scudi vj^{M} servito la Camera apostolica sopra la Thexoreria di Romagna et sopra del decto Luca per nostro conto sotto loro nome. Posto dare in questo a 94 702. 9. -

E addì detto scudi mille quattrocentoquaranta d'oro in oro fannoci buoni Salvestro da Montacuto e co. di Roma per nostro conto de' tempi et sono per tanti riscossine da' dohanieri della Salara di Roma per li interessi di scudi xij^{M} servito la Camera apostolica sopra l'augmento del sale di Roma et Romagnia sotto Benvenuto Ulivieri e co. fideiussori et amministratori. Posto dare a 99 1404.18. -

E addì xvj di magio ducati ducati dicassette s. viij di camera s'avanzò in conto a fructi di portione a 56 17. 8. -

E addì detto ducati iij in conto a Lotti di corte cexarea per 4 protonotari. In questo a 330 3. -. -

E in ddì primo di marzo ducati ventiotto s. xiij d'oro di camera facci buoni il Reverendo m. Giovanni Poggio per scomuniche et censure levate a più obligati per conto delli marchi 87 et darli a cambio. Dare a 277 28.13. -

E addì 30 di gugnio ducati millecento s. iij d. viij d'oro di camera fannoci buoni Antonio Covoni e co. et sono per la nostra rata delli utili fatti in quella ragione a buon conto fino addì ultimo di marzo che finì. Posto detti Covoni dare in questo a 274 1100. 3. 8

E in dì xvj detto scudi centocinquanta d'oro in oro facci buoni il Rev.mo cardinale Triultio per li cambii del partito per suo conto del servitolo sino a tutto gennaio paxato, a 204 146. 7. -

E addì v di luglio scudi ottanta d'oro in oro facci buoni Luca Iustiniani e co. per li cambi di scudi 1000 d'uno anno finito a 15 d'agosto 1542 servitoli sino a 15 d'agosto 1541. Dare a 76 78. 1. -

E addì v di luglio ducati quarantadua s. xviii.v di camera in conto a Monte nostro. In questo a 73 42.18. 5

E addì detto ducati millesexantaquattro.0.viiij d'oro in oro in conto allumi della scala di Roano Rocella et Potto per cantara 10258 finiti de primo et secondo anno de' Borghallesi. Posto dare a 133 1038. 1. 9

E addì detto ducati mille d'oro di camera si ragionono a buon conto in conto delli allumi della scala di Provenza el primo et secondo anno. Posto dare in questo 134 1000. -. -

E addì viij di luglo ducati otto s. viij.x di camera in conto a spese d'allumi. In questo a 81 8. 8.10

E addì detto scudi dugentoquaranta d'oro in oro in conto al R.mo Antonio Pucci cardinale Santi iiij, c. 89 234. 3. -

E addì 12 detto ducati trentatre s. xvij.iij d'oro di camera sono per l'utile di Monte preso per noi Ambrosio Spinula che n'era creditore al quaderno di cassa dove se n'è fatto creditore a 111. Cassa in questo a 364 33.17. 3

E addì 17 detto scudi ventidua s. xiiij.vj d'oro per scudi 25 di juli x per scudo hauti dal dipoxitario del Monte della Fede per salario di giennaio et febraro proximo paxato. Post cassa dare in questo a 364 22. 3. 6

E addì 23 detto scudi ventidua s. vij.vj d'oro inn oro per scudi 24 di juli x per scudo facci buoni Morello Morelli da Farnese per il quinto di scudi 123 di moneta che ha reso uno Cavaliere di Santo Paulo per scudi 200 servitolo. Posto li debba dare in questo a 350 21.16. 9

E addì detto scudi settantatre s. vj.viiij d'oro inn oro fannoci buoni Antonio Covoni e co. per l'assegnatione delli 293 ⅓ l'anno sopra la Thexoreria di Romagna per tre mesi finiti a l'ultimo di gugnio. Dare a 199 71.11. -

E addì detto ducati xiiij.xij.ij d'oro di camera s'avanzano al conto de' Giacomini. In questo a 324 14.12. 2

[fol. 362] yhs M.D.xLiii

Avanzi di nostro conto per conto corrente debano havere per resto di simil conto per tirarlo avanti. Posto dare a quello in questo a 311 20198. 6. 4

E addì 23 di luglio scudi ottantaquattro d'oro in oro ci fanno buoni e Castri e Malvendi di Burghus per li utili di scudi 1050 prestati a Luca Iustiniani in somma di scudi 4200 per uno anno finito all'utimo di gugno 1543. Posto dare a 177 81.19. -

E addì detto scudi quarantasei s. vij.iiij d'oro in oro per valuta di scudi 50.16 di moneta sono per li fruti a noi spettanti d'uno officio di Cavaliere di Santo Paulo in persona di Federico Buontempi, che ne pagò, solo scudi 500 per uno anno finito all'ultimo di gugnio 1543. Posto detto Federico dare in questo a 351 45. 4.10

E addì 8 d'aghosto s. xj.iij s'avanzano a uno conto delli Ulivieri di Firenze per noi. In questo a 324 -.11. 3

E addì detto ducati undici s. viij.viij d'oro di camera fannoci buoni li Ulivieri di Firenze per tanti che ci restavano debitori per più averi trovati a nostro che a lor danno nelle partite mandate loro che per non havere a ritochare scritture si lascieno stare come stavan. Detti Ulivieri a 318 11. 8. 8

E addì viij d'agosto scudi dugentocinquanta di juli a buon conto per la nostra rata della Dohana dello Studio per li utili del terzo anno. Posto Filippo Carducci dare a 35 243.18. 6

E addì 20 detto ducati tremilanovecento sessantaquatro s. x.iiij d'oro di camera sono che tanti restavan creditori provisione di nostro conto per conto corrente dare in questo a 368 3964.10. 4

E addì detto scudi quarantatre s. xj d'oro in oro sono per la nostra provision di scudi 871.5.6 d'oro riscossi de' mezzi frutti delle comende del 1542. Et li fa buoni il depositario a 292 42.10. -

E addì detto scudi centocinquantasei s. xiiij.viij d'oro in oro a buon conto de' cambii che ci à a fare buoni Antonio bergamasco per danari servitolo. Posto dare a 93 152.17. 1

E addì 30 d'agosto ducati sexanta s. vii d. x d'oro di camera s'avanzano in conto a' Captani per noi, a 370 60. 7.10

E addì vij di septembre scuti centoventi s. xiij.iiij di moneta sul galeone Santo Jovanni, a c. 180 116.15. -

E addì detto ducati sexantuno s. x di camera per provision in conto a' Venturi. In questo a c. 124 61.10. -

E addì viiij d'ottobre ducati quarantuno s. ii di camera in conto alla Congregatione di Valombrosa, a 149 41. 2. -

E addì xvii di gennaio scudi dieci d'oro in oro a compimento di scudi 250 ci fa buoni Rev.mo Santi 4 [Antonio Pucci], a c. 205 9.15. -

E addì xxxj detto ducati centottantuno s. -.viij di camera s'avanzano al conto delle speditione. In questo a carte 129 181. -. 8

Manuscript Sources

FLORENCE

ARCHIVIO DI STATO, FONDO GALLI TASSI

Galli Tassi (n. 1732-1733, 1806-1876, 1912-1962, 1976-1980, 2074, 2278-2282, 2294, 2310-2311); *filze* (bundles) are indicated in italic

OLIVIERI FAMILY
— Scritture e lettere varie, 1475-1595: *1808*
— Scritture relative a processi e cause, 1510-1619: *1938*
— Scritture varie, 1523-1619: *1807*
— Quadernuccio di ricordi di anonimo, 1530-31: 1816
— Scritture varie delle compagnie italiane ed estere, 1530-96: *1824*
— Lettere varie, 1531-96: *1961*
— Scritture e lettere varie, 1532-1604: *1962*
— Scritture varie, 1535-95: *1806*
— Lettere varie, 1537-96: *1960*
— Scritture relative a cause e processi, 1538-91: *1809*

GIOVANNI OLIVIERI IN FLORENCE
— Quadernuccio, 1511-14: 1913

MICHELE AND GIOVANNI OLIVIERI & PARTNERS IN FLORENCE
— Bilancio Libro bianco segnato C, 1543: 1926
— Debitori e creditori, 1544-47: 2294

ALESSANDRO DI PAOLO OLIVIERI IN NAPLES
— Debitori e creditori, verde segnato A, 1518-24: 1915

BENVENUTO OLIVIERI'S PERSONAL ACCOUNTS IN ROME
— Debitori e creditori, 1516-31: 1914
— Ricordanze [il volume è mancante], 1519-48: 1813
— Scritture varie relative ad acquisto casa, 1537: 1812
— Libretto di spese, 1539: 1820
— Entrata e uscita, 1547-49: 1819

BENVENUTO OLIVIERI'S HEIRS
— Debitori e creditori, bianco segnato A, 1549-53: 1822
— Scritture varie, 1549-87: *1810*
— Conti vari, 1550-62: 1928

— Scritture varie, 1551-66: 1811
— Entrata e uscita, segnato C, 1562-69: 1823

BENVENUTO OLIVIERI & PARTNERS IN ROME (MISCELLANEOUS DOCUMENTS)
— Conti vari, 1517-87: *1950*
— Conti vari, 1518-60: *1912*
— Conti vari, 1523-60: *1951*
— Conti vari, 1524-51: *1953*
— Conti vari, 1527-90: *1952*
— Conti vari, 1528-91: *1945*
— Conti vari, 1530-66: *1955*
— Scritte di compagnia, 1531-46: 1826
— Conti vari, 1531-57: *1942*
— Conti vari, 1531-75: *1949*
— Scritture varie, 1532-49: *1829*
— Conti vari, 1533-88: *1954*
— Conti vari, 1533-96: *1946*
— Conti vari, 1534-53: *1941*
— Conti vari, 1535-98: *1948*
— Scritture relative alla causa Olivieri-Del Nero, 1537-48: *1939*
— Contratti vari, 1537-53: *1828*
— Conti vari, 1537-93: *1947*
— Ordini e ricevute di pagamenti, 1539-49: *1958*
— Quaderno di debitori, 1540: 1916
— Debitori e creditori, libro azzurro segnato A secondo, 1542-44: 2278
— Scritture varie, 1542-49: *1825*
— Conti vari, 1542-59: *1943*
— Conti vari, 1543: 1931
— Ricordi e conti, 1544-51: 1814
— Spoglio del libro azzurro segnato A secondo e terzo, 1544-70: 1920
— Ordini e ricevute di pagamenti, 1544-87: *1957*
— Quaderno di listra, verde segnato C, 1545: 1929
— Copialettere, 1545-46: 1959
— Ricordi di cause, 1545-46: 1940
— Conti vari, 1545-87: *1944*
— Quadernuccio di listra, 1546: 1930
— Quaderno di cassa, 1547: 1818
— Debitori e creditori, libro giallo segnato B, 1548: 1918
— Spoglio del libro giallo segnato B, 1548-50: 1921
— Libro di spese di casa, 1548-49: 1821
— Conti vari, 1548-49: 1932
— Ricordanze segnato F, 1549: 1815
— Libro del negozio di vini greci, 1550: 1827
— Quaderno di debitori, s.d.: 1919
— Spoglio di debitori, s.d.: 1922
— Quaderno di oggetti venduti, s.d.: 1934

Olivieri family benvenuto olivieri & partners (depositary)
— Entrata e uscita, 1542-43: 1817
— Conti vari, 1530-48: *1843*
— Quaderno di conti, 1540: 1935
— Quaderno di cassa, 1540-41: 2279
— Quaderno di debitori e creditori, 1540-43: 1917
— Entrata e uscita per viaggio di Paolo III a Lucca e Bologna, 1541: 1855
— Quaderno di debitori e creditori, 1543: 1856
— Conti vari, 1543-51: *1844*
— Libro bianco C dei pagamenti, 1545-48: 2280
— Entrata e uscita, 1546-48: 2282

Benvenuto Olivieri & Partners (*Monti* of Rome)
— Conti miscellanei, 1532-50: *1836*
— Conti miscellanei, 1538-48: *1837*
— Conti vari, 1538-49: *2074*
— Conti vari, 1539-45: *1838*
— Scritture varie, 1541: 1840
— Spoglio di debitori e creditori, 1541: 1842
— Conti miscellanei, 1541-49: *1835*
— Scritture varie, 1542-43: 1841
— Conti miscellanei, 1543-49: *1839*
— Debitori e creditori, libro bianco C, 1546-49: 2281
— Giornale giallo E, 1549: 1933

Benvenuto Olivieri & Partners (Customs of Rome)
— Conti vari, 1533-54: *1832*
— Conti vari, 1539-55: *1833*
— Entrata e uscita, 1541-43: 1834
— Conti vari, 1542-50: *1831*

Benvenuto Olivieri & Partners (Treasury of Umbria and Perugia)
— Conti vari, 1529-49: *1847*
— Conti vari, 1539-47: *1845*
— Conti vari, 1540-42: *1846*
— Conti vari, 1541-46: *1848*
— Bilancio del libro paonazzo C, 1550: 1927
— Entrata e uscita della Camera di Todi, 1543: 1858
— Entrata e uscita della Camera di Assisi, 1544: 1860
— Cause varie, 1560: 1849

Benvenuto Olivieri & Partners (Treasury of the Romagna)
— Conti miscellanei, 1529-55: *1851*
— Conti vari, 1543-49: *1850*

BENVENUTO OLIVIERI & PARTNERS (SALT OF ROME AND THE ROMAGNA)
— Conti vari, 1531-45: *1865*
— Scritture varie, 1538-45: 1863
— Conti vari, 1539-44: *1864*
— Libro dell'aumento del sale di Bologna e Romagna segnato A, 1540-43: 1866

BENVENUTO OLIVIERI & PARTNERS (VARIOUS SERVICES PROVIDED TO THE APOSTOLIC CHAMBER)
— Libro sull'imposizione delle galere, 1542: 1857
— Libro su imposizione galere, entrate delle comunità e decime, 1542-44: 1859
— Quinterno dei «partiti» di scudi 55.000 e 28.000, 1544-48: 1862
— Quinterno del «partito» di scudi 128.000, 1548-49: 1861
— Spoglio di diversi libri, 1548-50: 1923

BENVENUTO OLIVIERI & PARTNERS (TITHES)
— Conti miscellanei, 1532-47: *1868*
— Conti miscellanei, 1537-47: *1867*
— Entrata nel bolognese (Cavalcanti-Giraldi e Strozzi), 1538-39: 1869
— Entrata nello Stato pontificio, 1538: 1870
— Entrata nello Stato del duca di Urbino, 1542: 1871
— Entrata nello Stato pontificio (Umbria), 1543: 1873
— Entrata nello Stato pontificio (Umbria e Marca), 1543-44: 1872
— Entrata in Romagna (per la guerra di Germania), 1546: 1874

BENVENUTO OLIVIERI & PARTNERS (TOLFA ALUM)
— Conti vari, 1537-51: *1830*

BENVENUTO OLIVIERI & PARTNERS (TRADE OF GRAIN)
— Conti vari, 1532-49: *1875*
— Libro per contratto di salme 10.000, 1540-41: 1876

BENVENUTO OLIVIERI & PARTNERS (EXCHANGE OPERATIONS)
— Lettere di cambio, 1541-49: *1956*
— Quaderno di cambi, bianco F, 1549: 1924
— Spoglio di debitori di cambi, 1565-69: 1925

BUSINI, FAMILY AND COMPANIES
— Scritture varie, 1537-50: *1733*
— Scritture varie, 1541-1600: *1732*

STROZZI, FAMILY AND COMPANIES
— Conti vari relativi alla Tesoreria della Marca, 1509-54: *1852*
— Scritture varie, 1521-46: *1976*
— Scritture varie, 1521-47: *1978*
— Quaderno di conti relativi alla Tesoreria della Marca, 1531: 1853
— Scritture varie, 1532-40: *1977*
— Libro di varie imposizioni fiscali nella Tesoreria della Marca, 1533-35: 1854

HEIRS OF FILIPPO STROZZI
— Quaderno di ricordi, 1514-39: 1937
— Quaderno di debitori della compagnia Strozzi, 1539: 1936

UBALDINI, FAMILY AND COMPANIES
— Scritture varie, 1355-1583: *1979*
— Lettere a Roberto Ubaldini, vice-tesoriere del Patrimonio, 1543-44: *1980*

INDEXES

— Inventario e indice dei nomi (A-I) delle scritture del fondo Galli Tassi, 1790: 2310
— Indice dei nomi (K-Z) delle scritture del fondo Galli Tassi, 1790: 2311

ARCHIVIO DI STATO

Carte Strozziane, serie III, 30
— serie III, 95
— serie III, 96
— serie III, 101
— serie III, 110
— serie III, 134

Catasto 77, *Santa Maria Novella*, *Lion Bianco*, year 1427
— 1013, *Santa Maria Novella*, *Lion Bianco*, year 1480
— 1014, *Santa Maria Novella*, *Lion Bianco*, year 1480

Ceramelli Papiani, 1390, famiglia Ceffini
— 4753, famiglia Ulivelli
— 4757, famiglia Ulivieri

Decima Granducale, 3624

Diplomatico, *Dono Torrigiani-Appendice*, 29 October 1533
Diplomatico, *Dono Torrigiani-Appendice*, 3 August 1534
Diplomatico, *Dono Torrigiani-Appendice*, 7 September 1536
Diplomatico, *Dono Torrigiani-Appendice*, 13 March 1544
Diplomatico, *Legato Torrigiani*, 24 May 1555

Eredità Lemmo Balducci, 74

Manoscritti 250, *Priorista Mariani*, tomo 3
— 351, *Carte dell'Ancisa DD*
— 353, *Carte dell'Ancisa FF*
— 357, *Carte dell'Ancisa II*

— 359, *Carte dell'Ancisa LL*
— 360, *Carte dell'Ancisa MM*
— 361, *Carte dell'Ancisa NN*
— 473 (*Armi di famiglie fiorentine raccolte da Gabbriello Landini piovano di Ripoli*)
— 603, *Carte Pucci*, scat. XII, 43
— 621 (*Sepoltuario della chiesa di S. Maria Novella*)
— 623 (*Sepoltuario della chiesa di S. Trinita di Firenze*)
— 625 (*Sepoltuario fiorentino del Rosselli*)
— 812 (*Sepoltuario della chiesa di S. Maria Novella*)

Mediceo Avanti Principato, filza 99, n. 42

Mercanzia, 10772
— *10832*

Notarile Antecosimiano, 5424, notaio Lorenzo Cioli, year 1535
— 9335, notaio Giovan Battista Giordani, years 1553-54
— 9338, notaio Giovan Battista Giordani, years 1557-58
— 15121, notaio Niccolò di Filippo di Pratovecchio, years 1547-48
— 15122, notaio Niccolò di Filippo di Pratovecchio, years 1548-49
— 15123, notaio Niccolò di Filippo di Pratovecchio, years 1549-51
— 15124, notaio Niccolò di Filippo di Pratovecchio, years 1551-52
— 15125, notaio Niccolò di Filippo di Pratovecchio, years 1552-53

Strozzi Sacrati, 528, years 1559-63
— 605, years 1559-63
— 606, years 1562-66

Torrigiani-Appendice, filza 1, years 1532-33
— filza 2, years 1531-35
— filza 3, years 1532-33
— filza 4, year 1534

BIBLIOTECA NAZIONALE CENTRALE

Poligrafo Gargani, scat. 2066
— scat. 2074
— scat. 2075
— scat. 2076

ROME

ARCHIVIO DI STATO

Camerale I, *Conti della Depositeria generale 1771*, years 1531-32

— *1772*, years 1533-34
— *1773*, year 1536
— *1774*, year 1538
— *1775*, years 1538-39
— *1776*, years 1539-40
— *1777*, year 1540
— *1777bis*, year 1541
— *1778*, year 1541
— *1779*, year 1542
— *1780*, years 1543-46
— *1781*, year 1545
— *1782*, years 1548-49
— *1783*, year 1549
— *1784*, year 1549

Camerale I, *Giustificazioni di Tesoreria*, busta 1, years 1431-1597
— busta 2, years 1547-54

Camerale I, *Mandati Camerali 867*, years 1533-39
— *868*, years 1534-37
— *869*, years 1535-37
— *870*, years 1537-41
— *871*, year 1539
— *872*, years 1539-42
— *873*, years 1540-41
— *874*, years 1540-43
— *875*, years 1541-43
— *876*, years 1541-43
— *877*, years 1541-48
— *878*, years 1542-46
— *879*, years 1543-45
— *880*, years 1541-45
— *881*, years 1545-46
— *882*, years 1545-46
— *883*, years 1546-48
— *884*, years 1546-51
— *885*, years 1548-49
— *886*, years 1548-51
— *887*, years 1548-52
— *888*, years 1549-50
— *889*, years 1549-50
— *890*, year 1550
— *891*, years 1550-51
— *892*, years 1550-51
— *893*, years 1551-53

Camerale I, *Tesoreria provinciale della Romagna*, busta 6, years 1494-1531
— busta 7, years 1517-40
— busta 8, years 1532-35
— busta 9, years 1532-37
— busta 10, years 1535-38
— busta 11, years 1536-38
— busta 12, years 1538-40
— busta 13, years 1540-43
— busta 14, years 1542-48
— busta 15, years 1545-60

Camerale I, *Tesoreria provinciale di Umbria e Perugia*, busta 29, years 1511-36
— busta 30, years 1533-51
— busta 31, years 1546-65
— busta 32, years 1546-52
— busta 33, years 1551-55
— busta 34, years 1555-61
— busta 35, years 1558-65
— busta 36, years 1564-73
— busta 37, years 1568-77
— busta 38, years 1574-80
— busta 39, years 1580-1609

Camerale I, *Tesoreria provinciale della Marca*, busta 22, years 1510-23
— busta 23, years 1518-26
— busta 24, years 1526-34
— busta 25, years 1532-39
— busta 26, years 1537-67
— busta 27, years 1547-62

Camerale I, *Tesoreria provinciale di Ascoli*, busta 6, years 1469-1531
— busta 7, years 1531-60

Camerale I, *Tesoreria provinciale di Camerino*, busta 1, years 1539-56

Camerale I, *Tesoreria provinciale di Fermo*, busta 1, years 1397-1542

Camerale I, *Tesoreria provinciale del Patrimonio*, busta 28, years 1515-47
— busta 29, years 1543-61

Camerale I, *Viaggi di Pontefici e Sovrani*, busta 1-2

Camerale II, *Gabelle*, busta 1, years 1322-1761

Notai segretari e cancellieri della R. Camera apostolica 1988, years 1543-45, notaio M. Tommasini

ARCHIVIO SEGRETO OF THE VATICAN

Camera apostolica, Diversa Cameralia 112, years 1537-46
— *127*, years 1541-43
— *131*, years 1542-43
— *133*, years 1542-47
— *134*, years 1543-44
— *139*, years 1544-45
— *141*, years 1545-46
— *142*, years 1545-46
— *147*, years 1546-47
— *153*, years 1546-48
— *157*, years 1546-48

BIBLIOTECA APOSTOLICA OF THE VATICAN

Vaticano latino 6190
— *7124*
— *9960*

ARCHIVIO DELL'ARCICONFRATERNITA DI S. GIOVANNI DEI FIORENTINI

vol. 321: *Statuti del consolato*, 1515-1727
vol. 339: *Libro del Provveditore*, 1546-52
vol. 344: *Ospedale e confraternita*, 1456
vol. 390: *Libro di instrumenti della Compagnia della Pietà*, 1403-1607
vol. 391: *Libro di instrumenti della Compagnia della Pietà*, 1403-1567
vol. 392: *Libro di instrumenti della Compagnia della Pietà*, 1534-61
vol. 393: *Libro di instrumenti della Compagnia della Pietà*, 1536-46
vol. 431: *Libro dell'elenco delli benefattori, contribuenti e sottoscritti per sovvenimento della fabrica*, 1518-21

ARCHIVIO STORICO DEL VICARIATO

S. Giovanni dei fiorentini. Battesimi, defunti, matrimoni e 'stato delle anime', I, years 1532-89

List of Cited References

Ait I., 'Credito e iniziativa commerciale: aspetti dell'attività economica a Roma nella seconda metà del XV secolo', in *Credito e sviluppo economico in Italia dal Medioevo all'età contemporanea* (Verona, 1988), pp. 81-95.

Ait I., 'Il commercio delle derrate alimentari nella Roma del '400', *Archeologia medievale*, VIII (1981): 155-172.

Ait I., 'La dogana di Sant' Eustachio nel XV secolo', in *Aspetti della vita economica e culturale a Roma nel Quattrocento* (Rome, 1981), pp. 81-147.

Ait I., 'La dogana di terra come fonte per lo studio della presenza di mercanti stranieri a Roma nel XV secolo', in *Forestieri e stranieri nelle città basso-Medievali*, pp. 28-44.

Ait I. – Esch A., 'Aspettando l'Anno Santo. Fornitura di vino e gestione di taverne nella Roma del 1475', *Quellen und Forschungen aus italienischen Archiven und Bibliotheken*, 73 (1993): 387-417.

Albèri E., *Relazioni degli ambasciatori veneti al senato (Relazioni della corte di Roma nel secolo XVI)*, s. II, voll. 3-4 (Florence: Tipografia e calcografia All'insegna di Clio, 1846).

von Albertini R., *Firenze dalla repubblica al principato* (Turin: Einaudi, 1970).

Arcelli F., *Il banchiere del Papa: Antonio della Casa mercante e banchiere a Roma, 1438-1440* (Soveria Mannelli: Rubbettino, 2001).

Arcelli F., 'La costituzione della compagnia di Antonio della Casa e Jacopo di Michele di Corso Donati presso la corte pontificia (1438-1440)', *Studi Romani*, 45 (1997): 5-26.

Aspetti della vita economica e culturale a Roma nel Quattrocento (Rome: Il Centro di Ricerca, 1981).

Avesani R., 'Appunti per la storia dello "Studium Urbis" nel Quattrocento', in *Roma e lo Studium Urbis. Spazio urbano e cultura dal Quattro al Seicento* (Rome, 1992), pp. 69-87.

Balbi De Caro S. – Londei L., *Moneta pontificia da Innocenzo XI a Gregorio XVI* (Rome: Quasar, 1984).

Banchi pubblici, banchi privati e monti di pietà nell'Europa pre-industriale. Amministrazione, tecniche operative e ruoli economici, Atti del Convegno, Genoa 1-6 October 1990 (2 vols, Genoa: Società Ligure di Storia Patria, 1991).

Bauer C., 'Die Epochen der Papstfinanz. Ein Versuch', *Historische Zeitschrift*, 138 (1928): 457-503 (reprinted in Id., *Gesammelte Aufsätze zur Wirtschafts- und Sozialgeschichte*, Freiburg-Basle-Vienna: Herder, 1965, pp. 112-147).

Bauer C., 'Studi per la storia delle finanze papali durante il pontificato di Sisto IV', *Archivio della Società Romana di Storia Patria*, L (1927): 319-400.

Belloni C., *Un banchiere del Rinascimento, Bindo Altoviti* (Rome: Cremonese Editore, 1935).

Berti G., 'Lineamenti di politica economica farnesiana nei ducati di Parma e Piacenza', *Archivio Storico per le Province Parmensi*, s. IV, 11 (1959): 65-88.

Bertolotti A., 'Speserie segrete e pubbliche di Paolo III', *Atti e memorie delle Deputazioni di Storia Patria per le province dell'Emilia*, n.s., 3, fasc. 1 (1878): 169-212.

Boyer-Xambeu M.T. – Deleplace G. – Gillard L., *Monnaie privée et pouvoir des princes* (Paris: Presses de la Fondation Nationale des Sciences Politiques, 1986).

Braudel F., *The Mediterranean and the Mediterranean World in the Age of Philip II* (2 vols, London: Collins, 1972).

Bullard M.M., 'Bindo Altoviti, Renaissance Banker and Papal Financier', in A. Chong – D. Pegazzano – D. Zikos (eds), *Raphael, Cellini & A Renaissance Banker. The Patronage of Bindo Altoviti*, pp. 21-57.

Bullard M.M., *Filippo Strozzi and the Medici: Favor and Finance in Sixteenth-century Florence and Rome* (Cambridge: Cambridge University Press, 1980).

Bullard M.M., 'Fortuna della banca medicea a Roma nel tardo Quattrocento', in *Roma capitale (1447-1527)*, pp. 235-251.

Bullard M.M., 'Grain Supply and Urban Unrest in Renaissance Rome: the Crisis of 1533-34' in P.A. Ramsey (ed.), *Rome in the Renaissance. The City and the Myth* (Binghamton N.Y.: Center for Medieval & Early Renaissance Studies, 1982), pp. 279-292.

Bullard M.M., *Lorenzo il Magnifico. Image and anxiety, politics and finance* (Florence: Olschki, 1994).

Bullard M.M., 'Marriage Politics and the Family in Florence: The Strozzi-Medici Alliance of 1508', *American Historical Review*, 84 (1979): 668-687.

Bullard M.M., '"Mercatores Florentini Romanam Curiam Sequentes" in the early sixteenth century', *The Journal of Medieval and Renaissance Studies*, 6 (1976): 51-71.

Bullarum Privilegiorum ac Diplomatum Romanorum Pontificum Amplissima Collectio cui accessere pontificum omnium vitae, notae & indices opportuni. Opera et studio Caroli Cocquelines (6 vols, Rome: Typis et sumptibus Hyeronimi Mainardi, 1739-62, reprinted Graz: Druck, 1964-67), *Tomus Tertius*, 1743.

Capasso C., *Filippo Strozzi, i fuoriusciti e la Corte pontificia* (Camerino: Tipografia Savini, 1901).

Caracciolo A., 'I Bilanci dello Stato ecclesiastico tra XVI e XVIII secolo: una fonte e alcune considerazioni', in *Mélanges en l'honneur de Fernand Braudel* (2 vols, Toulouse: Privat Editeur, 1973), II, *Méthodologie de l'Histoire et des sciences humaines*, pp. 99-103.

Caracciolo A., 'Sovrano pontefice e sovrani assoluti', *Quaderni storici*, 52 (1983): 279-286.

Caravale M. – Caracciolo A., *Lo Stato Pontificio da Martino V a Pio IX*, in G. Galasso (ed.), *Storia d'Italia*, vol. 14 (Turin: UTET, 1978).

Caravale M., 'Entrate e uscite dello Stato della Chiesa in un bilancio della metà del Quattrocento', in *Per Francesco Calasso. Studi degli allievi* (Rome: Bulzoni, 1978), pp. 167-190.

Caravale M., *La finanza pontificia nel Cinquecento: le province del Lazio* (Naples: Jovene, 1974).

Caravale M., 'Le entrate pontificie', in *Roma capitale (1447-1527)*, pp. 73-106.

Carboni M., 'Camere delle città e Camera apostolica: l'evoluzione dei rapporti finanziari fra centro e periferia nello Stato della Chiesa in età moderna', *Studi Storici Luigi Simeoni*, L (2000): 9-22.

Carboni M., *Il debito della città. Mercato del credito, fisco e società a Bologna fra Cinque e Seicento* (Bologna: Il Mulino, 1995).

Carocci G., *Lo Stato della Chiesa nella seconda metà del secolo XVI* (Milano: Feltrinelli, 1961).

Cassandro M., 'I banchieri pontifici nel XV secolo', in Gensini (ed.), *Roma capitale (1447-1527)*, pp. 207-234.

Cassandro M., 'L'irradiazione economica fiorentina nell'Italia meridionale tra Medioevo e Rinascimento', in *Fra spazio e tempo. Studi in onore di Luigi De Rosa* (3 vols, Naples: Edizioni Scientifiche Italiane, 1995), I, pp. 191-221.

Cassandro M., *Le fiere di Lione e gli uomini d'affari italiani nel Cinquecento* (Florence, Baccini & Chiappi, 1979).

Castagnoli F. – Cecchelli C. – Giovannoni G. – Zocca M., *Topografia e urbanistica di Roma* (Bologna: Cappelli, 1958).

Chacon A., *Vitae et res gestae pontificum romanorum et cardinalium* (3 vols, Rome: Cura et sumptib. Philippi et Ant. De Rubeis, 1677).

Chambers D.S., 'Studium Urbis and *gabella studii*: the University of Rome in the fifteenth century', in C.H. Clough (ed.), *Cultural aspects of the Italian Renaissance. Essays in honour of Paul Oskar Kristeller* (Manchester: Manchester University Press, 1976), pp. 68-110.

Chiacchella R., 'Per una reinterpretazione della "guerra del sale" e della costruzione della Rocca Paolina in Perugia', *Archivio Storico Italiano*, 145 (1987): 3-60.

Chong A. – Pegazzano D. – Zikos D. (eds), *Raphael, Cellini & A Renaissance Banker. The Patronage of Bindo Altoviti* (Boston: Isabella Steward Gardner Museum, 2003).

Coniglio G., 'I Medici, i Fiorentini e il Viceregno', in *Napoli nel Cinquecento e la Toscana dei Medici* (Naples: Edizioni Scientifiche Italiane, 1980), pp. 7-24.

Contini G., 'Contributo documentario per uno studio delle condizioni finanziarie del Comune di Perugia alla vigilia della "guerra del sale"', *Rassegna degli Archivi di Stato*, 30 (1970): 365-376.

Coppi A., *Discorso sulle finanze dello Stato Pontificio dal secolo XVI al principio del XIX* (Rome: Tipografia Salviucci, 1855).

Corbo A.M., 'La serie Viaggi di Pontefici e Sovrani del Camerale I', *Rassegna degli Archivi di Stato*, 25 (1965): 406-420.

Costamagna P., 'Portraits of Florentine Exiles', in A. Chong – D. Pegazzano – D. Zikos (eds), *Raphael, Cellini & A Renaissance Banker. The Patronage of Bindo Altoviti*, pp. 329-350.

Credito e sviluppo economico in Italia dal Medioevo all'età contemporanea, Atti del I Convegno nazionale della Società Italiana degli Storici dell'Economia, Verona 4-6 June 1987 (Verona: Società Italiana degli Storici dell'Economia, 1988).

Cristofori Mancia M. (ed.), *Il primo registro della Tesoreria di Ascoli (20 agosto 1426-30 aprile 1427)* (Rome: Ministero dell'Interno, 1974).

Da Silva J.G., *Banque et crédit en Italie au XVIIe siècle* (2 vols, Paris: Klincksieck, 1969).

De Luca G.B., *Tractatus de officiis venalibus vacabilibus Romanae Curiae* cui accedit alter Tractatus eiusdem Auctoris *De locis Montium non vacabilium Urbis* (Rome: Ex Typographia Reverendae Camerae Apostolicae apud Nicolaum Angelum Tinassum, 1682).

De Roover R., *The Rise and Decline of the Medici Bank (1397-1494)* (New York: W.W. Norton & Company, 1966).

Del Treppo M., 'Il re e il banchiere. Strumenti e processi di razionalizzazione dello Stato aragonese a Napoli', in G. Rossetti (ed.), *Spazio, società e potere nell'Italia dei comuni* (Naples: Liguori, 1986), pp. 229-304.

Del Treppo M., 'Stranieri nel regno di Napoli. Le élites finanziarie e la strutturazione dello spazio economico e politico', in G. Rossetti (ed.), *Dentro la città. Stranieri e realtà urbane nell'Europa dei secoli XII-XVI* (Naples: Liguori, 1989), pp. 179-233.

Delumeau J., *L'alun de Rome XVe-XIXe siècle* (Paris: S.E.V.P.E.N., 1962).

Delumeau J., 'Les progrès de la centralisation dans l'Etat pontifical au XVIe siècle', *Revue Historique*, 226 (1961): 399-410.

Delumeau J., *Rome au XVIe siècle* (Paris: Hachette, 1975).

Delumeau J., *Vie économique et sociale de Rome dans la seconde moitié du XVIe siècle* (2 vols, Paris: De Boccard, 1957-59).

Delumeau J., *Vita economica e sociale di Roma nel Cinquecento* (Florence: Sansoni, 1979).

Dini B., 'L'economia fiorentina e l'Europa centro-orientale nelle fonti toscane', *Archivio Storico Italiano*, 153 (1995): 633-655.

Esch A., 'Bankiers der Kirche im grossen Scisma', *Quellen und Forschungen aus italienischen Archiven und Bibliotheken*, 46 (1966): 277-397.

Esch A., 'Dal Medioevo al Rinascimento, uomini a Roma dal 1350 al 1450', *Archivio della Società Romana di Storia Patria*, 94 (1971): 1-10.

Esch A., 'Die Kirchenstaatsfinanz und das Bruttoprodukt der grossen Handelsunternehmen (14.-15. Jh.)', in A. Guarducci (ed.), *Prodotto lordo e finanza pubblica (secc. XIII-XVIII)*, Atti della 'Ottava settimana di studi' dell'Istituto Internazionale di Storia Economica 'F. Datini', Prato, 3-9 May 1976 (Florence: Le Monnier, 1988), pp. 487-506.

Esch A., 'Florentiner in Rom um 1400. Namensverzeichnis der ersten Quattrocento-generation', *Quellen und Forschungen aus italienischen Archiven und Bibliotheken*, 52 (1972): 476-525.

Esch A., 'Im heiligen Jahr am römischen Zoll. Importe nach Rom um 1475', in J. Helmrath – H. Muller – H. Wolff (eds), *Studien zum 15. Jahrhundert. Festschrift für Erich Meuthen* (Munich: Oldenbourg, 1994), II, pp. 869-901.

Esch A., 'Importe in das Rom der Renaissance. Die Zollregister der Jahre 1470 bis 1480', *Quellen und Forschungen aus italienischen Archiven und Bibliotheken*, 74 (1994): 360-453.

Esch A., 'Le importazioni nella Roma del primo Rinascimento', in *Aspetti della vita economica e culturale a Roma*, pp. 7-79.

Esch A., 'Roma come centro d'importazioni nella seconda metà del Quattrocento ed il peso economico del Papato', in S. Gensini (ed.), *Roma capitale (1447-1527)*, pp. 107-143.

Esch A., 'Roman Customs Registers 1470-80: items of interest to historians of art and material culture', *Journal of the Warburg and Courtauld Institutes*, 58 (1995): 72-87.

Esposito A., 'Note sulla popolazione romana dalla fine del secolo XIV al Sacco (1527)', in Ead., *Un'altra Roma. Minoranze nazionali e comunità ebraiche tra Medioevo e Rinascimento* (Rome: Il calamo, 1995), pp. 19-30.

Eubel A. – Van Gulik G., *Hierarchia Catholica Medii et Recentioris Aevi sive Summorum Pontificum, S.R.E. Cardinalium, Ecclesiarum Antistitum Series*, vol. 3 (Regensburg: Sumptibus et Typis Librariae Regensbergiane, 1923).

Falchi L. – Pastura Ruggiero M.G. – Sinisi D., 'L'Annona di Roma nel sec. XVI', in *Gli archivi per la storia dell'alimentazione*, Atti del convegno, Potenza-Matera 5-8 September 1988 (Rome: Ministero per i beni culturali e ambientali – Ufficio centrale per i beni archivistici, 1996), pp. 568-589.

Favier J., *Les finances pontificales à l'époque du grand Schisme d'Occident, 1378-1409* (Paris: De Boccard, 1966).

Forcella V., *Tornei e giostre, ingressi trionfali e feste carnevalesche in Roma sotto Paolo III* (Rome: Tipografia Artigianelli, 1885, reprinted Bologna: Forni, 1971).

Forestieri e stranieri nelle città basso-medievali, Atti del Seminario Internazionale di Studio, Bagno a Ripoli (Florence), 4-8 June 1984 (Florence: Salimbeni, 1988).

Fosi I. – Visceglia M.A., 'Marriage and politics at the papal court in the sixteenth and seventeenth centuries', in T. Dean – K.J.P. Lowe (eds), *Marriage in Italy, 1300-1650* (Cambridge: Cambridge University Press, 1998), pp. 197-224.

Frollière G., 'La guerra del sale sostenuta dai Perugini contro Paolo III nel 1540', ed. F. Bonaini-A. Fabritti-F.L. Polidori, *Archivio Storico Italiano*, s. I, 16, parts 1-2 (1850-51): 405-476.

Fumi L., *Inventario e spoglio dei registri della tesoreria apostolica di Perugia e Umbria dal R. Archivio di Stato di Roma* (Perugia: Unione tipografica cooperativa, 1901).

Fumi L., 'Ragguaglio della ribellione di Perugia (Nota dall'Archivio di Stato di Milano)', *Bollettino della R. Deputazione di Storia Patria per l'Umbria*, XIV (1908): 69-81.

Garampi G., *Saggi di osservazione sul valore delle antiche monete pontificie* (Rome: Niccolò e Marco Pagliarini, 1776).

Gardi A., 'La fiscalità pontificia tra medioevo ed età moderna', *Società e Storia*, 33 (1986): 509-557.

Gascon R., *Grand commerce et vie urbaine au XVIe siècle. Lyon et ses marchands (environs de 1520-environs de 1580)* (2 vols, Paris: S.E.V.P.E.N., 1971).

Gascon R., 'Les Italiens dans la renaissance économique lyonnaise au XVIe siècle', *Revue des études italiennes* (1958): 167-181.

Gensini S. (ed.), *Roma capitale (1447-1527)*, Atti del IV convegno di studio del Centro studi sulla civiltà del tardo Medioevo, San Miniato (Pisa), 27-31 October 1992 (Pisa: Pacini, 1994).

Gnoli D., 'Descriptio Urbis o censimento della popolazione di Roma avanti il Sacco Borbonico', *Archivio della Società Romana di Storia Patria*, 17 (1894): 375-520.

Goldthwaite R.A., 'Banking in Florence at the End of the Sixteenth Century', *The Journal of European Economic History*, 27 (1998): 471-532.

Goldthwaite R.A., *Private Wealth in Renaissance Florence. A Study of Four Families* (Princeton N.J.: Princeton University Press, 1968).

Goldthwaite R.A., 'The Medici Bank and the World of Florentine Capitalism', *Past and Present*, CXIV (1987): 3-31.

Goldthwaite R.A., *Wealth and the Demand for Art in Italy 1300-1600* (Baltimore and London: The Johns Hopkins University Press, 1993).

Gottlob A., *Aus der Camera apostolica des 15 Jahrhunderts: ein Beitrag zur Geschichte des päpstlichen Finanzwesen und des endenden Mittelalters* (Innsbruck: Wagner, 1889).

Guidi Bruscoli F., *Benvenuto Olivieri, i* mercatores *fiorentini e la Camera apostolica nella Roma di Paolo III Farnese (1534-1549)* (Florence: Olschki, 2000).

Guidi Bruscoli F., 'Der Handel mit Seidenstoffen und Leinengeweben zwischen Florenz und Nürnberg in der ersten Hälfte des 16. Jahrhunderts', *Mitteilungen des Vereins für Geschichte der Stadt Nürnberg*, 86 (1999): 81-113.

Guidi Bruscoli F., 'Drappi di seta e tele di lino tra Firenze e Norimberga nella prima metà del Cinquecento', *Archivio Storico Italiano*, CLIX (2001): 359-394.

Guidi Bruscoli F., 'Mercanti-banchieri e appalti pontifici nel Cinquecento', in A. Jamme – O. Poncet (eds), *Offices, écrit et papauté (XIIIe–XIIe siècle)* (Rome: Ecole Française de Rome, forthcoming).

Guidi Bruscoli F., 'S. Giovanni dei Fiorentini a Roma. Due secoli di finanziamenti tra pontefici e granduchi, prelati e *mercatanti*', *Quellen und Forschungen aus den italienischen Archiven und Bibliotheken*, 86 (2006): 294–320.

Guidi Bruscoli F., '*Se questi pagassino sarebbe già principio...* Il difficile finanziamento della chiesa di S. Giovanni dei Fiorentini in Roma', in A.M. Falchero – A. Giuntini – G. Nigro – L. Segreto (eds), *La storia e l'economia. Miscellanea di studi in onore di Giorgio Mori* (2 vols, Varese: Edizioni Lativa, 2003), I, pp. 355-369.

Guiral-Hadziiossif J., *Valence. Port méditerranéen au XVe siècle (1410-1525)* (Paris: Publications de la Sorbonne, 1986).

Holmes G., 'How the Medici became the Pope's Bankers', in N. Rubinstein (ed.), *Florentine Studies. Politics and Society in Renaissance Florence* (London: Faber and Faber, 1968), pp. 357-380.

Hoshino H., 'Interessi economici dei lanaiuoli fiorentini nello Stato pontificio e negli Abruzzi nel Quattrocento', *Annuario dell'Istituto Giapponese di cultura*, XI (1973-74): 7-51.

Hurtubise P., 'La présence des "étrangers" à la cour de Rome dans la première moitié du XVIe siècle', in *Forestieri e stranieri nelle città basso-Medievali*, pp. 57-80.

Hurtubise P., 'L'implantation d'une famille florentine à Rome au début du XVIe siècle: les Salviati', in S. Gensini (ed.), *Roma capitale (1447-1527)*, pp. 253-271.

Hurtubise P., *Une famille-témoin. Les Salviati* (Vatican City: Biblioteca Apostolica Vaticana, 1985).

Igual Luis D., *Valencia e Italia en el siglo XV. Rutas, mercados y hombres de negocios en el espacio economico del Mediterraneo occidental* (Valencia: Bancaixa – fundació Caixa Castelló, 1998).

Kellenbenz H., 'Gli operatori economici italiani nell'Europa centrale ed orientale', in '*Aspetti della vita economica medievale*', Atti del Convegno di Studi nel X Anniversario della morte di Federigo Melis, Florence-Pisa-Prato, 10-14 March 1984 (Florence: Università degli Studi di Florence – Istituto di Storia Economica, 1985), pp. 333-358.

Lee E. (ed.), *Descriptio Urbis. The Roman Census of 1527* (Rome: Bulzoni, 1985).

Lee E., 'Foreigners in Quattrocento Rome', *Renaissance and Reformation*, n.s., VII (1983): 135-146.

Lee E., 'Gli abitanti del rione Ponte', in *Roma capitale (1447-1527)*, pp. 317-343.

Levati S., 'La venalità delle cariche nello Stato pontificio tra XVI e XVII secolo', *Ricerche Storiche*, XXVI (1996): 525-543.

Litva F., 'L'attività finanziaria della Dataria durante il periodo Tridentino', *Archivum Historiae Pontificiae*, V (1967): 79-174.

Lo Sardo E., *Le gabelle e le dogane dei Papi in età moderna: inventario della serie Dogane della Miscellanea camerale per materie* (Rome: Archivio di Stato di Roma – Scuola di Archivistica Paleografia e Diplomatica, 1994).

Lodolini A., 'I "Monti Camerali" nel sistema della finanza pontificia', in *Archivi Storici delle Aziende di Credito* (2 vols, Rome: Associazione Bancaria Italiana, 1956), I, pp. 263-278.

Lodolini E., 'I libri di conti di Antonio Fatati tesoriere generale della Marca (1449-1453) nell'Archivio di Stato di Roma', *Atti e memorie della Deputazione di Storia Patria per le Marche*, s. VIII, vol. IV (1966): 137-176.

Lodolini E., 'Introduzione', in Archivio di Stato di Roma, *L'Archivio della S. Congregazione del Buon Governo (1592-1847). Inventario* (Rome: Ministero dell'Interno, 1956), pp. VII-CLXXVI.

Lodolini E., 'I registri delle Tesorerie provinciali dello Stato Pontificio (1397-1816) nell'Archivio di Stato di Roma', in *Studi in memoria di Federigo Melis* (5 vols, Naples: Giannini, 1978), II, pp. 431-439.

Lombardo M.L., *La Camera Urbis. Premesse per uno studio sull'organizzazione amministrativa della città di Roma durante il pontificato di Martino V* (Rome: Il Centro di Ricerca, 1970).

Lombardo M.L., 'La dogana di Ripa e Ripetta nel sistema dell'ordinamento tributario a Roma dal Medio Evo al sec. XV', *Archivi e cultura*, XII (1978): 9-100.

Lowe K.J.P., *Church and Politics in Renaissance Italy. The Life and Career of Cardinal Francesco Soderini, 1453-1524* (Cambridge: Cambridge University Press, 1993).

Lunt W.E., *Papal Revenues in the Middle Ages* (2 vols, New York: Columbia University Press, 1934).

Lupo Gentile M., *La politica di Paolo III nelle sue relazioni colla Corte Medicea* (Sarzana: Tipografia Lunense, 1906).

Il Magnifico Agostino Chigi (Rome: Associazione Bancaria Italiana, 1970).

Malatesta S. (ed.), *Statuti delle gabelle di Roma* (Rome: Tipografia della pace di Filippo Cuggiani, 1885).

La Marca e le sue istituzioni al tempo di Sisto V, Archivio di Stato di Macerata, Macerata 1991 (Pubblicazioni degli Archivi di Stato – Saggi, 20).

Maroni Lumbroso M.–Martini A., *Le confraternite romane nelle loro chiese* (Rome: Fondazione Marco Besso, 1963).

Martini A., *Manuale di metrologia, ossia, Misure, pesi e monete in uso attualmente e anticamente presso tutti i populi* (Turin: Loescher, 1883, reprinted Rome: Editrice E.R.A., 1976).

Martinori E., *La moneta. Vocabolario generale* (Rome: Istituto italiano di numismatica, 1914, reprinted Rome: Multigrafica, 1977).

Masi G. (ed.), *Statuti delle colonie fiorentine all'estero (secc. XV-XVI)* (Milan: Giuffrè, 1941).

Mazzei R., *Itinera mercatorum. Circolazione di uomini e beni nell'Europa centro-orientale, 1550-1650* (Lucca: Pacini Fazzi, 1999).

Melis F., *Aspetti della vita economica medievale (studi nell'archivio Datini di Prato)* (Florence: Olschki, 1962).

Melis F., 'Considerazioni su alcuni aspetti della nascita dell'impresa capitalistica', in Id., *L'azienda nel medioevo*, con introduzione di M. Del Treppo, a cura di M. Spallanzani, Florence, Le Monnier 1991 (Istituto Internazionale di Storia Economica «F. Datini», Prato – «Opere sparse di Federigo Melis», 1), pp 129-160.

Melis F., *Documenti per la storia economica dei secoli XIII-XVI*, con una nota di Paleografia Commerciale a cura di Elena Cecchi, Florence, Olschki 1972 (Istituto Internazionale di Storia Economica «F. Datini», Prato – Pubblicazioni, Serie I, Documenti, 1).

Melis F., 'Le società commerciali a Firenze dalla seconda metà del XIV secolo al XVI secolo', in *Troisième Conférence Internationale d'Histoire économique* (Munich 1965) (Paris: Mouton, 1974), pp. 47-62; reprinted in Id., *L'azienda nel medioevo* (Florence: Le Monnier, 1991), pp. 161-178.

Monaco M., 'Il primo debito pubblico pontificio: il Monte della Fede (1526)', *Studi Romani*, 8 (1960): 553-569.

Monaco M., *La situazione della Reverenda Camera Apostolica nell'anno 1525. Ricerche d'archivio (Un contributo alla storia delle finanze pontificie)* (Rome: Biblioteca d'arte, 1960).

Monaco M., 'Le finanze pontificie al tempo di Clemente VII (1523-1534)', *Studi Romani*, 6 (1958): 278-296.

Monaco M., *Lo Stato della Chiesa*, I, *Dalla fine del Grande Scisma alla Pace di Cateau-Cambrésis (1417-1559)* (Pescara: Libreria dell'Università, 1971).

Montenovesi O., 'Agostino Chigi banchiere e appaltatore dell'allume di Tolfa', *Archivio della Società Romana di Storia Patria*, 60 (1937): 107-147.

Moroni G., *Dizionario di erudizione storico-ecclesiastica* (103 vols, Venice: Tipografia Emiliana, 1840-61).

Mousnier R., 'Le trafic des offices à Venise', *Revue historique du droit français et étranger* (1952): 552-565.

Muntoni F., *Le monete dei papi e degli Stati pontifici* (4 vols, Rome: Santamaria, 1972-73).

Niccolini G.B., *Filippo Strozzi – tragedia* (Florence: Le Monnier, 1847).

Nina L., *Le finanze pontificie nel Medioevo* (3 vols, Milan: Fratelli Treves, 1929-32).

Palermo L., 'Aspetti dell'attività mercantile di un banco operante a Roma: i della Casa alla metà del Quattrocento', in *Credito e sviluppo economico in Italia dal Medioevo all'età contemporanea*, pp. 67-80.

Palermo L., 'Banchi privati e finanze pubbliche nella Roma del primo Rinascimento', in *Banchi pubblici, banchi privati e monti di pietà nell'Europa preindustriale*, pp. 435-459.

Palermo L., 'Espansione demografica e sviluppo economico a Roma nel Rinascimento', *Studi Romani*, 44 (1996): 21-47.

Palermo L., *Il porto di Roma nel XIV e XV secolo. Strutture socio-economiche e statuti* (Rome: Il Centro di Ricerca, 1979).

Palermo L., 'L'approvvigionamento granario della capitale. Strategie economiche e carriere curiali a Roma alla metà del Quattrocento', in S. Gensini (ed.), *Roma capitale (1447-1527)*, pp. 145-205.

Palermo L., *Mercati del grano a Roma tra Medioevo e Rinascimento*, vol. I: *Il mercato distrettuale del grano in età comunale* (Rome: Il Centro di Ricerca, 1990).

Palermo L., 'Ricchezza privata e debito pubblico nello Stato della Chiesa durante il XVI secolo', *Studi Romani*, 22 (1974): 298-311.

Palermo L., *Sviluppo economico e società preindustriali. Cicli, strutture e congiunture in Europa dal medioevo alla prima età moderna* (Rome: Viella, 1997).

Palermo L., 'Un aspetto della presenza dei fiorentini a Roma nel '400: le tecniche economiche', in *Forestieri e stranieri nelle città basso-Medievali*, pp. 81-96.

Pancaldi M.G., 'Militi lauretani', in *La Marca e le sue istituzioni al tempo di Sisto V*, pp. 317-319.

Partner P., 'Camera Papae: Problems of Papal Finance in the Later Middle Ages', *Journal of Ecclesiastical History*, IV (1958): 55-68.

Partner P., 'Papal financial policy in the Renaissance and Counter-Reformation', *Past and Present*, 88 (1980): 17-62.

Partner P., *Renaissance Rome 1500-1559. A Portrait of a Society* (Berkeley: University of California Press, 1976).

Partner P., 'The "Budget" of the Roman Church in the Renaissance Period', in E.F. Jacob (ed.), *Italian Renaissance Studies* (London: Faber and Faber, 1960), pp. 256-278.

Partner P., *The Lands of St. Peter. The Papal State in the Middle Ages and the Early Renaissance* (Berkeley: University of California Press, 1972).

Partner P., *The Papal State under Martin V. The Administration and Government of the Temporal Power in the Early Fifteenth Century* (London: The British School at Rome, 1958).

Partner P., *The Pope's Men. The Papal Civil Service in the Renaissance* (Oxford: Clarendon Press, 1990).

Passerini L., *Genealogia e storia della famiglia Altoviti* (Florence: M. Cellini e c., 1871).

von Pastor L., *The History of the Popes from the close of the Middle Ages* (40 vols, London: Routledge & Kegan Paul Ltd, 1949-53), vol. XII (1950), ed. R.F. Kerr.

Pastura Ruggiero M.G., *La Reverenda Camera Apostolica e i suoi archivi (secoli XV-XVIII)*, with essays by P. Cherubini, L. Londei, M. Morena and D. Sinisi (Rome:

Archivio di Stato di Roma – Scuola di Archivistica Paleografia e Diplomatica, 1984).

Pastura Ruggiero M.G., 'Lo Stato e la "res frumentaria" a Roma nella prima metà del Cinquecento', *Dimensioni e problemi della ricerca storica*, 2 (1990): 17-70.

Pastura Ruggiero M.G., 'Tesorerie e depositerie', in *La Marca e le sue istituzioni al tempo di Sisto V*, pp. 191-198.

Pavan P., 'Il Comune romano e lo "Studium Urbis" tra XV e XVI secolo', in *Roma e lo Studium Urbis. Spazio urbano e cultura dal Quattro al Seicento*, pp. 88-100.

Pecchiai P., *Roma nel Cinquecento*, Storia di Roma, vol. XIII (Bologna: Cappelli, 1948).

Pegazzano D., 'A Banker as Patron', in A. Chong – D. Pegazzano – D. Zikos (eds), *Raphael, Cellini & A Renaissance Banker. The Patronage of Bindo Altoviti*, pp. 59-91.

Pegazzano D., 'Il Gran Bindo Huomo Raro et Singhulare: The Life of Bindo Altoviti', in A. Chong – D. Pegazzano – D. Zikos (eds), *Raphael, Cellini & A Renaissance Banker. The Patronage of Bindo Altoviti*, pp. 3-19.

Pellegrini M., 'Corte di Roma e aristocrazie italiane in età moderna. Per una lettura storico-sociale della curia romana', *Rivista di Storia e Letteratura Religiosa*, 19 (1994): 543-603.

Picot E., *Les Italiens en France au XVI*^e^ *siècle* (Bordeaux: Imprimeries Gounouilhou, 1918, reprinted with an introduction by N. Ordine, Rome: Vecchiarelli, 1995).

Piola Caselli F., 'Aspetti del debito pubblico nello Stato Pontificio: gli uffici vacabili', *Annali della Facoltà di Scienze Politiche, Università degli Studi di Perugia*, 11 (1970-72): 98-170.

Piola Caselli F., 'Banchi privati e debito pubblico pontificio a Roma tra Cinquecento e Seicento', in *Banchi pubblici, banchi privati e monti di pietà nell'Europa pre-industriale*, pp. 461-495.

Piola Caselli F., 'Gerarchie curiali e compravendita degli uffici a Roma tra il XVI ed il XVII secolo', *Archivio della Società Romana di Storia Patria*, CXIV (1991): 117-125.

Piola Caselli F., 'La diffusione dei Luoghi di Monte della Camera apostolica alla fine del XVI secolo. Capitali investiti e rendimenti', in *Credito e sviluppo economico in Italia dal Medioevo all'età contemporanea*, pp. 191-216.

Piola Caselli F., 'La disciplina amministrativa ed il trattamento fiscale dei luoghi di monte della Camera apostolica tra il XVI ed il XVII secolo', in *Historia economica y de las instituciones financieras en Europa. Trabajos en homenaje a Ferran Valls I Taberner* (Barcelona: Archivo de la Biblioteca Ferran Valls I Taberner, 1989), vol. XII, pp. 3525-3549.

Piola Caselli F., 'L'espansione delle fonti finanziarie della Chiesa nel XIV secolo', *Archivio della Società Romana di Storia Patria*, CX (1987): 63-97.

Polverini Fosi I., 'I fiorentini a Roma nel Cinquecento: storia di una presenza', in *Roma capitale (1447-1527)*, pp. 389-414.

Polverini Fosi I., 'I mercanti fiorentini, il Campidoglio e il papa: il gioco delle parti', in *Roma e lo Studium Urbis. Spazio urbano e cultura dal Quattro al Seicento*, pp. 169-185.

Polverini Fosi I., 'Il consolato fiorentino a Roma ed il progetto per la chiesa nazionale', *Studi Romani*, 37 (1989): 50-70.

Polverini Fosi I., 'Pietà, devozione e politica: due confraternite fiorentine nella Roma del Rinascimento', *Archivio Storico Italiano*, 149 (1991): 119-161.

Pratesi L., *Il rione Ponte* (Rome: Newton & Compton, 1994).

Prodi P., *Lo sviluppo dell'assolutismo nello Stato pontificio (secoli XV-XVI)* (Bologna: Pàtron, 1968).

Prodi P., *The Papal Prince. One Body and Two Souls: the Papal Monarchy in Early Modern Europe* (Cambridge: Cambridge University Press, 1987).

von Ranke L., *Histoire de la papauté pendant les XVIe et XVIIe siècles* (4 vols, Paris: Débecourt, 1848).

Reinhard W., 'Finanza pontificia e Stato della Chiesa nel XVI e XVII secolo', in A. De Maddalena – H. Kellenbenz (eds), *Finanze e ragion di Stato in Italia e in Germania nella prima età moderna* (Bologna: Il Mulino, 1984), pp. 353-387.

Reinhard W., 'Finanza pontificia, sistema beneficiale e finanza statale nell'età confessionale' in H. Kellenbenz – P. Prodi (eds), *Fisco religione Stato nell'età confessionale*, Atti della settimana di studio, 21-25 September 1987 (Bologna: Il Mulino, 1989), pp. 459-504.

Reinhard W., 'Papal Power and Family Strategy in the Sixteenth and Seventeenth Centuries', in R.G. Asch – A.M. Birke (eds), *Princes, Patronage and the Nobility. The Court at the Beginning of the Modern Age, c. 1450-1650* (Oxford: Oxford University Press, 1991), pp. 329-356.

Reinhard W., *Papstfinanz und Nepotismus unter Paul V (1605-1621). Studien und Quellen zur Struktur und zu quantitativen Aspekten des päpstlichen Herrschaftssystem* (2 vols, Stuttgart: Hiersemann, 1974).

Renazzi F.M., *Storia dell'Università degli Studi di Roma* (4 vols, Rome: Stamperia Pagliarini, 1803-06, reprinted Bologna: Forni, 1971).

Renouard Y., 'Le compagnie commerciali fiorentine del Trecento', *Archivio Storico Italiano*, 96, vol. I (1938): 41-68, 163-179.

Renouard Y., *Les relations des papes d'Avignon et des compagnies commerciales et bancaires de 1316 à 1378* (Paris: De Boccard, 1941).

Reydellet-Guttinger C., *L'administration pontificale dans le Duché de Spolete (1305-1352)* (Florence: Olschki, 1975).

Rocchi E., *Le piante iconografiche e prospettiche di Roma del secolo XVI* (Turin-Rome: Casa editrice nazionale Roux e Viarengo, 1902).

Roma e lo Studium Urbis. Spazio urbano e cultura dal Quattro al Seicento, Atti del convegno, Rome, 7-10 June 1989 (Rome: Ministero per i beni culturali e ambientali – Ufficio centrale per i beni archivistici, 1992).

Romani M., *Pellegrini e viaggiatori nell'economia di Roma dal XIV al XVII secolo* (Milan: Società Vita e Pensiero, 1948).

Rosa M., 'La "scarsella di Nostro Signore": aspetti della fiscalità spirituale pontificia nell'età moderna', *Società e Storia*, 38 (1987): 818-845.

Rotelli C., 'La finanza locale pontificia nel Cinquecento: il caso di Imola', *Studi Storici*, IX (1968): 107-144.

Rufini E., 'L'Archivio di San Giovanni dei Fiorentini in Roma e la Compagnia della Pietà', in Archivio di Stato di Roma, *Scuola di Paleografia Diplomatica e Archivistica, Lezioni speciali*, 1962-63, pp. 108-134.

Rufini E., *Michelangelo e la colonia fiorentina a Roma* (Naples: Editrice Cultura e Vita, 1965).

Sapori A., 'La beneficenza delle compagnie mercantili del Trecento', *Archivio Storico Italiano*, 83 (1925): 251-272, reprinted in Id., *Studi di storia economica. Secoli XIII-XIV-XV* (3 vols, Florence: Sansoni, 1955^{3}-67), II, pp. 839-858.

Sapori A., *Studi di storia economica. Secoli XIII-XIV-XV* (Florence: Sansoni, vols 1-2, 1955^{3}, vol. 3, 1967).

Schulte A., *Die Fugger in Rom 1495-1523* (2 vols, Leipzig: Duncker und Humblot Verlag, 1904).

Solivetti G., *Un conto del banco Altoviti (1526-1530)* (Rome: Stab. Tip. Morara, no date).

Spallanzani M., 'Le aziende Pazzi al tempo della congiura del 1478', in *Studi di storia economica toscana nel Medioevo e nel Rinascimento. In memoria di Federigo Melis* (Pisa: Pacini, 1987), pp. 305-320.

Spallanzani M., 'Le compagnie Saliti a Norimberga nella prima metà del Cinquecento (un primo contributo dagli archivi fiorentini)', in *Wirtschaftskräfte und Wirtschaftswege. Festschrift für Hermann Kellenbenz* (5 vols, Nuremberg: Klett-Cotta, 1978), IV, pp. 603-620.

Spallanzani M., 'Tessuti di seta fiorentini per il mercato di Norimberga intorno al 1520', in *Studi in memoria di Giovanni Cassandro* (3 vols, Rome: Ministero per i beni culturali e ambientali – Ufficio centrale per i beni archivistici, 1991), III, pp. 995-1016.

Spallanzani M., 'Una grande azienda fiorentina del Trecento: Carlo Strozzi e compagni', *Ricerche Storiche*, VIII (1978): 417-436.

Stella A., 'Altoviti Bindo', in *Dizionario Biografico degli Italiani* (Rome: Istituto della Enciclopedia Italiana fondato da Giovanni Treccani), II (1960), pp. 574-575.

Stow K.R., *Taxation, Community and the State. The Jews and the Fiscal Foundations of the Early Modern Papal State* (Stuttgart: Hiersemann, 1982).

Stumpo E., 'Economia naturale ed economia monetaria: l'imposta', in *Storia d'Italia. Annali*, 6, *Economia naturale, economia monetaria* (Turin: Einaudi, 1983), pp. 523-562.

Stumpo E., *Il capitale finanziario a Roma fra Cinque e Seicento. Contributo alla storia della fiscalità pontificia in età moderna (1570-1660)* (Milan: Giuffrè, 1985).

Stumpo E., 'La gestione delle tesorerie provinciali nello Stato della Chiesa fra Cinque e Seicento', in *La Marca e le sue istituzioni al tempo di Sisto V*, pp. 49-62.

Tomassetti G., 'Del sale e focatico del Comune di Roma nel Medioevo', *Atti della R. Deputazione di Storia Patria per le Marche*, s. IV, 1/2 (1924): 313-368.

Villari P., *Niccolò Machiavelli e i suoi tempi* (3 vols, Florence: Le Monnier, 1877-82).

Weber C., 'Fünfzig genealogische Tafeln zur Geschichte der römischen Kurie in der frühen Neuzeit', *Quellen und Forschungen aus italienischen Archiven und Bibliotheken*, 73 (1993): 496-571.

Zippel G., 'L'allume di Tolfa e il suo commercio', *Archivio della Società Romana di Storia Patria*, 30 (1907): 5-51, 389-462.

Index

If not otherwise indicated, companies and partnerships are located in Rome